International Political Economy Series

Series Editor: **Timothy M. Shaw**, Visiting
Boston, USA and Emeritus Professor, Unive

The global political economy is in flux as a
organization and governance. The IPE serie
analysis and structure over the last three de ____ a concentration on the global South. Now the South increasingly challenges the North as the
centre of development, also reflected in a growing number of submissions and
publications on indebted Eurozone economies in Southern Europe.

An indispensable resource for scholars and researchers, the series examines
a variety of capitalisms and connections by focusing on emerging economies,
companies and sectors, debates and policies. It informs diverse policy communities as the established trans-Atlantic North declines and 'the rest', especially the
BRICS, rise.

Titles include:

Eris D. Schoburgh, John Martin and Sonia Gatchair
DEVELOPMENTAL LOCAL GOVERNANCE
A Critical Discourse in 'Alternative Development'

Jessica Chia-yueh Liao
DEVELOPMENTAL STATES AND BUSINESS ACTIVISM
East Asia's Trade Dispute Settlement

Richard Münch
THE GLOBAL DIVISION OF LABOUR
Development and Inequality in World Society

Jakub M. Godzimirski
EU LEADERSHIP IN ENERGY AND ENVIRONMENTAL GOVERNANCE
Global and Local Challenges and Responses

Md Saidul Islam and Md Ismail Hossain
SOCIAL JUSTICE IN THE GLOBALIZATION OF PRODUCTION
Labor, Gender, and the Environment Nexus

Geoffrey Allen Pigman
TRADE DIPLOMACY TRANSFORMED
Why Trade Matters for Global Prosperity

Kristian Coates Ulrichsen
THE GULF STATES IN INTERNATIONAL POLITICAL ECONOMY

Eleonora Poli
ANTITRUST INSTITUTIONS AND POLICIES IN THE GLOBALISING ECONOMY

Andrea C. Simonelli
GOVERNING CLIMATE INDUCED MIGRATION AND DISPLACEMENT
IGO Expansions and Global Policy Implications

Victoria Higgins
ALLIANCE CAPITALISM, INNOVATION AND THE CHINESE STATE
The Global Wireless Sector

Andrei V. Belyi
TRANSNATIONAL GAS MARKETS AND EURO-RUSSIAN ENERGY RELATIONS

Silvia Pepino
SOVEREIGN RISK AND FINANCIAL CRISIS
The International Political Economy of the Eurozone

Ryan David Kiggins (*editor*)
THE POLITICAL ECONOMY OF RARE EARTH ELEMENTS. RISING POWERS
AND TECHNOLOGICAL CHANGE

Seán Ó Riain, Felix Behling, Rossella Ciccia and Eoin Flaherty (*editors*)
THE CHANGING WORLDS AND WORKPLACES OF CAPITALISM

Alexander Korolev and Jing Huang
INTERNATIONAL COOPERATION IN THE DEVELOPMENT OF RUSSIA'S FAR
EAST AND SIBERIA

Roman Goldbach
GLOBAL GOVERNANCE AND REGULATORY FAILURE
The Political Economy of Banking

Kate Ervine and Gavin Fridell (*editors*)
BEYOND FREE TRADE
Alternative Approaches to Trade, Politics and Power

Ray Kiely
THE BRICS, US 'DECLINE' AND GLOBAL TRANSFORMATIONS

Philip Fountain, Robin Bush and R. Michael Feener (*editors*)
RELIGION AND THE POLITICS OF DEVELOPMENT
Critical Perspectives on Asia

Markus Fraundorfer
BRAZIL'S EMERGING ROLE IN GLOBAL SECTORAL GOVERNANCE
Health, Food Security and Bioenergy

Katherine Hirschfeld
GANGSTER STATES
Organized Crime, Kleptocracy and Political Collapse

Matthew Webb and Albert Wijeweera (*editors*)
THE POLITICAL ECONOMY OF CONFLICT IN SOUTH ASIA

International Political Economy Series
Series Standing Order ISBN 978–0–333–71708–0 hardcover
Series Standing Order ISBN 978–0–333–71110–1 paperback

You can receive future titles in this series as they are published by placing a standing order. Please contact your bookseller or, in case of difficulty, write to us at the address below with your name and address, the title of the series and one of the ISBNs quoted above.

Customer Services Department, Macmillan Distribution Ltd, Houndmills, Basingstoke, Hampshire RG21 6XS, England

Making Medicines in Africa
The Political Economy of Industrializing for Local Health

Edited by

Maureen Mackintosh
Professor of Economics, The Open University, United Kingdom

Geoffrey Banda
Research Fellow in Regenerative Medicine, University of Edinburgh, United Kingdom

Paula Tibandebage
Senior Research Associate, REPOA, Tanzania

Watu Wamae
Visiting Research Fellow, The Open University, United Kingdom

First published 2016 by
PALGRAVE MACMILLAN

Palgrave Macmillan in the UK is an imprint of Macmillan Publishers Limited, registered in England, company number 785998, of Houndmills, Basingstoke, Hampshire RG21 6XS.

Palgrave Macmillan in the US is a division of Nature American, Inc., 75 Varick Street, New York, NY 10010.

Palgrave Macmillan is the global academic imprint of the above companies and has companies and representatives throughout the world.

Palgrave® and Macmillan® are registered trademarks in the United States, the United Kingdom, Europe and other countries.

DOI: 10.1007/978-1-137-54647-0
E-PDF ISBN: 978-1-137-54647-0
Paperback ISBN: 978-1-137-57133-5

This book is printed on paper suitable for recycling and made from fully managed and sustained forest sources. Logging, pulping and manufacturing processes are expected to conform to the environmental regulations of the country of origin.

A catalogue record for this book is available from the British Library.

Library of Congress Cataloging-in-Publication Data
    Making medicines in Africa: the political economy of industrializing for local health / [edited by] Maureen Mackintosh, Geoffrey Banda, Paula Tibandebage, Watu Wamae.
        p. ; cm.—(International political economy series)
    Includes bibliographical references.
    ISBN 978–1–137–57133–5
    I. Mackintosh, Maureen, editor. II. Banda, Geoffrey, 1969– , editor. III. Tibandebage, Paula, editor. IV. Wamae, Watu, editor. V. Series: International political economy series (Palgrave Macmillan (Firm))
    [DNLM: 1. Technology, Pharmaceutical – economics – Africa. 2. Technology, Pharmaceutical – methods – Africa. 3. Diffusion of Innovation – Africa. 4. Drug Industry – standards – Africa. 5. Economic Development – Africa. 6. Pharmaceutical Preparations – supply & distribution – Africa. QV 778]
    RA401.A55
    338.4′76151096—dc23   2015025771

Contents

List of Figures   viii

List of Tables   ix

Preface   xi

Notes on Contributors   xiii

Introduction: African Industrial Development, Values and
Health Care   1
*Maureen Mackintosh, Geoffrey Banda, Paula Tibandebage and
Watu Wamae*

Part I   The Pharmaceutical Industry in Africa   5

1   Making Medicines in Africa: An Historical Political Economy
    Overview   7
    Geoffrey Banda, Samuel Wangwe and Maureen Mackintosh

2   Pharmaceuticals in Kenya: The Evolution of Technological
    Capabilities   25
    Roberto Simonetti, Norman Clark and Watu Wamae

3   Pharmaceutical Manufacturing Decline in Tanzania:
    How Possible Is a Turnaround to Growth?   45
    *Paula Tibandebage, Samuel Wangwe, Maureen Mackintosh and
    Phares G.M. Mujinja*

4   Bringing Industrial and Health Policies Closer: Reviving
    Pharmaceutical Production in Ethiopia   65
    Tsige Gebre-Mariam, Kedir Tahir and Solomon Gebre-Amanuel

5   South-South Collaboration in Pharmaceuticals: Manufacturing
    Anti-retroviral Medicines in Mozambique   85
    Giuliano Russo and Lícia de Oliveira

6   Can Foreign Firms Promote Local Production of
    Pharmaceuticals in Africa?   103
    Sudip Chaudhuri

7   Raising the Technological Level: The Scope for API, Excipients, and Biologicals Manufacture in Africa   122
Joseph Fortunak, Skhumbuzo Ngozwana, Tsige Gebre-Mariam, Tiffany Ellison, Paul Watts, Martins Emeje and Frederick E. Nytko III

Part II   Industrialization for Health   145

8   Health Systems as Industrial Policy: Building Collaborative Capabilities in the Tanzanian and Kenyan Health Sectors and Their Local Suppliers   147
Maureen Mackintosh, Paula Tibandebage, Joan Kariuki Kungu, Mercy Karimi Njeru and Caroline Israel

9   The Dissemination of Local Health Innovations: Political Economy Issues in Brazil   166
Erika Aragão, Jane Mary Guimarães and Sebastião Loureiro

10   Healthy Industries and Unhealthy Populations: Lessons from Indian Problem-Solving   183
Smita Srinivas

Part III   Industrial Policies and Health Needs   201

11   Policies to Control Prices of Medicines: Does the South African Experience Have Lessons for Other African Countries?   203
Skhumbuzo Ngozwana

12   Pharmaceutical Standards in Africa: The Road to Improvement and Their Role in Technological Capability Upgrading   224
Geoffrey Banda, Julius Mugwagwa, Dinar Kale and Margareth Ndomondo-Sigonda

13   Innovative Procurement for Health and Industrial Development   243
Joanna Chataway, Geoffrey Banda, Gavin Cochrane and Catriona Manville

14   Industry Associations and the Changing Politics of Making Medicines in South Africa   261
Theo Papaioannou, Andrew Watkins, Julius Mugwagwa and Dinar Kale

15 Finance and Incentives to Support the Development of
    National Pharmaceutical Industries 278
    Alastair West and Geoffrey Banda

Bibliography 298

Index 323

List of Figures

1.1   A timeline of selected pharmaceutical firm start-ups by
      country, 1930–2013   9
2.1   Local production of non-parenteral medicines in Kenya
      by type of product, 2007–13   30
3.1   The expanding local supply gap: total imports and
      exports of medicines and blood products   48
5.1   Timelines for the implementation of the factory project   87
7.1   Chemical synthesis to produce the anti-malarial APIs
      artemether and artesunate   126
7.2   Synthetic route for the manufacture of the API tenofovir
      disoproxil fumarate   128
9.1   The Brazilian pharmaceutical market (unit sales),
      1997–2013   173
9.2   Percentage of municipalities covered by the PFPB,
      2006–15   176
9.3   Pharmaceutical products: Balance of trade, Brazilian
      exports and imports   178
10.1 Institutional triad of health care   189
11.1 Medicine contribution to total private health care costs   218

List of Tables

1.1 Pharmaceutical production and exports, Tanzania, 2004–05 — 23

3.1 Decline in domestic market share of medicines made in Tanzania, 2006–12 — 49

3.2 Share of local manufactures among specified tracer medicines available in sample outlets, 2006–12 — 49

5.1 Estimated cost of setting up the factory — 91

5.2 Public sector drug import value, by source and type of health programme — 94

5.3 Unit price for selected SMM drugs — 96

6.1 Anticipated trends in global pharmaceutical markets — 107

6.2 Indian share of pharmaceutical formulations imports into Africa, 2012 — 110

6.3 India's pharmaceutical exports — 112

6.4 Comparison of retail formulations prices in India and Ghana — 118

7.1 Common excipients used in solid oral dosage formulations, their standard use and weight % content, and pricing on a per-kilogram basis — 125

7.2 Raw materials that contribute to the structure of the API tenofovir disoproxil fumarate (TDF) and their current commercial pricing — 129

8.1 Country of origin of tracer essential medicines, by procurement sector, Tanzania and Kenya, 2012–13 — 151

11.1 Pharmacy dispensing fee: fee in rands (R) plus permitted mark-up (%), by band of SEP in rands (R) and date of publication of schedule — 215

11.2 SEP increases since the implementation of the SEP — 216

12.1 Drug life cycle stages and regulatory requirements — 226

13.1 Donor support of local industry through contracting for local health supplies: Zimbabwe — 252

15.1 Finance capabilities at the firm and financial institution levels — 288

15.2   Finance capabilities required by financial institutions,
        mapped using Lall's (1992) firm-level technological
        capability framework   290
15.3   Recruitment of non-traditional banking skills to build
        finance capability by one Zimbabwean international
        bank in 1998–2000   292

Preface

This book is a collective project. It was designed and debated in a workshop funded largely by the United Nations Industrial Development Organization (UNIDO), in London in December 2014. We are grateful to UNIDO and to Juergen Reinhardt in particular for his support and encouragement. We also would like to thank the Open University and the Economic and Social Research Council, UK, for providing the funding that allowed this book to be published in open access form.

The book draws extensively on original research and on direct experience of involvement in policy making. Several chapters – and some of the broader framing of the book – have their origins in a research project on *Industrial Productivity and Health Sector Performance,* funded by the DFID/ESRC Growth Research Programme. The findings, interpretations, conclusions and opinions expressed in the relevant chapters (identified in notes) are those of the authors and do not necessarily reflect the views or policies of DFID or the UK ESRC. The views expressed throughout are the sole responsibility of the authors.

When a number of contributors to this book began to work on the *Industrial Productivity* project in 2012, it is fair to say that the international policy debates on access to medicines in African countries remained focussed on funding procurement of essential medicines from Asian manufacturers. The project aimed to explore the scope for local developmental synergy between industrial development of pharmaceutical production on the Sub-Saharan African subcontinent and improvement of the performance of health sectors suffering from chronic undersupply of essential medicines. As we have worked on the project, we have become part of a much wider movement to identify and generate these synergies. This book is an outcome of this networking, and we hope it will contribute to strengthening evidence, debate and policy making.

We have many people to thank. First, our extraordinary authors who have given their time and expertise to preparing the chapters and participating in the workshop debates. They have brought expertise in pharmaceutical research, manufacturing and policy making, as well as social science research. Among our African contributors, the editors would particularly like to thank Skhumbuzo Ngozwana and Tsige Gebre-Mariam for their commitment and for bringing in other expert colleagues also. We are also grateful to Alastair West of UNIDO for contributing his breadth of knowledge of this policy field, and to our Indian and Brazilian colleagues whose depth of historical understanding of interactions between industrial change and health sector values helped to shape the book's themes and objectives.

Much more widely, we owe a great deal to all the many manufacturers, distributors, health facility staff, pharmacy and drug shop staff, policy makers, regulators, researchers and others who have patiently answered the questions of authors of these chapters and participated in workshop discussions of the findings.

At Palgrave Macmillan, we thank our supportive publisher, Christina Brian; also Judith Allan, and our enthusiastic series editor Tim Shaw. Many thanks also to Radha Ray, who administered the London workshop with such welcoming efficiency, and to Jim McGinlay who has patiently chased endless manuscript detail.

We hope this book can make a real contribution to the search for better access to essential medicines alongside industrial development in Sub-Saharan Africa.

Notes on Contributors

Editors

Geoffrey Banda is a research fellow at the Innogen Institute within Science, Technology and Innovation Studies at the University of Edinburgh. He is currently working on an ESRC-funded regenerative medicine project looking at business models, value chains and innovation ecosystems for organizations involved in commercializing cell therapies. His doctoral and post-doctoral work at the Open University focussed on finance, innovation and development in the African pharmaceutical sector. He has previously worked in quality assurance in the food manufacturing and airline catering industries, focusing on microbial food safety, and has also been a corporate banker financing diverse industrial sectors.

Maureen Mackintosh is Professor of Economics at the Open University. She is a development economist specializing in the analysis of markets in health care and medicines, with particular reference to African contexts. She has just completed, with a number of collaborators including Paula Tibandebage, Samuel Wangwe, Watu Wamae and Norman Clark, a DFID/ESRC-funded project on Industrial Productivity and Health Sector Performance, the results of which inform a number of chapters in this book. Other recent collaborative research has focussed on the role of non-governmental public action in access to medicines, and on payments for maternal health care.

Paula Tibandebage is a senior research associate with REPOA, a non-government policy research institute in Tanzania. She has over 20 years research experience, specializing in issues of social protection and social services provisioning including health and education. Her most recent publication is entitled 'Can managers empower nurse-midwives to improve maternal health care? A comparison of two resource-poor hospitals in Tanzania', *International Journal of Health Planning and Management* 2015; it reports findings from her Wellcome Trust-supported project on ethics, payments and maternal survival in Tanzania.

Watu Wamae holds a PhD in the economics of innovation and development and is a visiting research fellow in the Department of Economics,

Faculty of Social Sciences at the Open University, Milton Keynes, UK. Her research expertise is in the area of industrialization and innovation policy, and she works closely with governments in Africa. She has strong interests in structural change and dynamics of growth in African economies and has held a number of honorary assignments including the Human Resource Development and Science and Technology Indicators programme in Africa.

Contributors

Erika Aragão is an associate professor at the Universidade Federal da Bahia (UFBA), Federal University of Bahia, Brazil. She is also a researcher at the Programme in Economics Technology and Innovation in Health Sciences (PECS/ISC/UFBA) and researcher at the National Institute for Neglected Diseases (INCT IDN – CDTS/FIOCRUZ). She has researched and published in the areas of technological innovation and health economics.

Joanna Chataway is Director of the Innovation, Health and Science Group at RAND Europe, a not-for-profit policy research institute, and Professor of Biotechnology and Development at the Open University. She has held senior positions and appointments across a range of academic, policy research, consulting and research funding bodies. She has particular expertise in the field of health innovation and has researched extensively the range of factors that influence the rate and direction of product and process innovation in health.

Sudip Chaudhuri is Professor of Economics at the Indian Institute of Management, Calcutta. His research interest includes matters relating to patents, the pharmaceutical industry as well as industrial and innovation policy. He has undertaken several studies for the United Nations Industrial Development Organization, Vienna and United Nations Development Programme, New York on the subject of promoting local production of pharmaceuticals in Africa.

Norman Clark is Emeritus Professor at the Open University where formerly he held a research chair in Innovation Systems and Development. He is a development economist whose research career has focussed mainly on academic and consultancy work dealing with science and technology policy issues in Africa and south Asia. In recent years he has acted as senior adviser to the DFID 'research into use' programme with special focus on technology development in East Africa.

Gavin Cochrane is an analyst at RAND Europe. His research interests are primarily focussed on innovation, global health and international development. At RAND he has worked on a variety of national and international projects, including a number of studies and evaluations examining the contextual factors involved with research, drug development and health systems strengthening in sub-Saharan Africa. He holds a BA in Economics and Japanese from the University of Leeds and an MSc in Asian Studies from Lund University, Sweden.

Tiffany Ellison is a doctoral candidate in the Department of Chemistry at Howard University in Washington, DC. She works under the supervision of Dr Joseph M. Fortunak. Her research interests include creating novel synthetic routes for HIV protease inhibitor drugs. Her goals are to make the drugs more affordable for people in low- to middle-income countries.

Martins Emeje holds a Bachelor's in Pharmacy with distinction from Ahmadu Bello University, Zaria, and a master of Pharmacy and PhD from University of Nigeria, Nsukka. He established an interdisciplinary group on nanotechnology at the National Institute for Pharmaceutical Research and Development (NIPRD). Prof. Martins' several international fellowships include the prestigious Raman fellowship. He has published over 100 primary scientific articles and patents. Prof. Martins who currently doubles as the Head in the Department of Pharmaceutical Technology and Raw Materials Development, Advanced Biology and Chemistry and NIPRD's Drug Manufacturing Unit, also holds the position of visiting professor at the University of Uyo. He coordinates Intellectual Property Rights matters and research collaborations at NIPRD.

Joseph Fortunak is Professor of Chemistry and Pharmaceutical Sciences at Howard University. He holds a PhD in Chemistry and did postdoctoral research at Cambridge University (UK). Dr Fortunak worked for many years in global pharmaceutical companies, most recently as Head of Global Chemical Development at Abbott Labs. He launched over a dozen new drugs, including major medicines for HIV/AIDS. Dr Fortunak now works with NGOs including UNITAID and the Clinton Foundation to promote access to medicines. He helped set up the Industrial Pharmacy Advanced Training (IPAT) with Sister Zita Ekeocha at the Kilimanjaro School of Pharmacy, where professionals are trained in medicines manufacturing and regulation to international standards of quality assurance.

Solomon Gebre-Amanuel is Research and Development Manager of the Ethiopian Pharmaceuticals Manufacturing Share Company. He has been in the Ethiopian pharmaceuticals manufacturing sector for the last 17 years. He has dedicated his career to the production and development of generic pharmaceutical products. He received his B. Pharm. (1997) and MSc (2005) in Pharmaceutics from Addis Ababa University.

Tsige Gebre-Mariam is Professor of Pharmaceutics at Addis Ababa University (AAU) and General Manager of the Regional Bioequivalence Centre. He also works as an independent consultant in the pharmaceutical sector including supply chain management and industry development. He has published extensively on conventional and modified drug release formulations, phytomedicines and alternative excipients, among others. He is co-author of *National Strategy for Pharmaceutical Manufacturing Development in Ethiopia* (2015) and a recipient of numerous awards and fellowships.

Jane Mary Guimarães is an associate professor at the Universidade Federal do Sul da Bahia (UFSB) – Federal University of Southern Bahia, Brazil. She is also a researcher at the Programme in Economics, Technology and Innovation in Health Sciences (PECS/ISC/UFBA) at the Federal University of Bahia, and a researcher at the Instituto Nacional de Ciência e Tecnologia em Saúde (CITECS) – National Institute of Science and Health Technology in Salvador, Bahia. She has researched and published in the areas of technological innovation and communication in health.

Caroline Israel is a researcher at UONGOZI Institute also known as Institute of African Leadership for Sustainable Development. Formerly she has worked as an assistant researcher in the Department of Social Protection at REPOA, Dar es Salaam, doing research on various social and economic policy issues including health and education. Currently her main areas of research are leadership, governance and sustainable development.

Dinar Kale is Senior Lecturer in Innovation and International Development at the Open University, UK. He has researched and published extensively in the areas of technological innovation, knowledge transfer and international development. His work concerns the issues that help or hinder innovation and development of the health care industries from developing countries.

Mercy Karimi Njeru is a senior research scientist and head of the Health Systems Research Unit at the Centre for Public Health Research in the Kenya Medical Research Institute (KEMRI). She holds a PhD and her work has recently received global recognition as one the best resources in mixed methods applications in health research. She has been involved in various research projects mainly from a health systems perspective and has also been involved in mentoring and supervising graduate students. She has participated in research involving countries in sub-Saharan Africa as well as Europe and has published in peer-reviewed international scientific journals.

Joan Kariuki Kungu is a research fellow at the African Centre for Technology studies. She has over eight years experience in multi-disciplinary research on environment, natural resources and sustainable development. She holds an MA in Development Studies with specialty in Environment for Development from the University of Nairobi, and a BSc in Environmental Science from Kenyatta University. She has particular interest in policy research for sustainable management of natural resources. She coordinated the Kenyan team's research on industrial productivity and health sector performance.

Sebastião Loureiro is a physician and holds a PhD in Epidemiology from the University of Texas Health Sciences Center. He is Emeritus Professor at the Universidade Federal da Bahia (UFBA), Brazil, and Executive Coordinator of the National Institute of Science and Health Technology. Recently his research has focussed on access to medical technology and health inequalities. He has contributed to the academic and institutional development of the fields of health economics and health technology at the Institute of Collective Health, University of Bahia, and is an active member of the Board of Directors of the Brazilian Association of Collective Health (ABRASCO) and Brazilian Association of Health Economics (ABrES).

Catriona Manville is a senior analyst at RAND Europe where she works in innovation and technology policy. She works on and manages research, policy analysis and evaluation studies across the sectors of health and higher education for clients in a variety of sectors including public–private partnerships, public health, the pharmaceutical industry and higher education institutions. In particular she has been involved in studies evaluating programmes and interventions in sub-Saharan Africa. She holds a PhD in Biochemistry from Newcastle University.

Julius Mugwagwa is a research fellow in the Development Policy and Practice (DPP) group and the INNOGEN Institute at the Open University, UK. He received undergraduate and postgraduate training in biological sciences, biotechnology and business administration in Zimbabwe before a PhD in Science, Technology and Innovation Studies at the Open University. Julius has worked in veterinary research, pharmaceutical production and quality assurance, medicines control, agricultural biotechnology research and biotechnology/biosafety governance. He is a recipient of Leverhulme Early Career Fellowship (2009–11) and the UK Economic and Social Research Council (ESRC) Future Research Leaders Scheme fellowship (2013–15).

Phares G.M.Mujinja holds a PhD in Public Health Economics from Heidelberg University and is Associate Professor of Health Economics and Public Health at Muhimbili University of Health and Allied Sciences, Dar es Salaam, Tanzania. His research interests are in health systems, health financing, health planning, monitoring and evaluation, pharmaceutical economics, and strategic project management. He has served as a consultant to various national and international organizations including the World Bank, EU, WHO, UNAIDS, UNDP, UNICEF, UNTAID. He has wide experience of designing and conducting health-related research; recent publications include pharmaceutical economics and consumer rights in health care.

Margareth Ndomondo-Sigonda has served as Chief Pharmacist (1998), Registrar of Pharmacy Board (1998–2003) and Director General of the Tanzania Food and Drugs Authority (2003–10). She then joined the African Union, New Partnership for Africa's Development (NEPAD) Agency, as their Pharmaceutical Coordinator (2010–to date) responsible for coordination of the African Medicines Regulatory Harmonization initiative. She holds an MSc in pharmaceutical services management (University of Bradford), an MBA from the Eastern and Southern Africa Management Institute-Tanzania/Maastricht School of Management-Netherlands; and Bachelor's in Pharmacy from the University of Dar es Salaam, Tanzania. Publications include: *The African Medicines Regulatory Harmonization Initiative: Rationale and Benefits, Clinical Pharmacology & Therapeutics* (2011).

Skhumbuzo Ngozwana is an internationally recognized expert on African pharma who has occupied various roles in the African pharmaceutical industry. He is the co-author of the *Pharmaceutical Manufacturing Plan for Africa* (2007), and the *National Strategy for Pharmaceutical*

Manufacturing Development in Ethiopia (2015). He holds qualifications in medicine, pharmacology and business administration.

Frederick E. Nytko III is a post-doctoral research fellow in the Chemistry and Pharmaceutical Sciences Department at Howard University. Dr Nytko received his PhD from the University of Maryland, College Park in 2014, with a specialization in synthetic organic chemistry and transition metal-catalysed coupling reactions. He currently works on both improving the syntheses of commercially available HIV/AIDS and tuberculosis active pharmaceutical ingredients (APIs), and also researching market trends for the international sale of APIs, in order to ensure that equitably priced treatments are available to at-risk individuals in the developing world.

Lícia de Oliveira is Director of the Fiocruz Regional Office for Africa in Maputo, Mozambique. A pharmacist by training, Lícia is currently a senior researcher at Farmanguinhos' Institute of Pharmaceutical Technology, Rio de Janeiro, Brazil. She has been the project coordinator for the implementation of SMM drugs factory in Mozambique since its inception.

Theo Papaioannou is Reader in Politics of Innovation and Development at the Open University, UK. He has researched and published extensively in the areas of technological innovation, political theory and international development. His recent publications include: 'How inclusive can innovation for development be in the 21st century?' *Journal of Innovation and Development* (2014); 'Innovation and development in search of a political theory of justice' *International Journal of Technology and Globalisation* (2014).

Giuliano Russo is Assistant Professor of Health Economics and Policy at Lisbon's Instituto de Higiene e Medicina Tropical. He has over 15 years of professional experience in the academia, public sector and pharmaceutical industry in Europe, Africa and Latin America. His recent research has focussed on the economics of human resources for health, on health systems and pharmaceutical markets in low-income settings, and on health-aid architecture, with a geographical focus on Portuguese-speaking countries.

Roberto Simonetti is Senior Lecturer in Economics at the Open University. He carries out research on industrial development, the economics of technological innovation and financialization. In the past, he has contributed to UNCTAD's Least Developed Countries

Report, various EU-funded projects on innovation, employment, finance and growth, such as AITEG and FINNOV, and to research on innovation in pharmaceuticals with the Edinburgh-OU ESRC INNOGEN Centre.

Smita Srinivas is a faculty member and Director of the Technological Change Lab (TCLab) at Columbia University. Her research centres on technological change and industrial transformation in the process of economic development. Her book, *Market Menagerie: Health and Development in Late Industrial States* (2012), pivots on pharmaceutical and biopharmaceutical capabilities and how nations reconcile their industrial and social goals. Smita sits on expert advisory boards or leads research programmes on industry sectors and inclusion questions in areas such as health, oil and gas, water and waste. She holds a PhD from the Massachusetts Institute of Technology (MIT), past fellowships at Harvard University's John F. Kennedy School of Government, and prior degrees in physics and mathematics. She is a frequent senior expert and advisor to multilateral organizations, development agencies and policy research institutes.

Kedir Tahir holds Bachelor's and Master's in Pharmaceutics from the School of Pharmacy, Addis Ababa University and diploma in Marketing Management from the Addis Ababa Commercial College. He combines experience in business development with professional knowledge in the field of pharmaceutical technologies. He is currently a business development manager at V-Tag International Trading PLC. He also works as an independent consultant in pharmaceutical industry development.

Samuel Wangwe is Executive Director of REPOA in Dar es Salaam. He has over 40 years' experience as an economist, policy researcher and analyst, policy and economic advisor to the Government of Tanzania. He has authored, co-authored or edited 13 books on development and economic management and over 70 published articles and chapters in journals and edited books.

Andrew Watkins holds a BA in Political Science, an MA in Science, Technology and Public Policy, and a PhD in Regional Planning from the London School of Economics. Andrew formerly worked at the National Science Foundation and the National Academy of Engineering in the US. He joined DPP in October 2013 as a research associate. His research interests involve the evolution of regional and sector-based innovation systems, with an emphasis on system functions, entrepreneurial capacity building and related political processes.

Paul Watts holds a first class Bachelor's in Chemistry and a PhD in Bio-Organic Natural Product Chemistry from University of Bristol. His PhD focussed on the synthesis of isotopically labelled compounds, for use in determination of biosynthetic pathways to polyketide-derived natural products. He pioneered organic synthesis in micro reactors at the University of Hull. As a lecturer and full professor (2011) he led the micro-reactor and flow technology group which published over 90 highly cited peer-reviewed papers on continuous-flow organic synthesis. In 2013, Prof. Watts moved to Nelson Mandela Metropolitan University (South Africa) to hold the distinguished position of Research Chair in Microfluidic Bio/Chemical Processing.

Alastair West is a senior technical advisor for UNIDO's pharmaceutical team. He holds a Bachelor's in Biochemistry from Oxford University and a MBA from IMD in Switzerland. He worked in the pharmaceutical and biotech industries for the first eight tears of his career. After his MBA he joined the World Bank as part of the vaccine team in Washington DC and later worked for the International Finance Corporation as Industry Expert for Life Sciences in the General Services and Manufacturing Division. He has been with UNIDO for six years and has worked on a number of pharmaceutical industry projects in Africa. As part of this work he co-authored the *Business Plan for the Pharmaceutical Manufacturing Plan for Africa* (2012).

Introduction: African Industrial Development, Values and Health Care

Maureen Mackintosh, Geoffrey Banda, Paula Tibandebage and Watu Wamae

This is a book about the industrial development of pharmaceutical production in Sub-Saharan Africa. Yet the values that drive this industrial enquiry are rooted in the needs of a subcontinent with the worst health status in the world. The central argument of this book is that industrial development in pharmaceuticals and the capabilities it generates are necessary elements in African initiatives to tackle these acute health care needs. A successful pharmaceutical industry is no guarantor of good health care: India indeed has managed to grow a highly successful industry while leaving many of its people without access to competent care. However, without the technological, industrial, intellectual, organizational and research-related capabilities associated with competent pharmaceutical production, the African subcontinent cannot generate the resources to tackle the needs and demands of its population.

The book is a collective endeavour, by a group of editors and authors with a strong African and more broadly Southern presence, to find ways forward that link technological development, investment and industrial growth in pharmaceuticals to improving access to essential good-quality medicines, as part of moving towards universal access to competent health care. This book presents original research, much of it from recent fieldwork in African contexts. The authors include academics, researchers and practitioners, including some who have been or are currently managing pharmaceutical firms in African contexts, and some deeply involved in policy formulation and implementation. We aim to shift the emphasis in international debate towards much more attention to the scope for sustained Africa-based and African-led initiatives to tackle this huge challenge.

In this we are contributing to a shift in mind-set that is already under way. African governments are increasingly considering medicines supply as a national security issue. African Heads of States have adopted the African Union's Pharmaceutical Manufacturing Plan for Africa (African Union, 2007), and regional African bodies are taking similar initiatives. There has also been a sharp shift in approach amongst UN agencies, including WHO and UNAIDS, from earlier critical stances towards support for the development of health sector manufacturing of medicines and supplies in Africa (Sidibé et al., 2014). That shift in turn has built on work by UNIDO with African governments and the African Union (e.g. African Union 2012a[1]; UNIDO, 2010; UNIDO/GoT, 2012). Bilateral donors, notably German and Japanese, are actively supporting upgrading in health-related industries.

The book's roots are in historical political economy. The process of building – or failing to build – industrial strengths and industry-health system synergies is long term, as the complex 30-year trajectory of Brazil's health-industrial complex illustrates. The book starts by challenging a highly persistent international myth: that Sub-Saharan Africa has no pharmaceutical industry. On the contrary, the industry has a long history and is strongly embedded in a number of African countries. Operating in a relatively high-skill, high-technology sector, pharmaceutical firms have faced all the well-known challenges of African countries' infrastructural weakness, in skills, utilities and transport, but many have built successful businesses and are investing in technological and product upgrading. Regional inter-country trade is expanding, and new investment opportunities are opening up.

The big challenges are twofold

First, there is the fight to sustain this industrialization effort in the current global market context – which is much more constraining to new competitors than the market context facing, for example, India in the years when it was building its pharmaceutical success story. Multilateral and bilateral policies have reinforced the stringent competition faced by Africa-based medicines producers. A core concept in our analysis is industrial capabilities. In Part I we explore the sources of the organizational, institutional, technical and human capabilities to make good products, to compete profitably in globalized markets that constantly force firms to upgrade, to overcome barriers to market entry and to distribute products effectively.

The second challenge is to ensure that the skills and competence built up by the manufacturers and distributors actually feed into better health care access for African populations. The institutional capabilities of the health system need also to be built up, to support, buy and use effectively locally manufactured supplies. Only on that basis can governments generate policies that bring the interests of the industrial and health sectors closer together, to collaborate for mutual benefit. In Part II we examine some country experiences of health-industry interactions, comparing East African countries' experience with Brazil and India, arguing that health system structure and initiative are as important as industrial policy to successful linkage. The values that underpin the importance of the pharmaceutical sector, its claim to policy priority, are rooted in the ethical requirement of universal access to competent health care.

The chapters in Part III therefore tease out experiences of some of the key aspects of health-industry interactions in more detail and identify some important policy issues to be tackled. All these issues are framed by political economy considerations of the ethics, interests and institutions involved. They include the highly contentious matters of price controls and standard setting for pharmaceutical products, plus examination of sources and problems of financing, the scope for innovative procurement processes that can reflect health system values while providing incentives for industrial investment, and the contested but important role of industrial manufacturers' associations and political lobbying.

This book is a loud challenge to pessimism about African industrial development and health care commitment. African governments have responsibility for their populations' health needs, and cannot address them without industrial expertise. The book explores the *conditions* under which industrial improvement can benefit those who need access to medicines and health care, pulling together the arguments for access and distribution with those for investment and industrial development. There are different routes by which improving supply capacities can generate local health improvement: this book is about how to generate local paths that work. It also identifies ways in which international donors and policy makers can shift from impeding to supporting the long-term development of local industrial and health system capabilities in African countries.

Note

1. See also http://www.local-pharma-production.net/index.php?id=97.

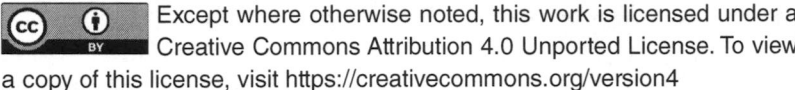

Part I

The Pharmaceutical Industry in Africa

Part I of this book aims to strengthen the inadequate evidence base on pharmaceutical manufacturing on the Sub-Saharan subcontinent. Throughout this book, 'local manufacturing' and 'African manufacturing' refer to manufacture physically located in Sub-Saharan Africa, whatever its ownership. The ownership structures are certainly relevant to understanding the development of pharmaceutical production, and indeed the extent to which the current industry is in African ownership is striking, while most output is produced for local and regional consumption. The African industry is, as we show, highly 'globalized' in the competitive pressures it faces, but also highly 'localized' in its markets and policy frameworks.

Part I therefore starts with an overview of the industry in Africa, tackling the recurrent myth that it barely exists. The four following chapters analyse aspects of the industrial experience of four countries in producing medicines: Kenya, Tanzania, Ethiopia and Mozambique. The chapters do not aim simply to describe the industrial evolution, though that is certainly one objective. They also explore in detail distinct aspects of the industrial histories: the evolution of technological capabilities in Kenya; the challenges in sustaining a relatively shallow industrial sector in Tanzania; the sharp turnaround of the industry in Ethiopia and its links to joint ventures and health sector change; and the immense challenge of starting from scratch in Mozambique, with Brazilian support. In each case, the authors are looking for wider lessons for policy and practice.

The final two chapters in this part are broader, and both also reflect some West African experiences. Chapter 6 asks an important question: What can help to bring more foreign direct investment to the pharmaceutical industry in Africa, with particular reference to Indian companies and Ghanaian experience? Finally, Chapter 7 addresses directly a question raised in several other chapters: What is the scope in African contexts for moving up the technological ladder, into producing the ingredients for medicines manufacture, and into more research and development activity?

1
Making Medicines in Africa: An Historical Political Economy Overview

Geoffrey Banda, Samuel Wangwe and Maureen Mackintosh

Introduction

This chapter sets out to show that, contrary to widespread misperception, pharmaceutical manufacturing in Sub-Saharan Africa is an established industry with a long history dating back at least to the 1930s. Data for the industry on the subcontinent are fragmented and incomplete (Berger et al., 2009; UNIDO, 2010a; 2010b; 2011a; 2011b), and this chapter and this book contribute to building a coherent historical picture and evidence base. This chapter presents some illustrative historical evidence, drawn from secondary data, reports and fieldwork by the authors and colleagues, as well as academic and non-academic literature.[1] We show that neither industrial capabilities in pharmaceuticals nor policy frameworks to support local pharmaceutical manufacture are a new phenomenon on the subcontinent.

The chapter takes an historical political economy lens to the development of the pharmaceutical industry, providing an overview and then examining three countries' industrial history in more depth. By a 'political economy lens' we mean a view of the evolution of the industry that replaces it within its historical political and economic context. Pharmaceuticals share many elements of the broader African experiences of industrialization. The industry also has, however, some very specific characteristics concerning technology and markets.

This chapter briefly traces the pharmaceutical industry's genesis and development in the context of colonial political history, independence and post-independence industrialization. We trace the development of the industry during the era of import substitution policies in the 1960s to 1970s, the economic crises of the 1980s and early 1990s, and the industrial rebuilding from the 1990s onwards. Some key political economy themes that are developed throughout the book are introduced here: the current context of international market liberalization, initiated in the era of economic crisis and structural adjustments policies, and its implications for manufacturing investment; the varying role of multinational corporations' (MNCs) investment in local manufacturing in Africa; the co-evolution and integration of the pharmaceutical industry with other manufacturing and industrial sectors; and the insertion of this relatively high-technology sector into local and international innovation systems and policies.

The chapter begins with an initial historical overview, based on firm-level evidence from nine Sub-Saharan African countries. It then compares and contrasts the industrial history of pharmaceuticals in three case study countries, Tanzania, Kenya and Zimbabwe, for which we have field data. These three countries cannot represent the highly diverse industrial history of Sub-Saharan Africa (henceforth often referred to as just Africa). Rather, they provide support and background for some of the generalizations suggested by the overview, and identify some illustrative similarities and differences in the pharmaceutical sector's roots and evolutionary trajectories across African countries. The case studies also identify a number of themes explored in depth in the rest of the book.

Pharmaceutical manufacturing in Africa: an historical overview

There has been substantial academic and policy questioning of the feasibility and desirability of African local pharmaceutical production (Kaplan and Laing 2005 is one of the most widely cited sources). We begin by countering this perception with evidence that pharmaceutical manufacturing companies have been setting up production facilities and manufacturing medicines in Africa since the 1930s.

A sketch of a pharmaceutical investment timeline

Figure 1.1 shows a time line of the pattern of establishment of pharmaceutical firms across different political and economic geographies on the African continent. It is drawn from a data base of start-up dates for manufacturing by larger pharmaceutical firms in a number of the major manufacturing countries in Sub-Saharan Africa, including South Africa, Nigeria, Kenya and Zimbabwe, and also some countries with smaller manufacturing sectors: Tanzania, Botswana, Uganda, Ethiopia and Ghana.

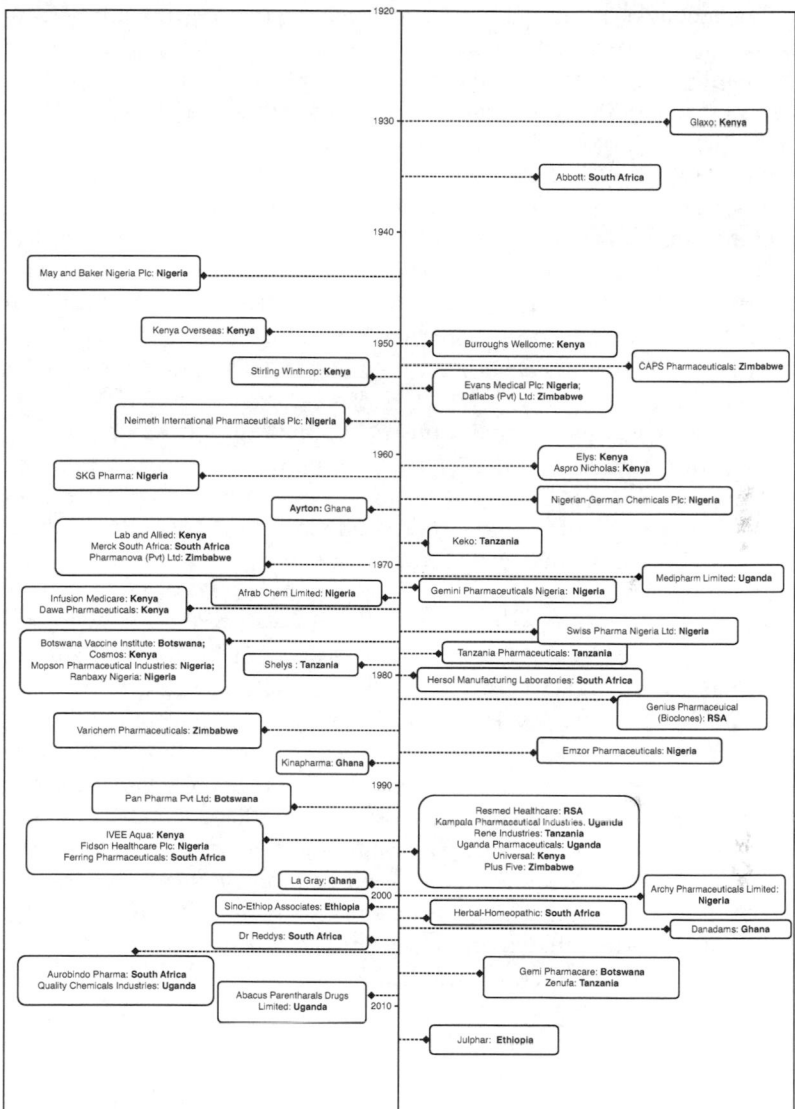

Figure 1.1 A timeline of selected pharmaceutical firm start-ups by country, 1930–2013

Source: drawn by author from created database.

The genesis of local pharmaceuticals manufacturing in South Africa, Nigeria and Kenya appears here as linked to multinational European companies setting up subsidiaries in colonies. In South Africa, Abbott was set up in 1935; in Nigeria, May and Baker was established in 1944; and in Kenya, Glaxo set up shop in 1930 (Figure 1.1). The whole period from 1930 to 1960 shows a slow take-off of local manufacturing in Kenya, Nigeria, South Africa and Zimbabwe. Historically these are the leading industrial countries in Sub-Saharan Africa. Local pharmaceutical industry set up did not occur in isolation, but was contemporary with the rise of other industrial sectors that supported mining and agricultural processing industries. Some of this industrialization was driven by pre-war supply chains with colonies and the disruptions of supplies during World War II.

Figure 1.1 suggests two major bursts of activity in setting up pharmaceutical firms. The first is the 1970s, starting in the 1960s and building up. Then there is a gap in the 1980s and early 1990s, when the rate of start-ups slows almost to zero. The second major burst of activity is from the mid-1990s and continuing into this century.

For most of the countries in Figure 1.1, the 1960s and 1970s were the early years of independence. Across the subcontinent, this post-independence era was characterized by efforts to tackle the challenge of industrialization and growth. Common approaches to industrial policy, promoted also in the development economics and planning literature, mixed public sector investment with import substitution policies, as briefly described in the case studies below. These were years of active developmental states in Africa (Mkandawire, 2001), which were also investing in public sector health and education provision to address the colonial legacies of inequality and discrimination. Domestic production of medicines, by public sector firms and locally owned private companies, found a market in expanding health sector demand.

By the late 1970s, however, this industrial development model was in trouble, and the impact of the economic crisis is reflected in Figure 1.1 by the dearth of new industrial investments in the 1980s. Key events included the oil crises of the 1970s, which severely inflated import bills, undermined balance of payments and fiscal balances and slowed down industrial activity through lack of foreign exchange. The early 1980s were years of severe economic crisis in many countries, exacerbated by severe drought.

The response across much of Africa took the form of structural adjustment programmes, linked to International Monetary Fund fiscal support and requiring extensive privatization and liberalization of trade. The timing varied: Ghana, for example, embarked on structural adjustment as early as 1983, whereas Zimbabwe only started in 1991.

The 1980s and early 1990s were, as a result, a period of deindustrialization across much of Africa. Previous industrial gains were eroded in many countries, and economic growth turned to decline, while health and education also suffered severely (Cornia et al., 1987). This is the context for the pause in industrial investment evident in Figure 1.1: the case studies that follow add some detail on this period, including the fate of existing firms and the distinctive experience of Zimbabwe.

From the mid-1990s, Figure 1.1 shows industrial investment in new pharmaceutical plants restarting across many countries. Much of this investment was by local investors. In some countries after independence, local entrepreneurs with working experience gained in multinational companies set up their own production facilities, a phenomenon not dissimilar to the Indian pharmaceutical industry evolution.

Pharmaceutical manufacturing capabilities in Africa: an overview

In 2005, a survey found that 37 of 46 African countries possessed some pharmaceutical manufacturing capability (Berger et al., 2009). Since then, numbers and activity have continued to expand (Figure 1.1). Almost all this manufacturing capacity produces generic medicines. Generic medicines are copies of originator or innovator branded medicines; generics have the same dosage form, therapeutic effect, delivery route, known risks and side effects as the originator drug. Local manufacturers in Africa import active pharmaceutical ingredients (APIs) and excipients mainly from India and China (UNIDO, 2010a; 2010b; 2011a; 2011b). Active pharmaceutical ingredients are the therapeutic component of the drug, while excipients are pharmacologically inactive substances used as a carrier for the active ingredients of a medication or as lubricants during the manufacturing process. Local firms import plant, equipment and machinery from India and China, while analytical equipment is sourced mainly from high-income countries such as Germany. Only South Africa and Ghana had built some technological capabilities to manufacture APIs locally, according to the 2005 survey (Berger et al., 2009), though other countries are now seeking to do so as well (see Chapter 7).

The pharmaceutical technologies in use, and the range of pharmaceutical drugs manufactured in African countries, are extensive. Firms have progressed from producing basic tablets and capsules to more complex technologies such as layered and sustained-release tablets. Product portfolios include suspensions and creams, syrups for children, sprays for inhalation and a range of sterile products such as injectables and ophthalmic preparations. The range of medicines includes anti-pain, anti-infectives including the penicillins, anti-worms and anti-virals, including anti-retrovirals for HIV/AIDS. There is a concerted effort to move into more products for chronic diseases such as hypertension and diabetes that are on the rise, implying a growing market.

Three indicative country case studies

The rest of this chapter briefly compares the industrial evolution of the pharmaceutical industry in three contrasting countries: Zimbabwe, Kenya and Tanzania. We show that their pharmaceutical sectors did not arise in isolation: in each case, the pharmaceutical industry co-evolved in important aspects with the broader industrial development. National patterns of industrial growth and periods of deindustrialization, along with shifts in industrial ownership and financing, are reflected in pharmaceutical firms' evolution. Broad industrial, macroeconomic and political economy influences are shared across industries in national industrial histories.

However, pharmaceuticals also display distinctive industrial characteristics that are observable across countries. The most striking are the technological challenges embodied in pharmaceutical production; the increasing regulatory impact on the African-based industry; and the implications of the health sector structure and funding, including the rise of donor funding, on the evolution of the local industrial structure. These issues are all explored in depth in the rest of the book. Here we present a comparative sketch of three pharmaceutical industrial histories, as an introduction to the analyses to come.

These historical sketches also employ some key concepts that will be used throughout the book, notably the concept of industrial capabilities. Given the high-skill, technologically demanding requirements of pharmaceutical production, as compared to widely produced consumer goods in these countries, the technological capabilities of the firms are key to their efforts to sustain competitiveness. By 'technological capabilities' we mean a set of skills and information the firm requires to operate a given technology and its associated organizational system efficiently (Wangwe, 1995). Firms' competitiveness in pharmaceuticals depends on their ability to obtain, absorb and use technological knowledge, capabilities which build on past skills and knowledge to cumulative effect. Successful firms' capabilities evolve from simpler to more complex activities in investment and process and product engineering (Lall, 1992).

Zimbabwe: the loss of early industrial advantage

There are elements of triumph and tragedy in the industrial history of Zimbabwe. As early as 1990, it was, after South Africa, touted as the next newly industrializing country (Pangeti et al., 2000; Phimister, 2000). The well-established and vibrant manufacturing sector was one of the most advanced and diversified in Africa (AfDB, 1994), contributing 30% to GDP and accounting for 35% of the country's gross export earnings. There were extensive linkages between manufacturing and key economic sectors such as mining, finance and agriculture. The manufacturing sector evolved to supply mining and agriculture, leveraging an extensive infrastructure (Mlambo, 2000; Phimister, 1988; 2000). Zimbabwe therefore provides a narrative of a pharmaceutical sector that arose in integration with other manufacturing and service sectors, illustrating the importance of linkages and support structures in an economy.

Early import substitution

The distinctive history of Zimbabwean manufacturing results from its political history and the related push towards industrial development through import substitution. The legacy begins from the Second World War era. Before then, the country was a destination for British and South African manufactures. During the war, the blockade of traditional trade routes from Britain and the resultant shortages prompted local industrial diversification and accelerated growth of local manufacturing. The average annual industrial growth from 1944 to 1948 was 24.4% (Pangeti et al., 2000). Later, the unilateral declaration of independence (UDI) from Britain in 1965, the trade with South Africa and the resulting UN sanctions (Pangeti et al., 2000; Phimister, 2000) reinforced the push towards industrial self-supply.

Zimbabwe's industrial history illustrates the potential benefits of import-substituting industrialization for countries that later liberalize trade. After 1945, imports from overseas recommenced, increasing competition. Local industry responded by turning to regional markets as an outlet for industrial overcapacity. The expanded markets included the 1953 Central African Federation (CAF) of Zambia, Zimbabwe and Malawi (then Northern and Southern Rhodesia and Nyasaland) (Pangeti et al., 2000). During this era, foreign direct investment by South African and British companies flowed into local manufacturing industry (Phimister, 2000). Industrial protection and import substitution were then vigorously pursued after UDI.

During the early expansionary phase, two of the five major pharmaceutical companies were established: CAPS Pharmaceuticals and Datlabs. The pioneer company, CAPS Pharmaceuticals (then Central African Pharmaceuticals [Private] Limited), was founded in 1953, manufacturing formulations and wholesaling (UNIDO, 2011b). In 1958, CAPS stopped general wholesaling and focussed on manufacturing (CAPS website, 2012). Datlabs (Pvt) Ltd was set up in 1954 as a subsidiary of Ingrams, a South African company (UNIDO, 2007; 2011b). These companies focussed on serving the regional market in the Central African Federation countries. A third major pharmaceutical company, Pharmanova (Pvt) Ltd, was established later, in 1970 in the UDI era (UNIDO, 2007). This period created an industrial base second only to South Africa in the region, including established pharmaceutical producers, inherited in 1980 by the independent government.

Industry–health care integration

A country's domestic market for pharmaceuticals is dependent on its health care spending and health care structure. At independence the new Zimbabwean government targeted the narrowing of the inherited racial gap in living standards by introducing free health care and education for all as key elements of social transformation (Davies and Ratso, 2000). Zimbabwe became renowned for high growth in education, health and public administration to promote social equity in development (Helmsing, 1990). The country also continued its inherited historically high level of reliance on domestically produced medicines (Turshen, 2001).

Zimbabwe also made a pragmatic and early shift to cheaper generic prescription policies to reduce cost of medicines: in 1981, the Ministry of Health produced an essential drugs list (EDLIZ) (WHO, 1995), and this formed the basis for local medicines production strategies. Zimbabwean entrepreneurs established Varichem Pharmaceuticals (Pvt) Ltd in 1985 to serve this expanding market (UNIDO, 2007).

The government also took industrial policy steps to address some of the consequences of 15 years of political unrest, liberation war and sanctions. Industrial machinery had become obsolete due to scarcity of foreign exchange, which continued into the early years of independence (Bond, 1998; Phimister, 1988; Chifamba, 2003). Companies struggled to import capital equipment and upgrade their technologies. The government partially eased foreign-exchange restrictions for verified export orders through an Export Revolving Fund (ERF) in 1983, followed by an Export Retention Scheme (ERS) in 1989 and later an Open General Import Licence (OGIL) in mid-1990s (Chifamba, 2003).

However, Zimbabwe was not spared the economic crises that swept across African countries from the mid-1980s. Expansion of social services without rising revenues led to budget deficits, forcing the government to abandon their initial resistance to economic structural adjustment programmes (AfDB, 1998). On the advice of the IMF and technocrats in the Ministry of Finance, the country embarked on a structural adjustment programme in 1991. Disastrous economic outcomes included deindustrialization, unemployment and deterioration of the health care system (AfDB, 1997; Brett, 2005; Richardson, 2005).

Despite the deteriorating industrial and economic conditions, however, Plus 5 Pharmaceuticals was established in 1996. The start-up used venture capital funding (UNIDO, 2007; 2011b), a testament to Zimbabwe's financial system's capability at the time, despite deindustrialization, and also to the continuing vibrancy of the pharmaceutical sector. The country continued to rely on locally manufactured medicines (Turshen, 2001), and Zimbabwe appears to have sustained some alignment of industrial and health policy goals through this tumultuous period.

Pharmaceuticals in an era of economic collapse

After 1997, however, economic collapse set in. The decade from 1997 to 2008 saw deindustrialization on a grand scale, as manufacturing decline was driven by hyperinflation (MTDP, 2010). Manufacturing real growth rates were negative every year from 1997 to 2008 except 2005, signifying declining manufacturing capacity as well as loss of skills and technological capabilities. Manufacturing share of GDP fell from 20% in 1997 to 11% in 2008 while GDP shrank annually. The manufacturing share of exports fell from 20% to slightly over 10%. The private sector declined to the point of operating at 10% capacity, faced with shortage of capital, foreign currency, and interrupted electricity supplies. Physical infrastructure crumbled, skilled people emigrated and incentives and institutions were severely debilitated (AfDB, 2009).

Yet even in this era, aligned industry, health and social development policies did create some positive feedback mechanisms, enhancing local manufacturers' innovative capabilities. This environment was instrumental in the country being one of the first in Africa to locally manufacture anti-retroviral medicines (ARVs) to address the HIV/AIDS pandemic (Banda, 2013). As Chapter 15 describes, in 2002 Zimbabwe issued a compulsory licence allowing its local manufacturers to produce ARVs.

This demonstrated purposive application of political will and policy infrastructure, associated with sustained local manufacturing capabilities, to meet a pressing health and social need.

However, the economic crisis created a cumulative collapse in the public health system's capacity to procure drugs over the period from 2003 to 2009. The country shifted to high donor dependence for public health care funding and drug procurement (Banda, 2013). In addition there was international political isolation, acute shortage of foreign currency and dwindling foreign direct investment (FDI) coupled with skilled resources flight (AfDB, 1997; Brett, 2005). The greatest challenge for local pharmaceutical industry was the loss of public health procurement as an industry policy tool (NECF, 2010). The increased reliance on donor funding posed a demand-side constraint for local firms: drugs for HIV/AIDS, TB and malaria were procured externally because the national procurement agency NATPHARM was incapacitated through lack of funds.

Current pharmaceutical manufacture in Zimbabwe

When the government of national unity was formed in 2009, there were various initiatives to resuscitate and rehabilitate the economy. Key strategies in the Short Term Economic Recovery Programme (STERP, 2009) were social protection, including food and humanitarian assistance and education. For health care, the focus was on building capacity in human resources, drugs and medical equipment availability, and reduction of preventable diseases. The health delivery strategy included addressing drug shortages: drug stocks in 2008 were just 36% of requirements, and stock-outs of essential drugs, vaccines and medical supplies had become common. The strategy also included capacitating NATPHARM, the national drug procurement agency, to supply government health institutions. There was a gradual improvement in the sector in the 2011–14 period.

The pharmaceutical industry in Zimbabwe now consists of nine pharmaceutical manufacturing companies registered with the Medicines Control Authority of Zimbabwe (MCAZ). Of these, five are the major generic manufacturers accounting for 90% of the formulation businesses (UNIDO, 2011b). The companies operate in a competition-intensive, low-margin commodity-type business, where profitability and long-term viability depend on economies of scale, assured demand and large markets (Berger et al., 2009). Currently the country is capable of producing 50% of all drugs on the essential drugs list, and if all research and development (R&D) activities in formulations are taken into account, the capability rises to supplying 75% (NECF, 2011). Firms used to export quite extensively in the East African region, and also to Namibia, Angola and South Africa (UNIDO, 2007; 2011b). In 2014, the local industry supplied medicines to the health sector valued at US$24 million compared to US$184.7 million of imported medicines and US$100.4 million of donated medicines (Zimstats, nd).

While Zimbabwe's experience shows that African countries can manufacture drugs for their local health system, and illustrates some ways in which health and industrial policies can be aligned, it is also a grim history of how economic crisis drives loss of industrial development opportunities in pharmaceuticals.

Kenya: creating the dominant East African producer

Kenya, like Zimbabwe, has a long history of pharmaceutical production. Local pharmaceutical manufacture can be traced back to the 1940s. The pioneer firm was the Kenya Overseas Company, established in 1947 and beginning local manufacturing activities in 1948. The next batch of firms included Sterling Winthrop (US), established in 1953; Burroughs Wellcome (East Africa) Ltd (UK) in 1955; and Aspro-Nicholas (EA) Ltd (Australia) in 1961 (Wamae and Kariuki Kungu, 2014). The early firms built up initial skills and experience in pharmaceutical manufacture in Kenya before independence in 1963.

After independence, Kenya also pursued policies of import-substituting industrialization (described and explained in Chapter 2). These policies supported manufacturing for the domestic market in the face of the 1970s balance-of-payments crises and rising oil prices. In this period pharmaceutical manufacturing expanded, benefitting from the industrial protection, and also from an active government policy to promote investment and technological upgrading. The government established the Industrial and Commercial Development Corporation (ICDC) to provide development finance, and supported a number of parastatal joint ventures, including Dawa and Infusion Medicare. The firms of Lab & Allied and Cosmos were also set up in this period.

The mid-1980s and 1990s saw in Kenya, as across Sub-Saharan Africa, a process of market liberalization, associated with structural adjustment programmes, and a shift to export promotion. In Kenya, export promotion included a number of schemes to allow bonded production for exports using duty-free inputs, but this had little impact on pharmaceuticals (Chapter 2). The early 1990s in Kenya also saw a push to 'buy local', using local health section procurement to benefit industrial development. There was industrial investment in pharmaceuticals production in this period, including Universal (Figure 1.1).

By the turn of the century, the Kenyan domestic medicines market was opening up in familiar ways to more global competition, notably from South Asia. Donors moved in to supply medicines for malaria, TB and especially HIV/AIDS, but this was later and more patchy in Kenya than in some neighbouring countries (Chapter 2). The relative strength of the production capabilities of the Kenyan industry by 2001 allowed the government to decide to permit compulsory licensing of generic production of HIV/AIDS medicines, and the subsequent issuing of voluntary licences (UNIDO, 2010a; see also Chapter 2). However import liberalization was by this date generating increasing competition from imports of finished formulations, and this seems to have been a factor in the departure of a number of multinational producers. In 2014, almost all pharmaceutical firms in Kenya were locally owned (Chapter 2).

A local industry with regional potential

In February 2014, Kenya had 39 pharmaceutical manufacturers registered with the Pharmacy and Poisons Board (PPB). Thirty-four were producing pharmaceuticals for human health, while the rest concentrated on veterinary products (Wamae and Kariuki Kungu, 2014). There were also 20 multinational firms with local representation for marketing purposes and /or involved in clinical trials.

Like the firms in Zimbabwe, Kenyan pharmaceutical activities are mainly production of finished formulations, with some reformulation and development activities. The industry mainly produces generic products, importing APIs, excipients and other raw materials from India, China and Germany. India dominates both raw materials and finished product imports, accounting for 40% of all pharmaceutical-related imports in 2008 (UNIDO, 2010a: 49). Few key inputs can be sourced locally; exceptions are maize starch, sugar and glucose syrup, rectified spirit and ethanol, as well as sodium chloride and quite a wide range of packaging materials.[2]

The Kenyan industry continues to suffer from relative low capacity utilization, and Chapter 2 explores the reasons for this in detail. They include limitations in the functioning state of machinery, delays in sourcing spare parts from abroad and human resource issues, in particular shortages of highly specialized skills in some critical areas such as product development.

Despite these constraints, Kenya's pharmaceutical sector is the strongest producer of pharmaceuticals in the East African region, and is upgrading to more demanding technological capabilities. In addition to the standard generic products in the dosage forms of tablets, capsules, creams and syrups, the industry in Kenya includes three firms producing injectable infusions (small and large volume parenteral preparations) and ophthalmic formulations. One firm (Universal) has achieved WHO prequalification for one of its products, allowing the firm to tender for donor contracts and also providing an indicator of the firm's technical capabilities and standards.

A further measure of the strength of Kenya-based pharmaceutical production is its export success, which accelerated from about 2002. Kenyan pharmaceutical producers' main export destinations are in the COMESA region: the Common Market for Eastern and Southern Africa, which does not include South Africa or Tanzania.[3] However, the Kenyan industry still supplies a tiny fraction of COMESA's medicines market, while provisioning only around a quarter of its own domestic market. There is substantial room for expansion. With supportive government policies, Kenya should be able to exploit effectively the integration of East African and Southern African markets to expand its role as one of the medicines production 'hubs' in Sub-Saharan Africa. Chapter 2 discusses the industrial challenges in depth.

Tanzania: a latecomer under stress

Tanzania has a shorter history of pharmaceutical manufacturing than the two countries just discussed. In the colonial period during World War II, facilities for manufacturing simple medicines were established to counter the risk of blockade. However, after the war, these closed, and the country reverted to imports. The mainland, then called Tanganyika, did not, unlike Zimbabwe and Kenya, have a large colonial settler population in the pre-independence period, and the level of industrialization at independence was correspondingly small.

Pioneering firms and public sector investment

The earliest pharmaceutical manufacturing firm in Tanzania seems to have been Mansoor Daya Chemicals Ltd., a privately owned firm. Mr. Daya, a pharmacist, began with a retail pharmacy in Dar es Salaam in 1959. He set up his own firm in 1962, originally in a small godown, later moving to his current production site.[4]

In the 1960s and early 1970s, the Nyerere government in Tanzania turned to the promotion of industrial development through public investment. In contrast to Kenya, the industrial policies were driven by a more explicitly socialist agenda, although, as the case studies in this chapter illustrate, the use of public investment to promote industrial development was a broadly implemented approach in these post-independence years (Lall and Wangwe, 1998). Manufacturing output rose from 4% of GDP at independence to about 8% or 9% in the 1970s. The production was mainly oriented to the domestic market, although there was a slow growth of manufacturing exports to East Africa, until these markets were lost with the break-up of the East African Community in 1977 (Bagachwa and Mbelle, 1995).

This was a period of import-substituting policies, paralleling those in Zimbabwe and Kenya, with an overvalued exchange rate, import controls, protective tariffs and administrative allocation of foreign exchange. It was also a period of state-led industrialization, including public sector investments in manufacturing plants. Two public sector pharmaceutical firms were established to provide essential medicines to a rapidly expanding public health sector. Keko Pharmaceuticals was opened as a production unit within the Ministry of Health in 1968 to supply tablets, capsules and large-volume parenterals for distribution to public sector health care facilities. Tanzania Pharmaceutical Industries Ltd (TPI) began as a public enterprise in 1978 with assistance from the Finnish government.

This was thus a period when the government was placing priority on expanding health care to serve a basic need, and the pharmaceutical industry responded to an alignment of industrial and health policies. The industrial strategy prioritized production to meet basic needs, including health care, creating a conducive environment for investment in pharmaceuticals. Private clinical practice was banned in 1977, except for some religious providers, and the main market for medicines was the public sector, plus retail pharmacies. However, the domestic market expansion was sufficiently attractive for a second private start-up, Shelys Pharmaceuticals, which began production in 1979. In 1984, Shelys was bought by the Tanzanian Sumaria Group of companies and built up into the largest pharmaceutical firm in the country.

Economic crisis and liberalization

Like our other other case-study countries in this chapter, Tanzania was hit by a major economic crisis in the 1980s. However, the impact in Tanzania was particularly severe, a result of a confluence of circumstances including a small and particularly internationally uncompetitive manufacturing sector focussing on consumer goods for the domestic market, and a liberalization process that was rapid and relatively unconstrained by transitional policy safeguards. The late 1970s and early 1980s were marked by severe shortages of goods, as foreign exchange constraints reduced inputs to local production and export manufacturing declined. Capacity utilization dropped dramatically, and manufacturing output fell back to 7% of GDP by 1985 (Bagachwa and Mbelle, 1995). Pharmaceutical manufacturers were badly affected by foreign exchange shortages that constrained their ability to import APIs and other key inputs.

The major policy framework reversal was signalled by the adoption of the Economic Recovery Programme (ERP) in 1986. This shifted policy sharply away from import substitution, liberalizing imports of final goods and providing export incentives for manufacturers. While there was some export recovery, production of consumer goods for the domestic market suffered badly as cheaper imports flowed in. Given the prior levels of industrial protection in Tanzania, the liberalization constituted a much more severe shock than in Kenya or Zimbabwe, where protection had been lower and transition was better managed. Firms in Tanzania had little time for adjustment (Lall and Wangwe, 1998: 93). The result in Tanzania was a swathe of deindustrialization, and firms serving the domestic market failed.

Pharmaceuticals faced a second challenge also: the 'battering' taken by public sector health care funding and other government provided social services as the government budget went into severe crisis (Kaijage and Tibaijuka, 1996). As a result, the two government firms, Keko and TPI, ceased to be able to compete with imported medicines, lost their markets, and closed in the early 1990s. However, the two private pharmaceutical producers, Mansoor Daya Chemicals and Shelys, survived the economic crisis years. Shelys in particular was built up into a successful business as the largest pharmaceutical firm in Tanzania and expanded exports to the region. Another privately owned local firm, Interchem Pharmaceuticals was set up in 1989 in Moshi, part-owned by the IPP group of companies.

The challenges of competitiveness and upgrading

Industrial research in the 1990s emphasized the importance of firms' technological capabilities for survival and competitiveness in a more open economy (Wangwe, 1995). In the late 1990s and early 2000s, some of these technological capabilities were rebuilt in Tanzania, in pharmaceuticals as in other industries. The challenge was particularly great in pharmaceuticals given its reliance on skills and ability to manage technological upgrading effectively.

However, from the late 1990s, the pharmaceutical industry in Tanzania was renewed and grew substantially, entirely through the efforts of local investors and managers. The government sold 60% of the equity in each of the inactive government firms, Keko and TPI, to private Tanzanian investors in 1995. Both reopened in the late 1990s. In 2003, Shelys bought Beta Healthcare International, a Kenyan pharmaceutical company (previously Boots), with private equity funding from Aureos Capital. This was the first cross-border merger whereby a Tanzanian firm purchased a Kenyan company, and it made Shelys Africa Group the largest East African pharmaceutical company at that time.[5]

By 2009, the high point of Tanzanian pharmaceutical production, there were eight firms producing for the local market and also exporting regionally. The new firms were started by a mix of local and international investment. Tanzansino started production in 2000 as a joint venture between the Tanzanian military and a Chinese provincial government body. In 2007, the ownership changed when the Chinese provincial government shares were bought by Holley Industrial Group Ltd., a Chinese industrial group including a firm producing and exporting one of the new artemisinin-based combination therapies for malaria.[6] AA Pharmaceuticals, a smaller firm established by a Tanzanian private investor who is a pharmacist, began production in 2002. And in 2007, a new plant, Zenufa Laboratories, was built and opened. Owned by a DRC (Congo)-based diversified family firm, Zenufa aimed for Good Manufacturing Practice status from the start. These new start-ups reflected the changed economic circumstances in Tanzania: faced with sharp external competition, they aimed for efficient manufacturing and regional export capability from the beginning.

Data are not easy to assemble, but Table 1.1 provides a summary overview of the pharmaceutical industry in Tanzania just before the start-up of Zenufa. Seven firms were then active. Shelys at that time was responsible for about half of local production by value (Table 1.1). Much of the rest of the output was supplied by TPI, Interchem and Keko. The main suppliers to the public wholesaler (MSD) were Shelys, TPI and Keko, while Shelys was also the main exporter. Chapter 3 analyses the Tanzanian industry after this date.

Conclusion: shifting the debate

This chapter aimed to dispel the persistent myth that pharmaceutical production is not an African industry, tracing the long industrial history of the production of medicines on the Sub-Saharan subcontinent. This

Table 1.1. Pharmaceutical production and exports, Tanzania, 2004–05

Producer	Value of production (US$ million)	Share of total production (%)	Sales to the public sector (US$ million)	Sales to private market (US$ million)	Exports (US$ million)
Shelys Pharmaceuticals	16.0	49.2	5.7	7.4	2.9
Tanzania Pharmaceutical Industries	6.7	20.4	4.0	2.5	0.2
Other firms	9.9	15.0	1.3	8.5	0.0
Total	32.6	100.0	11.0	18.4	3.1

Source: Compiled by the authors from data in MoHSW (2006). Data in Tanzanian shillings in that source converted to US$ using the average exchange rate of 0.00095 for the year July 2004–June 2005 obtained from www.oanda.com.

book aims to contribute to shifting the whole debate on *making medicines in Africa* definitively away from 'Should it be done?' to 'How can it be done well to the benefit of public health?' Despite the successes to date, local manufacturers serve only a small proportion of African domestic demand, let alone population need (Berger et al., 2009; UNCTAD, 2011; WHO, 2005; 2011). The bulk of medicines consumed are imported from India and China, and there is heavy reliance on disease-specific donor-funded imports. That situation is not sustainable. African countries need to grow their capabilities to address the health needs of their populations, and pharmaceutical manufacturing and its associated technical and scientific bases are needed for that effort.

Nationally and across the African subcontinent, efforts to expand local manufacturing and innovation are extensive. The business case for local drug manufacture – and its potential to enhance security of medicines supply – has gained ground within African Union (AU) and New Partnership for Africa's Economic Development (NEPAD) circles. Not all countries have the capacity and capability to embark on the full spectrum of pharmaceutical production, innovation and R&D. The *Strengthening Pharmaceutical Innovation in Africa* strategy report (Berger et al., 2009) and the UNIDO-AU-sponsored African Pharmaceutical Manufacturing Plan of Action (AU-UNIDO, 2013) propose a phased approach of working up the technological ladder (see Chapter 15). Given the current rates of investment and industrial development in pharmaceuticals, the debate now concerns the policy and business determinants of cost-effective manufacture of safe and efficacious medicines, and the conditions for aligning industry, finance and public health needs. The mechanics of achieving this become a matter of strategic intent at national, regional and continental levels. This is the terrain this book explores.

Notes

1. Part of this chapter draws on research undertaken for the project *Industrial productivity and health sector performance*. The findings, interpretations, conclusions and opinions expressed here are those of the authors and do not necessarily reflect the views or policies of DFID or the UK ESRC, whose financial support is gratefully acknowledged (project ES/J008737/1). Some of the evidence is drawn from fieldwork by Watu Wamae and Joan Kariuki Kungu for this project.
2. Source: UNIDO (2010a) and interviews.
3. Source: http://about.comesa.int/, accessed 12 April 2015.
4. Source: interviews.
5. Source: Sumaria Group website: http://www.sumaria.biz/our-businesses/, accessed 6 March 2014.
6. Source: interview with Tanzansino manager, 2010.

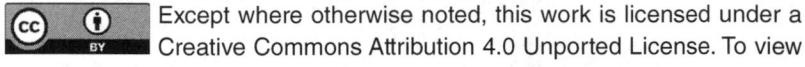

2

Pharmaceuticals in Kenya: The Evolution of Technological Capabilities

Roberto Simonetti, Norman Clark and Watu Wamae

Introduction

As Chapter 1 briefly outlined, Kenya has a strong and long-standing pharmaceutical industry. A 2015 Business Monitor report on pharmaceutical manufacturing in Kenya states that the country hosts the largest pharmaceutical industrial base in East Africa. The report also sees a bright future as a 'potential base for export across East Africa' (BMI Research, 2015). This chapter locates the Kenyan pharmaceutical industry within the country's historical context of industrial development and growth.

The features of the local production of medicines are shaped by the characteristics of the Kenyan economic and industrial systems, which in turn are the product of its economic history. To analyse this shaping, this chapter briefly presents and then applies an evolutionary economic understanding of industrial capabilities, focusing particularly on technological capabilities at the firm and industrial system level, their sources and evolution. This framework of industrial analysis is also used in a number of subsequent chapters in this book. It is particularly illuminating for the analysis of the development of an industry, pharmaceuticals, that is technologically demanding relative to the industrial and economic context in a low-income country such as Kenya.

Pharmaceutical manufacturers face constant competitive and regulatory pressure to upgrade their technological capabilities, and the evolutionary framework of analysis emphasizes the extent to which this upgrading relies on both firm-level investment building on existing capabilities, and also on the benefits that accrue from its surrounding industrial base. Chapter 1 briefly noted that African countries' broader industrial base frequently stems in turn from an era of policy-led import-substituting industrialization. This chapter explores in more detail how the pharmaceutical industry has built on this basis in Kenya, and the scope that gives the industry for exploiting the opportunities opened up by the subsequent more liberalized and competitive markets. It also outlines some of policy decisions that have shaped the industry's development, and some of the challenges for firms and policy makers.

This chapter draws on a range of sources, including trade and manufacturing data, secondary published and grey literature sources and also interviews with manufacturers and distributors and other field data collected in 2012–14.[1]

The evolution of Kenya's pharmaceutical industry in the context of post-colonial industrialization

The profile of the pharmaceutical industry in Kenya is influenced by the country's broader economic and industrial history. The post-independence industrial history of Kenya can be split into three periods according to the policy regimes adopted: the early years of import substitution industrialization (ISI), until the 1970s; the liberalization and gradual opening up of the economy in the 1980s and 1990s; and the new millennium (Chege, Ngui and Kimiyu, 2014).

Pharmaceutical production was already taking place before the advent of independence in 1963, as Chapter 1 described. The early firms were mainly foreign direct investments (FDI). The newly independent country then continued to implement policies of ISI that had started during the colonial period.

Import-substituting industrialization is a set of economic and trade policies that aim to promote domestic industrialization in order to reduce the country's dependence on manufacturing from abroad. The policies seek to promote the accumulation of skills, capital and knowledge for the production of manufacturing goods by limiting imports of selected manufacturing goods through a variety of trade restrictions and subsidizing domestic manufacturing enterprises. In the Kenyan case, local producers were shielded from foreign competition in manufactures in a variety of ways. High tariffs, even reaching 100% of the goods' value, and quotas were imposed on imported manufactures, which were also charged higher rail fares, with the result that their prices were high for Kenyan consumers. Domestic manufacturing firms were also helped with financial subsidies, allocated land for production facilities, and allowed to have import duties refunded on the inputs (raw materials and equipment) they had to import for production.

The Kenyan government also explicitly welcomed foreign-owned firms who set up production facilities in the country, as they contributed to the domestic industrial development. The large weight of FDI in Kenyan industry of the colonial period is also typical of the early years of independence, when it even reached half of industrial output (Maxon, 1992). Fearing a flight of FDI, a year after independence, in 1964, the government passed the Foreign Investment Act, which gave reassurances to foreign firms in areas such as repatriation of profits and protection from nationalization.

This policy orientation towards manufacturing for the domestic market was reinforced in the 1970s by balance-of-payments crises and rising oil prices which led to scarcity of foreign exchange. Manufacturing of consumer goods for the local market expanded rapidly in the early 1970s, and there was diversification into upstream supplier industries such as plastics. In this period, pharmaceutical manufacturing expanded, benefitting from the industrial protection, and also from an active government policy to promote investment and technological upgrading. Laboratories & Allied was incorporated in 1970. The government established the Industrial and Commercial Development Corporation (ICDC) to promote the inclusion of local people in industry by providing development finance and technical assistance. ICDC helped to develop pharmaceutical production in this period through parastatal joint ventures. Dawa was established as a 1970s joint venture between the ICDC and the Yugoslav government. A firm producing infusions, Infusion Medicare, began in the mid-1970s as a joint venture between the ICDC and Hoechst E.A. (the latter the East African arm of a German pharmaceutical producer now part of Sanofi).

ISI policy in this period successfully created an industrial base in Kenya, especially in light consumer industries such as textile and foodstuffs, but also in others such as metal products. Between independence and 1980, industrial output quadrupled, the share of GDP in manufacturing grew from 10.1% to 13.3% and the number of industrial establishments more than doubled (Ogonda, 1992: 297–98). The increase in local manufacturing reduced the multinational companies' (MNCs) share of industrial output, which however still accounted for 20% of industrial output in the early 1970s (Maxon, 1992: 385).

However, the protection from international competition encouraged local firms to focus on the protected local market and neglect exports. This created an anti-export bias that, together with external shocks such as the oil crises and a deterioration of terms of trade, led to a shortage of foreign exchange. In 1980 Kenya had to take a loan with the World Bank, which imposed structural adjustment conditions. This marked the beginning of the phase of liberalization and structural adjustment policies in the mid-1980s and 1990s, as it happened across Sub-Saharan Africa, and the beginning of a shift to export promotion. In Kenya, export promotion included a number of measures to allow production for exports using duty-free inputs, but the implementation was slow and tentative, with little impact on export.

The gradual opening up of local markets created competition that had an adverse impact on local industrial activity. Shortage in foreign currency contributed to the decline of domestic industry as firms found it difficult to buy foreign inputs and equipment, with adverse effects on capacity utilization and therefore productivity. After an economic crisis at the beginning of the 1990s, liberalization and export promotion accelerated with the creation of Export Promotion Zones (EPZs), participation in the Common Market for Eastern and Southern Africa (COMESA) and the East Africa Community (EAC), and the removal of price controls in 1994. Export promotion and international competition, however, had little impact on pharmaceuticals in that period. More important was a push in the 1990s to 'buy local', aiming, for example to ensure that basic medicines kits should be 50% local products (Wamae and Kariuki Kungu, 2014). Local pharmaceutical companies benefitted from this policy – an example of active use of health sector procurement as an industrial policy. Among the larger Kenyan manufacturers, Regal was established in the 1980s and Universal in the 1990s. Parastatal firms were privatized.

The third phase of industrial development, in the new millennium, saw an increase in exports especially in textiles through the United States' African Growth and Opportunity Act (AGOA), which facilitated exports to the US and increased activity in EPZs. In spite of this new push to promote exports, the pressure of global competition from other low-income countries has meant that the share of manufacturing in total GDP has not changed significantly, and much of industrial activity is still carried out in the informal sector by micro enterprises, whose small size makes it difficult to find funds for investment, expansion and upgrading. During these years, most of the foreign MNCs also ceased to produce in Kenya as they reorganized their supply chains globally in the light of competition from China and India to find cheaper locations for production. It is possible that local producers may have benefitted from the flight of production from MNCs, being able to take their place in some market segments and absorbing employees already trained by foreign MNCs.

The development of Kenya's pharmaceutical industry suggests that ISI policies were important to build an initial industrial base. Previous analyses of industrialization have argued the ISI policies followed by careful liberalization and export promotion might be useful to promote industrialization (see, e.g., Athreye, 2004, for the Indian software industry). So it is possible that ISI policies enabled Kenya to start the accumulation of basic technological know-how, perhaps through parastatal joint ventures, such as those formed by ICDC, in spite of their problems. The opening up of export markets, especially with the creation of COMESA and EAC and the policies that promoted exports such as the formation of EPZs, also enabled the strongest firms to adapt to international competition and offered opportunities for the expansion that is observed today, as the next section shows.

The Kenyan pharmaceutical industry and its market position

In historical studies of industrialization in Kenya, the pharmaceutical sector is rarely mentioned as it traditionally accounted for a very small share of industrial output. However, recently its status has been increasingly recognized. For example, pharmaceuticals are mentioned as one of the eighteen strategic sectors in the National Industrialization Policy 2011–15 (Ministry of Industrialization, 2010). Kenyan local manufacturers of medicines have shown great resilience during the years of economic difficulties and are now embarked on a process of growth and technological upgrading that, if successful, can establish them as a major player in the East African market for medicines.

Kenya's pharmaceutical production grew continuously from 2007 to 2013. As Figure 2.1 shows, in that period total production of tablets, capsules, liquid preparations for oral use and creams/ointments alone increased from US$34.1 million to US$154 million. The figure also shows that the composition of products has changed over these years, with creams and ointments becoming more popular, although virtually all product types have steadily increased with the possible exception of capsules.

Kenya has also seen strong growth in its pharmaceutical exports in the new millennium, especially since 2002. Exports started growing around 1992–93 thanks to the 'buy local' push, which promoted the expansion of local manufacturing. However, during the 1990s and early 2000s,

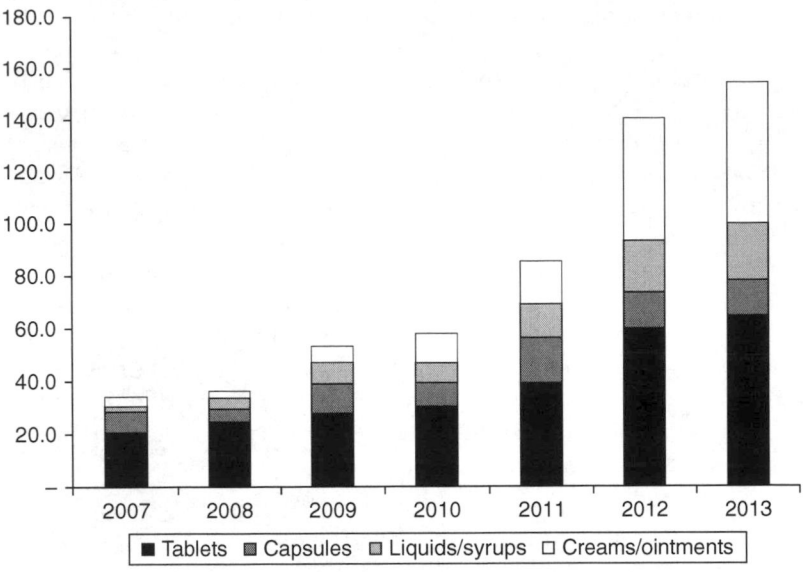

Figure 2.1   Local production of non-parenteral medicines in Kenya by type of product, 2007–13 (US$ million)

Source: Kenya National Bureau of Statistics, Production data for the period 2007 to 2013, Government of Kenya, Nairobi, obtained 4 September 2014.[2]

local production was affected by the adverse effects of liberalization policies described in the previous section, and exports remained stable. These years also saw a wave of divestments of production activities from foreign-owned companies that carried on in the new millennium as Kenya's industrial environment deteriorated and MNC producers moved out of Kenya to lower cost platforms. By 2014, only one MNC was still manufacturing in Kenya – GSK. Otherwise, pharmaceutical firms in Kenya are currently mainly locally owned.

The great majority of Kenyan's pharmaceutical exports are destined to Sub-Saharan Africa (SSA). COMESA is the main export destination for Kenya's pharmaceutical exports, with Kenya supplying about 50 per cent of the region's production. In relative terms, however, this translates into a minute share of the COMESA market.

With respect to the main importers of Kenya's pharmaceutical products, Uganda has remained a significant market over a number of decades. Somalia and Sudan have also seen significant growth of Kenyan products, particularly over the last two decades.

In spite of the growth in production and exports, the Kenyan pharmaceutical industry has to overcome important challenges in order to consolidate and expand its influence in the East African region. Kenya's pharmaceutical industry is still mainly oriented towards the home market, with an export share of domestic production only ranging between 15 and 20 per cent, at least up to 2010. Furthermore, the Kenyan producers' share of their own home market is estimated at around 25% of domestic demand (see also Chapter 8), leaving room for expansion (Wamae and Kariuki Kungu, 2014).

Kenyan manufacturers sell to the Kenyan public procurement agency KEMSA, and to the large non-profit wholesaler the Mission for Essential Drugs Supply (MEDS) that supplies predominantly the faith-based health care sector. They also sell into the large private sector (Chapter 8). Public procurement is regulated by the Public Procurement and Disposal Act of 2005, and tendering decisions are based mainly on pricing, though a 15% price preference for local manufacturers is available. Producers and distributors are free to set their own prices and mark-ups, and private mark-ups are, on average, high. The pricing of medicines in Kenya was completely liberalized in 1993.

In the new millennium the Kenyan domestic medicines market has been hit by more global competition, notably from South Asia. A key development for the pharmaceutical industry has been the large-scale movement of donors into supplying medicines for malaria, TB and especially HIV/AIDS. This has been a strong influence on the domestic market and pharmaceutical policies in a number of the countries discussed in this book. The arrival of the large donors was, however, somewhat later and more patchy in Kenya than in some neighbouring countries. PEPFAR, for example, the main US programme for funding HIV/AIDS medication, began to operate in Kenya only in 2008, and Kenya received no funding under Rounds 8 and 9 of the Global Fund financing (UNIDO, 2010: 41).

The production capabilities of the Kenyan industry were confirmed during this period by the companies' role in the campaigning that led to the 2001 government decision to allow compulsory licensing of generic production of HIV/AIDS medicines, and the subsequent issuing of voluntary licences (UNIDO, 2010). However, private importers from South and East Asia were increasingly generating price-based competition in the Kenyan medicines market as liberalization took hold. With export figures that in absolute terms remain very modest, it is essential that Kenyan manufacturers keep upgrading and also control costs in order not only to expand its foreign markets but also to keep up with increasingly demanding technological standards and cheap foreign competition that creates a serious challenge to local producers.

Technological capabilities and sectoral systems of innovation

The previous sections have shown that Kenyan pharmaceutical manufacturers are enjoying a period of growth. However they also face challenges that arise from cheap imports and the need to constantly upgrade their technology in order to keep up with global competition and increasingly demanding technical standards and to successfully exploit new market opportunities. A key factor in the future prospects of the Kenyan pharmaceutical industry is therefore the extent to which the local producers will be able to improve their technological capabilities.

The notion of technological capabilities, which has now entered the mainstream analysis of industrial development, can be traced back to the work of evolutionary economists such as Richard Nelson, Sydney Winter, Christopher Freeman and Giovanni Dosi (Dosi et al., 1988; Nelson and Winter, 1982). Evolutionary economics started as a critique of the dominant theoretical framework in economics, the neoclassical approach. The critique arose from the observation that the tools of neoclassical analysis were not well suited to the study of technological and industrial change. Neoclassical economics focuses on the working of the price mechanism in the coordination of economic activity but makes strong and unrealistic assumptions about the nature of technological knowledge and the way firms (and, in general, other economic agents) operate. Technology is seen as information, which has public good features and is therefore easily transferred between firms. Technology transfer is simplistically seen as the transfer of free information.

Evolutionary economists, however, argue that much of technological knowledge is tacit and hence difficult to articulate, let alone transfer easily. The effective use of technology requires that any publicly available technical information be processed using know-how and skills that not only are costly to acquire but also differ across firms, industries and countries. Firms and other organizations, like people, acquire skills, or capabilities, that become embedded in their procedures (also called routines) and people through a process of learning that is shaped by the history of the firm. Technological capabilities, therefore, are the organizational skills that enable firms to make effective use of technologies, including the ability to adapt them, improve them and even develop radically new products and processes. Because of their tacit nature, capabilities are costly to acquire, are learned over time and change slowly over time. An important consequence of this view is that since firms' histories and sources of learning differ, the capabilities that firms accumulate also differ. Indeed, industry studies have shown that firms within the same industry usually have many differences that are persistent over time: each firm is unique (Griliches and Mairesse, 1995).

The work on capabilities of early evolutionary economists originally focussed on advanced technologies and firms in industrialized countries. However, other scholars, such as Lall, extended this work into the context of developing countries. In an influential paper, Lall (1992) distinguished between firm-level and country-level capabilities. Firm capabilities include both investment and production capabilities and can be classified according to their degree of complexity, from basic, which involve experience-based tasks, to intermediate, which involve an element of search, to advanced, which are research-based and involve the creation of wholly new products and processes. Firm capabilities also include 'linkage capabilities', the way in which firms learn from and transfer knowledge to the external environment, that is, other organizations and institutions, including customers, suppliers, government agencies and science and technology providers. Countries also have distinctive national capabilities, which are more than the sum of the capabilities of their firms and other organizations because they also include they way economic agents interact and the features of the economic environment, such as the policies, incentives and institutions.

The early work on technological capabilities has been further developed by many scholars and has now entered mainstream thought in the field of science, technology and innovation studies (STI). A useful development of this theorizing is the recognition that industrial sectors have a set of institutions and organizations that differ across sectors and influence the way technological capabilities are accumulated and firms compete. In order to understand an industry's patterns of development and change, it is necessary to study the various agents that influence the accumulation of knowledge and the nature of competition in the industry and the way they interact.

The pharmaceutical sector is a typical example of the distinctiveness of sectoral institutions that shape technological learning and competition. Medicines are usually strictly regulated for their efficacy and safety by government agencies in a way that is unusual in other industries. The structure of demand is also distinctive because of the important role played by the state through the public procurement of essential medicines for the health system and, especially in low-income countries, the major role played by international donors in the purchase of key medicines. On the supply side, universities also play an important role as providers of skilled labour and scientific knowledge.

Technological capabilities in manufacturing of medicines in Kenya

This section draws on various sources, including firm interview data, in order to give an assessment of the Kenyan technological capabilities in the local production of pharmaceuticals. The technological capabilities of the Kenyan domestic pharmaceutical sector are analysed by looking at various dimensions of the production system in which local manufacturers of pharmaceutical operate.

The analysis starts with the description of the local producers because the firms are at the centre of the industrial system. A good starting point for the assessment of the manufacturers' capabilities is the analysis of the characteristics of their products in terms of quality and technological sophistication, the extent to which they achieve industry standards and their productivity. What firms can achieve, however, also depends on the capabilities of the system of suppliers, customers, regulations and institutions with which they interact, including the educational and financial systems, so these aspects will be included in the analysis.

Industrial structure

Local manufacturing of pharmaceuticals in Kenya is dominated by locally owned firms. In 2014 there were 39 local manufacturing firms with products registered with the Pharmaceuticals and Poisons Board (PPB), the agency that regulates the manufacture and trading of medicines in Kenya. Of these, 34 produced medicines for human consumption, whilst at least five firms produced animal health products. Of the 34 firms, only one producer is a foreign-owned MNC, GSK East Africa, which has not followed the exodus of other MNCs. Although MNCs dominated the local production of pharmaceuticals in Kenya in the 1990s, because of the unattractive economic conditions in Kenya in the 1990s and changes in global supply chains, most of them have moved production facilities to lower cost locations and are only present in Kenya for activities such as marketing and clinical studies (Wamae and Kariuki Kungu, 2014).

However, government policy has provided other incentives for local production by removing import duties and taxes from inputs to pharmaceutical products, such as APIs, excipients and packaging materials. The situation, however, changed in 2013 when the new VAT act reintroduced taxation for pharmaceutical inputs and only exempted finished products. This decision made locally produced medicines up to 22% more expensive, and the industry put pressure on the government to reverse the decision. This happened in the 2014 Act, but there are still some unresolved issues that are worrying local manufacturers (Wamae et al., 2014).

Studies of the Kenyan supply medicines chain show that Kenya has high margins for distributions, which raise the final price of the medicines to users in spite of fairly low manufacturing costs, in comparison to countries, such as Brazil, India, Indonesia, Kenya, Netherlands, Russia and South Africa. The study shows that the percentage of distribution costs is clearly highest in Kenya (see IMS Institute for Healthcare Informatics, 2014: 11). The high margins are a sign of the market power enjoyed by private distributors, who have a global reach and access to cheap imports, mainly from India.

Products and standards

Kenyan manufacturers are mainly engaging in activities that require basic to moderate technological capabilities, such as formulation activities, that is, converting manufactured bulk substances into final usable forms, and packaging rather than activities at the high end of the technological spectrum, such as R&D aimed at the discovery of new molecules and product development or the production of bulk pharmaceutical substances (APIs). The tablet is the most common dosage form; Kenyan firms also manufacture capsules, topical preparations (creams, gels, ointments or pastes), liquid preparations for oral use (including syrups), injectable infusions (small and large volume parenteral preparations) and ophthalmic formulations. Topical preparations have seen significant growth between 2007 and 2013 (Figure 2.1) (Wamae and Kariuki Kungu, 2014).

Formulations, however, can vary substantially in terms of the technological capabilities required for production. Products such as injectable infusions and ophthalmic formulations require sterilization, which is achieved through a production process that is technologically complex and demanding in terms of meeting standards of safety, efficacy and quality – particularly for injectable infusions. There are three local firms that manufacture injectable infusions and a few others that produce sterile ophthalmic products, including Laboratories & Allied (Wamae and Kariuki Kungu, 2014).

There are also important differences in the technological requirements within the group of non-sterile formulations. Some of the more technologically progressive firms have dedicated laboratories that undertake extensive product development activities with regard to existing products and are developing the capabilities for the production of more technologically sophisticated products. For example, some firms are moving from plain tablets to modified-release and sustained-release tablets. Some firms also engage in active process improvements. Some producers already meet WHO-GMP standards, and are also upgrading their production processes to gain WHO recognition, which could possibly open the door to funding by international donor agencies. One company, Universal Corporation, has already received WHO prequalification for its Lamivudine/Zidovudine anti-retroviral product in 2011, and other firms, such as Cosmos, are aiming to gain pre-qualification in the near future. Other firms are attempting to gain GMP standards with the help of PPB and international agencies such as UNIDO (UNIDO, 2014).

Formal R&D activity (the discovery and product development of new active pharmaceutical ingredients) is in its infancy, with only one firm engaging in R&D. Another firm, Botanical Extract EPZ (or BEEPZ), is the only Kenyan firm developing capabilities for the production of artemisinin, which is used in the production of anti-malarials. BEEPZ is the development of an industrial concern born in 1996 in Tanzania to develop the production of high-quality *artemisia annua* with improved yields and artemisinin content. The project expanded its facilities to produce the raw materials in Kenya and Uganda, and in 2007 BEEPZ commissioned its principal processing facility in the export processing zone (EPZ) in Athi River, Kenya, currently producing non-API-grade artemisinin for export (Botanical Extracts EPZ, 2015). The expansion of production of *artemisia annua* to Kenya and Uganda was possible thanks to grants from the UK Department for International Development (DFID) and the multinational company Novartis, a leading producer of artemisinin-based anti-malarial drugs, which also became a BEEPZ customer in 2009, when the EPZ plant started production (IRIN News Africa, 2015).

There are also three local firms that process some raw materials that are used to manufacture bulk pharmaceutical products. These raw materials are 100% destined for export, as the local capacity for manufacturing active pharmaceutical ingredients remains underdeveloped.

Productivity, capacity utilization and cost efficiency

Unfortunately, it is too difficult to obtain a direct measure of productivity for the various manufacturers, but it is well known that capacity utilization is an important determinant of productivity. Firms that only operate at a low level of capacity utilization are less efficient and can only achieve relatively low levels of productivity.

Annual capacity utilization for the manufacture of most dosage forms averages around 60%. Only injectable infusions experience higher capacity utilization ranging between 85 and 100%. A number of reasons have been identified from interview data. These include: the functioning state of machinery and equipment; delays in sourcing spare parts from abroad and specialized maintenance support from machinery and equipment suppliers; human resource issues and in particular highly specialized skills in some critical areas such as product development; perceptions of locally manufactured products by some market segments; and lack of policy coherence (Wamae and Kariuki Kungu, 2014). Some of these challenges have a direct impact on the competitiveness of locally manufactured products.

The interesting observation is that these factors seem to apply mainly to the supply side of the industry. In other words, limited capacity utilization does not seem to be due to lack of demand. The previous sections showed that local producers only supply a quarter of the domestic market and a very small fraction, less that 1%, of the COMESA medicines market, so there are plenty of opportunities for expansion. Indeed, Kenyan local manufacturers have the twofold challenge of having to increase capacity utilization and very importantly considering options for expanding their total capacity.

On the other hand, once the segments in which local producers operate, which are mainly fairly unsophisticated formulations of essential medicines, are taken into account, it is possible to see that Kenyan manufacturers operate in a very competitive sub-section of the market with many competitors, both domestic and importers, and where prices and therefore profit margins are low because of the low purchasing power of the consumers and the inability to access funding from donors because of lack of WHO prequalification (UNIDO, 2012). So the technological limitations of the manufacturers also contribute to relegating most of them to a narrow and highly competitive segment of the industry where demand for each firm's product might well be constrained in some cases.

Human resources and the educational system

Successful industrial production requires a range of different skills. Local universities, such as Jomo Kenyatta University of Agriculture and Technology, Mount Kenya University and the University of Nairobi, provide graduates with good-quality basic skills and training in pharmacy, engineering and chemistry. Top polytechnics such as the Kenya Medical Training College are good sources for mid-level training. Employees also use foreign universities, for example in the UK, Germany and India. All firms also have compulsory training in-house. However, the internal education system cannot meet all industry requirements, especially as upgrading is needed.

Official reviews (UNIDO, 2012) and interviews suggest that there is a scarcity of pharmacists specialized in industrial pharmacy. The educational system has a high literacy rate and provides people well qualified in clinical pharmacy, but newly qualified employees need extensive training in the industrial aspects of drug production, including specialized training in industrial quality assurance. A key issue is that the teachers were originally trained in clinical pharmacy, so there is not a long tradition of industrial pharmacy in Kenya. University graduates have a good training in basic skills and theory, but many firms make use of training programmes run both internally and externally by international organizations, such as GIZ, Action Medeor and UNIDO. The latter sponsors popular courses such as the industrial pharmacy advanced training course run in Tanzania at the Kilimanjaro School of Pharmacy with the support of US universities (UNIDO, 2015).

Firms use some local training institutions, both public, such as the Kenya Medical Research Institute (KEMRI) and the PPB, and private. For advanced skills, however, they need to bring in experts from abroad, usually from India but also from other countries. Expatriates are expensive but important for quality because they have rare skills and experience in industrial processes. Usually they are offered short-term contracts (two to three years), possibly renewed once but usually not longer because of permit limitations and because new people tend to have more up-to-date skills. Foreign experts are identified through various channels, such as suppliers, agencies, the Web, competitors and international agencies.

Finally, in some cases firms also use their informal networks to send employees to be trained abroad, with India being a popular destination because of the strength of the Indian pharmaceutical industry. So local manufacturers seem to be able to rely on solid internal supply of skills, although at a fairly basic level, and to access expertise at a global scale even though the latter is subject to intense scrutiny because of its high costs.

Equipment and inputs

The shallow level of the Kenyan industrial sector is an important factor when inputs to production and equipment are considered. Kenya's industry is one of the most developed in East Africa, and local producers can find local suppliers for basic inputs including packaging, with the exception of some more advanced packaging for sterile products, which is procured abroad, for example from China. Some more technologically complex packaging, such as over-pouches for injectables, used to be imported but are now produced locally.

Raw materials for production are mainly imported, due to the lack of producers of APIs and excipients. This dependence on imports is an important issue because it generates possible shortages which might influence production capacity, and additional costs even though pharmaceutical inputs are supposed to be exempted from duties. In addition, Kenyan firms compete with imports produced by vertically integrated companies who also produce APIs, and are likely to price this key ingredient above the competitive level.

Kenya does not have a developed industrial machinery sector, so the main machinery is imported from international suppliers. A popular source of equipment for pharmaceutical production is India followed by China, although language can be a barrier. India's machines have the advantage of being significantly cheaper than those from industrialized countries and basically do the work well enough for tasks that do not require a high level of technological sophistication. Europe (especially Germany and Italy) and other high-income countries are the sources of more advanced and reliable machinery. The choice of suppliers is sometimes dictated by financial considerations: higher-quality machinery might be not only more efficient but also more profitable in the long run. Companies, however, lack the resources for a high upfront investment in European machinery, in spite of the fact that the financial sector in Kenya is the most developed in East Africa.

The dependence on imports of machinery creates additional costs for local firms. Spare parts attract additional costs because imported products need to be checked and to obtain a quality stamp according to rules of the Kenyan Bureau of Standards. Additional inefficiencies are also created by the lags that occur in decisions during the process of import.

Machines are operated by local engineers, who also keep records for GMP inspections, and are usually installed by suppliers who offer a comprehensive package of support including training and maintenance, at least for the first few years of life of the machines.

Some companies are currently looking to automate their production processes. Reduction of labour costs is one of the reasons, but improvement of quality and productivity and reduction of human error and exposure in handling are more important factors.

Knowledge flows, linkage capabilities and innovation

As explained above, capabilities at the industry level depend not only on the capabilities of the various economic agents, such as manufacturers, but also on how effectively the various components of the industrial system interact and promote flows of knowledge. This section, therefore, looks in more detail at the flows of knowledge in the system and how these influence the accumulation of capabilities within firms.

Medicine producers develop their capabilities by acquiring knowledge from the external environment and through experience accumulated through a process of learning-by-doing over time. An important input to the firms' capabilities comes from the education and training activities of its workers, as discussed above. Firms, however, can step up their accumulation of knowledge by explicitly investing in learning. This can happen internally through formal or informal research activities and by acquiring knowledge from other firms – suppliers, customers and even competitors – or research institutions. Most of the firms interviewed mentioned the importance of suppliers as sources of useful knowledge. Suppliers regularly train manufacturers' employees to use their machinery. Furthermore, by coming into contact with many different firms, suppliers gain useful knowledge about the industry and can be used as sources of technological knowledge or to identify people and firms with specific expertise that is useful for a company. Since Kenyan firms use foreign suppliers, they have been able to tap into their suppliers' knowledge networks in order to identify foreign experts to hire, good training programmes and foreign firms where they can send their employees to learn more about advanced industrial technologies: some firms, for example, have mentioned examples of employees sent to be trained in Indian firms.

As mentioned above, firms also gain valuable knowledge by hiring international experts from countries such as India, South Africa and even European countries. Hiring expatriates and sending employees to train abroad are expensive investments, so firms have schemes in which the trained employees relay the knowledge learnt to their colleagues.

As the innovation literature has pointed out since the work of Von Hippel, firms also learn from the users of their products (Von Hippel, 1982). Some producers have stressed the importance of the feedback collected by their marketing teams. A firm selling sterile injectable products stated that important knowledge was learned from nurses who used their products, and changes were implemented following the nurses' feedback.

Other common channels through which firms learn useful knowledge are exhibitions (also abroad), websites, membership of professional associations and conferences. Manufacturers also learn from each other because employees move between firms or meet and have informal exchanges at training events and seminars. Flows of knowledge also occur through the industry associations, the Federation of Kenyan Pharmaceutical Manufacturers (KFPM) and the Federation of East African Pharmaceutical Manufacturers (EAFPM), which organize training events and other initiatives.

Regulatory agencies also provide firms with valuable knowledge. For example, PPB does not only carry out inspections but also helps manufacturers with advice, especially on issues relating to the acquisition of the GMP standard, including documentation relating to the audits, and on Good Laboratory Practice and Good Distribution Practice. Similarly, the National Quality Control Laboratory (NQCL) offers training and knowledge transfer in the areas of drug testing and medical instrumentation, and Kenya Medical Research Institute (KEMRI) collaborates in the areas of research and training (KEMRI, 2015).

Licensing and joint ventures: the role of government policy

As the previous section has explained, the accumulation of technological capabilities occurs over time, and the current capabilities are influenced by past events. Because of the cumulative nature of technological knowledge, policy initiatives can have a long-lasting impact on the capabilities of firms and industries. In the Kenyan case, there are two examples of policy intervention that can be said to have helped the development of technological capabilities in the industry: the provisions for compulsory licensing in the Trade-Related Aspects of Intellectual Property Rights (TRIPS) negotiations, and the policy of forming parastatal joint ventures with foreign MNCs in order to develop local capabilities based on foreign technology.

In the case of licensing of foreign technology, Kenya campaigned vigorously during the trade negotiations that led to the TRIPS agreement in order to be able to carry out compulsory licensing for some essential medicines. Compulsory licensing means that governments can issue licenses to manufacture medicines that are still protected by patents at more affordable prices than those set by foreign pharmaceutical companies that hold the patents, without receiving the latter's consent. Although in practice there has been no compulsory licensing in Kenya, it can be argued that the threat of compulsory licensing has enabled local firms to reach good licensing agreements with foreign MNCs. According to Garwood (2007), 'Kenya has never issued a compulsory license, but came close to in 2004 before the German pharmaceutical major Boehringer Ingelheim agreed to enter into a voluntary license agreement with Kenyan drug firm Cosmos to produce generic versions of its patented anti-AIDS drug nevirapine'. Cosmos went on to enter another technology transfer agreement with Roche and is now one of the most dynamic Kenyan manufacturers, also aiming to gain WHO prequalification for the production of ARVs. The 'buy local' drive or procurement approach of the 1990s was also significant. It helped to lay a strong basis for the mushrooming of private local manufacturers: thus Cosmos would probably not have had its advantageous licensing position were it not for the 'buy local' move that was in effect very much steeped in ISI thinking.

As the above historical background pointed out, during the import substitution period, the government established ICDC to promote the development of local capabilities partly through parastatal joint ventures with foreign organizations. Joint ventures formed through the 1970s with the Yugoslav government and a German firm are now the precursors of two dynamic Kenyan private firms: Dawa and Infusion Medicare, one of the producers of injectables. Cosmos was also originally formed as a joint venture. Now all three firms are wholly locally owned private firms, and critics of import substitution and ICDC interpret the fact that the joint ventures had to be privatized as a failure of import substitution and ICDC (see, for instance, Himbara, 1993). However, it can be argued that although the parastatal status might have hindered the business development of the joint ventures, ICDC can still be said to be responsible for the creation of organizations that developed local technological capabilities that were later further developed by private capital. Possibly, without the initial policy of forming joint venture, companies like Dawa, Infusion Medicare and Cosmos would not exist today.

The ISI policy involving joint ventures, of course, is not the only way to build industrial capabilities. In more recent years, Kenyan firms have found other ways to draw successfully on foreign capabilities. Two other producers of sterile products followed different strategies: one, facilitated by the assurance of a large government procurement, bought a South African firm outright and transferred the facilities to Kenya, whilst the other, which pursued an export-oriented strategy and is located in an EPZ, assembled a variety of suppliers and contractors to build a new plant with equipment sourced from various countries and drawing on international expertise.

Conclusions

This chapter has provided an outline of the local production of medicines in Kenya, which is the leading manufacturer of pharmaceuticals in East Africa, accounting for half of the local production in COMESA and boosting rising production and exports. The Kenyan pharmaceutical industry is still small in relation to imports into Kenya and the whole of COMESA. However it constitutes a story of successful development of technological capabilities with examples of firms that are upgrading their technology and might be able to become leading players in East Africa, such as Universal, which has achieved enough technological capabilities to be awarded WHO prequalification. Kenya's dynamic private sector and its access to COMESA and EAC are important strengths that suggest good prospects for Kenyan local producers.

However, obstacles and limitations remain, and the analysis in this chapter has shown that Kenyan firms have to upgrade successfully in order to compete effectively against strong imports. Kenyan pharmaceutical producers have not yet been able to access donor funding, with only one firm achieving WHO prequalification so far. Most of the firms also operate in a highly competitive segment of the industry, the production of formulations of essential medicines, which offers low returns and pits them against very efficient imports. There are, however, success stories of firms that have reached significant technological sophistication, as in the case of the producers of injectables, and the analysis paints the picture of an industry integrating in global value chains, with access to global networks of equipment suppliers, foreign experts and training centres.

Still, there is work to be done to improve the regulatory environment, such as making sure that the VAT regulations do not disadvantage local firms, reducing the dependence of local manufacturers on imported raw materials and promoting upgrading throughout the technologically weaker firms; the current strategy is to progressively move all firms from local to international GMP standards.

It is not straightforward to draw general lessons for the promotion of local production of pharmaceuticals in low-income countries given the messy economic history and diverse patterns of technological accumulation this chapter has presented. It is possible, however, to suggest some possible tentative reasons that might have contributed to the observed successes of Kenyan pharmaceutical production. The chapter has argued that ISI policies, including the use of joint ventures at an early stage of industrialization, followed by gradual liberalization, might have been a positive factor in the accumulation of technological capabilities. Kenyan producers seem also to access global networks that are useful to identify and tap into rare skills and identify good equipment suppliers. The openness of Kenyan manufacturers may also be assisted by India-linked networks of some manufacturers with accumulated family experience in capitalist production from older merchant enterprises (Himbara, 1993).

On the whole, this chapter suggests a positive future for broadening and deepening pharmaceuticals production in Kenya. Despite an international and national context that is often less than helpful, considerable progress has been made in the past few years and capabilities have been established that, while often unseen, are laying the basis for further growth. With a little extra help at the government level, Kenya might soon be a leading African nation in the field.

Notes

1. Research project *Industrial productivity and health sector performance*. The findings, interpretations, conclusions and opinions expressed here are those of the authors and do not necessarily reflect the views or policies of DFID or the UK ESRC, whose financial support is gratefully acknowledged (project ES/J008737/1). This chapter draws on fieldwork undertaken by Watu Wamae and Joan Kariuki Kungu as part of that research project.
2. An earlier version of this figure appears in Wamae and Kariuki Kungu (2014), reworked with permission.

3
Pharmaceutical Manufacturing Decline in Tanzania: How Possible Is a Turnaround to Growth?

Paula Tibandebage, Samuel Wangwe, Maureen Mackintosh and Phares G.M. Mujinja

Introduction

"This sector [pharmaceuticals] is going to die...A hundred percent reliance on imports is dangerous." (Tanzanian government official)[1]

As Chapter 1 described, Tanzania has a decades-long history of pharmaceutical production, the sector mirroring fluctuations in Tanzania's post-independence industrial history. By 2004–05, the sector was estimated to be producing pharmaceuticals worth US$32.5 million, supplying around 30% of the local market and exporting about 10% of local production (MoHSW, 2006). The subsequent rise and decline of the sector is analysed in this chapter, locating firms' sources of both market resilience and vulnerability in local patterns of ownership, finance and management, interacting with the internationalization of firms' domestic and regional markets. Finally, the chapter examines the 'turnaround' challenge facing the local industry. Concerned policy makers are aware, as the above quotation shows, of the health sector insecurity inherent in complete reliance on medicines imports.

Methods and sources

The chapter draws on extensive interviewing in 2013–14, some earlier interviews, unpublished research findings and feedback from involvement of the authors in policy debates in Tanzania.[2] Senior managers in all five pharmaceutical firms producing human medicines for the private and public market that were operating at the time of the research were interviewed. Interviews were conducted with CEOs and/or production managers, using a semi-structured interview schedule that focussed on firms' capabilities to supply the Tanzanian health sector. Interview data are not attributed to specific firms except by agreement; otherwise, firm-specific information is drawn from the public domain and referenced.

In addition, informants and stakeholders associated with the industry were interviewed, including policy makers, regulators, senior actors in business associations and wholesalers in public, non-profit and private sectors. Finally, seven firms producing non-pharmaceutical products relevant to the health sector were also interviewed.

Recent industrial rise and decline in pharmaceuticals

In 2004–05, seven pharmaceutical firms were producing medicines for human consumption in Tanzania (Chapter 1). There were no multinationals, and only one joint venture with an external partner. The years up to 2008–09 then saw substantial investment, upgrading and some consolidation and new entry in the industry: this was an optimistic period in the sector.

Investment and consolidation

The largest firm is Shelys Pharmaceuticals, a pioneering firm developed by the Sumaria group. Sumaria is a successful example of the large, diversified, family-owned conglomerates that dominate Tanzania's large industry sector (Sutton and Olomi, 2012). It is a regional multinational, producing plastics, cement and consumer goods, and moving into renewables. It built up Shelys as a wholly owned firm in Dar es Salaam; in 2003, Sumaria bought Beta Healthcare International, a Kenyan pharmaceutical company, with private equity funding from Aureos Capital, making Shelys Africa Group the largest East African pharmaceutical company at that time. Shelys built and commissioned a new plant for making penicillins in Tanzania in 2008, to international good manufacturing practice (GMP) standards, and at the time was planning diversification including parenterals and anti-retrovirals (ARVs) (Shelys, 2008). In 2008, Sumaria sold 60% of Shelys to Aspen, a South African multinational, allowing private equity to exit.[3]

Three other larger firms were developed by Tanzanian African capital. Interchem Pharmaceuticals, set up in 1989 in Moshi and part-owned by the IPP group of companies that includes large media interests, made substantial investments but closed in 2008. In 1995, the government sold 60% of the equity in two closed government pharmaceutical firms into Tanzanian private family ownership, and each reopened. Keko Pharmaceutical Industries then made substantial investments. Tanzania Pharmaceutical Industries (TPI) began production in 2008 of three first-line anti-retrovirals (ARVs) for HIV, the first such production in Tanzania. With European Union financial support and technical support from Krisana Krasintu of Thailand, TPI was upgrading its production and quality assurance and planning a new GMP-compliant plant for ARV production (Losse et al., 2007). In 2007, Zenufa, a firm with a family-owned parent company based in the Democratic Republic of Congo (DRC), invested in a new plant in Dar es Salaam, aiming for full GMP standards, with initial loan financing from the Belgian Investment Company for Developing Countries.

Also in this period, Tanzansino, a Chinese government–Tanzanian military collaboration, closed for planned major renovation,[4] while two family firms owned and run by Tanzanian pharmacists, Mansoor Daya and AA Pharmaceuticals, were investing and expanding supplies to the local market. Mansoor Daya is the oldest Tanzanian local producer, while AA was started in 2003.

By 2009, Tanzania-based production was supplying an estimated 35% of a local medicines market worth about US$140 million, and rising medicines exports had reached almost US$8 million.[5] A particular strength of the local firms was supply to the rural areas: rural availability relied quite heavily on local manufacturers, and interviews with rural medicines buyers in 2006–07 had found evidence of brand recognition and trust for locally produced medicines, especially those from Shelys (Chaudhuri et al., 2010; Mujinja et al., 2014). In 2009, Tanzanian pharmaceutical production looked like a relative success story.

Recent industrial decline

Yet between 2009 and 2013, this success story turned into rapid decline (Wangwe et al., 2014a). By 2013, just five pharmaceutical firms were operating. The rising trend of medicines exports to 2009 had reversed (Figure 3.1). By 2013, imports of pharmaceuticals had risen to US$286 million on the back of rising donor spending, while medicines exports had fallen to US$1.7 million. Informed local estimates[6] put the local producers' share of the domestic medicines market at under 20%.

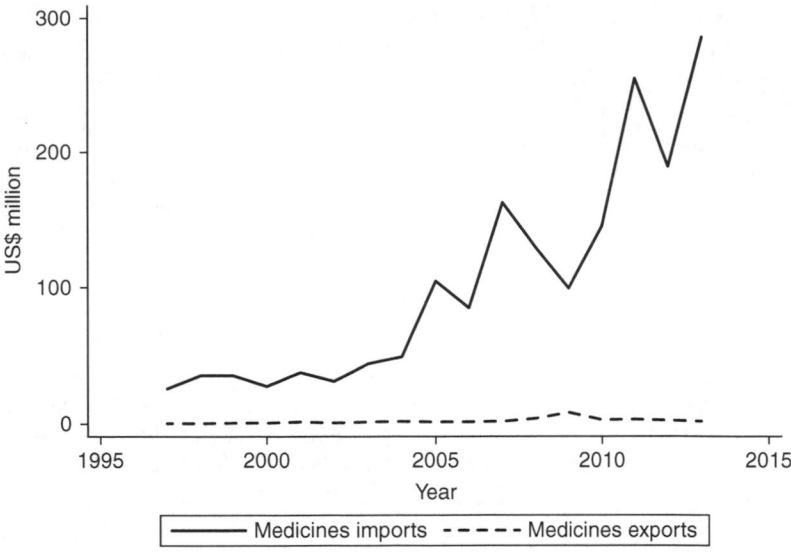

Figure 3.1   The expanding local supply gap: total imports and exports of medicines and blood products (US$ millions)

Source: Drawn from Comtrade data, http://comtrade.un.org/data/, downloaded 5 August 2014.

As the market has expanded, the local firms' share had fallen. Figure 3.1 shows the yawning trade gap.

Data on availability and sources of medicines in the Tanzanian public and private markets confirm this declining trend in local producers' market shares, for a matched sample of medicines and health facilities and shops (Table 3.1).

As the number of producers dropped, the product range narrowed. The only local producer of anti-retrovirals (ARVs) had been closed. All but one of the remaining firms had by 2013 largely ceased to produce basic antibiotics, and the largest firm was moving out of production of many other basic medicines. Local producers' share of public procurement had been falling, and only one local firm was tendering for public sector procurement contracts in 2013–14. A non-profit wholesaler estimated buying locally 'far less than half' than four years previously. A private wholesaler, who in 2010–11 had bought local medicines worth Tshs 1.5–2 billion, was, he said, now buying 'almost nothing, a few syrups'. The resultant decline in the local market share of a number of key essential medicines shows up in the survey data (Table 3.2). A

Table 3.1 Decline in domestic market share of medicines made in Tanzania, 2006–12

	Percent of sample medicines available on day of visit, by country of origin			
Year	Tanzania	Kenya	Other	Total
2006	33	14	53	100
2009	21	13	66	100
2012	12	11	78	100

Source: Authors' analysis of WHO/HAI survey data 2006, 2009, 2012.[7]

Table 3.2 Share of local manufactures among specified tracer medicines available in sample outlets, 2006–12

	Local share of available:				
Year	Amoxicillin capsules	Folic acid tablets	Albendazole tablets	Ciprofloxacin tablets	Diclofenac tablets
2006	79%	79%	81%	40%	45%
2009	74%	27%	33%	32%	26%
2012	13%	51%	43%	24%	4%

Source: Authors' analysis of WHO/HAI survey data 2006, 2009, 2012.

domestic medicines market, worth around US$250 million, had become supplied overwhelmingly from imports paid in dollars.

Industrial strengths and vulnerabilities: explaining sudden decline

The predominance of family ownership with diversified business activity, described above for the pharmaceutical firms, is characteristic of the Tanzanian industrial sector more broadly (Sutton and Olomi, 2012). Diversified family-run businesses have a number of competitive advantages in Tanzania's challenging business environment. Where bank finance is expensive and hard to access, diversified family firms can spread risk and provide access to financing which is both 'patient' (Goodluck, 2014) and also relatively low-cost and flexible. The business structure also reduces transparency and helps to weather crises. Tanzania has a shallow industrial structure: other than agro-processing, manufacturing relies heavily on imported inputs, so firms may integrate backwards to produce inputs such as packaging. Large diversified firms can gain competitive advantage by addressing in-house some 'institutional voids' (Khanna and Palepu, 1997) in their environment, such as market information sources, skilled labour pools or institutionalized working relations with government.

Some of these competitive strengths can be identified in Tanzanian family-run pharmaceuticals. Where market information is poor and consumers cannot judge quality directly, as in poorly regulated retail medicines markets, local brand trust and recognition is a powerful marketing tool (Khanna and Palepu, 1997). Where the domestic generics market is a firm's core business, investment in building a reliable generics brand benefits both consumers and manufacturer. All the pharmaceutical manufacturers interviewed had relied on capital from other parts of diversified family business, including property and trading. One firm was producing its own bottles, while two relied on overseas companies within a business group for quality assurance of inputs and access to technological information.

However, the vulnerabilities of family-based industrial organization, and of the shallow industrial structure, were also evident in the interviews. Reliance on imported inputs lengthens production schedules and increases quality risks. All firms had problems sourcing good packaging locally, and poor packaging of local products was a common complaint by Tanzanian health sector buyers. The financial and reputational risk associated with quality problems implied reliance on imported blister strips from India. Some firms had found locally bought bottles to be of unreliable quality and had switched to imports. While plastic containers for bulk tablets (sealed first into clean plastic bags) were made locally, the shallow industrial sector constrained improvements in local upstream supply. For example, a shift by pharmaceutical firms from glass to plastic bottles – desirable for safety and supply reasons – required substantial related investments by both pharmaceutical and plastics firms. At root of the problem was the small number of firms and a lack of mutual trust and coordination, posing a major hurdle to mutually beneficial industrial upgrading.

Access to technology and information was also generally constrained. Some firms relied on hard-pressed CEO's visits to trade fairs, and on established suppliers, for technical information, for training and upgrading support, and sometimes for trade credit. Ensuring quality of inputs from Asian suppliers was a constant challenge. Machinery suppliers – predominantly Indian or Chinese – installed, trained and provided spare parts and advice. Two firms had gained external donor support for technical upgrading and capacity expansion. All trained their own staff and complained of the difficulties of finding and retaining pharmacists and pharmaceutical technicians. This small cluster of Tanzanian pharmaceutical firms apparently collaborated rather little, and benefitted from few spill-overs or linkages between firms.

Changing context and responses

The Tanzania-based industry is operating in a very open market context, where shifts in the relevant international market segments are immediately experienced within Tanzanian domestic and regional markets. Structurally and technologically, several worsening pressures appear to be producing a tipping point. The first relates to size and market positioning. Pharmaceutical firms in Tanzania mainly produce basic essential generic medicines and over-the-counter items such as cough syrups. Economies of scale are limited in basic formulations (Chaudhuri and West, 2014) but are large in active pharmaceutical ingredient (API) production. While small firms can compete, therefore, in formulations, they are at a structural disadvantage to large Indian exporters since they buy small API lots from Asian suppliers, some of whom also produce formulations. As one manufacturer put it, the 'key constraint in this market is demand'. If firms cannot sell sustainably, they cannot grow, and they need their home market as a basis for expansion.

The second pressure is technological and regulatory: firms are forced into a cycle of constant upgrading, both to meet rising international standards that are requirements for different levels of market entry, and to meet competitors' quality standards. Constant upgrading of firms' technological capabilities (Bell and Pavitt, 1993; Lall, 1992) is central to firms' competitive survival in pharmaceuticals, to sustain quality at a competitive price and to retain market access. For all the firms, the technological challenge was framed by Good Manufacturing Practice (GMP) standards.

GMP constitutes a production *culture* to be attained (see also Chapter 12). GMP Guidelines[8] emphasize documentation and validation of the production flow, including effective quality control (independent of production management); high standards of hygiene and preventions of cross-contamination; effective and documented staff training and qualifications; and well-maintained equipment and premises. Our interviewees noted the extent of professional judgement in GMP implementation of, for example, 'adequate' ventilation, 'high' levels of hygiene, risk evaluation drawing on 'experience' and 'well-designed' documentation.

The Tanzania Food and Drug Authority (TFDA) presses for GMP adherence. Tanzanian firms either have attained locally acceptable GMP standards or are working towards them with TFDA support. Manufacturers agreed that TFDA required standards rise over time, just as do the standards achieved by international competitors and the expectations of international buyers. None, when interviewed, had WHO prequalification of individual products to allow them to tender for donor-funded contracts.

All firms reported recent and current substantial investment – relative to their capacity – in technological upgrading. Major investments included new machinery for expanding capacity or for automating processes to improve quality control and lower costs. Other investments included expensive improvements in air handling and plant standards (e.g. door seals and room separation) and production flow reorganization. One firm had just put in a new product line, and another was engaged in an expensive upgrade of tablet quality to produce higher compression. This last firm was aiming, with donor financial and technical support, for WHO product pre-qualification for a combination therapy. Most firms experienced financial stress in achieving these investments, which they saw as essential to stay in business.

A third interconnected pressure comes from donors' tendering processes. Donors such as the Global Fund[9] procure a large share of medicines used in Tanzania (see also Chapter 8). Their large-scale tenders and the market entry requirement of product-by-product WHO prequalification[10] shuts out local firms from markets for HIV, TB and malaria drugs. The effect has been most damaging in anti-malarials. In 2006, about 90% of the then first-line treatment for malaria (sulphadoxine-pyrimethamine [SP]) was sourced locally. From 2007, Tanzania shifted to the more expensive combination artemisinin-lumefantrine (AL) first-line medication. Subsidized supply by the Global Fund and other donors shut out local firms. Two firms developed AL formulations but concluded that pre-qualification (costing an estimated US$150,000) was unlikely to provide market access given the scale and pricing power of Asian competitors. One local firm lost an estimated third of turnover; others also suffered substantial losses.[11]

The final major contextual pressure reported by firms was a recent sharp increase in price competition from imports. This was particularly felt for 'beta lactam' antibiotics such as amoxicillin. These are produced in a separate plant from other medicines to prevent cross-contamination, and all the larger pharmaceutical firms interviewed had such production capability. All confirmed they were becoming increasingly unprofitable.

One has closed its beta lactams plant; another said it would do so 'in a couple of years, unless policy changes'. International tender prices for amoxicillin appear to have flat-lined since 2010 (MSH, 2010, 2013).[12] A local NGO wholesaler was buying at a landed import price well below a local firm's factory gate price. One informant stated some importers' landed prices were below his firm's full materials costs. Since about 78% of materials costs were calculated to be APIs in 2012–13, the latter allegation suggests dumping may be occurring. Local producers who up to 2009 were successfully competing to supply amoxicillin for domestic use had by 2012 largely left the market, as Table 3.2 also confirms.

At the national level, this move up-market leaves the domestic supply of basic essential medicines reliant on imports, which may not be sustainable at current low prices, and which may not reach rural areas as effectively as local supplies (Mujinja et al., 2014). The government official quoted at the beginning of this chapter saw this. Price pressure was also transmitted through private market competition. Around half of the Tanzanian medicines market is private (Chapter 8), and the number of competing wholesalers has been rising.[13] Interviewees contended that margins on private sales and public contracts had been severely squeezed. The financial risk attached to supplying the public sector had also increased, since payment delays by the public procurement agency (Medical Stores Department [MSD]) were increasing, driven partly by 'erratic disbursement' of treasury funding (MSD, 2013: 8; see also MoHSW, 2013). These pressures discouraged local firms from tendering, and MSD officials confirmed that the local share of their procurement was falling.[14]

The larger manufacturers were responding by moving up-market, towards more technologically sophisticated, higher-value products with export potential. All continued to supply some over-the-counter medicines, and some higher-value items such as ciprofloxacin, an anti-infective (Table 3.2). Firms were refocusing on the domestic and regional private market, narrowing their product range and investing in new products for export. Overseas partners could support moves into higher-value products.

This business strategy carries two kinds of risk. At firm level it abandons what one firm called the 'cash cows': the cash-generating basic commodities; this reduced their turnover and liquidity and hence capability to invest. Family firms may find this reduces their survival chances in the medium term. The largest firm, Shelys, had been sold 100% in 2012 to Aspen, the South African multinational firm now part-owned by GSK (Aspen Holdings, 2013). The Aspen annual report confirms the subsequent change in Shelys' business strategy: pursuit of higher margins by largely moving out of public sector supply (down to 5% of turnover in 2013), refocusing on the private market and dropping low-margin products. Shelys' recent investment has been largely in Kenya (ibid).

At the national level, this move up-market leaves the domestic supply of basic essential medicines reliant on imports, which may not be sustainable at current low prices, and which may not reach rural areas as effectively as local supplies (Mujinja et al., 2014). The government official quoted at the beginning of this chapter saw this trend as a national security issue.

Turnaround strategies: can the pharmaceutical industrial cluster be revived?

> Government policy is totally unfriendly to pharmaceutical manufacturing. (Experienced Tanzanian manufacturer)

Where industrial problems vary by activity, policy must vary too: selective intervention is an essential element of industrial policy. Lall and Wangwe (1997) argued this point nearly 20 years ago; it remains true today that distinct sectoral problems require distinctive sectoral solutions. Pharmaceuticals share characteristics with Tanzania-based industry generally but also face characteristic challenges (see also Chapter 1). Furthermore, some of the firms' problems, as the manufacturer quoted above implies, are policy-based and distinctive to the pharmaceutical and medical supplies sectors. Furthermore, clusters of firms create mutual benefits in terms of knowledge flows and spill-overs (Nadvi and Halder, 2007; Page, 2012; see also Chapter 2), and Tanzania risks losing these benefits as the number of firms falls. Turnaround for this sector needs to be policy-led.

However, a shift to active sector-specific support requires change in the current policy approach, which, as government officials confirmed, currently focuses on policies to influence the general business environment and does not address specific sectoral needs (Wangwe et al., 2014b). The two broad policy challenges are to reverse policies that have the largely unintended consequence of incentivizing imports over local manufacture, and to generate active policy support for the continuous upgrading of technological capabilities essential for local firms to compete in these highly globalized markets.

Sector-specific policy issues

Around half of essential medicines used in Tanzania are obtained via public and non-profit procurement. MSD's public sector procurement gives local firms a 15% price preference in competition with importers when both meet the quality hurdles. The effective preference rate is somewhat lower (one interviewee suggested around 9%), because importers' prices are landed prices at the port, while local firms' price includes delivery to MSD's zonal warehouses.

Manufacturers and other interviewees argued, however, that the procurement and tax regimes in Tanzania specifically disadvantage local firms in pharmaceuticals, as compared to other industrial sectors. The key decision that has generated these disadvantages is the removal of the import duty on all finished formulations. The decision to remove the 10% import duty on pharmaceuticals, applying the East African Community (EAC) Common External Tariff (CET) rate of zero per cent, was announced in the 2009 budget speech.[15] Since then, manufacturers supplying the private domestic market have no protection against finished imports.

Taxes and duties on imported inputs therefore specifically disadvantage local pharmaceutical manufacturers by raising their materials costs of production. The Customs Act 2008, recognizing this disadvantage, stated that where finished goods such as essential medicines are zero-rated for import duties, so are their inputs such as APIs, in order to ensure fair competition for local producers. However, as officials acknowledged, this commitment has proved 'complex' to administer in practice. While APIs are zero-rated, problems arise in identifying other inputs such as additives and excipients; manufacturers complained that highly refined sugar for syrups, for example, paid a high duty but could not be sourced locally. Manufacturers stated that efforts to put together a consolidated list of imported inputs to be zero-rated had not met with a positive response. Requests for zero rating could also be met by harassment and accusations of corruption and favour seeking.

Manufacturers also complained of uncertainty and instability in the tax and duty regime. VAT was payable on many imported inputs, and reimbursement was reported to be slow and often incomplete. Tax rules changed unpredictably. Proposals to impose duty on packaging were reported to have been raised, then withdrawn. 'Uplift', whereby customs officials increased the taxable value where under-invoicing was suspected, was unpredictable and sometimes punitive. Machinery, though exempt from duties in principle, required an import licence which could create delay, leaving a choice between paying duty or losing cash flow. One interviewee who was considering investing in manufacturing stated that in Tanzania the rules are not as clear as in Kenya, 'where it is clear' what taxes are to be paid.

Pharmaceutical manufacturers identified ways in which contracts to supply the public sector disadvantaged local suppliers. Trade credit rules were an example: an overseas supplier winning a public sector tender would be given a letter of credit. This meant the firm was paid as soon as the goods were delivered to the port, and it could also be used to raise working capital (see Chapter 15). By contrast, local manufacturers were paid only 30 days – or more – in arrears once goods were delivered, leaving working capital to be raised by the firm. If the order is large relative to a firm's capacity, that imposes a large financial burden. Smaller firms said the risk attached to public sector tendering had become unmanageable. One now preferred to supply the public sector via private wholesalers. A wholesaler who won a tender ordered from the manufacturer, who supplied and was paid, thus shifting the tender costs and some other financial costs and risks to the wholesaler.

This last strategy illustrates a more general trend. There appeared, anecdotally, to be a shift in public sector tendering practice towards buying from importers who would 'bundle' imports with (perhaps) some local supplies. Pharmaceutical wholesalers/importers in Tanzania are generally representatives of external, mainly Indian manufacturers. Tanzanian industry, however, has historically strong links to trading capital (Sutton and Olomi, 2012), and some local pharmaceutical manufacturers also import and distribute, with or without repacking. It follows that a policy tilt towards favouring importing over manufacturing may quite rapidly result in a shift towards much higher reliance on imported commodities as traders expand and manufacturers become more 'hybrid' in their activities, expanding more into importing.

Increasing sophistication: the capabilities squeeze

Tanzania has a low level of sophistication in manufacturing, that is, a low share of medium- and high-technology manufacturing within total manufacturing value added (UNIDO/GoT, 2012: 35–36). Its pharmaceutical sector produces products that are relatively unsophisticated by industry standards. However, within Tanzania, pharmaceuticals nevertheless represent a relatively high-technology, skill-intensive industrial activity as compared to much other Tanzanian manufacturing. The recent decline in this sector therefore threatens to reinforce a declining share of sophisticated manufacturing in total manufacturing value added. Tanzania may be losing technological capabilities at firm level, retreating to a lower level of manufacturing capabilities (Warren-Rodríguez, 2010). In this sense, the apparent crisis in pharmaceuticals identifies a more general problem.

Firms' technological capabilities (Lall, 1992) are core determinants of their ability to compete. Many of the challenges described above concern product and process capabilities: the ability to manage and document the work processes following GMP guidelines, to ensure and be able to demonstrate quality and safety of the final product. For pharmaceutical firms, these capabilities determine their market access, both locally (achieving product registration and sustaining quality when products are tested) and for access to the regional and international markets. All the firms interviewed reflected technological conditions in the international industry, in that they were chasing a moving target, facing constant pressure to upgrade. They also found it hard to sustain technological capabilities over time.

Lall (1992) distinguishes between production capabilities, investment capabilities and linkage capabilities at the firm level (see also Chapter 2). Most pharmaceutical firms interviewed in Tanzania were struggling with all three.

One of the most serious constraints on firms' capabilities in Tanzania is the low level of general and technical education in the country, implying shockingly high levels of innumeracy and illiteracy among production line staff (UNIDO/GoT, 2012: 68). Firms argued that they have more machine downtime than would be true elsewhere, given operators' limited capabilities. Lack of command of English was also a problem as compared, for example, to Kenya, especially when trying to promote people internally. The rigorous rule-following, documentation-centred culture required by GMP is unfamiliar for staff: one CEO wanted to send supervisors abroad so they could get a feel for a GMP factory. The firms all train internally the laboratory pharmacists and chemists they hire, in the equipment and techniques for the factory; they all lose these trained staff both to other firms and especially to NGOs and government, where work conditions are easier. Training is expensive and there is no local pool of skilled labour, constraining a firm, for example, from quickly adding an additional shift. Finally, there is a repeatedly reported problem in obtaining work permits for essential expatriates.

'Access to skilled labour is also a problem…. in Tanzania, which is compounded by refusal to grant work permits and where granted, they are expensive'. (Manufacturer)

Investment capabilities, including finance, technological information and management of investment projects, also become more demanding over time, as firms upgrade to meet rising required standards for exports. The large jump in production capabilities required to move from local market standards to international requirements imposed by donors involves investment financing, improvements in internal process operations, replanning factory layouts, retraining, improving factory infrastructure and changing marketing capabilities. This kind of investment can amount to a substantial proportion of a local firm's annual turnover and generally required funding support from outside the business and from non-bank sources. Examples cited in the interviews included financial transfers from other family businesses; external grant funding; a low-cost loan; and a joint venture partner with 'financial muscle', as one firm described it. The joint venture and grant routes to improvement can combine finance and access to technology.

Development of capabilities in production of combination therapies for anti-malarial medication, in the form of two-layer tablets, provides an example. One firm[16] was upgrading, with financial and technical support from Drugs for Neglected Diseases (DNDi), to produce a fixed dose artesunate/amodiaquine combination tablet, primarily for regional export through donor-funded procurement. The formulation was initially produced by Sanofi, in collaboration with DNDi, which then set out to transfer the technology to firms in Africa.[17] To achieve this, the firm must meet WHO-prequalification standards at competitive cost, requiring changes across the production process. DNDi support includes the formulation, technological support and training, new machinery, laboratory upgrading, raw materials for the batches and technical and training support right through to pre-qualification. The firm itself is also investing substantially in quality improvements and cost reductions across the plant. The upgrading therefore benefits the entire plant, with spin-offs in improved tablet production for the local market also.

A second example also relates to combination anti-malarials. Another firm was benefitting from a new formulation available from its parent company, alongside support from its international network to, for example, assure quality of APIs at source. A third firm (currently closed) had benefitted from an EU grant to fund a new turnkey plant to produce anti-retrovirals plant for HIV/AIDS treatment. Without this type of substantial external input, it is hard for the firms in Tanzania to enhance their capabilities sufficiently rapidly to regain access to the regional market for anti-malarials and other medication widely purchased by donors.

External networks and support are thus essential to survival in the race to upgrade and retain or regain market access. The Tanzanian pharmaceutical firms are caught in a capabilities 'squeeze': as process and product standards rise, and as the standards become more binding as requirements for market access, the constraints imposed by the firms' working conditions at home become more severe. Lack of a local skills pool, high and rising energy prices, lack of economies of scale for buying inputs and marketing output, poor transport and business infrastructure and a lack of local linkages – all these constraints have long existed, but have become increasingly binding in the new technological and market environment.

Policy to sustain upgrading and market access in pharmaceuticals: Can it be done?

It requires a change of mind-set for policy makers in Tanzania to turn to prioritizing and actively engaging in selective support of particular industrial sectors. The arguments for prioritizing pharmaceuticals include the national security issues raised at the beginning of this chapter. Loss of national ability to supply one of its population's basic needs increases reliance on exporters, notably from India, who may not be committed to production for this market medium term (Chaudhuri et al., 2010; see also Chapter 6). It may reduce availability and reliable supply especially in rural areas. The decline in the industry is also an element of deindustrialization and cumulative industrial decline, losing valuable skilled and semi-skilled employment opportunities, both in these firms and in upstream suppliers, for example in plastics and packaging firms. Tanzania is also losing opportunities to exploit synergies between health needs and financing and industrial development benefits, as compared to competing countries (see also Chapter 8).

Can this sector be turned around? A turnaround requires two key changes in mind-set and policy behaviour:

- an acceptance of the need for well-designed industrial protection mechanisms, and their effective implementation in stable and clearly explained rules;
- an active and sustained engagement with existing firms and their suppliers, in a determined effort to deepen and strengthen the local pharmaceutical production system.

There is principled opposition by some Tanzanian officials to protection of the market in essential medicines. Duties, argued one official, would raise prices, so 'people would die'. This echoes emotive WHO and inter-national NGO characterizations of tariffs on medicines imports as taxes that 'target the sick' (Olcay and Laing, 2005), or a 'sick tax'.[18] In practice, however, there appear to be no studies of the tax incidence of import duties on medicines in comparable contexts, though the most impor-tant influences on retail prices are likely to be the extent of domestic market competition, the purchasing power of out-of-pocket purchasers and the extent of competition between public or non-profit and private vendors[19] (see also Chapter 6).

It is, however, well established that 'infant industry' protection, to allow local firms to access markets, invest and grow *may* support both industrial growth and increasing industrial competitiveness, so long it is selective and temporary, and associated with incentives for domestic competition and export growth (Lall, 1992: 172). In the East African Community, of which Tanzania is a member, the common external tariff is set at zero for most essential medicines.[20] Tanzania could, without challenging the tariff agreement, institute a 'negative products' list of items that cannot be imported unless local manufacturers are unable to supply reliable quality at an acceptable price.

The key benefit of this change would be to allow local manufacturers to retain and grow their share of the basic essential medicines market. Without this market, the firms lose scale, cost efficiency and cash flow. The negative list would also be a relatively straightforward policy, in contrast to the complex efforts that would be required to identify and effectively exempt all essential inputs to local pharmaceutical produc-tion. Reducing or removing VAT on inputs to pharmaceuticals, or at least rapidly reimbursing the tax paid, would also shift the balance of incentives back towards manufacturers, as would raising the preference level above 15% for local suppliers in public procurement of medicines.

Additional practical changes that would shift the balance back towards local production include effective implementation by TFDA of their formal commitment to fast tracking of tests and registrations for local products (which may require additional TFDA resources). Providing trade credit for local suppliers to public procurement, as well as to over-seas importers, would also rebalance the incentive structure, as would more timely funding by the Ministry of Finance for procurement by MSD of locally contracted supplies.

All of these policy changes are feasible, and many are implemented by other African countries including Ethiopia and Ghana (see Chapters 4 and 6). However, they would quite sharply shift incentives against the wholesaler/importers who currently manage the bulk of private sector and substantial elements of public sector medicine supply. The changes would set manufacturing and importing interests against each other to some extent, posing challenges for policy makers.

Active engagement with existing firms in supporting upgrading of technological capabilities, local input sourcing and market access would also assist a shift in policy direction from trading to manufacturing, by engaging government officials more closely in manufacturing affairs. There are examples in Tanzania, outside pharmaceuticals, of success along these lines, such as the sustained consultations with manufacturers that led to the successful initiation of production of long-lasting insecticide treated bed nets. Manufacturing associations could strengthen their engagement with government. Current Tanzanian initiatives to create an active Task Force on Promotion of Local Pharmaceutical Production, including manufacturers, to improve policy and implementation in support of pharmaceutical manufacturing, could greatly enhance government-private sector collaboration.

Supporting continuous industrial upgrading requires a combination of types of support. Government policy can improve external constraints, for example by moderating utility cost increases, and streamlining slow, overlapping and expensive industrial licensing. Government can directly support areas where firms lack incentives and capability to invest themselves, such as industrial and vocation training schemes tailored to the needs of specific sectors, and funding for in-house training. Governments can work with donors to identify and tackle barriers to international market access for local firms. The large government shareholdings in pharmaceuticals, at present managed as passive holdings, could be actively used to support manufacturing improvement, or otherwise sold to support new joint ventures. Government could provide some direct financial support for investment.

The lack of industrial depth in this sector in Tanzania at present implies that government has a role in supplying missing 'public goods' of the type that larger clusters may generate locally: technological and market information; networks and introductions to help to generate joint ventures; active support for upgrading that would be available from consultants in more developed industrial contexts; and timely facilitation of external expertise when required. At present, in the small cluster of pharmaceutical firms, each was creating its own linkages; the mix of competition and beneficial externalities and collaboration characteristic of successful industrial clusters is missing here.

Two government bodies in Tanzania do provide some effective advice appreciated by manufacturers interviewed: the Japanese-supported

Kaizen unit in the Ministry of Industry and the TFDA. The manufacturers interviewed broadly appreciated the TFDA's practical and informed approach. TFDA officials are among the few in government who spend substantial time considering the requirements – and the point of view – of manufacturers. TFDA expertise could be brought into industrial policy implementation, perhaps through secondments, to help in changing the policy culture in support for pharmaceuticals.

Restructuring public procurement to support local firms' domestic market access can also help to stimulate and fund expansion and upgrading. This restructuring may include a policy already under development, to allow longer term contracts where procurement supports new local investment. This was being considered in relation to new investors, but could equally be applied to existing firms requiring longer contracts in order to fund upgrading. Manufacturers of medicines with longer public contracts could then be encouraged to use that stability to support their local suppliers' investments, for example in packaging. Given the shallow industrial structure of pharmaceuticals at present, industrial turnaround will need to address the local supply chain for pharmaceuticals, including local suppliers. Tanzania currently imports large quantities of glass, air, paper and water (bottles, packaging and intravenous fluids) in the pharmaceutical sector; even without any move into producing APIs, upstream improvement of input suppliers, and selective increases in sophistication of technological capabilities could cut industrial and import costs.

Conclusion: staying in the 'moving window'

Sutton (2012) argues that as markets integrate internationally, price competition intensifies and firms respond by investing in quality, producing better quality for a given cost. The net effect is to shift the market 'window' that firms must access upwards over time, dropping out of the window firms that can no longer meet the minimum quality/ price ratio required for market entry. Tanzanian firms, facing a combination of a shallow industrial structure with few supportive linkages, a highly liberalized market, a policy 'tilt' towards incentivizing imports, and a largely passive industrial policy approach, have been vulnerable to these rising barriers to domestic and international market entry. The observed industrial fragility – the vulnerability to sudden decline – is not a new industrial phenomenon in Tanzania: for example, a number of the exporting firms that were the subject of an earlier industrial study (Wangwe, 2003) are no longer operating.

This conjuncture urgently requires a more engaged industrial policy. However, the industrial policy literature remains thin on how to sustain continuous engagement between government and manufacturers to support constant upgrading.[21] The small, strategic, but currently shrinking pharmaceutical sector offers a good ground for experimentation in policy renewal, given its perceived strategic importance. Chapter 4, on Ethiopia, provides a comparative case study of an effective set of turnaround policies.

Notes

1. All quotations are from authors' fieldwork in 2012–14, unless otherwise stated.
2. This chapter is based on the research project entitled *Industrial productivity and health sector performance*. The findings, interpretations, conclusions and opinions expressed are those of the authors and do not necessarily reflect the views or policies of DFID or the UK ESRC, whose financial support is gratefully acknowledged (project ES/J008737/1). Particular thanks also to all our interviewees who gave time within very pressured schedules to talk to us at considerable length. Thanks also to Martin Bell, Paul Nightingale and other participants in a SPRU seminar in February 2014, and to participants in a Policy Dialogue workshop in Dar es Salaam in November 2014. The same disclaimer applies.
3. Source: Sumaria Group website: http://www.sumaria.biz/our-businesses/, accessed 6 March 2014.
4. Interview, 2010.
5. Sources: Comtrade data for imports and exports, http://comtrade.un.org/data/, accessed 5 August 2014; NBS (2009) manufacturing survey for pharmaceutical production data.
6. There was no available manufacturing survey later than 2009 at the time of writing.
7. Thanks to Mary Justin-Temu for access to these data; Table 3.1 uses the 2006 sample of facilities and medicines only, for comparability.
8. East African Community Secretariat (nd) *Guidelines on Good Manufacturing Practice for Medicinal Products within the EAC*, Arusha: late draft kindly made available in near-final form by a TFDA official, in 2014.
9. The Global Fund to Fight AIDS, Tuberculosis and Malaria, www.theglobalfund.org, henceforth 'the Global Fund' in this chapter.
10. See http://apps.who.int/prequal/, also Chapter 12.
11. Source: interviewing of firms previously supplying anti-malarials, 2010
12. Median selling prices USD/tablet 0.0171 2010, 0.0173 2013 (MSH 2010, 2013).
13. Sources: TFDA figures for wholesaler numbers cited in Mhamba and Mbirigenda (2010), and interviews.
14. An MSD accountant estimated for us that just 11% by value of MSD's new two-year framework contracts had gone to local firms in 2012–13.
15. Source: URT (2009: 67).

16. This example is reported with permission from the company's CEO.
17. http://www.dndi.org/diseases-projects/portfolio/asaq.html?highlight=WyJ0 YW56YW5pYSJd, accessed 23 February 2015.
18. http://www.haiweb.org/medicineprices/29012010/MPM_6.pdf, accessed 23 February 2015.
19. See Waning et al. (2010) for an interesting investigation of non-profit supply and its impact on competition. We have found no studies of import duties' incidence on medicines prices in low- and middle-income countries.
20. The currently available EAC tariff schedule, available from http://www.eac. int/customs/index.php?option=com_content&id=41:common-external-tariff-handbook&Itemid=141, sets antibiotics' import duties at 10%, but this does not appear to be implemented at present in Tanzania.
21. We owe that observation to Martin Bell.

4

Bringing Industrial and Health Policies Closer: Reviving Pharmaceutical Production in Ethiopia

Tsige Gebre-Mariam, Kedir Tahir and Solomon Gebre-Amanuel

Introduction

Manufacturing of medicines in Ethiopia started in 1964 with the establishment of one joint venture manufacturing company. This company remained the sole producer of medicines throughout the military regime (1974–91). Following the regime change in 1991, several manufacturing plants were established during the period referred to as the 'boom and crash' period, since, for reasons described below, some of the new companies were not successful. To respond to the crisis, the government took a mix of initiatives, simultaneously fulfilling its responsibility for health care improvement and industrial promotion. As a result of policy adjustments and attractive incentives, the environment for investment in pharmaceuticals became conducive, prompting private initiative to engage in industrial investment. Joint ventures that were realized have not only contributed to the pharmaceutical industry; they also effectively transferred skill and technology.

This chapter argues for the importance of integrating the health and industrial policies to foster local pharmaceutical production. We argue that local production of pharmaceuticals is justified from both industrial and health polices standpoints. From an industrial policy standpoint, local pharmaceutical manufacture is usually justified by its benefits for the local economy, such as savings on foreign exchange through import substitution, employment creation and the development of exports. From a health policy perspective, the rationale for local pharmaceutical manufacture is largely founded on increasing the access to essential medicines. Ethiopia is a country with high disease burden; it therefore considers development of the pharmaceutical industry a strategic endeavour.

The chapter is organized to demonstrate the close interconnections between industrial and health improvement in recent Ethiopian experience. After an overview of the stages of pharmaceutical industrial development in Ethiopia over the last 50 years, the chapter turns to an examination of the context and framework of Ethiopian health policies and the supply of medicines, describing the importance of medicines demand for the industry and industrial supply for health sector development. We describe how the health sector development programme is linked to the provision of essential medicines in the primary health care (PHC) system of the country, and the government's social responsibility in providing medicines to the population.

A key objective of the chapter is to argue, on Ethiopian evidence, that joint ventures in the pharmaceutical industry can be designed as strategic partnerships. It narrates some success stories in terms of technology transfer and upgrading manufacturing plants, and localization of knowledge within Ethiopia, and their roots in a conducive policy environment for private sector investment. A final section examines these developmental aspects of Ethiopian industrial policies. In conclusion we acknowledge the headway Ethiopia has made in manufacturing medicines and identify some issues to be addressed.

In the preparation of this chapter, policy documents, proclamations, regulations, guidelines and literature were reviewed. Key informant interviews were conducted and plant visits undertaken by the authors.

Pharmaceutical industrial development in Ethiopia

Phases of industrial development

The history of pharmaceutical manufacturing in Ethiopia is only half a century old and it may be classified into three periods: the establishment of the Ethiopian Pharmaceutical Manufacturing company (EPHARM), the subsequent boom and crash and the later 'reform and revival' period.

The first pharmaceutical manufacturing plant in Ethiopia, EPHARM was founded in 1964 as a joint venture by the Ethiopian government and the British company, Smith & Nephew. In 1971, Smith & Nephew was superseded by Teva Jerusalem of Israel. Following the overthrow of the monarchial government by the military in December 1975, the company was nationalized. Due to the socialistic policy of the military regime, private industrial investment generally stagnated and EPHARM remained the sole producer of medicines in the country until 1993. In February 1994, EPHARM was re-established as a public share holding company and recently it was sold to a local investor.

The period 1995 to 2004 experienced the boom and crash. Ten new pharmaceutical plants were established: Asmi Industry PLC, East African Pharmaceuticals (EAP), Addis Pharmaceuticals Factory (APF), ETAB PLC, Pharmacure PLC, BioSol PLC, Life-Line PLC, Fews PLC, Sino-Ethiop Associate (Africa) PLC (SEAA) and Bethelehem PLC. However, the new factories faced daunting challenges, as there were neither policies nor regulatory mechanisms to control dumping of cheaper and substandard products. The prices of local products were not competitive. In addition, most of the new factories were poorly organized and managed. Consequently, four companies were foreclosed for failure to service their loan obligations.

According to the secretary of the Ethiopian Pharmaceuticals and Medical Supplies Manufacturing Association (PMSMA), the production capacities of the majority of the industries at the time was below 50% of their installed capacity. There was a high tariff on raw materials and a chronic shortage of experienced human resources, associated with high turnover of technical staff, shortage of technical manpower, and an absence of any training centre on good manufacturing practices (GMP) and pharmaceutical management. In addition there were no GMP-certified inspectors at the regulatory authority. It was hard to get working capital from banks, there were management problems in the industries, an absence of qualified equipment calibration and maintenance centres, and university-industry linkages were weak.

Established in 1996, East African Pharmaceuticals (EAP) was one of the companies that survived the 'crash' period. EAP was an initiative of British and Sudanese nationals. It had difficulties at the outset when the cost of the investment was driven up due to the decision of Drug Administration and Control Authority (DACA) that EAP should reconstruct its plant to comply with GMP, shortly after it started operation. In 2009, the factory was operating at 30% of its capacity. EAP produces human and veterinary medicines mainly for the local market, although a small portion is exported to Sudan and Somali. Being the only local manufacturing company producing veterinary medicines, EAP enjoys market monopoly. Hence, it is currently considering increasing its production to meet the market demand. At the time of writing EAP has just achieved a GMP Certificate from the Pharmaceutical Inspection Convention and Pharmaceutical Inspection Co-operation Scheme (PIC/S).

Established in 1997, Addis Pharmaceuticals Factory (APF) Sh. Co. is the largest pharmaceutical manufacturing plant in Ethiopia. It is located in Adigrat, Tigray Regional State, northern Ethiopia. Though the plant was constructed and equipped with high-tech production facilities, at the start it faced financial and management crisis. In 2009, it acquired a second factory located at Akaki at the outskirts of Addis Ababa, which is dedicated to the manufacturing of large-volume parenterals. APF manufactures about 90 products. It has nine production lines with a capacity to produce 1.2 billion tablets, 19 billion ampoules, 10 million vials, 500,000 capsules, 4 million ointment tubes and 9.6 million bottles of syrup. It has fully equipped laboratories. APF is owned and managed by the Endowment Fund for the Rehabilitation of Tigray (EFFORT).[1]

Sino-Ethiop Associate (Africa) PLC (SEAA) was established in March 2001 as a joint venture between an Ethiopian company, Zaf Pharmaceuticals PLC, and two Chinese companies (China Associate Group and Dandong JINWAN Group). SEAA produces empty hard gelatin capsules and sells them to pharmaceutical factories in Africa and the Middle East. Recently, SEAA completed its expansion project and doubled its production capacity, to 2.4 billion capsules annually. SEAA has recently acquired Certificate of PIC/S conformity. It will be shown later that companies established through joint venture have been generally successful.

The 'reform and revival' period began in 2005. The Ethiopian Pharmaceutical and Medical Supplies Manufacturers Association (EPMSMA) and other key stakeholders appealed to the government for appropriate measures to be taken in support of local manufacturing. To address the crisis the local manufacturers were facing, the government created benefit packages and undertook policy reforms. This improved the business environment, resulting in some new joint ventures.

In 2007, Cadila Pharmaceuticals Ethiopia PLC (CPEL) was established by Cadila Pharmaceuticals Ltd (India) and Almeta Impex PLC (Ethiopia), owning 57% and 43% of the company, respectively. The market size, including easy access from Ethiopia to other East African countries, motivated the investment. All machines and raw materials were imported from India. CEPL has the capacity to manufacture 390 million tablets, 165 million capsules and 1.44 million litres of liquid per annum. In 2011, CEPL acquired a GMP certificate.[2]

Established in 1998, Pharmacure PLC, a Swedish turnkey plant, is an Ethiopian-Saudi investment. It produces large-volume parenterals. Rx Africa (Ethiopia) PLC, an Ethiopian-US joint venture was commissioned in 2007 through the acquisition of a local company called Sunshine Pharmaceuticals. Rx Africa launched 36 products in 2009. Another local manufacturer, Fews PLC, produces syrups.

In 2013, Julphar (Gulf Pharmaceutical Industries) commissioned its pharmaceutical manufacturing facility[3] in Addis Ababa. The facility has the capacity to produce 150 million bottles of suspension and syrup, 500 million tablets and 170 million capsules annually.

One unique local manufacturer is the National Veterinary Institute located in Bishoftu, 40 km south of Addis Ababa. With its well-equipped diagnostic and research laboratories and production plants, the NVI is currently producing 19 R&D-based veterinary bacterial and viral vaccines for both domestic and international markets to more than 25 countries in Africa and the Middle East.

The Ethiopian industry today

Today, the Ethiopian pharmaceutical industry consists of 15 pharmaceutical manufacturers, of which nine produce medicines, one manufactures empty gelatin capsules, and the rest are engaged in producing medical supplies such as syringes, absorbent cottons, gauzes, bandages and sanitary products. Though significant expansion of the industry is taking place, as such the base is not yet well developed, and the companies have relatively low production capacities.

The therapeutic categories of local production include antibiotics, gastrointestinal drugs, central nervous system drugs, cardiovascular drugs, anti-diabetic agents, antihistamines, anthelmintics, analgesics and antipyretics, antiprotozoals, respiratory drugs, dermatological preparations, minerals and vitamins, large-volume parenterals as well as veterinary vaccines. None of the manufacturers produces medicines against tuberculosis, HIV/AIDS and malaria. Since the local manufacturers were not GMP-compliant, they could not make use of the donor funding made available for the procurement of medicines for these diseases. Hence these medicines are being imported from abroad, mainly from Indian manufacturers.

The Ethiopian pharmaceutical industries are small- to medium sized industries. Most use labour-intensive, step-by-step manual manufacturing, with semi-automated production lines. Manufacturers mainly focus on tablets, capsules, powder and liquid preparations. A few produce parenteral preparations, creams and ointments. Production is limited to secondary manufacturing that involves combining and processing pharmaceutical active ingredients (APIs) and excipients into dosage forms. There is no active pharmaceutical ingredient (API) plant in the country. Almost all input materials (APIs and excipients), including primary packaging materials, are imported, mainly from India and China. According to an interview with the procurement department manager of EPHARM, input materials are purchased in small quantities, at times too small to attract suppliers, and as a result manufactures have no power to negotiate better prices. This situation tends to increase the cost of input materials. Hence, most of the finished products are not competitive as compared to products imported from China and India. Just a few inputs such as sugar (for syrup production), empty hard gelatin capsules and secondary packing materials are locally produced. There are new packaging manufacturers who have begun producing PVC and empty bottles for pharmaceutical use replacing some of the imports (Sutton and Kellow, 2010). Cardboard boxes for bulk packaging are manufactured locally.

Although most of the manufacturers operate below their respective capacities, the capacity utilization of the manufacturers has shown improvement during the 2005–14 period, increasing from a mere 29.3% in 2008 to 79.0% in 2013. This is indicative of the growing market for locally produced pharmaceuticals – an opportunity lying ahead for the sector (CSA, 2014).

As regards quality issues, there are three manufacturers that comply with basic GMP standards, one of whom is to acquire PIC/S Certification soon, while two others are expected to acquire the same in the near future. One of the main issues that must be addressed by local manufacturers is the need to access updated technology. In terms of personnel, however, Ethiopia seems to have sufficient trained pharmacists, though there is a dire need for those with industrial and managerial skills.

Developing and supplying the health sector

This section analyses the interaction of health care development and industrial market development, aiming to show how health and medicines policies influenced the development of the local pharmaceutical industry.

The National Health Policy (NHP) launched in 1993 includes as core elements the development of preventive, promotive and curative health care; assurance of health care accessibility for all segments of the population; and the promotion of private sector and NGO participation in the health sector (TGE, 1993a). In order to achieve these goals, a 20-year Health Sector Development Programme (HSDP) consisting of a series of five-year rolling programmes was established in 1997/98. The HSDP has been aligned with the wider frameworks of the Plan for Accelerated Development to End Poverty (PASDEP), and a Growth and Transformation Plan (GTP) has been formulated and implemented.

HSDP implementation takes a sector-wide approach encompassing the following components: service delivery and quality of care; health facility rehabilitation and expansion; human resource development; pharmaceutical services; information, education and communication; health sector management and management of information systems; monitoring and evaluation and health care financing.

Over the last two decades the government has been engaged in health facility construction, expansion, rehabilitation, furnishing and equipping. From 2003/04 to 2011, the number of health posts increased from 4,696 to 17,972 and the number of public health centres from 519 to 3,871, while the number of hospitals (public and private) rose from 126 to 194 (FMOH, 2011). Health service coverage increased from 45% in 2001 to 95% by 2011. The rise in health service coverage necessitated an increased demand for pharmaceuticals. Hence, the number of pharmaceutical manufacturers, importer/distributors and retail outlets increased significantly during the same period to serve an expanding market.

Targets set by HSDP IV with respect to pharmaceutical supply and services include increasing the availability of quality pharmaceuticals at an affordable price and in a sustainable manner, and achieving improved rational drug use. In the design of HSDP III and IV, the SWOT analysis made indicated increasing domestic manufacturing capacity of drugs as an opportunity to be explored (FMOH, 2011/12). Recognizing the importance of the supply of pharmaceuticals in the overall health policy, the government decided to increase the availability of essential pharmaceuticals from 75% to 100% and improve the efficiency of regulatory activity (MOFED, 2006). Moreover, the Growth and Transformation Plan (GTP) anticipated increasing the domestic market share of the local pharmaceutical industry from the baseline year 2009/10 share of 15% to the target 50% (MOFED, 2012).

The market for pharmaceuticals in Ethiopia is met through import (purchase and donation) and local production. Local manufacturing still represents less than 15% of the total market for pharmaceutical products. Governmental organizations, private importers, non-government organizations (NGOs) and international agencies such as the UNICEF and WHO used to participate in the import and distribution of pharmaceuticals. In order to streamline the supply and distribution of essential medicines to the public health care facilities, the former PHARMID was transformed into the Pharmaceutical Fund and Supply Agency (PFSA), as established by Proclamation in 2007 (FDRE, 2007).

Today, local and international procurement for the public health facilities is mainly provided by the PFSA which operates with a revolving fund. PFSA procurement is done through international and local tenders as well as through direct purchasing. The PFSA also receives some pharmaceuticals through donation from sponsors of vertical programmes such as those for ARVs, TB and malaria medication and reproductive health commodities. From its central hub in Addis Ababa and the regional hubs, PFSA distributes medicines and medical supplies directly to health care facilities. Private companies import directly from their respective suppliers and distribute to wholesalers, and these in turn sell to retailers.

The PFSA has designed and implemented different strategies to support local manufacturers of pharmaceuticals and medical supplies. These include the provision of 30% advance payment for the purchase of products won through national bidding and 25% price preference when local manufacturers participate in international bids. Although not yet implemented, a tripartite agreement (PFSA as a collateral, pharmaceutical companies and the Development Bank) has been signed, providing local manufacturers with a loan for 70% of a bid that has been won. Furthermore, to increase local production of pharmaceuticals and medical supplies and create market linkages with consumers, the type and amount of products given priority by the health services have been identified. Based on this, a list of 124 pharmaceuticals and medical supplies produced in the country has been prepared to serve as a guide for the procurement process.

With an estimated population of 95 million in 2014, Ethiopia has the potential to become a significant market for pharmaceutical products in Sub-Saharan Africa. Although the Ethiopian pharmaceutical market grew on average by 20% per annum from 2007 to 2011, it is still rather limited, estimated at around US$500 million, due mainly to low per capita income. Currently, there is slightly higher total health expenditure as a share of GDP, at 4.9% in Ethiopia, as compared to other countries in Africa (excluding South Africa), but the per capita health expenditure remains among the lowest in the region (Wamai, 2009).

Joint ventures and strategic partnerships: fostering technology transfer

The revival of the pharmaceutical industry of Ethiopia after the boom and crash is largely attributed to policy reforms, investment and manufacturing incentive packages. One important phenomenon that stands out is joint ventures. Through the initiative of joint ventures, a foreclosed factory revived, an old factory was upgraded, new factories were established, and enhanced technology transfer included localization of technical knowledge within Ethiopia.

One of the shortcomings of the local manufacturers is that they are organized at the secondary level and hence dependent on foreign companies for raw materials and technology sources. In order to overcome this problem, some local manufacturers established joint ventures as a strategic partnership with foreign companies. These joint venture investors gain access to both local and regional markets, and Ethiopia's cheap labour force, as well as a number of investment incentives that the country offers in exchange for raw materials, know-how, technology transfer and pre-established market networks. This kind of strategic partnership can be considered as a key factor for long-term success. The joint ventures between the Ethiopian company, Zaf Pharmaceuticals PLC, and two Chinese companies, China Associate (group) Co., Ltd and Dandong Jinwan (Group) Co., Ltd (Sino-Ethiop Associate Africa PLC), and between Medtech (Ethiopia) PLC and Gulf Pharmaceuticals Julphar of UAE (Julphar Pharmaceuticals Manufacturing Ethiopia PLC) are based on this principle.

Sino-Ethiop Associate Africa PLC, the sole empty hard gelatin capsules (EHGCs) manufacturer in Africa, was established at the outskirts of Addis Ababa in March 2001 and became operational in June 2003. China Associate (Group) Co., Ltd. is a 35% shareholder of Sino-Ethiop Associate Africa PLC. It is a diversified enterprise engaged in manufacturing of bulk pharmaceuticals and finished formulations and has a trading business. This company has more than ten years of business relationship with the pharmaceutical companies of some African countries, including Ethiopia. Dandong Jinwan (Group) Co., Ltd. is the other partner holding 35% of the shares. It is a diversified enterprise engaged in the production of EHGCs itself and manufacturing of equipment for capsules production. Zaf Pharmaceuticals PLC, engaged in importing of pharmaceuticals, is the Ethiopian counterpart in the joint venture, having 30% of the shares.

The company currently has five automatic capsule production lines to produce EHGCs, with a total capacity of 2.4 billion EHGCs of size 0, size 1 and size 2 per year. The continuous batch system is applied in the production process; as a result, production is not interrupted except during regular preventive maintenance schedule and size part changes. Its capacity utilization is normally more than 95%, operating in three shifts. On average, there are more than 300 production days per year. The company covers 100% of the local EHGCs demand and exports to Sudan, Kenya, Uganda, South Africa, Ghana, Zimbabwe, Democratic Republic of Congo, Yemen and Saudi Arabia, among others.

The company has recently undergone a major expansion that transformed the overall capacity of the company, doubling the annual output. It has also done the civil engineering required to accommodate three more production lines. The director of the company revealed that the expansion has transformed the company in terms of both quality and productivity, including:

- state-of-the-art manufacturing equipment which is automatic and fully synchronized;
- Programmable Logic Controller (PLC) systems: advanced from push-button to touch-screen, enabling easy process monitoring and record keeping;
- heating, ventilation and air conditioning (HVAC) system: programmed based on a one-year study made on the climatic condition of the location in order to improve its overall efficiency;
- water treatment system: use the double-reverse osmosis system along with electro-deionization system that reduced the use of different chemicals and improved the quality of the water; and
- energy utilization: integrated a solar energy source with the existing grid supply.

After the expansion, the manufacturing lines were moved to the new plant, leaving the old facility empty. Although the company is working three shifts at full capacity, it is still unable to meet market demand for EHGCs. It is therefore planning to increase its capacity from five to eight lines at the new plant. Further, the company plans to convert the old facility into a formulation plant for contract manufacturing. The other plan of the company, which is also of interest to the government, is to look into the possibilities of developing gelatin raw materials from cattle bone, which is abundant in the country.

Skills and technology transfer has been extensive. Over a period of ten years, the Chinese technical and managerial staff have been completely replaced by Ethiopian staff (today there is just one Chinese engineer). The technology has been totally transferred (by Dandong Jinwan), signifying the critical role that joint ventures can play in the development of the pharmaceutical industry. According to the general manager of the company, such a smooth transfer was possible due to several complementary reasons, including the trust developed among the partners, the government policy to limit the number of foreign employees in a company, training of personnel locally and abroad, and government insistence that the transfer of skills and technology by partners should take place.

Julphar Pharmaceuticals Manufacturing Ethiopia PLC is another company established as a joint venture. Its vision is to become one of the leading pharmaceutical companies in Africa by the year 2020 with a number of product portfolios. The joint venture is formed between an Ethiopian company, Medtech Pharmaceuticals PLC, that holds 45% of the shares, and a United Arab Emirates (UAE) company, Gulf Pharmaceuticals (Julphar), that holds 55% of the shares. The UAE partner is producer of various pharmaceutical products in the Middle East and in its other subsidiaries in Algeria. Julphar maintains a network of 11 manufacturing plants based in the UAE, with developments under way to open additional facilities in strategic countries such as Saudi Arabia, Ethiopia and Algeria. It supplies its generic pharmaceutical products to the global pharmaceuticals markets. The Ethiopian partner has been exclusively importing and distributing Julphar products and continued to do so for products being produced locally by Julphar Ethiopia as well.[4]

This joint venture transformed a previously bankrupted manufacturing facility, Bethelehem Pharmaceuticals, into a viable, state-of-the-art facility at a cost of about US$9.17 million. Currently, it is running at full capacity and producing and supplying the Ethiopian market with 25 different products (25 million bottles of syrup/suspension, 500 million tablets and 170 million capsules per year). In order to reach the international market, the company has already fulfilled GMP requirements and is expected to be fully certified with PIC/S.

The company has upgraded the facility with new utilities and machineries as per GMP requirements. It has put in place new HVAC system, state-of-the-art and fully automated reverse-osmosis water treatment system, and boilers for generation of pharmaceutical grade steam. Furthermore, to increase its product portfolio and production capacity, a new closed and fully automated oral liquid preparation and filling line, tablet compression and blistering machines, and ointment filling machines have been installed and made operational. To upgrade the quality control system, Julphar has introduced high-performance liquid and gas chromatography systems and computerized stability chambers. To enhance the quality assurance (QA) system, the company is transferring QA documentation systems such as product dossiers, procedures and validation protocols from the mother company in the Gulf.

According to the country director of Julphar UAE, the joint venture has been highly encouraged by Ethiopian market access and by the investment policy of the government. Accordingly, Julphar has also earmarked an additional investment worth US$50 million to establish an insulin plant. To facilitate the expansion, the government of Ethiopia availed a plot of land for Julphar adjacent to its existing facility. This new investment is the first of its kind in Africa and it aims at making Ethiopia an insulin hub for the growing African insulin demand.[5] This move is heralding the beginning of advanced manufacturing of pharmaceuticals of biological origin in Ethiopia.

To achieve its vision, Julphar Ethiopia PLC is interested in launching new investment in additional plant to produce products like B-lactams and small-volume injectable products. The director reiterated the challenges the company has been facing, including lack of trained and skilled engineers to install and maintain pharmaceutical machineries and facilities and the unavailability of spare parts and consumable materials in the local market. To deal with these challenges, the company has assigned engineers and technicians from the mother company. This arrangement has helped with technology and skill transfer for Ethiopian engineers. To overcome the shortage of trained and skilled manpower in the pharmaceutical industry, the company has made arrangements with local universities for the provision of on-the-job training within its facility and abroad in its mother company. Accordingly, a team of selected students from different universities were fully funded by the company for their stay in Julphar UAE to acquire knowledge and skill in the pharmaceuticals manufacturing sector.[6] From the foregoing it is apparent that integrating health and industry polices is highly beneficial for industrial development, since it can attract and make good use of joint ventures.

Socio-economic policies and the investment environment

The last section referred to the Ethiopian government's incentives for local industry. This section explores those industrial and socio-economic policies in more depth. The Ethiopian government's industrial policies are developmental in nature, and pharmaceuticals are a key aspect of that broader approach. Consequently, the current investment climate of the country is considered propitious, since the country has several competitive advantages. Ethiopia has sizeable young and educated, trainable human resource and a large number of inexpensive labourers; rapidly developing green energy, as well as modest transportation infrastructure and trade logistics; and duty-free, quota-free access to the US and EU markets under the African Growth and Opportunities Act (Assefa et al., 2013).

Both the National Health Policy (NHP) (TGE, 1993a) and the National Drug Policy (NDP) (TGE, 1993b) emphasize the importance of local pharmaceutical production. The NHP states: 'Availability of drugs, supplies and equipment shall be assured by encouraging national production capability of drugs, vaccines, supplies and equipment by giving appropriate incentives to firms which are engaged in manufacture, research and development' (TGE, 1993a). One of the objectives of the NDP also specifies: 'To develop a domestic drug manufacturing capacity and gradual supply to the export market' (TGE, 1993b). Given the significant headway Ethiopia has made in availing access to PHC for its people, and given the country's ambitious local pharmaceutical manufacturing plans, the NDP is currently being revised to lead GTP II and GTP III.

The regulatory body previously known as DACA was restructured (with greater mandates including improved regulation, and setting standards in health care facilities as well manufacturing companies) and re-established as the Food, Medicine and Healthcare Administration Control Authority (FMHACA) by Proclamation, and has set standards for manufacturing facilities, among others (FDRE, 2009). Even though the primary responsibility of FMHACA is to regulate and control medicines, it has been building the capacity of the local manufacturers in GMP in collaboration with the WHO and the United States Agency for International Development (USAID) programme 'Promoting the Quality of Medicines' and United States Pharmacopeial Convention (PQM/USP).

The other sectoral polices that Ethiopia has put in place that in one way or another have contributed to the overall socio-economic developments (including the local pharmaceutical industry) are trade policies (focusing on business transactions such as the pharmaceutical supply chain), industrial policies (focusing on fostering manufacturing and technology transfer) and investment and labour policies. Since the implementation of the 1991 Trade Policy, Ethiopia has made significant progress in opening up its economy and notable improvements have been recorded in its international trade.

Industry Policies

Ethiopia's Industry Policy dates from August 2001 and is designed within the framework of a free market economy. The key principles of the strategy include recognition of the role the private sector as an engine of industrial development and facilitation by the government towards that end; an agricultural development-led industrialization strategy; and ultimately export-led industrialization. It focuses on labour-intensive industries and aims to coordinate foreign and domestic investment.

Local pharmaceutical production in developing countries has always been a debatable issue. On one hand, there are opinions that argue against local pharmaceutical production for lack of comparative advantage, including absence of GMP and inadequate drug regulatory systems. These critics are also concerned with the immediate and long-term threats posed by low-quality medicines manufactured by African countries. People on the other side of the debate consider essential medicines as strategic commodities and seek to foster self-reliance and hence local production (Bate, 2008). The Ethiopian industry policy fosters the latter approach.

The investment policy within Ethiopia's industrial policy framework encourages the private sector to invest in almost all areas of economy. The policy does not impose local content, technology transfer (although encouraged) or export performance requirements on foreign investments. Export-oriented sectors receive long-term credit with low interest, export incentives, customs duty privileges and provision of land at competitive rents. The Development Bank of Ethiopia offers up to 70% of the investment capital for new investments or expansion projects in the pharmaceutical sector, with a 7.5% interest rate and a long-term repayment horizon. Investors in the manufacturing sector will have customs duty privileges for capital goods and construction materials necessary for the investment, spare parts whose value is not greater than 15% of the total value of the capital goods and tax holiday privileges between two and seven years. There are no restrictions on repatriation of earnings, capital, fees or royalties (EIC, 2014).

Recognizing the role of the private sector in the economy, the government of Ethiopia revised its investment law at least three times between 1992 and 2012. The revisions rendered investment incentives more transparent, attractive and competitive. Major positive changes regarding foreign investments have also been introduced through Investment Proclamation No.769/2012 and Regulation No. 270/2012, which detail the tax incentives and duty-free privileges for investors.

In general, there are a number of reasons for potential investors to consider Ethiopia as a desirable location for pharmaceutical investment, including factors such as investor-friendly policies, conducive macroeconomic policies and stable foreign exchange rates, a sizeable local market, access to the markets of several African countries through COMESA, preferential trade treatment to the EU, ACP-EU, a favourable export market under the US Generalized System of Preference, abundant and inexpensive skilled and trainable workforce, strategic location with proximity to the lucrative markets of the Middle East, Europe and Asia and attractive incentive packages for investment.

Ethiopia is a member of the World Bank–affiliated Multilateral Investment Guarantee Agency, which gives foreign investors guarantees against non-commercial risks. Ethiopia is a signatory to several bilateral and multilateral investment promotion and protection treaties. Ethiopia has also signed the World Bank Treaty on 'The Convention on Settlement of Investment Disputes between States and Nationals of other States'.

The country's current labour policy is based on Labour Proclamation No. 377/2003 which calls for workers and employers to comply with basic principles of rights and obligations, through co-operative efforts (FDRE, 2004) in conformity with international conventions and other legal commitments to which Ethiopia is a party. Abundance of inexpensive and disciplined labour together with the introduction of the revised labour proclamation is believed to contribute positively towards competition in the industry and other sectors.

Science and technology policies

One of the key indicators of the socio-economic development and technological progress of a country is the contribution of the industrial sector to the economy. The Ethiopian government has recognized that science and technology are the major driving forces behind industrialization. It is taking steps to foster the growth of science, technology and innovation (STI), including the promotion of indigenous knowledge to tackle the country's needs (see also Chapter 7).

The Ministry of Science and Technology (MoST) recently published a document called the 'Green Paper on Science, Technology and Innovation Policy of Ethiopia-Building Competitiveness through Innovation' (MoST, 2012). In this document the pharmaceutical industry has not only been listed as one of the high-level technology industries but also identified as an area in which efforts will be geared to building domestic technological capability. According to the paper, the pharmaceutical industry is among the National Priority Technology Capability Programmes of Ethiopia.

The national science and technology policy of the country dates from 1993. Although this policy served to provide general directions to guide scientific and technological activities, it was not followed by implementation strategies and programmes aimed at achieving the envisaged policy objectives. It was therefore revised in 2012. The revised policy directives and strategies indicate, among other things, that at least 1.5% of the country's gross national product (GNP) will be allocated annually to support and sustain the different STI activities in all sectors. A centralized innovation fund for R&D activities will be created through a contribution of 1% of the annual profit of all productive and service sectors, and banking and financial institutions will be encouraged through various legal and incentive mechanisms to improve their role of fostering technological innovation (MoST, 2013).

The policy landscape of Ethiopia entered a new phase when the Ethiopian government launched the GTP I (2010/11–2014/15). As the highest national policy framework, the GTP governs Ethiopia's developmental policies, budgets and government organizations, as well as actions of development partners and foreign investors. Among other things, the GTP is tuned to expand infrastructure significantly and increase the role of the manufacturing industry in employment and economic development. The GTP identifies the pharmaceutical industry as a priority sector. Moreover, government support for the priority sectors will focus on, among other things, expanding modern systems in the sector by using local and external technical support and ensuring foreign technical support and investment, focusing on management skills and transformation, technological transfer and capacity building. The market share of local pharmaceutical producers is targeted to reach 50% by 2015 (MoFED, 2010).

For this set of objectives, regulatory support is essential. As part of the GTP, the FMHACA has been implementing a five-year project which states: 'The main aim of the pharmaceutical industry is substituting essential medicines imported to the country and setting the ground for export of local products by building the capacity of existing pharmaceutical and medical device manufacturers and establishing new ones'. Notwithstanding the responsibilities vested in the authority by Proclamation 661/2009 to ensure the safety, efficacy and quality of products, the FMHACA together with stakeholders has been exerting efforts to build the technical capacity of local manufacturers.

The FMHACA's ambitious project envisioned 17 local GMP-certified pharmaceutical manufacturers by the end of 2015; at least five pharmaceutical manufacturers pre-qualified by WHO by 2015; seven newly established pharmaceutical manufacturers by the end of 2015; and two newly established pharmaceutical raw materials manufacturers and two newly established traditional medicines manufacturers (FMHCA, 2011). To build the capacities of the local pharmaceutical manufacturers, FMHACA also prepared the Medicine Manufacturing Establishment Directive, and it has made it mandatory for any person engaging in manufacturing medicines to obtain a Certificate of Competence from the Authority (FMHCA, 2013a).

FMHACA, working together with the WHO and USP/PQM and local manufacturers, prepared a five-year GMP Road Map (2013–18). It has assessed and mapped the GMP status of the local manufactures and categorized them into three GMP compliance levels (Level I with up to 50% GMP compliance; Level II with 60–80% GMP compliance; and, Level III with more than 80% GMP compliance). As per their levels, FMHCA and its partners are building the capacity of the local manufacturers for them to be GMP compliant by 2018 (FMHACA, 2013b).

A major scientific and technological project is the establishment of a Regional Bioequivalence Centre (RBEC) in Ethiopia. This presents yet another major opportunity for upgrading. To serve as substitutes, generic products should be bioequivalent or therapeutically equivalent to the originator/comparator products. Consequently, bioequivalence becomes even more crucial for generic products such as medicines for critical use (e.g. anti-retroviral, anti-tubercular), medicines with a narrow margin of safety (e.g. cardiovascular drugs), sustained or modified-release products and medicines with inherent solubility and permeability problems.

To obtain marketing authorization in different countries, manufacturers have to get their products approved and registered by the national drug registration authorities. Under normal circumstances, manufacturers are expected to present product pre-qualification for bioequivalence. However, local regulatory authorities could not enforce bioequivalence testing thus far, because the service fees charged by international contract research organizations are not affordable to the local manufacturers. Hence, the absence of a local bioequivalence testing facility in the subregion has been a big hurdle in the enforcement of the bioequivalence testing requirement of the generic medicines.

To assist local manufacturers, the Regional Bioequivalence Centre Sh. Co. (RBEC) was recently established in Addis Ababa as a public-private partnership. GIZ provided the basic instruments and equipment for the bio-analytic laboratory and technical training to key staff. Addis Ababa University made available laboratory space and furnished offices. Two pharmaceutical manufacturing companies in Kenya (Universal Corporation Ltd and Skylight Chemicals Ltd), one local manufacturer in Ethiopia (Addis Pharmaceutical Factory PLC) and one generic manufacturer in Germany made modest financial contributions to cover the running costs of the Centre until it acquires the WHO prequalification and thereby begins to generate its own revenue. The Centre has a clinical partner, Armauer Hanssen Research Institute, where the clinical studies are being conducted.

Since RBEC is the first of its kind in the Sub-Saharan region (except for South Africa), the centre anticipates an overwhelming demand for BE studies. The Centre will also offer services related to assessment of quality of medicines. In the long run the RBEC would also play key role in clinical trials as well as in pharmaceutical research and development activities aiming at product development and drug discoveries.

The other important entity that has been recently (2013) established by Proclamation is the Food, Beverage and Pharmaceuticals Industry Development Institute, which has the objective of transforming the food, beverage and pharmaceutical industries through accelerated technological development and transfer. Currently, the Institute is preparing a 10-year strategic plan for the development of the pharmaceutical industry.

Conclusion: future pathways and challenges

Ethiopia is making substantial headway in all areas of socio-economic development. It is in the midst of a sustained growth surge that is becoming increasingly broad-based, building on major improvements in educational attainment, improved health outcomes and improved infrastructure capacity (power, transportation and telecommunications). The GTP sets ambitious targets for further improvements in these areas, together with significant reforms aiming to improve local manufacturing capacities (including pharmaceuticals) and trade logistics by rolling out various export-oriented economic programmes (Assefa et al., 2013).

Despite all these achievements, however, there are still outstanding issues to be addressed, such as the low production capacity and overwhelming dependence on importation of medicines; shortage of qualified management and technical personnel; and inadequate continuing professional development for practising professionals.

Asked about challenges and limitations faced by the local manufacturers, the plant technical manager of EAP reiterated the following: limited working capital of the factories; conflicts of interest with the suppliers of raw materials in India and China (as they are also producers of medicines, so they charge higher prices); paying VAT that is not reimbursed; shortage of foreign currency and hence longer lead time in foreign purchase resulting in price fluctuation and ultimately purchase reorders; small bulk orders with no economy of scale; low manufacturing capacity and hence high production cost; and limited capacity for troubleshooting and management.

Finally, based upon the assessment in this chapter, we suggest the following ways forward.

Strengthen local production: Although some progress has been made over the past few years, the development and local production of medicines is still marginal. Consequently, Ethiopia is relying heavily on imports for medicines and medical supplies. It is therefore crucial to build and strengthen national capacity to manufacture affordable, safe, efficacious, high-quality generic essential medicines which can significantly contribute to the simultaneous achievement of public health and industrial development objectives (MoST, 2012).

Competitive and efficient local pharmaceutical production should be promoted by strengthening local producers' capacity to meet WHO-GMP and WHO prequalification standards, promoting regional and international collaborations and facilitate technology transfer; fostering pooled procurement of raw materials and other inputs.

Establish raw material manufacturing plants: The fact that most raw materials have to be imported has made the local pharmaceutical manufacturers less competitive against imported generic products from Asia. Therefore, looking for alternative local sources of some of the excipients and APIs is one important strategy to improve the competitiveness of the local manufacturers (Gebre-Mariam and Schmidt, 1996, 1998; Gebre-Mariam et al., 1996) (see also Chapter 7). The government should foster such an endeavour.

Build human capital: The availability of adequate, appropriately trained and well-motivated personnel endowed with requisite knowledge, skills and attitude to provide effective and efficient services is of paramount importance for the development of the pharmaceutical industry. Some manufacturers report that local personnel are not adequately trained to carry out pharmaceutical production and business development. To rectify this, formal pharmaceutical training should be based on the needs of the industry. Strategies should be devised and implemented to update professionals who are in service.

Enhance research and development: R&D on raw materials (APIs and excipients) should be fostered and long-term strategy for their local production should be planned and implemented. Research on product development to make local products competitive should be enhanced. More favourable conditions should be created for the introduction of appropriate technology and know-how to vitalize the industry. To develop the raw material base for the pharmaceutical industry and to enhance the growth of a viable domestic pharmaceutical industry and manufacturing capacities, the government should extend its support to the private sector engaged in raw materials production. Research collaboration between universities, research institutes and local manufacturers should be promoted.

Notes

Acknowledgements: The authors would like to extend their gratitude to Mr. Asmelash Gebre (Secretary, EPMSMA), Mrs. Zaf Gebre-Meskel (General Manager, SEAA), Mrs. Muna Ahmed (Technical Director, EAP), Mr. Shimelis Mamuye (General Manger APF), Mr. Mukemil Abdella (Country Director, Julphar), Mr. Shegaw Adreaw (Deputy General Manager, SEAA) and Mr. Girma Aweke (Procurement and Supply Head, EPHARM) for accepting interviews, for their valuable time and for providing us with invaluable information on the pharmaceutical sector and their respective companies.

1. http://effortinvestments.com/new/index.php/officer, accessed 10 December 2014.
2. http://www.rttnews.com/1687014/cadila-pharma-s-ethiopian-jv-receives-cgmp-certificate.aspx, accessed 10 December 2014.
3. This facility used to belong to 'Bethelehem Pharmaceuticals PLC'. It was foreclosed during the crisis period, the Ethiopian Development Bank sold it out to Julphar, and the latter renovated the plant to meet GMP standards.
4. http://www.julphar.net.
5. http://www.pharmaceutical-technology.com/projects/julphar-manufacturing-facility-addis-ababa/.
6. http://allafrica.com/stories/201501190895.html Ethiopia: Julphar to Build Africa's Largest Injectable Medicine Plant.

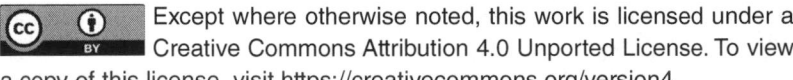

5

South-South Collaboration in Pharmaceuticals: Manufacturing Anti-retroviral Medicines in Mozambique

Giuliano Russo and Lícia de Oliveira

Introduction

Back in 2003, Brazil's and Mozambique's presidents, Luiz Inácio Lula da Silva and Joaquim Chissano, agreed to set up the first pharmaceutical factory in Mozambique, to be entirely owned by the national government. The project – widely known as the Brazil-Mozambican anti-retroviral factory because of its commitment to produce AIDS drugs – still represents the single most expensive and eye-catching project of Brazil's South-South cooperation programme in the health sector.

Part I of this book examines the complexities of African pharmaceutical markets and some practical aspects of setting up and developing pharmaceutical industries in the subcontinent. This chapter's contribution is to present the experience of establishing a pharmaceutical factory in Mozambique through industrial and official development collaboration between two national governments. Uniquely, this is a case study of an attempt to kick-start, through an innovative South-South partnership, pharmaceutical production in a country that previously had none. This chapter therefore discusses an experience sharply distinct from most of the countries' experiences discussed in the book, since they have pharmaceutical industries dating back to the 1950s, and with substantial numbers of firms in their industries.

This chapter draws on multiple sources such as official technical cooperation documents and the published literature on the subject, as well as on the authors' direct experience of the Mozambican pharmaceutical markets, of Brazil's development cooperation programme and of the factory's implementation project. It aims chiefly to discuss whether foreign lessons about the development of the pharmaceutical sectors can be learned for African countries, and the extent to which similar experiences of industrialization and health policy development can be exported from Brazil to the complex African environment. Two main contributions to the making medicines in Africa debate emerge from the analysis of this case study: one is the absolutely key role of the innovative South-South collaboration to the nascent pharmaceutical industry in Mozambique in terms of both financial subsidy and technical support. The other is that, while the technical collaboration with Brazil remains highly positive, the link to the market in Mozambique seems to have been a major problem, as the health-industry link so fundamental in the Brazilian pharmaceutical development experience seems to have worked less well here, at least in the early years of the project.

After a description of the evolution of the cooperation project and of the collaboration between the two countries to set up a factory in Mozambique, this chapter presents details of the technical investment needed to start such a complex enterprise in a country with a less-than-ideal business environment. The crucial link between the factory and the local as well as regional pharmaceutical markets is then analysed. The chapter ends with a discussion of the issues still hampering the development of the factory in Mozambique, and of the insight to be gained from such an experience, including insights for those countries in the subcontinent with a rather more established pharmaceutical industry.

The Brazil-supported pharmaceutical factory in Mozambique

Official reports show that back in 2003, the initiative to set up a pharmaceutical factory in Mozambique originally had the following stated objectives. It aimed to secure the supply of anti-retroviral medicines (ARVs) for HIV/AIDS treatment in the country, and to jump-start pharmaceutical generics' manufacturing in Mozambique, enabling the fulfilment of the objectives of the national primary care and pharmaceutical policies. It also aimed to reduce the country's dependence on pharmaceutical donations and imports and to contribute to the creation of local capacity for pharmaceutical production and industrial management (de Oliveira, 2013).

Following an informal agreement between the two presidents, diplomatic and international cooperation efforts were stepped up from both the Brazilian and Mozambican governments to iron out the details of the project from 2003 onwards. Figure 5.1 summarizes the long timeline of the project from its inception to 2014.

The Oswaldo Cruz Foundation (Fiocruz) – Brazil's leading public health institution (Roa and Baptista e Silva, 2015) – was appointed in 2004 to conduct the factory's feasibility study. This was completed and approved three years later. *Farmanguinhos* – Fiocruz's pharmaceutical arm, and a key instrumental actor in Brazil's national pharmaceutical policy – was charged with the pharmaceutical technological transfer, technical training and the wider project implementation. These two institutions are directly linked to the Brazilian Ministry of Health and have been credited with playing a pivotal role in the development of domestic

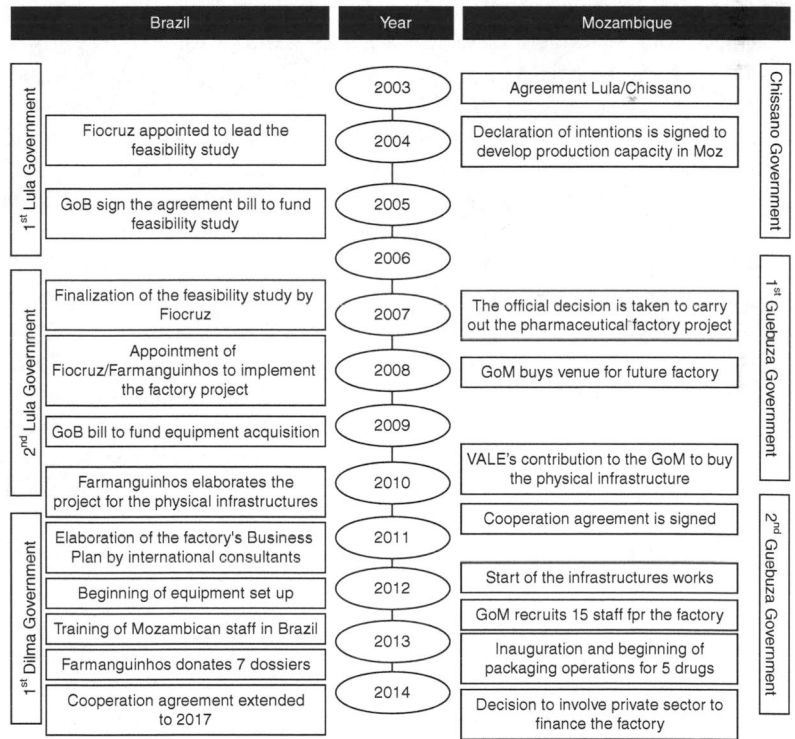

Figure 5.1 Timelines for the implementation of the factory project
Source: drawn by the authors.

pharmaceutical regulation as well as of the pharmaceutical market in Brazil (Flynn, 2008). (Their role is discussed further in Chapter 9). These institutions' early involvement in the factory project in Mozambique was considered instrumental in seeking to replicate that experience back home.

Meanwhile, in the field, a number of cooperation agreements and spending authorizations had to be sought by both the Mozambican and Brazilian sides, as the project was to be funded through multiple sources. The process was lengthy. VALE S.A. – Brazil's largest mining company with ongoing operations in Mozambique – was also recruited by President Lula to support the national government in financing the factory's infrastructure works, which were only finalized in 2012. In the same year, the majority of the pharmaceutical equipment was procured in the international market, donated by *Farmanguinhos*, and shipped to the future factory venue. The government of Mozambique recruited the first 15 local staff in the same year, and *Farmanguinhos* donated the pharmaceutical production technology files and provided the technical assistance required to start production of Nevirapine, Lamivudine, Captopril and Hydrochlorothiazide in 2013 (Russo et al., 2014).

In 2008, the enterprise was officially registered as Mozambique Pharmaceuticals Ltd (*Sociedade Moçambicana de Medicamentos*, SMM), as it planned to extend production beyond anti-retroviral drugs. SMM is owned by the government of Mozambique's State Assets Management Institute (IGEPE), which appoints the executive director and chair of its administrative board from candidates put forward by the Mozambican Ministry of Health (MISAU). In addition to the short-term Brazilian technical assistance necessary for training and setting up operations, four full-time Brazilian consultants in pharmaceutical manufacturing, quality assurance, technical engineering and maintenance have been appointed for the coming years, with the objective of steering the factory towards sustainable production and WHO Quality Certification (Russo et al., 2014).

According to official documents (de Oliveira, 2012), the government of Brazil (GoB) originally agreed to take responsibility for the project's staff training, for procuring equipment and raw materials, for providing technical assistance and for designing the factory and managing the project. Meanwhile the government of Mozambique (GoM) was to be responsible for purchasing the physical infrastructure for the factory, for undertaking rehabilitation works, for funding the factory's recurrent expenditures and for buying the bulk of the factory's pharmaceutical output. The first three-year cooperation agreement was signed in

2011. Extensions of the original 2011 agreement were to be negotiated every three years through official Complementary Agreements (*Ajustes complementares*).

In 2014, procurement contracts were signed by MISAU for the acquisition of locally produced hospital serum bags and imported but locally packaged generic drugs from the factory. Although disruptions were experienced in 2014 in the production lines, a fresh cooperation agreement was signed the same year to extend Brazil's support to the factory until 2017. Towards the end of the same year, following a visit of Mozambican officials to the Brazilian Ministry of Health and Ministry of Foreign Trade, Industry and Development, a decision was taken by IGEPE – the institution in responsible for the factory – to seek capital to finance the factory from the Mozambican banking sector, and at the time of writing this seems to be the path identified for the development of the project in the near future (Figure 5.1). In the process of developing the factory, more than ten years and three presidential terms have elapsed both in Mozambique and Brazil, and administrative, political and foreign affairs details have had to be ironed out across two countries and four different political administrations.

The new pharmaceutical factory is located in Matola City within Mozambique's capital's metropolitan outskirts, on a 20,000-square-metres allotment close to the capital's commercial port and to the South African border. The factory currently engages both in secondary and tertiary pharmaceutical production. That is, it produces its own formulations from imported active pharmaceutical ingredients (APIs) and raw materials, as well as packing imported finished formulations. Twenty-one generic drugs are planned to be produced in the next two years, including ARVs (Nevirapine, Zidovudine and Lamivudine combinations), hypertension drugs (Captopryl and Propanolol) and a list of antibiotics, antimycotics and anti-diabetic compounds specifically requested by the MISAU as currently in wide use in the country's public National Health Service (NHS). Such a list can be expanded on demand to include generic drugs to meet the WHO requirements for ARV treatment and generic formulation to be sold by third parties. All the formulations (pharmaceutical dossiers) belong to *Farmanguinhos* and are transferred for free to MISAU. A laboratory for the control of medicine quality has been already established, equipped to test drugs for efficacy and safety. When fully functional, the laboratory will be capable of providing information on the quality of all the drugs imported into the country and of contributing to the development of new drug testing methodologies.

The technical investment

So far the factory's overall set-up costs have been estimated at US$ 39.6 million (de Oliveira, 2013). Capital investment (land, infrastructures, machinery and implementation of production lines) amounted to approximately 46.5% of overall expenditures and pledged funds, while technological transfers and technical assistance represented a substantial cost item (13.0%), including the value of compounds dossiers for the 21 generic drugs, as well as personnel costs for the expatriate staff who helped setting up the operations. Running costs for the first year (API procurement, training and maintenance) represented 23.7% of present and future expenditures (Table 5. 1).

Although the Brazilian government funded the majority of the project's set up costs (62.7%), the government of Mozambique contributed through buying up land and some existing infrastructure for the establishment of the factory, while a donation from VALE, a Brazilian mining company operating in Mozambique, supported personnel and infrastructure expenditures (Table 5.1).

As Brazil still lacks a comprehensive legal framework to provide funds and procure goods for its international cooperation programme (Cabral, Russo and Weinstock, 2014), funds for the project had to be channelled through the implementing public institutions linked to the Brazilian Ministry of Health – Fiocruz, Fiotec and Farmanguinhos – and through the Brazilian Development Cooperation Agency (ABC), linked to the Ministry of Foreign Affairs (*Itamaraty*). On the Mozambican side, the costly acquisition of the infrastructure from a former hospital serum bags factory (*Final Farmacêutica)* was directly managed by the government, while IGEPE funded the capital rehabilitation and maintenance costs. The donation to the venture by VALE S.A. was expressly solicited by the government of Brazil and channelled through the government of Mozambique Treasury to set up the factory's early production lines and pay for some Brazilian personnel as part of the running costs. With the extension of the cooperation agreement to 2017, both governments agreed to further the funding of the project.

Although according to the business plan the factory would require 88 full-time staff to manufacture at full capacity (24 for direct production, 4 for quality-control-related services, and 18 for management and administration), at the time of writing only 55 had been recruited, and a team of 8 Brazilian technical assistants based in Maputo were still providing key management and technical expertise for the factory's operations. Given the limited development of industrial capabilities in Mozambique,

Table 5.1 Estimated cost of setting up the factory (current US$ million)

Source of funding	Implementing agencies	Activities	Type of expenditures	Spending (to 2013)	Pledged (2017)	Total
Government of Brazil	Fiotec/Fiocruz/MoH of Brazil	Transfer of Technologies; Technical assistance	Technology transfer	6.3	6.7	13.0
	Farmanguinhos/ Fiocruz/MoH of Brazil	Equipment	Capital	4.0	1.0	5.0
	Brazilian Cooperation Agency / Ministry of Foreign Relations (ABC/Itamaraty)	Procurement of raw products	Running costs	1.0	2.0	3.0
		Capacity building	Running costs	0.2	0.5	0.7
Government of Mozambique	GoM	Purchase of land and infrastructure from Final Farmacêutica Lda	Capital	8.0		8.0
	IGEPE	Maintenance of infrastructures	Running costs	2.0	2.0	4.0
		Development of existing infrastructure	Capital	1.4		1.4
VALE S.A.	Support to the GoM for the project	Setting up production lines	Capital	4.0		4.0
	Support to the GoM for personnel expenses	Payment of Brazilian technical director for 4 years	Running costs	0.250*	0.250*	0.5*
Total				27.2	12.5	39.6

Note: *SMM Accounting Report SMM.

Sources: Respective implementing agencies, unless otherwise stated.

technical personnel as well as senior managers for the new factory had to be either summoned from the Brazilian public sector or recruited in the local market and provided for extra training abroad.

In terms of technological transfer, until March 2015, *Farmanguinhos* had donated for free 10 out of 21 technological dossiers for the production of specific pharmaceuticals, to include results from pharmaceutical equivalence tests, quality control procedures for APIs and other ingredients, manufacturing process specifications and test failure reports. The next steps for technological production are still under way and include:

- adaptation of the Brazilian dossiers to the MISAU's specifications;
- training local personnel to the local production of the pharmaceutical dossier;
- assisting production for the drugs' first three pilot batches, following production as well as commercialization of the products;
- establishing a pharmacovigilance system.

In terms of pharmaceutical production equipment, 18 high-tech pieces have been procured internationally by *Fiocruz/Farmanguinhos* and donated by Brazilian cooperation. This included main production line equipment such as compression, coating and blender machines, packing equipment – blisters, labelling and capping machines – as well as quality and in-process control equipment – tablets' hardness and dissolution testers, chromatography and centrifuges. Given the total absence of up-to-date manufacturing machinery in the infrastructures inherited from *Final Farmacêutica*, basic non-specific equipment such as water purification machines also had to be brought in.

The machines presently installed in the factory in Maputo have an estimated market value of US$4 million, with an additional list of equipment worth approximately US$1 million to be procured and bought by 2017. All the machines were purchased by *Farmanguinhos/Fiocruz* through international tenders and donated to the government of Mozambique, including installation services and personnel training for its use and maintenance. SMM technical personnel were all trained in Brazil on the use of the specific machines, and on-site ongoing technical assistance is provided for specific manufacturing.

The company and the market

This section details a key – and often overlooked – aspect of the Brazil-Mozambique collaboration to produce pharmaceuticals: the link to the market. A feasibility study was conducted in 2007 looking at the likely costs of setting up the factory in Maputo and its specific production capacity for ARVs, but it failed to analyse the market conditions in Mozambique and in the wider Sub-Saharan region (Fiotec/Fiocruz, 2007).

Mozambique's pharmaceutical policy in the 1970s and 1980s focussed on procuring and using generic drugs, to extract the best possible value from its drugs budget (Barker, 1983). However, as Mozambique became after Independence one of the world's largest recipients of health-aid funds, international finance for drugs began to be handled, first through an externally managed Drugs Common Fund (Pavignani and Durão, 1999), and subsequently through an MoH-managed Sector Wide Approach common fund agreement (PROSAUDE). Currently, with the global push for AIDS fight and the introduction of anti-retroviral treatment (ART) in 2003, the country is enjoying a considerable injection of AIDS funds, with anti-retroviral drugs procured in the international market by organizations such as the Global Fund, the World Bank and USAID.

In 2012, the national drugs market in Mozambique was estimated to be worth approximately US$140 million in terms of the value of drugs imported (COWI, 2012), which represented a drugs expenditure of US$5.55 per capita. Eighty-five per cent of the total market value was represented by public sector imports, mostly funded by external funds and donations, some of them managed by the local Ministry of Health through the sector budget support fund, PROSAUDE (CMAM, 2011). In recent years public drugs expenditures have gone from US$78 million in 2004 to US$122 million in 2012 (Table 5.2), the increase being driven by in-kind AIDS drugs donations that rose from the original US$4 million to the current US$49 million in eight years (COWI, 2012).

As shown in Table 5.2, AIDS drugs represent the largest single item of the national public pharmaceutical expenditures, and enter the country exclusively as in-kind donations procured and managed directly by foreign organizations. Public funds pay for roughly a quarter of the overall public sector drug expenditures, with North-America-based organizations (USAID, Supply Management Systems and the Clinton Health Access Initiative) contributing to purchase 67% of all the public sector drugs procured in the country. In this respect, the local funding environment appears still to represent a critical limitation for pharmaceutical production in Mozambique. Given the typical consumer's limited ability to pay, and the relatively small size of the local private

Table 5.2 Public sector drug import value, by source and type of health programme (2012 US$)

Health programme and associated drugs	Internal and external funds managed by MISAU (drug pool and state budget)	In-kind donations	Total
Hospital drugs	11,861,471	1,200,883	13,062,354
Primary care drug kits	8,708,824	0	8,708,824
Community health	3,870,588	7,217,900	11,088,488
STD and HIV-SIDA	0	48,750,977	48,750,977
TB	0	249,550	249,550
Malaria	0	24,124,599	24,124,599
Blood banks	967,647	0	967,647
Oral health	290,294	0	290,294
Surgical supplies	10,111,912	0	10,111,912
Laboratory supplies	2,497,000	0	2,497,000
Imaging devices and supplies	1,741,765	0	1,741,765
Total	40,049,500	81,543,908	121,593,408

Source: CMAM, 2012.

sector, selling to the public sector is obviously the only way for local producers to go to scale and access a local market worth in excess of US$140 million. However, the lack of flexibility of the international drugs financing environment is pointed to by many as a key limiting factor for the development of local production of pharmaceuticals in the country; even if locally produced drugs were made available at competitive prices, the manner in which external funds for AIDS drugs are currently regulated would stand in the way of procuring, or offering preferential procurement terms to buy, locally produced drugs. As a side effect, free internationally procured ARVs also end up crowding out the local private sector, which is traditionally a key customer for locally produced goods (Herzer and Grimm, 2012; Rajan and Subramanian, 2011).

Little consolidated data exist about the private pharmaceutical market in Mozambique. Some estimates put it at approximately US$20 million, calculated on the basis of the drugs value declared on the import documents submitted to the pharmaceutical department in 2012 (COWI, 2012). Although 54 private importers are officially registered in Mozambique, a 2010 study found that the private sector is highly concentrated, with the four largest firms handling more than 50% of the drugs imported (Russo and McPake, 2010).

As for the regional market, according to some industry pundits (IMS, 2012), with its 10.6% yearly growth rate by volume, Africa is the world's fastest-growing pharmaceutical market after Asia, and is estimated to reach a value of US$30 billion next year. With specific reference to the ARVs market in the Southern African Development Community, the SMM business plan estimated in 2012 that a sufficiently homogeneous regional demand for ARVs existed for SMM to serve. Previous studies of the regional market (COWI, 2012) suggested that across the neighbouring countries of Mozambique, Tanzania, Zambia and Zimbabwe, AIDS treatment lines were relatively similar and reliant on standard Lamivudine-Zidovudine-Nevirapine combinations. This would have implied access to sizeable market for HIV/AIDS drugs of approximately 6 million treatment doses per year across the four countries. However, there is little recognition in SMM's viability study and subsequent business plans of the complexity of those markets, of the possible regional and international competition to be faced, as well as of their regulation and of the role played by national governments in supporting the local industry.

Currently, SMM's business plan expects to sell its products in the Mozambican market in the short term, particularly to the NHS. It aims to sell into the regional pharmaceutical market only in the medium term, once the required certifications are obtained to allow the firm to compete in international tenders (COWI, 2012; SMM and Farmanguinhos, 2013). SMM unit prices, listed in Table 5.3, reflect the initial production costs calculated on the basis of APIs imported from Brazil. As production goes to scale and APIs are bought in from the global competitive market, SMM is projecting lower selling prices reflecting the lower API costs. SMM also enjoys most of the standard preferential policy interventions already adopted in the East Africa Community: an ad hoc tax exemption regulation on imported APIs and other manufacturing product and a preferential buying regime from the government, according to which, when procuring drugs for the National Health care Service, the National Drugs Acquisition Agency is required to give preference to locally produced drugs as long they are no more than 15% more expensive than the products of their international competitors.

The prices listed in Table 5.3 represent SMM's factory gate selling prices for public procurement; a comparison with the Management Science for Health international median reference prices for procurement is also shown. It is worth noting that although in the same price range, SMM prices for ARVs, particularly those involving Lamivudine, appear to compare less favourably with international reference prices than do those for the other generic drugs (Table 5.3).

The factory's business plan predicted wholesale selling price levels at which the factory would break even, on the basis of the cost structure model used for the production of ARVs in Brazil's state pharmaceutical factories adapted to the Mozambican context (Pinheiro et al., 2006). Although SMM drugs face higher costs because of Mozambique's burdensome import duties on non-API production materials, as well as high maintenance costs, according to the factory's business plan these will be offset by lower capital costs and smaller operating margins, typical of a state-owned company (MacDonald and Yamey, 2001).

Table 5.3   Unit price for selected SMM drugs (US$)

Product	Package (Units)	SMM's selling price to the NHS (US$)	MSH* median price (US$)
Amoxicillin caps 500 mg cx c/500	500	0.0502	0.0313
Glibenclamide tab 5 mg cx c/500	500	0.0035	0.0042
Hydrochlorothiazide tab 50 mg cx c/500	500	0.0047	0.0050
Metronidazole tab 250 mg cx c/1000	1000	0.0116	0.0061
Prednisone tab 5 mg cx c/500	500	0.0077	0.0108
Lamivudine 150 mg 60 tab – 3TC	60	0.1152	0.0508
Lamivudine 150 + Zidovudine 300 mg 60 tab	60	0.4354	0.1714
Lamivudine 150 mg + Zidovudine 300 mg + Nevirapine 200 mg	60	0.2754	0.1654
Lamivudine 30 mg + Zidovudine 60 mg + Nevirapine 50 mg	60	0.1015	0.0726
Nevirapine 200 mg 60 tab – AD	60	0.0849	0.0611

Note: *Management Science for Health Drug Price Database.
Source: SMM.

According to the factory's business plan, SMM furthermore will be able to sell its products at prices comparable to those from the international market, thanks to savings in the initial investment in infrastructures and equipment, donated by the Brazilian cooperation, and in national transport charges and taxes, which are particularly favourable to business in Mozambique, since the original tax rate on chemical products was scrapped. In comparison to the typical cost structure for ARVs (Pinheiro et al., 2006), SMM's production costs will be largely driven by active pharmaceutical ingredients' (APIs) import prices, and less by taxes, profit margins, research and development and local production mark-ups (SMM and Farmanguinhos, 2013).

The South–South collaboration in context

'Emerging donors' and 'South-South cooperation' are terms usually referring to providers of development assistance and forms of cooperation that have recently become prominent in the international aid architecture, due to a recent expansion in resources allocated to development cooperation with poor countries (Manning, 2006). Thanks to their recent economic growth, emerging economies like China, India and Brazil are boosting their cooperation programmes (Brautigam, 2009; Cabral, 2010), and according to one estimate, the volume of aid from emerging donors reached between US$9.5 billion and US$12 billion in 2006, corresponding approximately to 8–10% of total aid flows. The recent literature on the subjects shows that some common features among these emerging aid players are discernible. One of the most salient is the emphasis on horizontal (South-South) cooperation between developing countries and the principle of non-interference in the internal affairs of recipient countries. Related to this aspect, emerging donors tend to have no policy-related conditionality, such as standards of governance and macroeconomic requirements, and fewer procedural conditions, such as counterpart funding or separate bank accounts, relative to traditional donors. More controversially, there is a more evident and openly acknowledged association between commercial interests, geo-strategic objectives and development cooperation than is the case for traditional donors (Kragelund, 2008).

Brazil's overall cooperation programme is still relatively small, estimated to be worth between US$350 million and US$1 billion per year, with a substantial component of support to international organizations and humanitarian assistance and a smaller proportion directed to technical cooperation projects (IPEA, 2011). South-South relations play an important part in Brazil's strategy of diversification of diplomatic and economic relations, and technical cooperation provides an expedient way of taking forward such an agenda. Brazil's South-South technical cooperation programme has as key features the emphasis on exchange of experiences between equal partners (or 'horizontal cooperation', as it is usually referred to), respect for the partner country's sovereignty and non-conditionality of support, with a dominant but not exclusive geographical focus on Latin American and Portuguese-speaking African countries and on the agriculture, education and health sectors (Cabral, Russo and Weinstock, 2014).

Government figures put the value of Brazilian technical health cooperation at approximately US$12 million between 2006 and 2009. However, recent independent reports estimated that Brazil spent between US$12 million and US$14 million in technical health cooperation projects in Portuguese-speaking African countries alone for the same period (Russo, Cabral and Ferrinho, 2013). Brazil's health-sector-specific characteristics and claimed principles suggest some important departures from the ways in which development cooperation has been traditionally practised. A key feature of Brazil's cooperation is that it is openly driven by foreign policy goals, and development cooperation is seen as instrumental in promoting Brazil's image and interests abroad. Brazil openly adopts the notion of 'health diplomacy' for its health projects (Roa and Baptista e Silva, 2015), implying that health development cooperation can be informed by international health objectives, following the recognition that national health problems need to be dealt with in the global health arena. Brazilian cooperation officials also dispute the use of the term 'aid' to define their work, as that would impose industrialised countries' 'world views, agendas and pre-defined objectives' (Buss, 2011). Instead, 'horizontal partnership' is Brazil's preferred terminology to indicate the wish to draw on principles of non-interference and mutual advantage. Brazilian projects are also claimed to promote 'structural cooperation in health', a concept defined by some as building local capacity for development (Buss, 2011). It begins from the premise that health cooperation should focus on integrating human resources for health and institutional development, developing local capacity to avoid dependency from foreign expertise and promoting internal collaboration between local health institutions to elaborate their own health system development agenda.

As for the relation between national business interests and cooperation goals, Brazilian cooperation in health openly claims to be inspired by the concept of the 'health-industrial complex for health development', according to which individual countries need to invest in the national health care industry and R&D capacity if they want to develop their health systems (see also Chapter 9). Such an emphasis on self-sufficiency is also aimed at avoiding costly dependency on foreign health care technologies (Gadelha, 2006). This approach happens to be particularly relevant for the pharmaceutical and biotechnology business in Brazil, as, besides being worth approximately US$24.5 billion in 2012, these two sectors are considered to be instrumental in the implementation of the Brazilian Unified Healthcare System's objectives of free and equitable access to health care services (Gadelha et al., 2013). Brazil's position on HIV/AIDS drugs appears in line with its support for strong government involvement in the provision of health care services, underpinned by a constitutional framework that establishes a universal citizen right to health and places a duty of health care provision on the state. The growing roles of the Brazil's Ministry of Health research and training agency, *Fiocruz*, and its pharmaceutical arm, *Farmanguinhos*, influential government institutions behind the development of the ARV industry in Brazil as well as in the factory project in Mozambique, are exemplifications of the strength of this paradigm of state-led health development (see Chapter 9).

Local production of pharmaceuticals: issues raised by the case study

In contrast to the experiences described in other chapters, the Maputo factory story provides a case study of an attempt to kick-start, through an innovative South-South partnership, pharmaceutical production in a country that previously had none. Our narrative of development and implementation of the project has shown the key role of the innovative South-South collaboration for the nascent pharmaceutical industry in Mozambique in terms of both financial subsidy and technical support. However, while the technical collaboration with Brazil remains highly positive, the link to health markets in Mozambique seems to have been a major problem, as the health-industry link so fundamental in the Brazilian pharmaceutical development experience seems to have worked less well here, at least for these early years.

The experience of the Brazil-Mozambique collaboration details the challenges of starting up such a complex enterprise from scratch, in an environment often lacking the basic infrastructural pillars for industry development. Human resources were identified as the single most important bottleneck for SMM development. As the majority of the staff recruited locally had to be sent for training abroad, some of those employed have been poached by competing businesses in wholesaling and retailing, and highly specialized positions in the factory are still covered by expatriate staff. Although personnel with middle-management skills should be already supplied by the local labour market, experienced executives with a track record of management in comparable industries are acutely lacking in Mozambique, given the country's relatively recent history of industrial development.

Mozambique's particular industrial environment was recognized as another factor hampering the development of the pharmaceutical factory. In comparison to other African countries with a more established industry, Mozambique seems to be lacking a critical mass of suppliers, products and services needed for the development of a competitive pharmaceutical business. All the primary products needed for Maputo factory's manufacturing are, up to now, imported from Brazil; all the basic maintenance and technical services are contracted to South African firms, and resorting to lower cost Indian and Chinese equipment has not been an option, given the limited equipment maintenance services provided by such suppliers in Mozambique.

Strengthening the government's current quality control of pharmaceutical manufacturing processes and final products is needed, as this was also reported to be a hurdle for the long-term development of pharmaceutical manufacturing in Mozambique. A lack of quality regulation *de facto* allows competitors to employ cheaper substandard machinery in pharmaceutical production and produce substandard – and, crucially, cheaper – generic products. The factory's case study shows that lack of effective quality regulation ends up benefitting those importers of non-branded generics for whom an ability to cut costs and offer wildly discounted generics represents the core of their market strategy in Mozambique.

This experience, however, also identifies a path to local industry development based on foreign assistance but also on national governments' willingness to support local procurement of drugs (Russo and Banda, forthcoming). As is already well known in those African countries with a more established pharmaceutical industry, this case study reaffirms that only through preferential pricing and reduced profit margins can local medicine production be competitive in Mozambique, but that the spill-over information-related benefits from local production can be substantial for epidemiological surveillance as well as for governments' price negotiations (Russo et al., 2014). However, a number of points of discussion are raised by this case study on the feasibility, sustainability and opportunity of local pharmaceutical production in Africa.

At the time of writing, the factory's sustainability after the likely end of Brazil's support in 2017 remains an issue. Brazil's original objective was to provide MISAU with enough production capacity to carry out its medicine policies; however, the GoM's appointment of IGEPE, together with the conspicuous absence of references to the factory in MISAU's policy documents, seem to signal a more pronounced interest in the factory's contribution to the country's industrial assets rather than to its public health goals. To this respect, the GoM will have to decide whether it is still in its interest to keep the factory as a public enterprise, or to attempt a privatization with a degree of public sector involvement, in the way similar experiences developed in Uganda and South Africa (Rajagopal, 2013; World News, 2013).

Finally, this case study raises questions about the suitability of foreign health policy and production models to the African context. If Brazil's original plan was to help Mozambique to replicate its own domestic experience in the AIDS fight and in pharmaceutical production, the implementation of this factory project exposed Brazil's limited familiarity with the development cooperation conundrum, but also the relevance of the differences between the two contexts (Russo et al., 2014). If some of the holdups in the project could be attributed to the relative lack of experience of Brazilian civil servants borrowed from their domestic duties to implement a cooperation project in the African continent, this case study probably shows that solutions that have proved effective elsewhere are hard to replicate in Mozambique for more than just one reason.

First, there is evidence from this experience that MISAU's engagement with the project and enthusiasm for using the factory as an implementation tool for its own national drug policy has not been the same as that which motivated the creation of public pharmaceutical laboratories in Brazil in the past decades (Russo et al., 2014; Flynn, 2010). Second, in stark contrast to what happens in the Brazilian pharmaceutical market, the majority of medicines in Mozambique are imported and paid for by the international community, so it is easy to understand why the government of Mozambique failed to see short-term gains in acquiring national production capacity and paying for something – ARV drugs –already provided for free. Finally, the human capital and manufacturing environment fundamentals that made possible the development of the pharmaceutical industry in Brazil are, in all likelihood, not yet in place in Mozambique. As a result, setting up a factory project already tested back home became highly cumbersome in a context where lack of skills, funds and services is the norm rather than the exception (Cabral, Russo and Weinstock, 2014).

Conclusion

Contrasting with other chapters in Part I that discuss very different experiences in African countries with a more established pharmaceutical industry, the present chapter has presented an original experience of developing local manufacturing from scratch through collaboration between two national governments. By describing the decade-long process through which Brazil and Mozambique cooperated to set up *Sociedade Moçambicana de Medicamentos* in Maputo, we aimed to illustrate the complexity of shoring up such an ambitious development cooperation project. Our analysis suggests that national and regional demand may justify SMM's production of ARVs and other generic drugs, but that public purchase of drugs remains essential to guarantee the sustainability of the business. We have also highlighted the differences between the two settings, Mozambique and Brazil, and have drawn attention to the possible risks involved in putting emphasis on the development of an enterprise without linking up adequately with local pharmaceutical markets. We believe that such an experience offers an insight into the complexities of developing pharmaceutical manufacturing operations in Sub-Saharan Africa, and into the options that the international community has to support it. The hope is that this will contribute to advancing the debate on local pharmaceutical manufacturing and on paths to its development.

6

Can Foreign Firms Promote Local Production of Pharmaceuticals in Africa?

Sudip Chaudhuri

Introduction

African countries, particularly the smaller ones, suffer from various disadvantages that prevent local producers from serving a substantial proportion of their domestic markets for pharmaceuticals. How to take care of these disadvantages to promote local production and to reduce dependence on imports is an important political and economic issue in Africa today. Most of the countries with developed industries have used foreign investments and technology in the process of their development. Is a similar trend likely in Africa? Are foreign companies likely to invest there to undertake manufacturing of pharmaceuticals? Can they be induced to do so? The objective of this chapter is to understand the prospects for foreign direct investment (FDI) in the pharmaceutical industry in Sub-Saharan Africa, particularly in smaller countries such as Ghana.

The foreign firms which are active in Africa can be broadly classified between the multinational corporations (MNCs) and the Indian generic companies. These two types of firms are quite different in terms of background and behaviour, and in the next section some of these differences are briefly outlined. The environment for pharmaceutical production and manufacturing is changing quite rapidly, both in Africa and abroad, and that is having an impact on the behaviour of both the MNCs and the Indian companies. The chapter first focuses on the MNCs and discusses the implications for the pharmaceutical markets in Africa. It then focuses on the Indian companies. We will see in the discussion that follows that on their own initiative, Indian companies may not be very keen to undertake investments for manufacturing in Africa. But given a conducive environment, they may not be averse to initiating manufacturing in Africa on a greater scale. The final section of the chapter takes up the case of Ghana, a relatively small African country. After a brief introduction to the structure of pharmaceutical market and industry in Ghana, the chapter analyses some policies which may be undertaken to promote local production, particularly in order to induce foreign firms to invest in Ghana.

MNCs, generics companies and the international pharmaceutical industry

Traditionally, pharmaceutical companies are classified between a small number of big MNCs that do research and development (R&D) for new drugs and aim to get these patented, and a large number of smaller generics companies that manufacture products that are not patented or products for which patents have expired. The MNCs are exceptionally large in size. The head offices are located in developed countries, mainly in the US, the UK, Switzerland, France, and Germany. They operate all over the world. The largest pharmaceutical MNC, Novartis (headquarters: Basel, Switzerland) reported US$46 billion in pharmaceutical sales in 2013. Each of the other top five MNCs – Pfizer (US), Roche (Switzerland), Sanofi (France), Merck (US) and GlaxoSmithKline (UK) – individually had sales worth more than the entire pharmaceutical market of the Middle East and Africa in 2013.[1]

The patent system and marketing power are at the root of the worldwide dominance of the MNCs. Naturally, for the products patented by the MNCs, they enjoy a monopoly status. They also use an elaborate marketing infrastructure to maintain dominant market shares even after patents expire. Even when the product is protected through patents, the MNCs promote their drugs under brand names, that is, through trademarks, rather than under generic names, which are commonly used in scientific literature. They continue using these brand names and try to take advantage of continuing brand loyalty when generic companies enter the market after the expiry of patents.

Traditionally MNCs have relied for their growth on patented drugs, and have focussed mainly on the large developed country markets. The largest pharmaceutical market is in US (US$343 billion), and this together with Western Europe (US$241.4 billion) and Japan (US$129.5 billion) accounted for about two-thirds of the global pharmaceutical market of US$1,052.1 billion in 2012 (BMI Espicom, 2013).

Like most other countries in the world, India after independence initially recognized product patent protection in pharmaceuticals, and the MNCs dominated the Indian market too. However, the abolition of product patents in 1972 eliminated the monopoly status that the MNCs enjoyed until then. Indian firms started manufacturing and marketing the latest drugs and were able to dislodge the MNCs from their position of dominance in the domestic market. India became self-reliant in drugs. The country furthermore emerged as a major player in the global pharmaceutical industry, receiving worldwide recognition as a low-cost producer of high-quality drugs. India now supplies medicines not only to other developing countries such as those in Africa but also to developed countries such as the United States.

The Indian pharmaceutical industry is highly heterogeneous. Most of the firms are small in size and operate only in the domestic market or in other developing countries. But some of the companies are large and not only compete with these small firms in these markets but also are active in regulated markets in developed countries. Two companies from India – Sun Pharmaceuticals (rank 48) and Ranbaxy (rank 50) – are among the 50 largest pharmaceutical companies in the world.[2] With the acquisition of Ranbaxy in 2014, Sun Pharmaceuticals will make a significant jump in the rankings. Other major Indian companies include Dr Reddys Laboratories, Cipla, Lupin, Glenmark and Cadila Healthcare. The larger Indian companies not only manufacture drugs in India and export these to different parts of the world. They have also started acquiring companies abroad to expand their manufacturing and marketing operations.

The changing marketing strategy of MNCs in Africa

Due to colonial or other links, some of the MNCs, for example GlaxoSmithKline (Glaxo as the firm then was known), had offices in some African countries. But as the MNCs started focusing more on the larger and more lucrative developed country markets, the African markets, especially in small countries, became less and less important for them and they started closing down their offices. Of course, their products were still available, but these imports were managed by their agents – local importers/distributors.

In recent years, however, the MNCs are returning to Africa and are focusing more on the subcontinent. Both push and pull factors are in operation. The most important push factor is that developed country markets have become less attractive, and the main pull factor is the better growth prospects in Africa (Mckinsey and Company, 2013; Tempest, 2011).

The cost of developing new drugs has gone up, but the introduction of new patented drugs in the market has slowed down. Earlier, as mentioned above, because of the steady flow of new patented drugs, the MNCs focussed mainly on the large markets for patented medicines in high-income countries. But in view of the declining productivity of R&D, MNCs can no longer afford to ignore the generics markets. Their turn to generics markets includes not only the patent-expired markets in the high-income countries but also the generics markets in emerging economies. The centres of economic activity are changing, with most of the growth expected to come from emerging markets (Mckinsey and Company, 2013).

Among emerging markets, Africa is still relatively small. The combined size of the market of the top ten African countries is about US\$14 billion, compared to US\$343 billion in the US and US\$129 billion in Japan (Table 6.1). However, the future growth is expected to take place in emerging countries, including in Africa, rather than in the developed countries. It has been estimated that between 2012 and 2018, major developed country pharmaceutical markets will remain stagnant (as in Japan and the UK), increase marginally (as in the US), decline marginally (as in Germany and France) and decline significantly (as in Italy and Spain). In contrast, the top ten African countries are expected to grow at 11% annually (Table 6.1). Quite understandably, therefore, while preparing their strategies for future, the MNCs are focusing more on the emerging countries, including in Africa.

The major drivers of growth in pharmaceutical markets in Africa have included increased disease burdens, particularly HIV/AIDS. The private markets have been expanded by developments in health insurance schemes, and some countries' health systems have seen large investments in public health. Political stability and rapid economic development, improving business climate, a maturing regulatory environment and increased confidence in generic products have all also contributed to market expansion (African Union and UNIDO, 2012; Mckinsey and Company, 2013).

The changes are having a variety of different impacts on the behaviour of the MNCs in Africa. The MNCs are no longer relying only on their agents. They have started opening offices and staffing these with their own employees. Marketing expenses for brand promotion have risen. To push up their sales they have also started offering credit facilities. Another notable development is that the MNCs are toning up their

Table 6.1   Anticipated trends in global pharmaceutical markets

Country	Market size 2012 (US$ billion)	Estimated market size 2018 (US$ billion)	Anticipated annual growth rate*, 2012–2018 (%)
Emerging markets			
China	82	164	12
Russia	22	39	10
India	16	28	10
Brazil	27	39	7
Africa**	14	26	11
Developed markets			
US	343	360	1
Japan	129	129	0
Germany	49	47	–1
France	43	41	–1
UK	38	38	0
Canada	26	25	–1
Italy	28	22	–4
Spain	23	16	–6

Note: * Compound annual rate of growth
** South Africa, Algeria, Egypt, Morocco, Tunisia, Sudan, Nigeria, Libya, Ivory Coast and Kenya.

Source: Mckinsey and Company, 2013.

distribution networks. They have started using the services of specialized supply chain organizations such as Imperial Health Sciences. The latter has operations in South Africa, Kenya, Ghana, Nigeria and Malawi, where medicines are received, stored and distributed in countries across Africa.

Perhaps the most significant development of all is that MNCs have started introducing new brands to compete in the generic markets. As mentioned above, when MNCs market new patented drugs, they sell these in brand names and continue to do so even after the patents expire. The patented drugs in monopoly markets are high priced. For patent-expired products too, the MNCs participate in the higher end of the market that has more limited competition. Even after the patents expire, the firms typically continue to use the same brands and continue to charge a very high price.

This strategy on the part of the MNCs has, in fact, helped the Indian generic companies. The large Indian companies typically adopt the strategy of charging a price lower than that of the MNCs to enter and grow market share in the patent-expired products. Armed with lower prices and active brand promotion, Indian companies such as Cipla, Ranbaxy, Sun Pharmaceuticals, Cadila and Glenmark have been able to dominate the markets in many products.

Particularly for Sub-Saharan African countries, India is the predominant supplier. In Tanzania, for example, the Indian generics company Cipla was the second-largest company in the retail market in 2010 with a market share of 16%, next only to the local firm, Shelys (21% market share), and ahead of MNCs such as Novartis (10%) and GSK (6%). Among the other notable Indian participants are companies such as Ranbaxy (8%), Sun Pharmaceuticals, Unichem Laboratories, Cadila Glenmark and Ajanta Pharma (Frost and Sullivan, 2010: 151; 2012: 81–83). As in most African countries, local firms in Tanzania manufacture a relatively simple list of formulations such as simple antibiotics, cough and cold preparations, analgesics antipyretics, sedatives, nutraceuticals, anthelmintics and anti-malarials (see Chapter 3; Chaudhuri et al., 2010). For technologically more sophisticated formulations, the competition is mainly between the MNCs and the Indian companies.

The MNCs are now increasingly trying to make their presence felt in these generic markets. They are reluctant to dilute their innovator brand by lowering the price to compete against generic products. There is a brand loyalty associated with innovator products and there is a price-insensitive market segment where MNCs continue to sell despite high prices and despite the availability of cheaper generic products. To enlarge their market, the MNCs are introducing new brands and selling these at prices significantly lower than their innovator brands. The dual-brand strategy enables them to be present not only in the price-insensitive segment of the market but also in the price-sensitive segment.

The most active MNC in this game is GSK. The innovator brand for their anthelmintic drug, albendazole, is Zentel. They have introduced a new brand for the same product, named Alzental. Another example is the antibiotic amoxicillin/clavulanate. The GSK innovator brand is Augmentin. They also sell the same product in the brand name Clavulin to compete against similar-sounding generic brands such as, for example, Clavam of India's generics company Alkem. These MNC generic brands are priced significantly below the innovator price, often 50% or less. These are still priced above the brands of generic companies. But with the price differential much smaller and their better reputation, the MNCs hope to prevent the slide in their sales in the generics markets.

Now that they have started competing on prices, the matter of costs has become important. Another important trend observed is that the

MNCs are trying to get their generic products manufactured in cheaper locations. The Ghanaian company LaGray has entered into an agreement with Sandoz, the generic arm of Novartis. The former will manufacture products to be marketed in their brand names by the latter. India offers an even cheaper location. MNCs such as GSK, AstraZeneca and Abbott have entered into supply agreements with Indian companies such as Dr Reddys, Aurobindo, Cadila Healthcare and Torrent. Dr Reddys, for example, will supply about 100 branded formulations to GSK for marketing in different emerging markets including in Africa. These deals enable the MNCs to get access to low-cost reliable products without undergoing the lengthy process of getting regulatory approvals in different markets and without incurring any capital expenditure for setting up manufacturing plants. The Indian companies gain by having access to the formidable marketing resources of the MNCs (Chaudhuri, 2012).

However, what these trends indicate is that although MNCs are targeting African markets, they are unlikely to make any significant investments to manufacture drugs in Africa, at least not in the near future.

Indian generic companies in the African market

European countries, mainly France, Germany and Switzerland, are the most important suppliers for some relatively large North African countries such as Algeria, Morocco and Egypt (UNCOMTRADE). But for Sub-Saharan Africa, India is the predominant supplier of medicines. As Table 6.2 shows, in 2012 India contributed more than 50% of the formulations imports in Uganda and Mozambique and more than 40% in Nigeria, Ghana and Rwanda. Its share was also substantial in countries such as Ethiopia, Tanzania and Zimbabwe. If we could exclude the imports of high-priced patented medicines and focus only on generics, India's contribution to Africa would be much larger than Table 6.2 suggests. Where drugs are purchased from multiple sources, as for example for ARVs, India has turned out to be the dominant supplier, accounting for more than two-thirds of Africa's imports (Chaudhuri, 2008).

Indian generic companies exporting medicines to Africa can be classified into two broad categories: those which are active also in the regulated markets in developed countries such as the United States, and those which are not yet present in these markets. The larger and more reputed companies belong to the first category. These more dynamic Indian

Table 6.2   Indian share of pharmaceutical formulations imports into Africa, 2012

Country	Total imports, US$ million	Imports from India (%)
Uganda	204	57.6
Mozambique	50	52.6
Nigeria	263	43.7
Ghana	126	42.7
Rwanda	55	40.4
Ethiopia	154	39.3
United Rep. of Tanzania	161	36.8
Zimbabwe	170	36.6
Mauritius	103	34.7
Burundi	42	33.3
Cameroon	168	25.0
Botswana	124	23.1
Niger	44	21.3
Côte d'Ivoire	259	19.1
Madagascar	49	18.9
South Africa	1,890	15.9
Namibia	142	13.1
Mauritania	15	10.4
Togo	68	6.2
Senegal	167	4.5
Mali	142	4.1
Morocco	360	3.6
Algeria	1,879	2.6
Cabo Verde	8	1.3
Egypt	1,498	0.5
Total (25 countries)	8,139	13.7

Source: Calculated from UNCOMTRADE database (http://comtrade.un.org).

generic companies have been more interested in the patent-expired markets in high-income countries such as the US and in Europe because of the larger markets and better prices realized. Prices achieved are higher in these markets because regulatory requirements to enter these markets are stricter and so entry is more difficult. The Indian companies active in the African markets also primarily target the markets where entry barriers are higher and hence competition is less strong. These companies promote their products through brands and their main competitors are the MNCs (and also generics companies from other countries). As mentioned above, these companies often try to enter and grow in these markets by charging a price lower than that of the innovator MNC. The smaller Indian companies are more active in over-the-counter medicines and in markets for simple products where they compete mainly against the local manufacturers and other smaller generic companies.

The changing composition of Indian companies

The composition of Indian generic companies is however changing in Africa. With improvements in the regulatory environment in Africa, the not so quality-conscious Indian companies are increasingly finding it difficult to operate there. Allegations have been made from time to time that some Indian companies have taken advantage of the regulatory environment in India and in Africa to export poor-quality drugs. In fact, it has been a very common complaint in Africa that India has not been taking initiatives to regulate the quality of drugs exported. This is now changing. Due to the efforts of the government in India and also some steps taken in some African countries, the quality standards have improved. Most African countries, for example, do not permit imports into their countries from India without a Certificate of Pharmaceutical Product (COPP). This is given by the drug control administration in India to units that qualify for the WHO-GMP standard. This standard is stricter than Schedule M, the Indian version of GMP, and hence exporters are required to satisfy higher standards than in the domestic market.

Like the MNCs, the more serious Indian players are also getting more involved in Africa. Here too both push and pull factors are in operation. An important push factor arises from the fact that earlier expectations of huge gains in the patent-expired markets in large markets such as in the United States have not materialized. Those markets have turned out to be very competitive, despite some value-added market segments where competition can be limited and where gains are still substantial.[3] However, with the declining R&D productivity and a reduced flow of new patented drugs in the market, the MNCs are aggressively trying to make the entry of generic companies more difficult in these markets.

The better regulatory environment in Africa has improved the attractiveness of the market for the larger Indian companies and is acting as an important pull factor there. Perhaps more important is the anticipated future growth in the pharmaceutical market in Africa. The African market is still relatively small for Indian companies. Africa accounts for about 15% of India's exports (Table 6.3). But Africa is an expanding market for India. The growth of India's pharmaceutical exports has been quite spectacular, and Africa has been able to increase its share from about 10% in 1994–95 to 15% in 2011–12. The growth of the African market has in fact been faster than all other regions except America

Table 6.3   India's Pharmaceutical exports

	1994–95	1994–95	2011–12	2011–12
	(Rs million)	(%)	(Rs million)	(%)
Europe	10,663	42.4	90,964.35	29.6
America	3,661	14.6	90,147.29	29.3
Asia	7,941	31.6	77,886.87	25.3
Africa	2,676	10.7	45,280.45	14.7
Oceania	182	0.7	2,949.168	1.0
Others	0	0	368.29	0.1
Total	25,123	100	307,596.4	100.0

Source: India's Directorate General of Commercial Intelligence and Statistics (DGCI&S) trade data, accessed from the 'India Trades' database of the Centre for Monitoring Indian Economy.

(Table 6.3). In 1994–95, just Nigeria and Kenya accounted for about 50% of India's exports to Africa, and the share of top five countries was nearly three-quarters of the total. However India's exports now are more diversified. Among the countries which are relatively more important are Ghana, Benin, Sudan, Angola, Malawi and Cameroon.[4]

Are Indian companies likely to invest in manufacturing in Africa?

It is clear that Indian companies will continue to play a very active role in the African markets. Indeed, because of the factors mentioned above, they are likely to expand their operations there. Some Indian companies have already been actively involved in foreign direct investments (FDI) in Africa. Notable examples are Cadila in Ethiopia, Cipla in Uganda and South Africa and Ranbaxy in Nigeria. Other Indian companies too may be involved in the future in setting up manufacturing plants in Africa. But are Indian companies in general likely to be involved in any significant scale in investing in Africa? R Modi, chief of the Indian company Cadila, mentioned during his presentation at the African Pharmaceutical Summit in Hammamet, Tunisia, on 23–24 September 2013 that profit has not been the main motivation for Cadila's investments in Ethiopia. It is possible that beyond narrow financial reasons, some Indian companies will invest in Africa. But if Africa is to benefit in any significant way from Indian companies to further develop the industry there, what is required is more systematic investments. Unless Indian companies find Africa commercially attractive, it will be difficult to sustain such investments.

Unless the policy environment changes in Africa, the indications are that Indian companies in general will continue to find exporting a better option than investing in Africa. The main reasons are the following.

Perhaps most importantly, Indian companies essentially face a free trade regime in Africa. Some countries impose tariffs on imports of finished formulations. Some countries have a restricted list, as in Ghana, as discussed below. But in general, imports are not otherwise controlled or prohibited. This implies that from the Indian firms' point of view, it is easier to export than to undertake direct investments. Export activity does not involve huge investment, nor is it risky. Lately, as just discussed, African countries are trying to improve their drug registration and regulatory systems, but traditionally it has been very easy to enter most of the African markets.

The most common model followed by Indian firms is for the Indian exporters to tie up with local importers/distributors. In some African countries, this trade is dominated by people of Indian origin, so that linking up with traders is not a difficult proposition in these countries. Again in comparison to China, the main competitor in Africa, India has the advantage of more exposure to the English language, which is understood and used in many African countries. The main role of the Indian company is therefore restricted to getting the product registered and manufacturing and supplying to local partners. This hardly requires much investment: Indian companies do not create separate plants for the African markets. They use their existing capacity – often excess capacity – for the purposes. It is also practically riskless. Many exporters insist on advance payment. Even where the medicines are supplied on credit, at worst the Indian company will lose money for that consignment, and then they can stop supplying medicines in the future.

Investments abroad, on the other hand, involve more risks. It is very important for foreign investors to be assured of the safety of their investments. Africa is now politically much more stable. But foreign investors seem to expect some proactive steps on the part of the government to instill confidence that their money will be safe and that, if necessary, they can take money out of the country. There are also risks related to volatility of foreign exchange rates. Perhaps most important, the local partnerships required for direct investments carry higher risks. Export activities of Indian companies are carried out through local partners, as mentioned above, and in such cases the roles are clearly defined and risks are fewer. In case of joint ventures, however, the success of the company will depend much more on the local partners. The question of reliability of partners becomes more important in the case of investments abroad, since substantial investments would be involved and it is not easy to get rid of undesirable partners.

It follows that it is still quite a challenge to undertake manufacturing activities in Africa. Most of these countries suffer from various disadvantages, discussed in the preceding chapters. They include lack of technical know-how and trained manpower in the local African labour markets and the low levels of development of support industries including suppliers of APIs, other materials and machinery. Production costs may be higher than in India because input costs and utility costs are higher, and also because productivity may be lower. In some smaller countries, the market is considered too small for profitable operations.[5] It is therefore much easier for Indian companies to manufacture in India and then to serve the African markets through exports.

This current status and set of perceptions can however be changed through policy interventions. Left to themselves, foreign firms may not be keen to invest. But if proper conditions are created, if the above-mentioned issues and factors are taken care of, then they might be induced to do so. If the experience of other countries is any guide, then neither the inflows of FDI nor the benefits from FDI result from a passive open-door FDI policy (Lall and Narula, 2004; Chang, 2004). What is required is an active industrial policy.

The last section of this chapter develops this argument for the case of Ghana.[6] It discusses how foreign firms can help to develop a local pharmaceutical industry, and how they can be induced to contribute to promote local production.

Ghana, industrial policy and foreign direct investment

Ghana is a relatively small African country. The size of its total formulations market was estimated at about US$329 million in 2012 (BMI, 2013: 16). There are about 38 pharmaceutical manufacturing units in Ghana of which about 20 are actively involved in manufacturing formulations. Only one company, LaGray, started manufacturing an API (erythromycin) for their own use in formulation manufacturing. Local production caters to about 30% of the market, with the remaining 70% of demand being met from imports. Some of the local firms, for example Kama and Ernest Chemists, are involved in both manufacturing and importing.

India is a major source of Ghanaian imports not only of formulations but also of the APIs and other materials required for the local production of formulations. Out of the 30% of the market which is supplied by local manufacturers, 25% are over-the-counter (OTC) medications and the remaining 5% are simple prescription formulations. About two-thirds of drug purchase in Ghana are financed through out-of-pocket expenditure, the remaining being financed through public procurement, donor-funded purchases and reimbursement by the National Health Insurance scheme. Ghana has an elaborate drug distribution system dominated by importers/distributors/wholesalers. The branded generics segment of the market is large, and both imported products and locally manufactured generic products are sold as brands. Local manufacturers are actively involved in sales promotion, particularly for OTC items.

The Ghanaian government has put in place a number of policies that have helped the local industry to grow to attain its present status. Among these policies, one of the most important steps taken to promote the pharmaceutical industry was to ban the imports of finished formulations of 14 widely used products including ampicillin, tetracycline, chlordiazepoxide, indomethacin, paracetamol, aspirin and diazepam. Domestic formulations manufacturing has also benefitted substantially from the industrial protection provided by combination of zero import duties on materials and machinery required for formulations production with 10% import duty on imports of finished formulations. Another important advantage that domestic formulations manufacturers have been enjoying was the refunding of the 15% VAT imposed on all materials and machinery required for formulations production. However, in 2013, the government has withdrawn this benefit, as has also happened elsewhere (see Chapter 2).

Like other countries discussed in this book, Ghana also offers a 15% price preference for domestic suppliers in public procurement. This has also helped manufacturers, though the system has not always functioned properly. Local manufacturers complain that the procurement system is not very transparent, and especially when the government buys at regional and local levels there is suspicion that the 15% advantage is often not provided. The government does not reveal the prices at which it actually procures. Perhaps if such information is made public the situation will improve.

Industrial policy in Ghana

What can be done to further increase the share of local production in the Ghanaian domestic market? What is fundamentally important for promoting an industry is to put in place policies to provide access to three key aspects of business activity: finance, technology and markets.

This section first discusses the problems of finance and technology in the context of Ghana. It then explores the ways in which a policy of ensuring a larger market for local producers can prompt FDI to assist the development of the pharmaceutical industry in Africa.

Under the conditions in which they operate, the local firms hardly earn adequate profits to plough back into investments. Furthermore, the rate of interest charged by banks in Ghana is exorbitant, often exceeding 30% per annum. As shown below, to set up Good Manufacturing Practice (GMP)-compliant manufacturing plants, to develop products for getting regulatory approval and for marketing these products, huge funds are required. Taking loans at such high interest rates is simply not a viable option, so that exploring other funding options is vital. The more resourceful foreign firms with access to diverse sources of funding offer one of the possible policy options.

Technology, furthermore, is a fundamental constraint in Africa today. When pharmaceutical manufacturing started in Ghana, technical requirements were simpler and technology was often arranged through informal channels. The promoters of local companies such as Amponsah Efah, LaGray and Pharmanova are themselves technologists, and they have used their knowledge and contacts to set up small-scale plants. But the technological scenario in recent years has changed fundamentally. Current requirements are significantly tougher. If local manufacturing in Ghana is to make a significant difference to the industry, then technical knowledge and expertise need to be available qualitatively and quantitatively on a big scale.

The first technological requirement is that the manufacturing plants need to be GMP compliant. To set up a GMP-compliant plant, significant additional costs, particularly investment costs, have to be incurred. Moreover, the products manufactured need to be approved for marketing by the local drug control administration. The companies are required to undertake various types of studies (e.g. bioequivalence studies) and to generate data and submit dossiers to the drug control authorities. Marketing approval is granted after various types of review by the latter, including chemistry review, bioequivalence review and after-plant inspection.

The technical knowledge required to set up and run GMP-compliant plants and to develop products for getting regulatory approvals for marketing are not widely available in Ghana and other African countries. It is vitally important to arrange this if the local industry is to develop.

A possible solution is to use the technological resources of foreign firms for the purpose. Manufacturing operations by Western MNCs are carried out in quite a different environment, while the situation in India is much closer to that in Africa. Pharmaceutical technical knowledge is furthermore highly diffused in India, so if Indian companies invest in Africa, then a major constraint will be lifted.

Furthermore, as Chapter 5 has emphasized, market access and serving the local market effectively are essential elements of business success. If the African governments can initiate policies to substantially limit the access of foreign firms to the domestic market, then Indian (or other foreign) companies will lose out unless they undertake investments in Africa to cater to that market. Where the loss is substantial, as in the cases of larger countries or regional markets, chances of FDI will be much higher. How can a country manage its domestic market to induce foreign firms to invest?

Policy makers in developing countries often are reluctant to impose import controls on the grounds that such an action may lead to shortages and/or lack of import competition may lead to higher prices. But this need not necessarily be the case, as Ghana shows. The products on its banned list are manufactured adequately in the country, and the country did not suffer from shortages after the policy was imposed. Lack of import competition has not resulted in higher prices. Importantly, import competition has been replaced by domestic competition, leading to competitive prices in the domestic market.

To explore the question of pricing further, Table 6.4 compares the retail prices of selected products in India and Ghana. The products include some of those which are manufactured in Ghana, for example ciprofloxacin, paracetamol, amlodipine, diazepam, metformin and also some of those that are not currently manufactured in Ghana, for example anastrazole, granisetron, losartan, rabeprazole and rosuvastatin. As Table 6.4 shows, the extent of price differentials between India and Ghana is quite different, depending on whether these products are manufactured in Ghana or not. For the products not manufactured in Ghana, the price differentials are significantly larger. For the products manufactured in Ghana, not only is the price differential much narrower – less than 1.5 times – but it is in fact the case that for three products, Ghanaian prices are lower than those in India. These include diazepam and paracetamol, which are products reserved for local manufacturers. Thus Table 6.4 suggests that local production in Ghana has contributed to affordability.

Table 6.4   Comparison of retail formulations prices in India and Ghana

	India: Median price in INR (1 tablet) 2013	Ghana: Median price in INR (1 tablet) 2011	Ghana/India price ratio: Col(3)/col(2)
Tablets manufactured in Ghana			
1. Ciprofloxacin, 500 mg	6.18	9.11	1.5
2. Amlodipine, 5 mg	2.36	3.64	1.5
3. Metformin, 500 mg	1.46	1.52	1.0
4. Diazepam, 5 mg	2.90	0.30	0.1
5. Paracetamol, 500 mg	1.14	0.30	0.3
6. Diclofenac, 50 mg	1.43	1.82	1.3
7. Lisinopril, 5 mg	4.58	6.07	1.3
8. Atorvastatin, 10 mg	8.60	9.11	1.1
9. Cetirizine Hcl, 10 mg	3.10	3.04	1.0
10. Metronidazole, 200 mg	0.39	0.61	1.6
Tablets not yet manufactured in Ghana			
1. Anastrazole, 1 mg	48.50	182.10	3.8
2. Cepacitabine, 500 mg	150.05	267.08	1.8
3. Granisetron, 1 mg	14.05	409.73	29.2
4. Itraconazole, 100 mg	47.50	182.10	3.8
5. Losartan, 50 mg	5.65	12.14	2.1
6. Rabeprazole, 20 mg	2.75	75.88	27.6
7. Risperidone, 2 mg	3.80	75.88	20.0
8. Rosuvastatin, 20 mg	20.36	69.81	3.4
9. Tindazole, 500 mg	5.52	69.81	12.7
10. Sertraline, 100 mg	6.3	98.64	15.7

Sources: 1. For Indian prices in col (2): median prices of retail brands accounting for 1% or more of the market. Market share data have been obtained from the *Sales audit data* of AIOCD Pharmasofttech AWACS Pvt. Ltd (AIOCD-AWACS), a pharmaceutical market research company; Price data have been obtained from CIMS (2013).

2. For Ghana prices in col (3): 'Medicines List', February 2011 of the Ghana National Health Insurance Scheme (http://www.nhis.gov.gh/_Uploads/dbsAttachedFiles/1(3).pdf). Prices in Ghana cedis (GHC) have been converted to Indian rupee (INR) using the annual average exchange rates for 2011 from www.oanda.com. The list specifies the maximum prices at which the medicines purchased at the retail level are reimbursable. Pricing data are collected from manufacturers, wholesale distributors, private pharmacies, government, mission and private health facilities and the median prices are set as the maximum price reimbursable under the insurance scheme.

3. Since the Ghana prices refer to 2011 whereas the Indian prices refer to 2013, depending on the extent to which Ghana prices have gone up since 2011, the price differential in fact may be larger than the figures show.

If the number of products on the banned list is increased, and if free flow of imports into the economy is controlled, then not only will domestic producers find a larger market. Import restrictions may also induce foreign firms exporting to the country to undertake manufacturing within the country.

Imports can also be controlled in several other ways. Ghana has introduced a National Health Insurance Scheme (NHIS), which covers about half the population. About 40% of the funds paid out by health insurance are for medicines. The NHIS-funded formulations market has therefore emerged as a major market segment in Ghana accounting for about 23% of the market (Seiter and Gyansa-Lutterodt, 2009: 19). The NHIS has expanded since that 2009 study, and the share of insurance-funded medicine purchase has risen. The substantial bargaining power of the NHIS agency can thus be used to enlarge the domestic market. The NHIS does not currently differentiate in its procurement between medicines according to whether they are manufactured locally or imported. However, after allowing some time for capacities to develop, NHIS reimbursement could be restricted to locally manufactured products. Since the prices to be reimbursed are being fixed by NHIS in any case, the possibility of such actions leading to higher prices will not arise.

A further policy option available is to use the instrument of government procurement. So far as the institutional market is concerned, the only benefit the local manufacturers receive is the 15% price preference, and that too, as noted above, does not operate properly. An important flexibility that the World Trade Organization (WTO) provides concerns public procurement. The WTO Agreement on Government Procurement (GPA) is a plurilateral agreement which is applicable only to the member countries which have signed the GPA. African countries, including Ghana, have not yet joined the GPA.[7]

Public procurement of drugs (and other goods) in Ghana is currently guided by the provisions of the Public Procurement Act. This provides for three types of competitive tendering: international, national and restricted. 'International tendering' means that organizations responding need not necessarily be located in Ghana. 'National tendering' means that the tendering can be restricted to organizations located in Ghana, but the organizations need not be manufacturers. They can be importers located in Ghana.

A simple step that could be initiated in Ghana for the further development of the pharmaceutical industry is to introduce tendering restricted to local manufacturers. This might be a two-stage tendering process: a technical evaluation and then evaluation of the financial bid. At the first stage of technical evaluation, tenders may be accepted only from those local manufacturers that are GMP-compliant and that have the manufacturing capacities to satisfy the procurement requirements. The financial bid may be restricted to the companies which qualify in the technical evaluation. Based on the widely used International Reference Prices,[8] maximum purchase prices may be also specified. This will ensure a larger domestic market for local manufacturers, and hence a more attractive market for FDI, without compromising on prices.

Conclusion

This chapter can be appropriately concluded with a quotation from the Chairman of an Indian company currently exporting pharmaceuticals to Africa. He summarized the prospects of FDI in Africa. He told us during an interview that if imported products including those from India are freely available in Africa, then it is difficult to induce Indian companies to go to Africa and set up plants. But if local production is somewhat protected, and if this is supplemented with few steps to take care of the disadvantages of local production in Africa including some incentives, for example some income tax benefits particularly in initial years and infrastructure support (land, water, roads, electricity), then the prospects of FDI from India will be brighter. In fact, his company will be willing to explore the possibility actively.

Notes

Acknowledgements: In writing this paper, the author has used the results of interviews carried out in India, Ghana and Tanzania in connection with other studies including those funded by ESRC (UK), UNIDO and UNDP. The author benefitted immensely from the comments and suggestions from Maureen Mackintosh. The author would also like to thank Alastair West, Juergen Reinhardt and Cecilia Oh for discussions and Geoffrey Banda and Watu Wamae for comments.

1. Wasem Noor, 'Pharm Exec's Pharma 50 2014', 9 June 2014 (accessed 17 April 2014 from http://www.pharmexec.com/pharm-execs-pharma-50–2014?id=&sk=&date=&&pageID=2); BMI Espison, 2013.
2. See note 1 above.
3. For example, after the expiry of the basic patent for a chemical, generics companies that can successfully challenge some of the secondary patents can prevent other generic companies from entering the market for a limited period of time, gaining substantial additional value-added.
4. Source: as in Table 6.3.
5. See Guimer et al. (2004); Kaplan and Laing (2005); Losse et al. (2007); Chaudhuri et al. (2010); Abbott (2011); Moon (2011); UNCTAD (2011); African Union and UNIDO (2012); Chaudhuri and West (2014) for further insights into local production in Africa.
6. The case study on Ghana relies to a great extent on the information collected through interviews while doing studies for UNIDO, Vienna and UNDP, New York.
7. Mostly developed countries are currently members of GPA; for the list of those who have joined, see https://www.wto.org/english/tratop_e/gproc_e/memobs_e.htm

8. Management Sciences for Health (MSH), *International Drug Price Indicator Guide* (annual) http://apps.who.int/medicinedocs/documents/s19968en/s19968en.pdf, accessed 20 April 2015.

7

Raising the Technological Level: The Scope for API, Excipients, and Biologicals Manufacture in Africa

Joseph Fortunak, Skhumbuzo Ngozwana, Tsige Gebre-Mariam, Tiffany Ellison, Paul Watts, Martins Emeje and Frederick E. Nytko III

Introduction

This chapter discusses raising the technological scope for locally manufacturing active pharmaceutical ingredients (APIs), excipients and biologicals in Africa – a hitherto nascent industry. It also discusses African drug development and manufacturing through the standardized use of 'reverse pharmacology' to bring new treatments for neglected diseases to the point of regulatory approvals. Currently there is very modest production of APIs on the African continent, although a few significant projects exist,[1] (such as LaGray in Ghana and Fine Chemicals in South Africa), or are in the planning stages.[2] Generic producers in India and China supply nearly all of the APIs used in African pharmaceutical manufacturing. Most African companies cannot afford the heavy investment and research and development activities required for API production.

Two strategies are suggested to help to address these issues: first, the introduction of technology transfer (product development) packages at centres of excellence, with each package being transferred to several manufacturers; second, the use of 'leap-frogging' technologies to reduce capital investment, minimize the environmental footprint and enhance competitiveness. Leap-frogging technologies have the advantage that Africa can skip technology and investment legacy issues. Leap-frogging technologies can also narrow the gap between rich and poor economies in drug discovery/development and pharmaceutical manufacturing by taking advantage of the rich diversity of natural products sources and indigenous knowledge in disease treatment.

In this chapter we tackle API, excipient and biologicals manufacture by considering the science, technology and human as well as institutional and organizational capabilities needed to raise Africa's technological levels in API, excipient and FPP manufacture. This chapter is informed by the laboratory and practice experience in API, excipients and biological manufacture.

APIs and excipients: important components of producing medicines

A medicine may be broadly defined as any substance or substances used in the treatment, diagnosis, prevention, mitigation or cure of a disease. Drug molecules that exert a biological effect are known as active pharmaceutical ingredients (APIs). APIs alone are unsuitable for human use as medicines. Various additional ingredients (excipients) are formulated in combination with APIs to manufacture finished pharmaceutical products (FPPs). An FPP contains one or more APIs and is the form in which a medicine is presented to the patient. FPPs can be tablets, capsules, oral liquids (suspensions or solutions); creams/ointments for topical administration; injectable solutions; or patches, suppositories or inhaled-delivery forms. Some delivery forms are inherently easier than others to manufacture, but each combination of API and delivery form requires an individual development program to assure the identity, stability, safety, purity, potency and efficacy of the final product. The number of APIs used for the treatment of all human diseases is relatively small. The various major pharmacopoeial compendia (international, European, US or British) list fewer than 2,500 different APIs that are approved for use as medicines. APIs are formulated in order to assure their stability, uniformity and reproducibility, to enhance patient compliance and to maximize efficacy by optimizing dissolution, absorption and bioavailability.

APIs alone are unsuitable for direct patient dosing, because FPPs must be stable, convenient, palatable and uniform in their dosage and content. Since the amount of drug dissolved in stomach fluid after oral dosing is a direct measure of how much drug is available for absorption, the use of different excipients/formulations may control solubility and whether a drug is available for immediate release, extended/sustained release or even delayed release. Tablets typically contain 20–60% loading of API content by weight. Pre-formulation studies involve the evaluation and establishment of target ranges for the physicochemical properties of an API (salt selection, crystal form, particle size distribution [PSD]and level of hydration/solvation).

Every solid oral dosage form contains at a minimum excipients that serve as a binder, filler, lubricant and disintegrant. Excipients that serve as surfactants, compression aids, desiccants, glidants, dissolution enhancers, taste modifiers, colorants and coatings are also very often employed. Many hundreds of excipients of various types are used in pharmaceutical formulations. These ingredients are generally regarded as safe (GRAS) when present below established permissible daily exposure (PDE) limits. Quality by design (QbD) at this stage involves careful evaluation and selection of critical quality attributes (CQAs) of the API, and matching of the desired performance characteristics of the FPP with selection and grade of excipients used.

Table 7.1 shows a range of excipients commonly used in FPPs, typically used as weight percentages of a tablet, and price ranges (prices obtained from import-export data at www.infodriveindia.com). If these costs are compared with API pricing in Table 7.2, it is readily seen that excipients are normally much less expensive than APIs as a contribution to the cost of producing FPPs.

For solid oral FPP manufacturing the API and excipients are blended together, often as powders with unlike properties. Along with blending, there is a massing process of bringing these powders together to form larger particles of uniform content, known as granules. Wet granulation is possibly the most commonly used technique for granulation. Although this process is very reliable, a subsequent drying step is required that is both process intensive and must be carefully controlled so as not to cause risk of degradation. Granules are either filled into hard gelatin capsules or compressed into tablets. Tablets may be coated in order to improve their appearance, impart distinctive identifying characteristics or enhance stability. Compression into tablets does not destroy granules. The disintegration of tablets in the stomach after ingestion releases these granules at an early step in the process of dissolution and absorption of drugs. Soft gelatin capsules are filled with a solution or suspension of API(s) in a liquid-fill process, and the technology used for these formulations is somewhat specialized.

Manufacturing active pharmaceutical ingredients

Almost all small-molecule APIs are prepared by chemical synthesis, fermentation or extraction and purification of natural products from

Table 7.1 Common excipients used in solid oral dosage formulations, their standard use and weight % content, and pricing on a per-kilogram basis

Excipient	Utility in tablet or capsule FPPs*	Typical weight% in FPP	Cost per Kg**
Cellulose or Microcrystalline Cellulose	Diluent, disintegrant	10–60%	$2.00–3.22
Lactose	Binder, diluent, compression aid	5–40%	$3.03–3.77
Calcium phosphate, dibasic	Filler, diluent	5–50%	$2.46–5.70
Carboxymethylcellulose Sodium (Carmellose Sodium, CMC)	Binder, disintegrant, coating agent, desiccant	5–25%	$3.25–5.99
Croscarmellose Sodium (cross-linked CMC)	Disintegrant	1–5%	$6.56–9.51
Sodium Starch Glycolate (SSG)	Disintegrant	1–5%	$0.96–4.93
Potassium Sorbate	Anti-oxidant	Up to 2%	$18–37
Povidone (poly(vinyl) pyrrolidinone; PVP)	Binder, disintegrant, dissolution enhancer	5–20%	$8.59–17.11
Crospovidone (cross-linked povidone)	Disintegrant	2–5%	$3.03
Magnesium Stearate	Lubricant	0.25–4%	$4.30 – 23.50
Methyl paraben	Antimicrobial	1–2%	$11.50
Sodium Lauryl Sulfate	Anionic Surfactant, emulsifying agent, lubricant	1–2%	36–51
Starch, pregelatinized	Binder, diluent, disintegrant	5–35%	2–9
Talc	Glidant, anti-caking agent	0.2–2%	$2.00–3.57
Aluminum Oxide	Adsorbent, dispersing agent	Less than 5%	
Sodium Benzoate	Antimicrobial, lubricant	1–3%	$1.62–2.19
Xanthan Gum	Stabilizer, suspending agent, viscosity enhancer; often used for extended release products	5–15%	$5.02–7.44
Xylitol	Sweetener, diluent, coating agent, antimicrobial	5–10%	$2.20–5.75

Note: *Summarized from Rowe, Sheskey, Cook and Fenton (2012). **Data summarized from www.infodriveindia.com

plant sources. A number of APIs are produced by some combination of these techniques. Plant cultivation and extraction of the natural product artemisinin, for example, is combined with chemical synthesis to produce the anti-malarial APIs artemether and artesunate (USNLM, 2014), as shown in Figure 7.1.

The cost of manufacturing an API depends on the raw material pricing, yield, processing time and volume efficiency of each manufacturing step. Other cost drivers are the cost of operating the manufacturing facility (overheads and labour: OHL) and capital investment required to build and equip the manufacturing plant. Overheads and labour include costs of personnel, energy, waste disposal, shipping and eventual cost of decommissioning the facility. Higher volume demand generally decreases the proportionate cost contribution of raw materials and overheads and labour. Substantial production volumes are therefore required to obtain full economy of scale (Jayaraman, 2012). Producing 1–5 metric tons per year is more expensive than producing 100 metric tons of an API in appropriately sized facilities. The efficiency of a synthesis is often quoted in terms of overall yield and as an E-factor (Sheldon, 2007) representing the kilograms of waste produced per kilogram of product manufactured. Waste management is expensive in chemical manufacturing, and increasing the overall yield or the

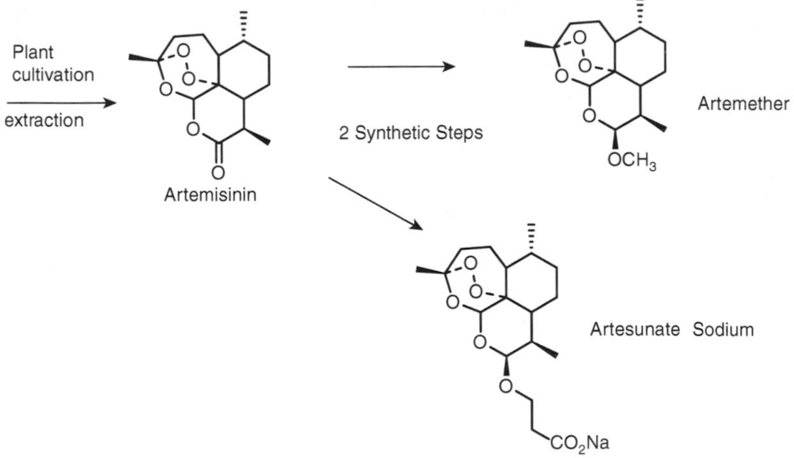

Figure 7.1 Chemical synthesis to produce the anti-malarial APIs artemether and artesunate

Source: Compiled by authors

E-factor of an API synthesis reduces costs. With a continued growth of volume demand, improved chemistry and competition from multiple suppliers, the cost of raw materials and APIs can decrease over time. For example, the cost of the API for the HIV/AIDS drug efavirenz at launch by the originator company (Dupont Pharmaceuticals) in 1998 was about $1,600/kg at a first-year demand of about 150 tons (Personal recollection from the author, JF). Generic producers in India estimated their API costs at about $1,100/kg upon first generic introduction in 2005 (Personal communication, Mr D.R. Rao, Cipla). Currently, the API can be purchased for about $120/kg, a 13-fold decrease in cost of API in 17 years (import-export data at www.infodriveIndia.com). Notably, the volume demand of efavirenz in 2015 is also estimated at about 2,000 tons, since this drug is a standard component of first-line AIDS treatment in low- and middle-income countries.

As a rule of thumb, the overall cost of raw materials for an efficient process will represent about 50–70% of the total cost of API manufacturing, signifying the important role of smart procurement. This rule of thumb is applicable to high-volume generic production of synthetic APIs. Smaller-volume APIs – those produced by fermentation or natural products extraction, or APIs used in sterile products – can have much higher proportionate cost contributions for overheads and labour and capital investment. The synthetic route of manufacturing the HIV/AIDS API tenofovir disoproxil fumarate (TDF) (Figure 7.2) is a typical example. The key raw materials – adenine, (R)-propylene carbonate (RPC), diethyl p-toluenesulfonyl(oxymethyl)phosphonate (DESMP), chloromethyl isopropyl carbonate (CMIC) and fumaric acid – contribute to the molecular structure of the API. Each step uses multiple additional materials as solvents or reagents, which are omitted from this simplified synthesis scheme.

The final crystallization or precipitation step of API manufacturing is the stage at which the physicochemical properties of an API are determined and the last stage at which related substances (impurities) can be removed or reduced to acceptable limits. The crystalline form and PSD of an API are often critical to the formulation, dissolution, absorption and bioavailability of a drug. Bioavailability is the fraction of a drug dose that reaches systemic circulation (blood plasma) upon human dosing (USFDA). By definition, any drug is 100% bioavailable when administered by injection.

API cost reductions reflect improvements in production efficiency, procurement and economies of scale. The overall yield of TDF (Figure 7.2) from adenine was less than 25% when the generic product

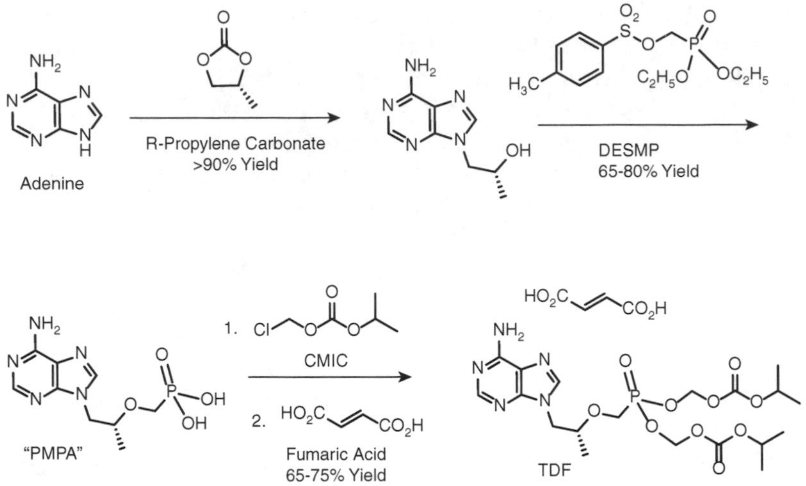

Figure 7.2   Synthetic route for the manufacture of the API tenofovir disoproxil fumarate

Source: Compiled by the author

was launched in 2006; it is currently in the range of 43–54%, a doubling of efficiencies. During this time the API pricing of TDF has decreased by 65% from more than $600/kg to about $210/kg. Undoubtedly a lot of research and development effort went into improving yields, reducing use of solvents and reagents and decreasing processing times (Ripin et al., 2010). Improved procurement – a critical finance capability (see Chapter 13) – greatly reduced the cost of most of the key raw materials; this was probably the biggest contributor to cost reductions (Jayaraman, 2012). Table 7.2 provides a range for the per-kilogram pricing of the key raw materials for TDF synthesis. These prices are given for purchasing ton-scale amounts of each raw material in the timeframe of January–December 2014 (import-export data available at www.infodriveIndia.com). When generic versions of TDF were first launched in 2006, the pricing for both RPC and DESMP, for example, was more than $20/kg.

API costs are often the largest component of the overall cost of a corresponding finished pharmaceutical product (FPP). API producers generally operate on smaller margins than FPP producers. A well-established, competitive market for anti-retroviral (ARV) APIs for the treatment of HIV/AIDS in low- and middle-income countries illustrates this. Target margins for generic APIs are typically 20–33%. The actual margins on

Table 7.2 Raw Materials that contribute to the structure of the API tenofovir disoproxil fumarate (TDF) and their current commercial pricing

Raw Material	Price per Kg (ton scale)	Kgs used per Kg of TDF produced	Raw Material. Price Contribution /kg of TDF
Adenine	$34.34–38.97	0.64	$21.98–24.94
R-Propylene Carbonate (RPC)	$7.88–9.75	0.50	$3.94–4.88
DESMP	$6.40–6.98	1.22	$7.81–8.52
CMIC	$8.79–9.24	1.61	$14.15–14.88
Fumaric Acid	$1.53–1.87	0.23	$0.35–0.43
Total:			$48.23–53.65

Source: Compiled by the author using data from www.infodriveIndia.com, April 2012–July 2014.

ARV drugs with several approved suppliers, however, can be far lower. It is generally agreed that margins for the well-established ARV APIs zidovudine (AZT) and lamivudine (3TC) do not exceed 10%.

Can Africa expand local production of APIs?

APIs are sold in bulk, typically as powder in a drum. Global demand for very common APIs such as paracetamol, erythromycin or ibuprofen is as high as 60,000 tons per year. Volume demand for most APIs is in the range of 10 to 500 tons per year. Economies of scale are important for both API and FPP production. A manufacturing facility must be operating at close to its full capacity to maximize operational efficiency. Companies that manufacture both APIs and FPPs possess a competitive market advantage because there is one less commercial transaction where profit is taken in the value chain.

In order to be successful, African API production must be priced similarly to that of Indian and Chinese competitors. The quality must also match or exceed the standards of competitor products in the market. Procurement information is becoming widely available, and therefore African producers potentially have access to knowledge of the best available pricing for raw materials. African producers are potentially able to obtain competitive pricing on APIs and key raw materials, because these items are not sold in huge quantities on a single-transaction basis. For solvents and reagents that require very large-volume purchases to obtain best pricing, however, African producers can be at a disadvantage relative to Indian and Chinese counterparts.

There are many products, however, for which it is realistic that Africa production can be price-competitive with India and China. Low-dose APIs are one set of medicines. Entecavir, for example, is a very useful product for the treatment of hepatitis B virus (HBV). Entecavir is also a very important drug for Africa, since the continent bears a very large share of the global burden for HBV. Entecavir is delivered at a dose of 0.5 mg/day. At this extremely low dose, the API contribution to FPP pricing is potentially so small that the only important cost contribution to manufacturing an FPP is the inherent efficiency of formulating the tablet FPP. African pharmaceutical manufacturers do not, however, presently hold in their organizations the experienced, knowledgeable scientific staff to optimize API production processes in the same manner as Indian and Chinese producers are able to do.

African manufacturing of APIs and FPPs might be successful for a large range of moderately priced products that are no longer of high priority for Indian generics manufacturers. Many Indian companies target exports of more lucrative FPPs (such as gleevec or imatinib for cancer) and target high-priced markets in the US and Europe. For well-established generic products manufactured in large volumes, it is quite conceivable that African companies can purchase APIs at equal pricing to Indian FPP producers (Table 7.2). Metformin (diabetes), naproxen sodium (analgesic), amoxicillin (anti-infective), metronidazole (anthelmintic) and lumefantrine (malaria) are examples. Under these circumstances, local manufacturing may actually be less expensive than importation because of differences in added-on pricing due to shipping and import duties. This aspect of pharmaceutical pricing is commonly overlooked. The associated costs of shipping and tariffs or other duties associated with importation of APIs or FPPs can readily amount to a 30% add-on for pricing; this can potentially create a pricing advantage for local manufacturing. International donor agencies that purchase essential medicines for Africa and African national procurement programmes often do not take into account this potential advantage for local manufacturing when issuing tender offers for purchase.

'Leap-frogging' technologies as opportunities for local API manufacture

Leap-frogging technologies are advances in manufacturing technology that provide large improvements over current techniques and avoid legacies of industrial organic growth. These advances can be related to chemistry, formulations or techniques for manufacturing. Global pharmaceutical companies are traditionally late adopters of new technologies because manufacturing costs are not closely tied to their product pricing or their profit model; furthermore, originator companies have huge investments in their current manufacturing facilities. For Indian companies, investment in new technologies can be unattractive unless it pays for the high cost of decommissioning existing 'legacy' manufacturing facilities. African companies do not largely suffer from such a high degree of captive 'legacy' investment in existing facilities. Continuous manufacturing of FPPs, for instance, is one area where African production can be both environmentally and cost-preferred versus global competition.

A number of patents and publications (Chava et al., 2014; Datta et al., 2014; Ripin et al., 2010) have disclosed information about TDF process optimizations that have reduced the API pricing by more than 70% since initial generic launch, as discussed earlier. New technologies for API production for TDF and EFV include biotechnology for the production of intermediates and 'greener' chemistry that reduces the E-factor of API production. In the case of EFV, this reduction is from about 55 to about 12 (Bolu et al., 2012; Jian, 2008). Green chemistry (GC) includes the use of catalytic amounts of amino acids and their derivatives (organocatalysis) to reduce the number of steps and the cost of API processing. GC also includes continuous or 'flow' processing (Hebrault, 2014). Both of these technologies are in early stages of implementation and their full impact on API pricing is not yet being felt.

Flow chemistry is being used in one step of the commercial production of an intermediate for the synthesis of the HIV-1 protease inhibitors atazanavir and darunavir (Pinho et al., 2014). Flow chemistry can be broadly summarized as an engineering approach to improved synthesis. Organocatalysis is a more chemistry-based approach to improved synthesis. Flow chemistry for commercial manufacturing is a special expertise owned by at least one African R&D centre, the Green Center for Chemical Manufacturing. Advanced technologies are not mutually exclusive and can often be employed together to improve API manufacturing efficiencies.

Taking advantage of these leap-frogging technology opportunities implies adoption of machinery, equipment and processes with higher efficiencies and lower environmental impact. This opportunity exists for African manufacturing of APIs. However, there is need for integration of API and FPP production to accommodate the scale needed for

API manufacture, requiring in turn financial incentives and supportive procurement to leveraging the huge intra-African medicines market.

Assuring the quality of APIs: Quality management systems and GMP

The quality of APIs and FPPs is assured by manufacturing under good manufacturing practice (GMP), including process validation, testing against previously established specifications and the demonstration of clinical bioequivalence (FDA, 2014). The investment and operating costs of a quality management system (QMS) for GMP contribute significantly to the cost of pharmaceutical production. Producers must designate and justify to regulatory authorities a starting point or stage in the API synthesis from which GMP is applied.

Janice Berger, a well-known former USFDA field inspector, often remarked: 'You're either GMP or you're NOT'. In a very real sense, this is the true. Companies cannot choose to move back and forth from GMP to non-GMP activities in the same manufacturing facility. The requirements for a QMS and documentation for GMP do not allow switches of this type. The general feeling in the industry is that additional investment in GMP compliance enables companies to gain market share and increase sales by differentiating them from their competitors based on quality. National drug regulatory agencies (NDRAs) bear the primary responsibility of working with companies to evolve their GMP practices to meet international standards (Chapter 12). The United States Pharmacopeia (USP) sponsors training programmes in GMP. Over the longer term, African nations must assume full responsibility for their own regulatory needs. The emerging Regulatory Sciences Institute (RSI) in South Africa is potentially an important player in promoting global standards for pharmaceutical manufacturing on the continent. It follows that a sustainable African generic pharmaceutical industry must be able to:

- develop products and processes meeting SRA standards of quality;
- continuously manufacture under GMP;
- compete with other quality-assured producers on price;
- operate without legal encumbrances (dependent on intellectual property).

Regulatory sciences and rigorous product development are critical for obtaining generic drug approvals by SRAs. Originator companies employ a very large number of skilled scientists to develop and launch new medicines. One of us (JF) managed a scientific staff of over 350 chemists and engineers to support the filing of, on average, only 1–3 new marketing applications per year. Indian and Chinese generic companies also hold very substantial staff (60 or more development chemists) to launch 8–12 new generic FPPs per year. Indian and Chinese generic companies also routinely outsource substantial R&D activities to regional centres of excellence (universities or technology development centres) to leverage their in-house capabilities. It is essential to build a pool of skills with capabilities in drug registration and regulation to support research and development as well as drug authorizations.

The IPAT program at the St. Luke Foundation / Kilimanjaro School of Pharmacy in Moshi, Tanzania is a UN ANDI Centre of Excellence training pharmaceutical and NDRA experts in GMP drug manufacturing, regulatory sciences and leap-frogging technologies since 2008. It was awarded a USFDA 'Honor Award' in 2013 for Excellence and Innovation in Regulatory Sciences training. The IPAT programme is partially funded by UNIDO and its approach has also been adopted by the University of Ibadan School of Pharmacy.

Opportunities for reverse pharmacology and traditional medicine for local drug development

Reverse pharmacology

Reverse pharmacology (RP) integrates traditional knowledge into drug discovery, development and production (Patwardan, 2009; Wambebe, 2001). This approach identifies natural products or mixtures of natural products based on traditional knowledge combined with screening in biological assays. This green approach to drug discovery takes advantage of cultural and ethno-botanical knowledge of a region to shortcut the lengthy, expensive, resource-intense process used in rational drug design.

The 'hits' identified by reverse pharmacology are further developed into drug candidates by exploratory studies including safety and activity testing, combined with clinical (human) dosing. During clinical development, mixtures of compounds obtained as crude extracts are often used, but the classical activities of isolating compounds with biological activity and elucidating their structure remains a part of reverse pharmacology. The correlation of API content with biological activity, safety, the development and validation of analytical methods, process validation and the setting of specifications for the active ingredients present are all steps in the RP process.

Drugs from traditional knowledge

Phytomedicines, or herbal medicines, are plants, herbs, extracts and purified natural products used for the prevention or treatment of disease, most often identified and derived from traditional knowledge. The regulatory requirements for approving phytomedicines are lower than for new chemical entities (NCEs), although the label claims for efficacy are also much more cautious. More than 80% of people in developing countries depend on herbal medicines (Iyamu, 2003; Patwardan, 2009; Perampaladas, 2010; Wambebe, 2001; Willcox, 2011). The World Health Organization has issued guidance on (1) quality assessment (WHO, 2007), (2) pharmacovigilance (WHO, 2004) and (3) good manufacturing practices (WHO, 2007) for herbal medicines. However, processes to regulate the registration, approval and standardization of such products are only now being made universal (WHO, 2007).

Phytomedicines are typically purified by short, simple processes such as aqueous or aqueous alcoholic decoction, followed by solvent removal. This is very different from pharmaceutical natural product isolation from plants, such as the vinca alkaloids, taxol or camptothecins. These are typically present as much less than 1% of the dried weight of their respective plant sources and are purified by expensive, resource-intensive procedures.

Nigerian experience with Niprisan™

A major centre for herbal medicines exists at the National Institute for Pharmaceutical R&D (NIPRD) in Nigeria. NIPRD utilizes a systematic approach to gathering, classifying, extracting, testing and identifying the therapeutic elements present in plant sources. A quality management system is in place at NIPRD, and standard operating procedures (SOPs) are followed by a multi-disciplinary team of scientists. This standardized approach has resulted in the launch of several effective medicines for treating malaria, sickle-cell anaemia, pain, inflammation and immunological diseases (Emeje, 2005; Emeje, 2011; Wambebe, 2001a; 2001b). The development of the herbal medicine Niprisan™ for treating sickle-cell anaemia is described below.

Niprisan™ is a combined extract of four plants traditionally used in Nigeria to prevent sickle-cell disease (SCD) (Iyamu, 2003; Wambebe, 2001). SCD is caused by a point mutation in the gene encoding for the beta globin chain of hemoglobin, distorting red blood cells into an elongated, 'sickled' shape. SCD causes impaired circulation, tissue and organ damage, severe anaemia and increased mortality. *In vitro* studies showed that Niprisan™ possesses potent anti-sickling effects. One or more of the active ingredients contained in Niprisan™ enhances the solubility of deoxy-HbS, retarding polymerization and increasing oxygen affinity (Wambebe, 2001). Controlled clinical trials conducted in Nigeria showed that Niprisan™ significantly reduces vaso-occlusion in SCD patients (Iyamu, 2003; Wambebe, 2001b).

Niprisan™ was standardized by extracting various seeds, fruits and stems from *Pterocarpus osun, Sorghum bicolor, Piper guineensis and Eugenia caryophyllum.* Data from animal testing and using blood from sickle-cell patients showed that the standard extracts prevent cell sickling. The safety of these extracts was demonstrated by animal testing before human use to demonstrate the absence of overt toxicities and lack of tissue and organ effects (Perampaladas, 2010; Wambebe, 2001a; 2001b). An initial human safety study was carried out in twenty patients, with the product already being used by thousands of people in Nigeria in an unstandardized product presentation (Wambebe 2001a).

Clinical phase II/III trials (in sickle-cell patients) using a capsule dosage form began about 18 months after the start of the discovery program at NIPRD. In that time, the product was identified, extracts were standardized, assays were developed, safety assessment was carried out, an initial manufacturing process was identified and clinical supplies were prepared. The extraction process for Niprisan™ is quite efficient, and extraction is not destructive of the cultivated plants. The dried extract represents about 20% of the collected biomass. One kilogram of Niprisan™ is therefore obtained utilizing about 5 kilograms of biomass and 10 litres each of water and ethanol.

A randomized, double-blind, placebo-controlled, crossover trial was conducted to support the approval of Niprisan™ (Perampaladas, 2010; Wambebe, 2001b). Patients with homozygous SCD in one group took the test drug (12 mg/kg body weight) daily for six months before crossing over to placebo for another six months. Another group took placebo for six months before crossing over to active drug for six months. There was a one-month washout period between crossovers. Niprisan™ use reduced the mean number of crises by 55% from placebo – a highly significant improvement ($p < 0.05$). Patients taking Niprisan™ generally rated their health as better and reported less sickness and absenteeism versus placebo. Apart from headache (12%), patients reported no significant adverse effects (Perampaladas, 2010; Wambebe, 2001a; 2001b). It was concluded that Niprisan™ was efficacious for the prophylactic management of SCD.

SCD patients can, to a substantial degree, recognize the symptoms of impending SCD attacks. The occasional prophylactic use of Niprisan™ with chronic, intermittent dosing by approximately 90,000 people in Nigeria has resulted in the reduction of SCD attacks by 98% in this population.

Herbal extracts almost always contain several compounds, so the attribution of biological activity to a single particular compound can be difficult. Experience at NIPRD has shown that some phytomedicines are more active as crude extracts than as purified entities. As in the case of Niprisan™, some extracts contain multiple closely related molecules with similar biological activity. Niprisan™ was approved by the Nigerian National Agency for Food and Drug Administration and Control (NAFDAC) in 2006 (see http://nafdac.org.ng/). The estimated total discovery and development costs of Niprisan™ were approximately US$28 million (out-of-pocket), including US$8 million to build a manufacturing facility (Pandey, 2009). This figure is much lower than the figures for rational drug discovery and development.

The following conclusions can be offered when comparing reverse pharmacology with rational drug discovery and manufacturing:

- Medicines from traditional knowledge/reverse pharmacology can be standardized in production and demonstrated to be safe by current standards.
- It is possible to prove that phytomedicines are effective in clinical trials.
- Phytomedicines production can be much less expensive than common means of pharmaceutical production.
- Reverse pharmacology can be highly effective and much less expensive than rational drug design for discovery and development.

Not all emerging economies, especially those in Sub-Saharan Africa, can afford to extensively adopt rational drug design to discovering and developing new medicines for their unique health needs, whereas global pharmaceutical originator companies cannot invest heavily in neglected tropical diseases (NTDs). Reverse pharmacology is a much less expensive approach to drug discovery and pharmaceutical manufacturing. Failure rates in RP development are reduced by evidence of human safety from traditional use. Clinical trials using an RP approach are not as rigorous as those for rational drug discovery. Yet it is possible to design and successfully execute placebo-controlled, crossover studies to demonstrate clinical efficacy for herbal medicines. Ultimately, drugs derived from RP are more accessible and affordable than those from pharmaceutical origi-nator companies, and some compromises must be made to provide new medicines for these significant, unmet medical needs. This only empha-sizes the need for green chemistry in drug discovery, to make all valid forms of drug discovery much more efficient.

African capacity for API pharmaceutical manufacturing

South Africa has invested heavily in research of medical significance, with a large number of research units funded by the Medical Research Council. The country has worked to build the capacity for national pharmaceutical manufacturing of APIs and FPPs, as small-molecule biological therapeutics, largely through the Department of Trade and Industry (DTI). The national government has sustained, for example, an investment in BIOVAC for several years in an attempt both to minimize reliance on imported vaccines and to generate foreign exchange by export of vaccine products. BIOVAC is presently manu-facturing the final stages of vaccine production for local and external use under license from at least one global, originator pharmaceutical company.

The only South African-based API manufacturer, Fine Chemicals Corporation (FCC) was founded in 1962 in Cape Town. At incep-tion, FCC produced codeine phosphate, morphine sulphate and para-cetamol exclusively for the South African market. The product range was expanded in the 1980s with the development of a number of generic APIs, primarily for the US market. In the 1990s, FCC invested heavily to meet emerging international standards of GMP production. Since then, the company has been successfully inspected by various regula-tory authorities including the USFDA in 1996, 1999, 2002 and 2006.

The company currently has 79 installed reactors with a capacity of 125,000 litres, with individual reactor capacities ranging from 100 litres to 6,000 litres for glass-lined and stainless steel. The company has significant expertise internally and supplements this with partner-ships with local and international contract research organizations and organizations with expertise in chiral separations and catalysis. The use of APIs is typically regulated by the filing of a drug master file (DMF) that fully describes the route of synthesis, controls, CQAs, testing and specifications. FCC has in excess of 150 DMF submission in more than 16 countries around the world. Therapeutic uses for locally manufac-tured APIs are as immunosuppressants, anticancer, muscle relaxants, anti-psychotics, anticholinergic, bronchodilators, carbonic anhydrase inhibitors, analgesics, antihypertensive, antianginals and anaesthetics, among others.

Bioclones was founded in 1982 with the aim of developing monoclonal antibodies and manufacturing biotechnology-derived products for human use. The company became one of the first in the world to develop recombinant human erythropoietin, which was registered by the MCC in 1997 and marketed in South Africa in 1998.

LaGray Pharmaceuticals in Nsawam, Ghana, is unique among African pharmaceutical manufacturers. LaGray was founded in 2002 by Alexandra Graham and Paul Lartey, a wife-husband team with extensive experience in drug discovery, development and manufacturing of both APIs and FPPs in the global pharmaceutical industry. Dr. Lartey is the former director of anti-infective drug discovery at Pfizer Corp. Dr. Graham held several management positions at Abbott Labs. LaGray aims to differentiate the company from its competitors by meeting international standards of GMP. LaGray products for topical use include a number of anti-infectives. The company's early approach focussed on new products whose quality could be assured without the added investment of human bioequivalence trials. LaGray has implemented advanced processes for waste management and wastewater remediation, an area which is often ignored in African pharmaceutical manufacturing. LaGray is presently cooperating with the USP (United States Pharmacopeia) to train operators – the skilled workers who do the actual pharmaceutical manufacturing, a critical training need in West Africa. LaGray also has a small-scale manufacturing facility for APIs and is producing commercial amounts of the macrolide antibiotic azithromycin in Ghana.

Leap-frogging technologies and training in new technologies for competitive advantage

Manufacturing processes for APIs typically reflect the standard of chemistry available at the time the corresponding FPPs were first registered and approved for use. Although API processes evolve over time to give improved yields, reduce solvent use and reduce manufacturing time, the routes of synthesis generally are those as registered by originator companies. Malaria drugs are one therapeutic area for which this is true. Artemisinin combination therapies (ACTs) for malaria treatment consist of older drugs that were combined in fixed-dose combination or co-packaged FPPs for use. The Global Fund and other non-governmental organizations sourced approximately 389 million ACT treatments in 2013 (UNITAID, 2013). Artesunate: amodiaquine (ASAQ) and dihydroartemisinin: piperaquine (DHAP) are two standard ACTs. ASAQ is the second-most used ACT behind artemether: lumefantrine (ALU).

The Kilimanjaro School of Pharmacy has trained participants in the IPAT program to synthesize these APIs during laboratory exercises in API manufacturing. Trainees have also used the API they synthesized to manufacture DHAP and ASAP FPPs in the Kilimanjaro School of Pharmacy pilot plant. One of us (JF) has created new chemistry for the synthesis of these two APIs that is used by participants in the IPAT training. One of these exercises has been published (Fortunak et al., 2013). The new chemistry utilized for this purpose has simplified the manufacturing process for amodiaquine from five steps to two steps with no intermediate isolations; this synthesis is also readily adapted for continuous-flow chemical reactors (Fortunak, 2014). The overall yield of this synthesis is about 93% as compared with 65% for the previous route. New chemistry discovered for synthesizing piperaquine has the same number of steps as the commercial synthesis, but completely eliminates the presence of a genotoxic impurity previously present at a level of more than 2% in an intermediate stage of the synthesis. This has allowed an overall improvement in the E-factor of the synthesis from more than 45-plus kilograms of waste to approximately 8 kg of waste generated per kilogram of API produced. The overall yield of this process again has improved, from approximately 55% to 93% on a five-kilogram demonstration scale (Fortunak, 2014).

To address the challenge of cost-competitive production of APIs in South Africa, one of us, PW, and researchers at Nelson Mandela Metropolitan University (NMMU) are working to provide a step-change in pharmaceutical manufacturing technology that will increase the availability and affordability of APIs. This step-change will result from the continuous production of APIs in small, modular units known as flow reactors. Flow reactors operate continuously on a small scale, for extended periods of time. Production carried out on a 24/7 basis reduces the size of reactors needed for production and thereby reduces the capital investment needed for production start-ups. Although flow chemistry is engineering-intensive and the individual reactors are more expensive than traditional, chemical stirred tank reactors, this upfront investment in advanced science can create substantial efficiencies in manufacturing footprint and production costs as well as capital investment. Waste generation during flow processing can often be significantly less than for traditional 'batch' processing of APIs.

Compared to stirred batch reactor methodology, the benefits of MRT/ flow chemistry are:

- increased reaction control and reproducibility by:
  - efficient mixing
  - accurate control of time, temperature and pressure
  - increased catalyst lifetime and activity
- enhanced safety due to:
  - rapid dissipation of heat
  - low reactant volumes at any given time
  - real-time analytical evaluation
- lower cost due to
  - higher chemical yield
  - reduced material use and waste generation
  - reduced investment

This system's flexibility has the potential to reduce the time and risk associated with transferring technology from research into production. This methodology is being exploited profitably by fine chemical companies in Europe. The aim of this project is to exploit this technology to reduce cost of drugs of importance to South Africa making the country more self-reliant. In the first instance NMMU are focusing on three anti-HIV drugs, but the technology could readily be applied to other drugs of relevance to African needs.

Ethiopia: Research on local sources of starch as an excipient

Excipients used in FPPs may originate from natural sources, chemical synthesis or biotechnology. Since excipients are ingested every time a patient takes an FPP, safety, quality and price are important. Most excipients are generally regarded as safe (GRAS) for humans because of a long history of use in the food, flavourings and cosmetics industries. One of us (TGM) is researching the development of inexpensive local sources of excipients in Ethiopia for pharmaceutical production, with a focus on starch and starch derivatives, gums and resins.

There is a huge potential for the development of new and alternative local sources of excipients in Africa. Starch is used as a component in the manufacture of pharmaceuticals, food, textiles, paper and adhesives. The use of native starch or its modified forms is based on its adhesive, thickening, gelling and film-forming properties. Starches are readily available, low cost and can be processed to provide high-quality materials of varying grades for a variety of uses. Although starch is a major component in most plants, the main commercial sources are the seeds of cereal grains (maize, wheat and rice), tubers (potato) and certain roots (sweet potato, cassava and arrow roots). Over the last ten years, native (*enset*) starch has been produced on commercial scale in Ethiopia for the food and beverage industries.

The worldwide market for industrial starches is expanding, and the industrial trend is towards the use of commercially viable raw materials other than maize, wheat and potato, which have competing food uses. Some tropical plants including *enset, dioscorea*, cassava and *godare* have been investigated. *Enset* starch extracted from *boulla* provided a 99% yield (recovery) of available starch on dry weight basis. Scanning electron microscopy (SEM) of *enset* starch granules showed characteristic morphology that was somewhat angular and elliptical. Laser diffraction studies revealed normal granule size distribution with a mean particle size of 46 μm (Gebre-Mariam and Schmidt, 1996a). Evaluated as a binder and disintegrant for compressed tablets, *enset* starch was found to compare favourably with potato and maize starches (Gebre-Mariam and Nikolayev, 1993; Gebre-Mariam and Schmidt, 1996b).

Super-disintegrants are modified polymers that rapidly absorb water and swell in the aqueous environment of the stomach. Sodium starch glycolate (SSG) is the sodium salt of the carboxymethyl ether of native starch. SSG rapidly absorbs water and swells, causing tablets and capsules containing these excipients to break apart rapidly, enhancing their release properties for improved drug absorption. *Enset* starch was modified into sodium starch glycolate and evaluated as a super-disintegrant in compressed tablets. SSG of *enset* starch was found to be at least as efficient as commercial grades of SGG, Primojel® or Croscarmellose sodium. In soluble tablet formulations, sodium starch glycolate of *enset* was more efficient than Primojel® or Ac-Di-Sol®. Tablets prepared with sodium starch glycolate of *enset* exhibited shorter disintegration times and faster rates of swelling and water uptake. Similarly, the sodium starch glycolate of *dioscorea* starch was found to be more efficient than EXPT® (the 'Explo-tab' brand of SSG) in soluble and insoluble tablet formulations (Gebre-Mariam et al., 1996b).

Comparative studies of the starch in tablet formulations indicated *dioscorea* starch has practically identical binding and disintegrating ability to that of potato starch (Gebre-Mariam and Schmidt, 1998). Drug release studies from matrix tablets revealed that the rate of release changed from rapid release to sustained release as the degree of substitution increased. Dissolution studies showed that *enset* starch acetates with high degree of substitution could act as matrix-forming agents in tablets, where the release of a drug can be significantly sustained (Nigussu et al.,

2013). Efforts are under way to progress the work for adoption in local pharmaceutical production.

Conclusion: building skills for API manufacture and drug discovery

African pharmaceutical companies largely employ excellent scientists – their staff are often the equal of scientists anywhere. A major gap, however, is one of experience. The USFDA commonly notes that an appropriate combination of 'education, training, and experience' is needed to operate under GMP. Another challenge for pharmaceutical production is that African companies rarely are able to apply substantial resources to developing new products. It is common for companies to purchase technical development packages from Indian generics producers as the source of their process descriptions. These packages are not nearly as detailed as needed for the full process understanding and control needed for SRA approvals. It is also difficult for African companies to expend equivalent resources on laboratory and pilot scale equipment and on preparing pilot- and commercial-scale development batches to optimize their manufacturing processes.

This chapter pinpoints two important strategies by which existing capabilities can be leveraged to support the emergence of a sustainable API, excipients and generic pharmaceutical industry on the African continent. Both of these approaches are suitable for implementation by regional centres of excellence (CoEs) in drug development and regulatory sciences. Regional CoEs are recognized by the PMPA and by the United Nations African Initiative for New Drugs and Diagnostics (ANDI) Program as important for developing African capabilities in pharmaceutical innovation.

The first of these strategies is to develop education and training curricula at universities and academic Institutions. These programs must initially borrow from the experience of external experts to reduce the gap in hands-on experience in manufacturing technologies API, excipients and FPP as well as regulatory science. There are substantial numbers of African nationals working in important positions in global pharmaceutical companies today. Active recruitment of some of these experienced scientists to 'return home' – a process known as braingain – could be an important point of leverage for promulgating, implementing and improving international standards for product development and SRA approvals. A number of African countries have courses in pharmacy, industrial chemistry, fermentation technologies, microbiology, biochemistry (including immunology) and process engineering, among others. As alluded to earlier, what is missing is hands-on industrial experience and learning-by-doing (DUI) mode of innovation.

A second strategy to promote African API, excipient and FPP development is to fund regional CoEs to develop Technology Transfer Packages (TTPs) that enable pharmaceutical companies to implement quality-assured manufacturing of a specific API, excipient or FPP. If adequately funded, equipped and staffed with competent people, the CoEs could develop pharmaceutical manufacturing processes, analytical test methods and specifications for essential medicines. They can serve as clinical trial coordinators and knowledge brokers. With such an approach it should be feasible to sustainably raise the technological scope for locally manufacturing APIs, excipients and biologicals and to support a broader value chain of local pharmaceutical production on the continent.

Notes

1. See, for example, Bioclones (South Africa), manufacturing erythropoietin, http://www.bioclones.co.za/, and LaGray Chemical Company (Ghana), manufacturing azithromycin, http://www.lagraychem.com/.
2. See, for example, South Africa: Ketlaphela – South Africa Government's ARV Manufacturing Project Enters Next Phase, all Africa, 16 May 2013,http://allafrica.com/stories/201305211581.html; Sarah Wild, 'ARV plan bounces back', *Mail & Guardian*, 24 May 2013, http://mg.co.za/article/2013–05–24–00-arv-plan-bounces-back.

Part II
Industrialization for Health

In Part II of this book we turn from the challenges of industrialization to the theme at the heart of this book: how to industrialize for health. Chapter 4 already explored the interactions between health and industrial policies within one African country. The next three chapters ask how the aim of universal access to health care, and the needs of populations frequently denied competent care, can become the values that shape the industrialization drive.

Chapter 8 returns to two East African countries whose pharmaceutical industries have already been analysed, Kenya and Tanzania. Drawing on the framework of capabilities analysis developed and applied in Part I, this chapter asks: How can two sectors, health and industry, develop collaborative capabilities – the ability to work together? Industrial and health managers, like industrial and health policy makers, live in different silos across the world. Just bringing officials from the relevant ministries into the same room can feel like a major innovation. This chapter argues that while dialogue across these boundaries is essential, what has to follow is institutional change in both sectors to progressively generate capabilities to work together.

In addressing the challenge of linking industry and health, in Part II we turn explicitly to learning from other continents. Chapters 9 and 10 present a historical perspective on the experiences of, respectively, Brazil and India. The experiences are very different. Brazil can track a progressive coming-together of industrial policy and industrial development with the needs of health care, rooted in the development of a universalist health care system. India, in contrast, has developed a major export industry in pharmaceuticals, but has been much less successful in meeting its population's health needs. A common theme of these two chapters is the necessity of an historical under-standing of cumulative change, economic incentives and key policy interventions in explaining outcomes in both health and industrial development.

8

Health Systems as Industrial Policy: Building Collaborative Capabilities in the Tanzanian and Kenyan Health Sectors and Their Local Suppliers

Maureen Mackintosh, Paula Tibandebage, Joan Kariuki Kungu, Mercy Karimi Njeru and Caroline Israel

Introduction: health sector organization as implicit industrial policy

A recognition that the demand patterns and investment incentives generated by health care and health policies constitute an 'implicit' industrial policy for manufacturers of medicines and medical supplies is not new. In a European context, Thomas (1994) argued that post-1945 UK health care pricing and regulation policies drove a shift to global competitiveness in the locally based pharmaceutical industry, while French post-war health policy did not. Reich (1990) has argued that Japanese success in pharmaceuticals was nurtured, not by the MITI's industrial policy, but mainly by government regulation and funding of the health sector and manipulation of pharmaceutical pricing.

The most sophisticated analyses of the health-industry relationships are by Indian and Brazilian scholars. Srinivas (2012) has analysed in depth the changing institutional relationships in India among the 'triad' of industrial production, health care provision/delivery and consumption of health care (Chapter 10) through three historically distinct 'market environments'. Brazilian scholars and policy makers have been addressing for three decades the development of a 'health-industrial complex' (Chapter 9) consisting of a health sector aiming at universalization of access and framed by the constitutional right to health, the development of pharmaceutical, biotech and other medical supplies industries, and the supporting governmental institutions (D'Ávila Viana and Elias, 2007, citing pioneering analysis by Cordeiro, 1985; see also Gadelha et al., 2012; Shadlen and Massard da Fonseca, 2013).

This chapter examines health-industry interactions in two East African countries. The chapter traces the ways in which the health sector's institutional organization in each country influences the domestic markets for industrial supplies. We argue that the recent institutional evolution in the health sector has tended to undermine local manufacturers' linkages with their domestic health sectors in both countries, with a progressive disconnection in particular between public and non-profit health care procurement of medicines and supplies and local manufacturers seeking market access. Coupled with rising external competition in the private medicines markets in each country (Chapters 2 and 3), these institutional changes have driven a process of partial disconnection of domestic industrial-health market linkages in the two countries. The effect is most striking in Tanzania, where the industrial structure is less robust (Chapter 3).

We argue that to achieve better developmental synergies between industrial development in manufacturing medicines and health system performance, both health and industrial sectors have to strengthen what we call 'collaborative capabilities': the capability to respond effectively to the opportunities offered by the other sector. We identify key elements of these collaborative capabilities in each sector and trace some ways in which institutional evolution and changing market structures can move health and industrial supplier sectors towards or away from mutually beneficial trading and working relations with each other.

We then go on to explore the mediation of these interactions via the under-researched institutions of procurement and local marketing. Procurement and marketing, we argue, are culturally and politically rooted institutions, not mere policy instruments. We aim to demonstrate that policy coherence, which is essential to incentivizing health-industry collaboration, is not only a matter of political will: it is itself a social construct that has to be built through institutional generation of collaborative capabilities and compatible incentive structures between health and industry at national level.

These conceptual arguments are developed through engagement with the findings from research undertaken in 2012–13 in Kenya and

Tanzania, which investigated supply chains from local producers and importers into the health sector.[1] Qualitative interviews and quantitative data collection on availability, source and price of a checklist of 'tracer' medicines[2] and other essential supplies were conducted in both countries. In Tanzania, 42 health facilities (public, faith-based and private), pharmacies and drug shops across four very diverse districts were visited (Tibandebage et al., 2014), while in Kenya, 55 health facilities, pharmacies and shops were interviewed in a comparative study (Kariuki et al., 2015). Following these supply chain studies, wholesalers, manufacturers and policy and regulatory stakeholders were interviewed in both countries in 2013–14. This chapter draws also on some of these interviews, alongside secondary data sources.

Health sector market structure

In political economy terms, health sectors are *not* best understood as 'delivery systems' – the linear and top-down framing favoured in much of the global health literature.[3] Rather, they represent complex and culturally embedded social institutions and important sectors of the economy whose evolution can be analysed using the tools of industrial economics. In almost all low- and middle-income countries, health sector institutions include widespread markets in services as well as commodities.

A key determinant of a health sector's capacity to procure and use medicines and other medical supplies effectively, and to develop good local suppliers, is therefore its market structures. These determine how the population's demand for and need for medicines feeds through (or fails to feed through) into wholesale purchasing; who are the resultant wholesale buyers of essential supplies; what market power those buyers exercise; and how they select and distribute supplies.

Market and supply chain segmentation

The Tanzanian and Kenyan health sectors, like many others in Africa, rely heavily on private individual expenditure for financing; hence, fees and charges operate as barriers to access to adequate health care for much of the population (Chuma and Okungu, 2011; Maluka, 2013). WHO data for 2012 estimate that private out-of-pocket (OOP) spending funded 48% of Kenyan health care, with another 6% from private insurance. The figures for Tanzania were 32% OOP, with negligible private insurance.[4] Charges are applied quite widely in the public as well as private sectors in both countries.

Private health care facilities, including for-profit, and faith-based and non-governmental non-profit facilities play a quite substantial role in each country. Private for-profit providers in Kenya run 27% of the hospitals and virtually all the nursing homes and clinics. Over half of Kenyan hospitals and over 75% of the health centres and dispensaries, however, are government-owned and run, with the rest (around 17% of each category) in the faith-based sector.[5] Tanzanian data are not strictly comparable, but the for-profit sector in Tanzania appears relatively smaller, owning 16% of dispensaries, 3% of health centres and 15% of hospitals (but only 4% of hospital beds). The faith-based sector is relatively larger in Tanzania, including 42% of hospitals, some funded and run as part of the government system (MoHSW, 2009).

These differentiated health care sectors buy medicines through quite segmented supply chains in each country. In the 2012–13 study outlined above, the public sector sourced supplies overwhelmingly from one large public wholesaler in each country.[6] Public facilities in Kenya had sourced 91% of the set of 'tracer' essential medicines from the public sector wholesaler, KEMSA. In Tanzania the comparable figure for public sector sourcing from the Medical Supplies Department (MSD) was 97%. In Kenya, private facilities sourced 99% of these essential medicines from private wholesalers, in Tanzania 94% (the main exception in each case was anti-retrovirals (ARVs) for HIV/AIDS sourced through the public sector). Only the non-profit facilities in Kenya had diverse wholesale sources, buying 44% from a faith-based, non-profit wholesaler (MEDS), about one-third from private wholesalers, and sourcing the rest from the public sector. In Tanzania there is no large non-profit wholesaler; the faith-based facilities' medicines came largely (83%) from private wholesalers, and the rest from the public sector.

However, a substantial proportion of essential medicines used by the population in these two countries, as across Sub-Saharan Africa (Wafula et al., 2013), is not accessed as part of treatment at a facility: rather, the medicines are bought in retail drug shops and pharmacies. Availability of essential medicines is limited and variable in the public sector in both countries, and public sector patients are often sent to shops to buy medicines out of pocket.[7] There are no reliable estimates of the percentage of essential medicines accessed through the private shops in either country, in part because of gaps in household budget survey data (MoHSW, 2012). National Health Accounts do not separate medicines purchase from other facility spending (MoMS and MPHS, nd). The private shops were found to be entirely reliant on private wholesalers to source medicines.

Market power and local purchasing

The implication of these market structures is that, with exceptions noted below, the final users and consumers of essential medicines exercise little influence over the sourcing and pricing of their medicines. That market power lies with the wholesalers and with some large funding bodies. The different sectors in the two countries exercise that market power to different effect in terms of local procurement of medicines.

Our supply chain data (Table 8.1) show that the public sector wholesaler in each country had bought a higher proportion of the tracer essential medicines from local manufacturers than had the private wholesalers. The faith-based wholesaler in Kenya (MEDS) was the most likely of all to source these medicines locally. All Kenyan wholesale sectors, furthermore, were more likely than their Tanzanian counterparts to buy these essential medicines from their local manufacturers (Table 8.1). Finally, while Tanzania buyers sourced medicines from Kenya ('other African' for Tanzania in Table 8.1 is largely Kenyan), the Kenyan buyers bought little from non-Kenyan African suppliers.

To what extent are these different patterns of local purchasing summarized in Table 8.1 generated from the health sector side, from the manufacturing capabilities side, and from effective institutional cross-sector interaction? We begin by examining in turn the public, donor, non-profit and private purchasing practices and their implications for health system capability and willingness to purchase effectively and economically from local suppliers.

Table 8.1 Country of origin of tracer essential medicines, by procurement sector, Tanzania and Kenya, 2012–13 (% by sector)

	Tanzania		Kenya		
	Wholesale sector		Wholesale sector		
Country					
Source	Public	Private	Public	Faith-based	Private
Domestic manufacturers	22	11	53	76	33
Other African	10	21	0	0	6
India and Pakistan	49	50	30	11	31
China	6	6	8	1	4
EU and Switzerland	7	11	1	4	19
Other	6	0	7	8	7
Total	100	100	100	100	100

Note: Numbers may not add to 100 because of rounding.

Public sector procurement capabilities

The view from 'below'

Interviews with clinical and administrative staff in public sector facilities in both countries about their experiences of procurement belie the image in the aggregated data above, of clearly segmented supply chains. The view from 'below' was not of a single linear public sector ordering process, but was more like navigating an interactive maze while constantly distracted by clinical demands.

In all the lower-level health facilities (dispensaries, health centres, smaller clinics), most people doing procurement were nurses and clinical officers doing it as part of the day job[8]:

> Like me now, who is a clinician, I do almost everything, I am the procurement person, I am seeing the patients. (Clinical officer, Kenyan public health centre)

The only institutions that might have procurement officers with specialist training were larger hospitals: there, pharmacists, laboratory in-charges, nurses and medical directors would be involved, and teamwork was emphasized. A high-end private hospital in Nairobi felt they were coping:

> I can tell you in a hospital like this you will really need team work. We have trained everybody on inventory management. What they need to keep in terms of safety stock versus ensuring they have re order levels. (Hospital pharmacist, Kenyan private hospital)

Procurement staff in a stressed Tanzania urban district hospital by contrast felt they lacked the capabilities needed to do this well:

> This is a big hospital that has different departments. ... Some are slow while some are sharp. This delays the process... departments that were quick in submitting their items... keep knocking at our doors asking for their order. We have to tell them, procurement process is under way, while waiting for other department to submit theirs. They get angry because patients are waiting at their doors. (Procurement officer, Tanzanian public hospital)

Procurement, like all aspects of health care, is social and relational. Though form-filling is required, the ordering and control systems work well only where institutional relationships stitch them into responding to health care needs on the one hand, and into effective and timely supply systems on the other hand.

In both countries, there were almost universal complaints about long delays and incompletely or inaccurately filled orders from the public wholesaler. Availability of our tracer medicines in public hospitals was 61% in Kenya and 86% in Tanzania; these were all items hospitals should have held. The corresponding figures for the lower-level public facilities were 48% in Kenya and 58% in Tanzania. The prevalence of 'stock-outs' at the public wholesaler was thus a fact of life in both countries, forcing a search for alternative sources of supply. Patients were sent to shops to buy missing medicines, and in both countries many found it unaffordable. Among many examples, a health centre interviewee serving low-income patients in Kenya commented that in cases of antibiotic resistance, 'sometimes you are forced to write a prescription to that patient [for another type of antibiotic] but you see the patients we deal with are the less privileged people', so some just went untreated.

Keeping essential items on the shelves was a constant struggle. The alternatives public sector staff turned to when stocks failed included spending user fees to fill gaps, using other pockets of public and donor-supported funds, borrowing between public sector facilities, soliciting personal and institutional donations and even spending their own money.

How these pressures feel can be illustrated from interviews in two public dispensaries and a public hospital in a single rural district of Tanzania. In the two dispensaries, procurement was done by a clinical officer in-charge. They had no procurement training. They ordered most of their medicines from the public wholesaler every three months, via the district medical officer (DMO), and struggled with missing essential items and resultant accusations from patients of mismanagement or corruption. Opening the consignments was overseen by a local village health committee.

All collected fees from patients, but only the hospital retained them; the dispensaries deposited them with the DMO. The DMO had access to a donor-supported 'basket' fund; like the budgets for the district at the public wholesaler, these were sometimes deposited with a delay. The dispensaries applied to the DMO for gap-filling from the 'basket'; the hospital also used its fees for this purpose. The hospital pharmacist would cycle off directly to buy urgent essentials at district-designated pharmacies. In the hospital, most essential medicines on our list were there, but barely, with little backup stock.

An exception was items provided by 'vertical programmes' via the DMO, such as test kits for HIV, malaria and pregnancy. These were generally available but had to be collected from the district centre – a challenge for rural dispensaries with no petty cash and no means of transport. Staff paid for their own transport if no lifts could be found: one remarked, 'this is not correct'. Medical equipment was the most problematic item: 'even if you order them, you do not get them, so we do not order them … we ask donors to help'. One clinical officer displayed thermometers obtained from a Dutch personal donor, a blood pressure machine sent to him by a friend in the United States and a stethoscope he had bought himself: individual networks of local rural sourcing were thus quite globalized.

Kenyan local-level experience echoes this complexity. There, public sector lower-level facilities obtained their KEMSA supplies through the local district hospital. The parallels to the 'basket funds' were the Health Sector Services Fund (HSSF) and Facility Improvement Funds (FIF), and they also used fees and charges. In addition, there was in Kenya a widespread local culture of borrowing between public facilities, especially when patients could not afford to buy medicines in the shops, and especially in the rural districts: in these circumstances,

> We usually borrow from other facilities, and they also borrow from us. (Nurse in-charge, Kenyan rural public dispensary)

Donor influence and government leverage

Local-level public sector procurement staff had little influence over decisions on wholesale procurement of medicines from different manufacturing sources. Some, when asked, had views and preferences on where medicines should be bought, commenting for example on problems of packaging of locally manufactured items, or positively on patients' acceptance of local brands. But decisions on manufacturing source of medicines in both countries were taken at wholesale level with little or no reference to facility-level views.

The public sector procurement bodies, KEMSA and MSD, sourced their medicines largely through international open tenders.[9] MSD is an autonomous government department working on a commercial basis[10]; KEMSA was, until 2013, a government agency, and is now an authority. Tendering by both authorities is strongly price-focussed, and most tenders are very large. The emphasis on open tendering has effectively liberalized the public sector medicines market in both countries. Both bodies can give 15% price preference to local manufacturers in competition with imported products. In Tanzania, local manufacturers argue, this equates to around 9% effective preference, since they deliver to MSD, while overseas suppliers deliver to the port of entry.[11] In Kenya, some local manufacturers complain the preference is not reliably applied (UNIDO, 2010: 9).

In both countries, public procurement practices for medicines are strongly influenced by tendering rules promoted by the multilaterals and other donors; they are also shaped by requirements of the large donors providing medicines funding. The very large international tenders have helped to control tendering costs and improve confidence in the public procurement process.[12] The biggest institutional evolution in both countries' medicines markets in the last decade has been the growth of large-scale donor-funded procurement of medicines for TB, HIV/AIDS and malaria. Around 63% of MSD's income from medicines and medical supplies came from these 'vertical programmes' in 2011–12, and this percentage varies sharply year on year (MSD, 2013). In Kenya, the latest estimate we have found is for 2005–06, when the government budget share of total public expenditure on medicines was estimated at 21.6%, the bulk of the expenditure being donor-financed (MMs and MPHS, 2010: 53).

For donor-funded medicines, there is substantial international participation and control of pooled procurement processes by organizations such John Snow International and Management Sciences for Health within the Partnership for Supply Chain Management.[13] The donors' emphasis has been on generating a global supply management chain for very high volumes of imports into East Africa, from 'pre-qualified', generally Asian suppliers to regional level in Africa. The pre-qualification process, run by the World Health Organization (WHO)[14] to approve specified products of individual suppliers, has in practice largely excluded local manufacturers in both countries from the domestic markets for these products (see also Chapters 2, 3 and 5).

International donors also fund other essential medicines, including other public medicines' procurement. The 'basket' fund in Tanzania, mentioned above, is donor-funded. The flows of support are complex, erratic, poorly documented, generally unconsolidated and uncoordinated, and sometimes provided in-kind, as shown by 'spaghetti' diagrams of hugely complex financing and in-kind flows for medicines supply in each country (KEMSA Task Force, 2008: 28; MoHSW, 2008: 23).

In these circumstances, how much leverage do national governments exert over their domestic medicines markets and procurement? Leverage over procurement patterns can be exerted through national regulatory policies – for example, by setting tendering rules and coordinating funding flows. However, the extent to which the national governments contribute funds to the medicines procurement 'pot' remains an important element of policy leverage. Data are poor, but estimates drawn from national health accounts and policy documents suggest that in each county, only around 5% of the domestic medicines consumption is currently funded by the government taxes.

For Tanzania, the domestic market size for medicines was estimated at around US$250 million in 2011–12.[15] Of this market, public wholesaler (MSD) sales were around 50% (US$125 million), of which 70% in turn were donor-funded vertical programme sales (MSD, 2013). That leaves just US$37.2 million as government-funded MSD procurement, or 15% of the total market. However, the Ministry of Health and Social Welfare has estimated that only around 30% of the pooled public funds held by public health facilities in accounts at MSD for medicines and medical supplies were locally tax funded, equating to around US$11.3 million, the rest coming from donor basket funds (MoHSW, 2013: 4–5). The implication is that just 5% of Tanzanian medicines were tax-funded in 2011–12.

A parallel calculation for Kenya could only be drawn from the most recent Kenyan National Health Accounts (MMS and MPHS, nd). They show total health spending (THE) for 2009–10 as US$1.62 billion. The Kenyan National Pharmaceutical Policy (NPP) (MoMS and MPHS, 2010: 53–54) estimates total pharmaceutical expenditure (TPE) at around 20% of THE, or US$324 million; of that 'about 15–20%' was public expenditure, or around US$64.8 million. Finally, the same document states (p. 53) that government spending was estimated in 2005–06 at 21.6% of public spending on medicines, the rest being donor funded. If that percentage were stable over time, it would imply a government tax-funded share of the Kenyan domestic medicines market in 2009–10 of under 5%.

None of these calculations is at all secure. But they are sufficiently similar and striking to indicate a strategic policy constraint for both governments. The market size estimates are likely to be low rather than high: UNIDO's Kenyan review (2010: 36) concluded of their own calculations that 'not all, if any, of the donor-funded supply of medicines is included in such [market size] estimates'. Policy documents in both countries indicate very high reliance on donor funding of medicines (MoMS, 2010). The robust conclusion for both countries is that the governments exercise very little tax-funded leverage over their domestic medicines markets in relation to both need and demand. Both governments' leverage at present depends almost solely on regulatory interventions. These data also suggest that, over time, it will be important to shift tax resources into the medicines funding stream.

Non-profit wholesaling: a case study of local procurement

Non-profit wholesalers and distributors can have a beneficial impact on essential medicines markets, providing low-priced competition in the supply of quality-assured medicines (Mackintosh et al., 2011). Both Tanzania and Kenya have non-profit medicines wholesalers supplying the faith-based and NGO sectors. Those in Tanzania, Action Medeor and MEMS, are small, while MEDS in Kenya is a large wholesaler with a turnover of about US$15 million in 2012[16] and therefore with substantial market impact. Action Medeor was supplying both faith-based and government facilities, and also selling to the Accredited Drug Dispensing Outlets (ADDOs), the regulated drug shops in Tanzania. It was, however, too small a supplier to appear in our Tanzania facility survey data. MEDS, on the other hand, supplied most of the faith-based and NGO facilities interviewed in Kenya.

The interviews showed that MEDS had a good reputation among those procuring medicines for faith-based and non-profit facilities. The two main reasons given for reliance on MEDS were price first and also reliance on their quality assurance. There was general agreement that they were cheap: not always the cheapest, but a combination of cheapness and reliability of quality and supply.

MEDS was also regarded as responsive to its clients on quality, responding to queries and complaints, taking back problematic supplies, and consulting on its stock lists. MEDS is working in a market context, where facilities have a choice of supplier, and it also responded to requests concerning the brands and origins of specific medicines, and to consider suggestions for new items. They would also order items not held in their stocks, and they maintained short delivery times (1–3 days) for stocked items. They were serving a differentiated faith-based health sector, with facilities serving higher-income groups and those serving the very disadvantaged, and they might stock more than one brand of the same item if preferences of customers require. They warned in advance when phasing out items from their stock lists, or when a shortage arose. They gave some credit: 'we pay at the end of the month and they do not push us' (Kenya, faith-based clinic). 'They are very reliable', one interviewee remarked. This was a remarkably positive set of assessments.

Both Action Medeor and MEDS had a strong orientation towards buying locally, subject to quality and price considerations. Action Medeor stated on its website: 'Most of our products are purchased locally in line with Action Medeor's policy to support local manufacturers – however, without compromising on quality'.[17] Given the limitations of Tanzanian suppliers (Chapter 3), Action Medeor was in practice buying from manufacturers in the East African region, notably Kenya and Uganda, as well as Tanzania.[18] Both Action Medeor and MEDS organized their procurement by 'pre-qualifying' local suppliers, using their own technical staff for inspections, site visits and questionnaires. MEDS kept suppliers 'on their toes' through batch testing of supplies on-site in their WHO-prequalified laboratory.

As Table 8.1 showed, MEDS was buying a high proportion of their basic essential medicines from local manufacturers. This success in local purchasing reflected a strong capability for local procurement built up over a number of years.[19] In contrast to the Kenyan public wholesaler, MEDS issues only local tenders for medicines and supplies, with no direct importing. Two local tenders a year go only to MEDS's pre-qualified supplier pool of local manufacturers and distributors.

Price is a very important component of MEDS's tender acceptance, but as private businesses, non-profit wholesalers such as MEDS can make their own supplier decisions, and price may not be the only consideration.[20] Both quality and supplier performance, including lead times and meeting delivery deadlines, influence MEDS's supply decisions. Local manufacturers can provide short lead times and reliable quality if working relationships are good. Furthermore, MEDS sustains its working relationships with suppliers through an annual invitation-only suppliers' conference during which issues are discussed and tender documents are generally available so that suppliers can plan ahead.

In our 2012–13 data, two local manufacturers had supplied nearly 70% of the tracer items sourced from MEDS: local firms producing a broad range of basic formulations can generally compete on the required mix of price and performance, though they can be beaten on price by imports. While MEDS leans towards regularly inspected local suppliers for basic essential medicines, donors' subsidized procurement arrangements, for example of the first-line anti-malarial medication, has meant a lack of local supply, and local distributors import those items for MEDS.

This case study of MEDS suggests some lessons about effective local procurement and supply, working with local suppliers and faith-based facilities. That capability is now being tested, as the decentralization reforms allow counties to switch suppliers, causing demand for MEDS' services to rise sharply from new buyers who lack experience in quantifying demand, and may delay payment.[21] The market segmentation identified from our data is now breaking down, as MEDS and KEMSA are effectively in competition (PSP4H, 2014; Yadav, 2014).

Private sector procurement and local products

The public, donor and non-profit procurement of medicines is important for medicines access. However, in both countries, half of medicines access or more relies on private sector wholesaling and importing. The interviews with private facilities and shops demonstrate that, in both countries, private retailers and clinicians rely almost wholly on private wholesalers. While most smaller buyers had little influence over the sources of the medicines they bought, many had opinions on the best sources of medicines, as did their patients. Asked systematically about the comparison between locally produced and imported medicines, the respondents' views varied according to their clientele. Some high-end private hospitals in Kenya, when procuring medicines, specified brands preferred by their patients, notably from European suppliers. Some pharmacies in better-off areas also said there was resistance to locally made branded generics.

Generally, however, the facilities and shops with lower-income clientele, who were buying from private wholesalers, would focus on price. Where the local items were price competitive, their clients would generally accept local brands, especially some, such as Shelys in Tanzania, which had built up a strong brand image (Mujinja et al., 2014). While in Tanzania opinions varied as to whether locally made medicines were cheaper or more expensive than imports, the consensus in Kenya was that local items tended to be cheaper:

> By the way the locally manufactured drugs are cheap and the people who go for them are the health facilities in upcountry. ... mission hospitals, clinics, district hospitals and local pharmacists in upcountry, they really support local manufacturers. (Private hospital, Kenya)

Most private retailers and facilities in both countries had built up long-term relationships with one or a few private wholesalers/importers, from whom they bought most of their supplies. The determinants of choice of supplier were predominantly price and credit terms, followed by issues such as transport arrangements and variety of items available. None could judge quality except through expiry dates and experience of clinical effectiveness, and only one interviewee had changed supplier for quality reasons: they found near-expiry drugs repackaged, more than once, as longer-dated on the external packaging, and changed supplier as a response.

The interrelated issues of price and credit terms were key: private shops and facilities are often struggling to maintain cash flow themselves, so they are looking for credit from suppliers. This was quite a typical comment:

> The main reasons why I chose those wholesale pharmacies are the prices of the drugs, quality and the convenience each of them offers. [Pharmacy X] is my number one priority because for most medicines they have the lowest prices. (Tanzanian rural private dispensary)

This was the type of credit relationship that sustained many small drug shops:

> [Pharmacy Y] can give medicines on a loan basis without any collateral provided what you take from the pharmacy does not exceed 400,000/= [Tanzanian] Shillings, and you pay after selling, in one or two months' time. (Rural drug shop,[22] Tanzania)

The main criticisms of locally manufactured medicines raised by private sector respondents in both countries concerned packaging, which was said to compare poorly with imported competing items, putting off users. In Tanzania, there was repeated criticism that some locally manufactured tablets tended to disintegrate too easily, and some unfavourable comparisons with the quality of Kenyan manufactured tablets.

The decisions of private wholesalers were therefore important to the local manufacturers' domestic market demand. Kenyan manufactured medicines were quite widely imported into Tanzania by the private wholesalers (Table 8.1; see also Chapter 2), while there were few Tanzanian items found in the Kenyan market. The Tanzanian private market was more heavily reliant on India (Table 8.1).

In both countries, many private wholesalers are also importers, who act as representative agents for Indian and European manufacturers. If margins are better on imported items, then importers will lack incentives to source and distribute local manufactures. Some large wholesalers/ importers supply only imported products, while others also deal in local products. Some importers, such as Phillips, have worked closely with a number of donor-funded projects, for example distributing imported subsidized anti-malarials and importing items for PEFAR-funded gap-filling supplies for donors' projects.

There are also wholesalers who have retail chains, and supply other retailers, and in both countries they buy locally as well as from importers. One such pharmaceutical wholesaler in Tanzania explained that there was demand for both Tanzanian and Kenyan medicines; however, there were constant shortages of Tanzanian items, whereas 'Kenyan products are always available in the market'. Kenyan suppliers such as Elys have representatives in Tanzania, and their products are widely distributed there.

Local manufacturers' collaborative capabilities

An important difference between the two countries is in the scale of the local pharmaceutical industry and the range of products the firms have the capability to supply (Chapters 2 and 3). While Tanzania had just five operating firms when the 2013 research was done, Kenya had about 40 producers, including firms capable of supplying parenterals manufactured in sterile conditions. The density in itself meant that Kenyan firms were more able than Tanzanian firms to supply their local market. However, they still currently (2013) supply only around 25% of the domestic demand (Chapter 2). There is clearly room for expansion of local supply in both countries.

In both countries, local manufacturers are strongly oriented to supplying the private market. Despite sharp price competition from imports and a lack of trade protection in the private market, Kenyan producers are continuing to compete successfully. One contribution to this price competitiveness appears to be export success: Kenyan manufacturers have expanded exports to the region (Chapter 2), allowing them to build up economies of scale and keep prices down. In addition to sales through local wholesalers, at least one large manufacturer in Tanzania had developed its own marketing teams to ensure wide product availability and brand recognition across the very large geographical distances in that country.

However, in both countries, there were problems concerning supply to the public wholesaler, and also problems of policy directions that were undermining the competitiveness of the local industry. The problem was sharper in Tanzania (Chapter 3). Even in Kenya, however, at least one large manufacturer had moved away from public sector tendering, citing KEMSA's focus on the lowest possible price, in order to build up higher-margin exports. Some larger Kenyan firms, with an expanding product range, continued to tender successfully. In Tanzania, some local manufacturers had shifted to supplying the public sector through local private wholesalers, who could carry the costs of bundling local and imported items and also carry some of the tendering costs and associated risks.

Furthermore, in both countries, there had been tax and tariff decisions that had undermined local manufacturers' competitiveness. In Kenya, manufacturers and distributors noted that the 2013 decision to impose VAT on inputs for pharmaceutical production was forcing up prices and undermining market access. In Tanzania, as Chapter 3 documents, the removal of tariffs on final goods, associated with VAT and tariffs on some inputs, was a substantial problem for the sustainability of the whole industry. In Kenya, however, the manufacturers' associations had made strong representations, and in 2014 this was amended to exempt inputs or raw materials for pharmaceutical manufacturing in Kenya.[23] However, the amendment was silent on packaging: the Kenyan manufacturers had previously fought successfully to remove taxes from packaging inputs, and had then seen those gains reversed. It appears that Kenyan manufacturers' associations are able to exert more influence over relevant policies than their equivalents in Tanzania.

However, local manufacturers in the two countries have historically struggled to exert influence over policies of donors. Many donor policies have excluded local firms from domestic market segments, the most damaging having been the loss of most of the regional anti-malarials markets to donor-subsidized, WHO-prequalified external suppliers. The extent of local firms' collaboration with external donors and multilaterals has, however, been increasing recently. Examples include working with WHO and UNIDO projects to support technological upgrading; working with charities such as Drugs for Neglected Diseases (DNDi) to implement new formulations and achieve pre-qualification; and working with PEPFAR to supply gap-filling medicines to donor projects. This process of learning to exert influence and benefit from collaborative projects is an important element of firms' learning and upgrading in the strongly donor-influenced regulatory and policy environments within which these firms work.

Conclusion: building collaborative capabilities

The sharp process of institutional change in the health systems and medicines financing in Kenya and Tanzania has faced the largely locally owned manufacturers of medicines currently working in the two countries with major shifts in market structure, regulation, demand patterns and the political economy of policy influence. The big changes have included increasing liberalization and 'globalization' of the domestic markets for medicines, associated with a growing private health and retail pharmacy sector, especially strong in Kenya, and a sharp rise in the variety and volume of imports on the market.

The public sector market has also been globalized, with increasing donor pressure for large-scale open international tenders, pooled procurement and a ruthless focus on price. Donors have been able to exert leverage for this evolution because of the huge increase in external funding provided for medicines and the need for reform because of earlier problems with public tendering processes. One outcome has been a dominant international 'framing' of the supply chains and procurement issues as a challenge in linking 'pre-qualified' external suppliers to local patients. Barriers to domestic market entry for local firms were raised by these institutional changes, and domestic market linkages disaggregated.

Now, these disaggregated linkages need to be substantially and collaboratively rebuilt, and then sustained in a very open market environment. For this purpose, there is a highly important role for government. Key policy objectives should be to institute and enforce measures to enhance medicines access through public and faith-based facilities in the health sectors within both countries, and to shift procurement incentives towards encouraging purchasing from local suppliers.

At the same time, these policies can only be effective if they are designed in collaboration with the market actors who must build and manage the market linkages that allow effective domestic market supply. The MEDS example, though operating in a specific niche, suggests some of the key elements for the rebuilding of market linkages between health and industrial sectors. They include active consultation and working relationships between procurement agents and supplier firms; pre-qualification of local suppliers, with a strong element of quality control; and a necessary level of business autonomy in procurement decisions on price/quality trade-offs.

Some of these elements are observable also within public sector procurement and can be built upon to create cumulative improvement. Some medical and other supplies (such as furniture items) are bought by the public wholesalers from local suppliers under more flexible purchasing arrangements. Local firms actively produce and supply emergency items (and resent being called upon in this way after they have lost earlier tenders). Furthermore, the public wholesalers have the financial capability to offer more active collaboration, in the form of longer contract to incentivize suppliers' investments, and better credit terms, if they wish to do so. In Kenya, the decentralization reforms have given KEMSA more autonomy while shifting some demand to MEDS (PSP4H, 2014).

This (re)building of domestic linkages has to be done in the context, not only of high levels of external competition but also in the face of the very high level in each country of 'fragmentation' (Chuma and Okungu, 2011; McIntyre et al., 2008) in health financing, procurement, service supply and management, and in a context where government expenditure exerts little domestic market leverage, as documented above. Policy coherence between health and industrial policies, an essential objective for governments seeking developmental synergies, is not merely a set of government decisions, but a social construction that has to be built over time through institutional generation of collaborative capabilities in both sectors, and associated incentives for extracting mutual benefit. The Ethiopian governments' effort to combine health-sector improvement with industrial-sector support (Chapter 4) identifies the relevance of health-sector restructuring for strengthening local health-industry collaboration. The Brazilian experience explored in the next chapter reinforces this point.

Notes

1. This chapter is based on the research project *Industrial productivity and health sector performance*. The findings, interpretations, conclusions and opinions expressed are those of the authors and do not necessarily reflect the views or policies of DFID or the UK ESRC, whose financial support is gratefully acknowledged (project ES/J008737/1). Particular thanks to all our interviewees, who gave time within very pressured lives to talk to us, often at considerable length. Thanks also to participants in a Policy Dialogue workshop in REPOA, Dar es Salaam, June 2013, at which early findings from these surveys were presented and discussed, and to Watu Wamae for research collaboration and for comments on an earlier draft. The same disclaimer applies.
2. In Kenya, a set of 29 essential medicines, including ARVs, were used for the quantitative data collection (Kariuki et al., 2015); in Tanzania, a comparable set of 24 medicines was used (Tibandebage et al., 2014); the differences were largely the result of differing treatment regimes between the two countries.
3. For example, the WHO Health Systems Framework and its 'building blocks' are a framework for service delivery; http://www.wpro.who.int/health_services/health_systems_framework/en/. See also Kim et al. (2013) for the rise of 'health care delivery science' in the global health field.
4. WHO Global Health Observatory, http://apps.who.int/gho/data/node.main.78?lang=en (accessed 3 March 2015) (Kenya); http://apps.who.int/gho/data/node.main.75?lang=en (accessed 20 November 2014) (Tanzania).

5. Calculated by the authors from Ministry of Health, Health Management Information Systems data for 2010.
6. These data were collected in Kenya before the decentralization reforms that have allowed counties to diversify procurement sources for public health sector supplies.
7. Source: quantitative data and interviews, 2012–13.
8. All quotations are from fieldwork unless otherwise stated.
9. Source: interviews, KEMSA website, http://www.kemsa.co.ke/, UNIDO (2010).
10. http://www.msd.or.tz/index.php/aboutus/msd-organizationconsulted (accessed 27 March 2015).
11. Source: interviews.
12. Source interviews, see also Yadav (2014) and MSD (2013).
13. http://pfscm.org/pfscm consulted 6/3/15.
14. See http://apps.who.int/prequal/ consulted 27/3/15.
15. Source, interviews.
16. Calculated from MEDS (2013: 38), from sales of KShs 1.413 billion.
17. http://medeor.de/en/medeor-tanzania/purchasing-information.html (accessed 1 April 2015).
18. Source: interviews.
19. Source: interviews.
20. An HAI/WHO assessment of medicines procurement prices in 2004 confirmed this perception independently: MEDS procurement prices were somewhat higher than KEMSA procurement prices, though both were paying low prices by international standards; http://www.who.int/medicines/areas/technical_cooperation/MedicinepricesKenya.pdf (accessed 29 March 2015).
21. MEDS (2013) confirms a problem of rising debt that has to be addressed.
22. This shop was an Accredited Drug Dispensing Outlet (ADDO).
23. By the Value Added Tax (Amendment) Act, No. 7 of 2014, Kenya. Inputs or raw materials (either procured locally or imported) supplied to pharmaceutical manufacturers in Kenya for manufacturing of medicaments, as approved from time to time by the Cabinet Secretary for National Treasury in consultation with the Cabinet Secretary responsible for health, were added to list of exempts.

9

The Dissemination of Local Health Innovations: Political Economy Issues in Brazil

Erika Aragão, Jane Mary Guimarães and Sebastião Loureiro

Introduction

In a book exploring the scope for mutually supportive integration between addressing health care needs and promoting industrialization, Brazil's experience offers an important case study.[1] This chapter presents Brazil's main strategies to ensure access to medicines to tackle the population's principal health problems. It particularly aims to show how the principle of the universality of care has influenced industrial policies and production in the pharmaceutical sector. Although more than 25 years have passed since Unified Health System (*Sistema Único de Saúde*: SUS) was established, and much progress has been made, a great many challenges remain. This chapter focuses particularly on those related to access to health technologies.

The underlying premise of the Brazilian approach is that health is a social right and improving the health of individuals has a positive impact on society as a whole. Yet the sustainability of the health system depends on a domestic production system capable of producing the needed technologies for health care. That production system in turn constitutes an important economic sector, generating employment and income and capable of reducing external dependence in strategic areas. This chapter explores how this relationship is configured within Brazilian society, the progress made and challenges faced by attempts to guarantee a reduction in health inequalities, with the aim of increasing policy dialogue between Brazilian, African and other policy makers and researchers. Brazilian experience in the dissemination of local innovations to meet health needs could be learned from and drawn upon by other countries, including recognition of the huge challenges that remain.

New medical technologies hold great promise for improvements to the population's health, but they accentuate concerns about the amplification of already significant health inequalities, since their consumption is determined by a range of factors, including the socio-economic status of the patient and the existence of public systems that guarantee patient access (Goldman and Smith, 2005). The impact of new technologies on health disparities depends on how hard they are to adopt and who effectively receives treatment. They are not uniformly absorbed into health systems, nor is there a guarantee of access for all, even in systems with universal coverage (Loureiro et al., 2007).

In high-income countries, research and development (R&D) efforts may result in innovations driven by technology, despite a high degree of uncertainty. However, in developing countries, demand constitutes the principal stimulus for innovation. From this perspective, the legal framework and the organization of health systems may either direct the diffusion of technologies towards social interests or allow the process to occur in a manner more closely aligned with market interests.

For its part, health care is increasingly expensive and dependent on a series of technologies such as diagnostic and surgical equipment and pharmaceutical products. The factors responsible for significant increases in health spending as a proportion of a country's domestic income and which may compromise the sustainability of its health system, include: the cumulative nature of the use of medical technologies; the oligopolistic structure of the sector, which often includes temporary monopolies obtained via intellectual protection; increases in per capita income and life expectancy; and changes to the epidemiological profile.

The sustainability of health systems is therefore one of the greatest challenges for public administrations at a global level, particularly for countries with universal systems such as Brazil, a middle-income country. Since 1988, the Brazilian state has considered health as a right and its provision as a duty that must be guaranteed to all its citizens; this includes pharmaceutical health care, which is considered necessary for the guarantee of comprehensive services.

Given significant pressure for the systematic incorporation of new medicines into the Brazilian health system, the country has sought to incentivize the growth of domestic technological capability, reflecting the demands of its Unified Health System. From this perspective, innovation within this industry has significant relevance for Brazil's social and economic development and presents huge challenges, given the complexity of scientific and technological development activities, the political and institutional coordination required, the scarcity of resources and the nature of mechanisms for knowledge production and appropriation.

This is, therefore, a field that allies economic dimensions with a strong social dimension, requiring the mobilization of a broad regulatory and institutional apparatus. In this way, despite the crisis in the both the Keynesian and the welfare state, health continues to be one of the most significant areas of state intervention, both in the service sector and in scientific and technological activities (Aragão et al., 2014; Gadelha and Costa, 2012).

Pharmaceutical health care in Brazil: seeking to link economic and social logic

The logic of social rights

The Unified Health System (SUS) was instituted by the 1988 Federal Constitution, as a result of a widespread movement for the democratization of society and another within the health sector, known as Sanitary Reform, which sought to create a public health system for all the country's citizens (Paim, 2009). Since 1988, health has been considered an inalienable right, and the state is responsible for guaranteeing universal, comprehensive and equitable access to activities and services that include the prevention of diseases and the promotion and restoration of health.

Through the 1988 Federal Constitution, the health system was integrated into the social security system and the social care and welfare systems (Federal Constitution 1988, art. 194), becoming a sector without restrictions on beneficiaries, where access did not require users' contribution (Brasil, 1998, art. 196).

The interpretation of the concept of social justice in the Brazilian Federal Constitution is innovative, since it views social security as 'an integrated series of activities initiated by the public authorities and by society, aimed at security rights related to health, welfare and social care',[2] introducing the notion of universal social rights as a condition of citizenship. It recognizes social rights and asserts that it is the duty of the state to guarantee such rights.

In the case of the SUS, universality represents the opportunity for all citizens to use public health activities or services without barriers to access of an economic, physical or cultural nature; comprehensiveness is understood in relation to a series of coordinated and continuous preventative and curative, individual and collective activities and services, at all levels of system complexity; and equity contains within it a certain notion of justice. It recognizes that individuals are different from each other, and therefore deserve differentiated treatment. In this sense, access to medicines begins to constitute a right, in that it is a health care component at all levels of complexity.

The 1990 Organic Health Law (*Lei Orgânica da Saúde*: LOS) asserts that the execution of comprehensive therapeutic care activities falls to SUS, and this includes pharmaceutical health care, given that medicine is a strategic ingredient to support health activities and its absence may compromise treatment, affecting both the patient's quality of life and the problem-solving capacity of health activities.

To secure this, it is envisaged that the SUS, amongst other bodies, formulates public policies; develops programmes that enable the population's access to medicines, equipment, vaccines and other supplies to meet its health needs; and participates in their production, either directly through public laboratories, or indirectly, acting jointly with those economic and science and technology bodies aimed at guiding research, development and production in the public interest. Furthermore, it operates through agreements and partnerships with private pharmacies, enlarging distribution channels. This is regarded as a tense arena of negotiation between collective and private interests, highlighting the need for state action to ensure that the institutional framework functions adequately (Gadelha, 2006; Gadelha et al., 2012; Oliveira et al., 2006).

Brazilian pharmaceutical health care policy

The integration of pharmaceutical management with production policy is distinctive of the Brazilian approach. To secure its guarantee to supply medicines to the Brazilian population, the Ministry of Health needed to work with, amongst others, the economic and science and technology spheres as core elements in the conduct of policies that guarantee the production of pharmaceutical products designed to meet SUS needs.

Although the right to pharmaceutical health care has been enshrined in the SUS since its creation, a specific policy – the National Medicine Policy (*Política Nacional de Medicamentos*: PNM) – was only created in 1998. In 2004, this was superseded by the National Policy of Pharmaceutical Care (*Política Nacional de Assistência Farmacêutica*: PNAF) (Brasil, 2004a). Overall, this strategy extends the Brazilian population's access to medicines and is therefore based on the same principles that guide SUS. This policy is based on the promotion of the rational use of medicines. It includes a range of adjustments to pharmacy practices and regulation, the production of essential medicines and scientific and technological development. Thus several initiatives were taken to enhance the national production of pharmaceutical drugs such as qualifying the public laboratories, and incentives to private groups to produce priority drugs to meet the SUS demand with financial support from distinct governmental agencies and offices other than the health sector.

The financing of public pharmaceutical health care programmes is the responsibility of the three spheres of SUS management: the federal, state and municipal governments. The allocation of resources to finance the acquisition of medicines and supplies is organized into three pharmaceutical health care components: basic, strategic and specialized. Each component includes resources for financing one or more programmes or activities, and each has its own features related to planning and administration. Medicines for HIV/AIDS, cancer and coagulopathy are not included within any of these components, but are funded exclusively by the federal government.

The federal government also bears the cost of supplying medicines through the Brazilian Popular Pharmacy (*Programa Farmácia Popular do Brasil*: PFPB) and the *Here There Is a Popular Pharmacy* (*Aqui Tem Farmácia Popular*) programmes (described below), which provide certain medicines either free of charge or at low cost, making them more accessible to the population (Brasil, 2004b).

Links to technological development in medicines

With the implementation of the PNM, Brazil expanded a strategic project for the technological development of medicines, initially through public production of essential medicines by laboratories belonging to the SUS (currently 19 SUS public laboratories). Two notable health policies in this initial period were investments by the Ministry of Health to allow public laboratories to produce less-expensive versions of anti-retroviral drugs, beginning in 1996, and the implementation of the Generic Medicines Law in 1999.

Brazil's policy of universal access to free anti-retroviral treatment supplied directly to the public sector has been in force since 1996, and has been an exemplary model for global efforts to reduce the HIV epidemic. However, it has also involved a significant increase in Ministry of Health spending on medicines, which rose from approximately US$35 million in 1997 to a landmark US$305 million in 1999 (Loyola, 2008). The vast majority of these medicines were imported, implying that fluctuations in the dollar led to interruptions in supply. The response was investment in the domestic production of medicines.

This initiative inaugurated the systematic establishment of agreements between the public and private sectors for the transfer of technology to public laboratories that manufacture medicines. Currently, the country is capable of producing 10 of the 23 medicines that constitute the HIV/AIDS treatment cocktail. Farmanguinhos alone, the Oswaldo Cruz Foundation (FIOCRUZ) Laboratory and part of the Ministry of Health, produces and distributes seven of the ten anti-retroviral drugs produced in the country (Fiocruz, 2014). FIOCRUZ is the largest public health institution in the country, for research, education, health care, development and pharmaceutical drugs production. Farmanguinhos is the unit for the production of pharmaceutical chemicals, and Biomanguinhos for the production of biologicals. These units, like others public laboratories, supply the specific programmes of the Ministry of Health.

The Generic Medicines Law enabled competition on the part of the public and private domestic industry in the market for drugs with expired patents. On the other hand, from 1996 onwards, the Patent Law (1996) recognized pharmaceutical patents in Brazil by adhering to the Trade-Related Aspects of Intellectual Property Rights (TRIPS). This had a negative impact on the domestic industry, one of whose competitive pillars was the commercialization of similar medicines (copies of the branded drugs) and which could not compete with the large international oligopolies in the production of innovative medicines. The domestic market configuration changed as a result. National companies focussed on the production of generic versions and multinationals increased their share in reference products that are more expensive that generic versions (Capanema and Palmeira, 2004; Gomes et al., 2014)

Strengthening industrial policy for pharmaceuticals

However, the right to pharmaceutical assistance within the SUS and the need to provide essential products to the Brazilian population at accessible prices required a series of measures to strengthen the pharmaceutical industry in Brazil, particularly in sectors serving the principal public health requirements. In the face of these challenges, the strengthening of the pharmaceutical chain became a strategic objective of Brazil's industrial and development policies.

Several public bodies, including the National Development Bank (*Banco Nacional de Desenvolvimento:* BNDES), started to support the development of the country's pharmaceutical chain. The Support Program for the Development of the Pharmaceutical Productive Chain (*Programa de*

Apoio à Cadeia Farmacêutica: ROFARMA), launched in 2004, provided specific BNDES credit support to contribute to growth in the domestic pharmaceutical industry.

Between 2004 and 2013, BNDES invested almost 5 billion Brazilian Reals in approximately 110 operations, spread across lines of support aimed at production, innovation, restructuring and biotechnology, and focusing on domestically owned companies and public laboratories. In its first phase, PROFARMA constituted an important source of funds to ensure that the national pharmaceutical complex complied with the new regulatory demands, which had become much more rigorous after the 1999 creation of the National Health Surveillance Agency (*Agência Nacional de Vigilância Sanitária*: ANVISA). However, throughout its existence, the programme adapted to industry needs, focusing on the production of generic medicines, on innovation and on the development of biotechnology, due to the increasing application of biopharmaceuticals in the treatment strategies for a range of diseases, particularly chronic non-communicable illnesses (Palmeira Filho et al., 2012).

These and other initiatives resulted in increased investment in research and development (R&D) within the Brazilian pharmaceutical industry. According to the Survey of Technological Innovation (*Pesquisa de Inovação*: PINTEC), in 2003, R&D investment by the pharmaceutical industry corresponded to 0.5% of net revenue, slightly lower than industrial sector average. In 2011, this had risen to 2.4% of net revenue, while the average for the industrial sector remained at around 0.7% (PINTEC/IBGE, 2011).

Local production for domestic requirements

The combination of the legal framework and the SUS organizational system has sought to direct the diffusion of technologies towards social interests, rather than allowing the process to occur in a manner aligned only with market interests. The data show that the investments in the pharmaceutical supply chain have been reflected in the consolidation of the local generic medicine sector. Since 2004, the total pharmaceutical market in Brazil has grown exponentially, both in number of units sold (9% per annum) and in real value (10% per annum), reaching almost R$ 40 billion in 2013 (Gomes et al., 2014; Interfarma, 2014). The market for generic medicines has provided a significant element of this growth, since in terms of unit sales, generic drugs' share of total sales leapt from 9% in 2004 to 27% in 2013 (Figure 9.1), while sales of both brand-name drugs and similar drugs fell (Gomes et al., 2014; Kaplan et al., 2013).

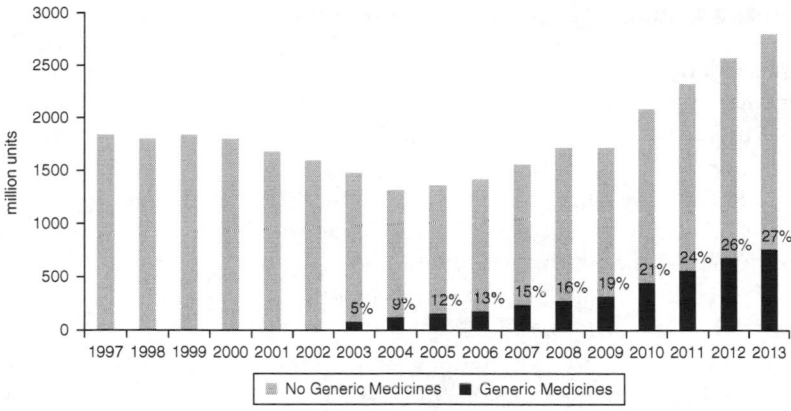

Figure 9.1   The Brazilian pharmaceutical market (unit sales), 1997–2013

Source: Drawn by the authors from data sourced from Progenericos (2014) and Gomes et al. (2014).

As the Gomes et al. (2014) study points out, the opportunities generated by the dynamism of the internal market, increasing improvements to sanitary regulation in Brazil and public policies have all been exploited by domestically owned companies, whose domestic market share rose from 30% at the beginning of the 2000s to over 50% in 2012.

In 2013, five Brazilian pharmaceutical companies were among the ten biggest companies in the Brazilian national market, measured by total sales. Generic drugs had almost 30% of the Brazilian market, measured in units sold, 15% by total sales. Furthermore, 85% of the drugs available in the Popular Pharmacy Program are generic drugs. As regards the origin and ownership of the capital invested, about 90% of the companies producing generic drugs are Brazilian, 6.3% are from India, 0.8% from Germany, 0.6% are Canadian and 0.5% Spanish (Progenericos, 2014).

The share of household income spent on medicines is higher in Brazil for those on lower incomes. Medicines account for 4.2% of spending in households with a monthly income of up to US$452.20. This corresponds to 76.4% of health expenditure for households within this income bracket. For those with a monthly income over US$5,655.20, spending on medicines is only 1.9% of income (IBGE-POF, 2008–09). Therefore, the SUS is a decisive instrument for the reduction of inequalities, in coordination with the economic and science and technology fields, and for the promotion of health as a priority for the sustainable development of the country (Gadelha et al, 2014).

Public demand and domestic medicines production

The enlargement of the state's purchasing power has been a fundamental strategy for extending access to medicines and strengthening the production base to address SUS interests, both public and private. Out of a range of important inter-sectoral initiatives (Aragão et al., 2014; Gadelha and Costa, 2012), two programmes particularly help to understand how current initiatives to strengthen the health sector in Brazil have had an impact on the domestic production of medicines.

The first, the Brazilian Popular Pharmacy Programme (*Programa Farmácia Popular do Brasil*: PFPB), was established in 2004 within the Ministry of Health in order to extend the population's access to essential medicines. It was hugely important in the growth of the generic medicines sector in Brazil, since its establishment relied heavily on the extension of the domestic production base. The second, the Partnerships for Productive Development (*Parcerias para o Desenvolvimento Produtivo*: PDPs), begun in 2012, aimed to strengthen the domestic pharmo-chemical and medicine industries, particularly in more innovative areas such as biotechnology, in order to reduce external dependence in key strategic areas.

Industrial policy in Brazil generally recognizes the potential of public procurement to promote competition in markets where government demand is significant, such as health. Rules have been defined for the use of public purchasing power, which allow a price preference of up to 25% for purchases from domestic producers, using a method of calculation that takes into account employment and income generation, impact on tax revenues, national development and other factors.[3]

The Brazilian Popular Pharmacy Programme (PFPB)

The PFPB expanded access to medication for the most common diseases, benefitting people on low incomes and enabling access to low-cost medicines for users of the private health network. Federal government initiatives included centralization of the medicines procurement and administrative improvements. Medicines were acquired, distributed and managed centrally by FIOCRUZ, a unit of the Ministry of Health. This procurement strategy was underpinned by a guarantee of state funding.

In order to meet the pharmaco-therapeutic needs of PFPB users, the Ministry of Health established a list of medicines based on the National Essential Medicines List, which was defined using epidemiological criteria, taking into account the principal diseases that affect the Brazilian population and the treatments that have the greatest impact on household budgets. The list also considers the medicines contained within the Ministry of Health's Welfare Programmes, the production capacity of the Official Pharmaceutical Laboratories and registration as a generic medicine (Brasil, 2005; 2010).

Initially restricted to the SUS network, from 2006 the Programme was extended to the private sector through partnerships with pharmacies. In 2011, with the launch of the Brazil Without Extreme Poverty Plan (*Plano Brasil Sem Miséria*), the municipalities included in this plan to eradicate extreme poverty were prioritized by the PFPB, in line with criteria adopted by the Ministry of Social Development and Combating Hunger.

Given the country's epidemiological profile, one programme priority is to extend access to hypertension and diabetes medication. About 33 million Brazilians have been diagnosed with hypertension and 80% (or approximately 22.6 million hypertension sufferers) are treated within the public health network. According to 2011 data, more than 7.5 million Brazilians have a diabetes diagnosis and about 6 million of these patients are treated within the public system. These diseases are included in the risk factors for cardiovascular problems, the greatest cause of mortality in Brazil (WHO, 2012). Through the activities of the PFPB aimed at non-communicable diseases (NCDs), medicines for the treatment of hypertension, diabetes and, latterly, asthma began to be dispensed to patients free of charge. In 2011, respiratory diseases were the third cause of death in the country (MS/PFPB, 2014; WHO, 2012).

Currently, the PFPB provides access to essential medicines for a wide range of patients with a private medical prescription, complementary to SUS, at low cost or free of charge. The initial list of medicines included 84 pharmaceuticals, dispensed to the population using their generic names, representing more than 1,200 commercial medicine brands registered in the pharmaceutical market. The PFPB provides for the inclusion of new products and takes into account regional variations, given its territorial coverage and the diversity of the epidemiological profiles across the different regions of the country. The first additions to the PFPB list of medicines occurred in 2004, when seven new items were added. Since then, new updates to the list have been made in order to increase its coverage. By 2013, more than 550 medicines had been made available (Brasil, 2004b; MS/PFPB, 2014).

It is worth noting that the products distributed through the PFPB are acquired through specific procurement processes, not to be confused with public procurement by federal, state, federal district and municipal governments. The programme prioritizes purchase of medicines produced by official government laboratories (public industrial units) and generic medicines (acquired through a bidding process); a pharmaceutical's availability as a generic medicine is therefore a factor for inclusion into the PFPB medicine selection process.

The expansion of the PFPB budget, of the accredited network and of the number of municipalities served has both reflected demand and coincided with growth in the generics market in Brazil (Figure 9.2).

By March 2015, more than 33,000 establishments had been accredited by the PFPB, distributed across 4,351 of the 5,570 Brazilian municipalities and providing almost 80% coverage in municipalities with Popular Pharmacy establishments. This is in contrast to 2006, when 2,955 establishments were accredited in 594 municipalities, with coverage of only 11% of municipalities. To this end, the programme's budget has increased significantly over the years.

Federal spending on the PFPB, in real terms in 2013 prices, has jumped from a little over R$35.7 million in 2006 to R$879.5 million in 2011, R$1.4 billion in 2012 and R$1.9 billion in 2013. In 2013, total spending on medicines rose to slightly over R$10 billion (Sala de Situacão em Saude, 2015). These data demonstrate the programme's importance and the need to coordinate it with production development policies, since rising demand has driven the increased production of generic medicines.

In turn, the Ministry of Health budget grew from R$59 billion in 2006 to R$100.5 billion in 2013, also in real terms. By 2013, the amount

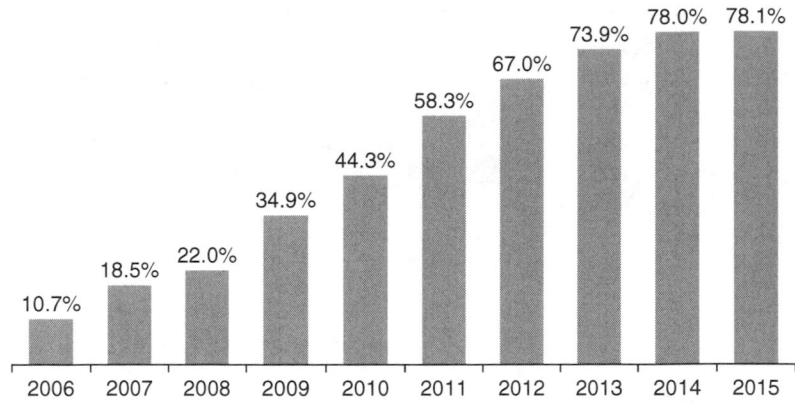

Figure 9.2   Percentage of municipalities covered by the PFPB, 2006–15

Source: Drawn by the authors from data from Sala de Situacão em Saude (2015), accessed 8 March 2015.

spent on medicines represented more than 10% of the total Ministry of Health budget. Public purchasing is responsible for 30% of the country's demand for medicine (Interfarma, 2014).

Strengthening public industrial production units has been a strategy to secure production in less intensive knowledge areas, such as generic products, in several Ministry of Health programmes. This approach also applies in more intensive knowledge areas, such as biological products, where the proportion of total Ministry of Health medicines expenditure has grown significantly, due to high prices, and contributed to the health sector's trade deficit. The Partnerships for Productive Developments (PDPs) were launched as a response to this.

Inter-sector coordination has enabled the creation of significant regulatory frameworks, which have tended to have a positive impact on the strategic sectors for the country's development. Significant features of these regulatory frameworks of support for innovation are Law 10973 of 2004 (Brasil, 2004c), known as the Innovation Law,[4] and the Goods Law of 2005 (Brasil, 2005), which were important for the development of Brazil's health-related goods industry. Furthermore, the PDPs have been the object of inter- and cross-sector policies aimed at reducing external dependency, in favour of innovation and the extension of domestic capacity to produce strategic technologies, including biologicals, for SUS.

Partnerships for productive development (*Parcerias para o Desenvolvimento Produtivo*: PDPs)

The PDPs form part of the policies in the Greater Brazil Plan, which contains guidelines that focus on innovation and productivity growth in the Brazilian industrial complex. They are one of the components of the Programme for Investment in the Health Industrial Complex (*Programa de Investimento no Complexo Industrial da Saúde:* PROCIS). The latter was launched in 2012 to coordinate the national strategy for development and innovation in health through investment in public producers and in public infrastructure for production and innovation. It is thus aimed at strengthening Brazilian industry, providing the country with greater autonomy for the production of strategic SUS technologies.

There are currently 19 SUS public laboratories involved in PDPs. They are responsible for the production of medicines, serum and vaccines to meet the country's public health needs. However, many products are still imported from other countries, and gaps in domestic production as well as the high cost of medicines may hinder access. Through PROCIS, the Ministry of Health has invested in public companies' infrastructure and workforce training (MS/DECIIS, 2015).

The partnerships are established between public drug production companies and the private production sector, aiming to absorb the technology to make new formulations. Thus, foreign companies with technological dominance commit to transferring to domestic companies the technology required to produce the medicine, as well as to produce within the country, to some degree, the active pharmaceutical ingredients (APIs) (the substance responsible for the treatment), over a five-year period. In return, the government guarantees exclusivity in procuring these products – at values below those quoted in the global market – over the same period. Until this point, since 1985, when the self-sufficiency programme in immunobiologicals was launched, there had been no other stimulus or public production investment programmes (Brasil, 2012 – Portaria nº 837/2012).

At the end of the technology transfer period, the domestic public laboratory will initiate autonomous production of the medicine in order to meet domestic demand. With production conducted inside the country, public laboratories will begin reducing dependence on imports (as illustrated by Figure 9.3), extending their competitive advantage and technological capacity.

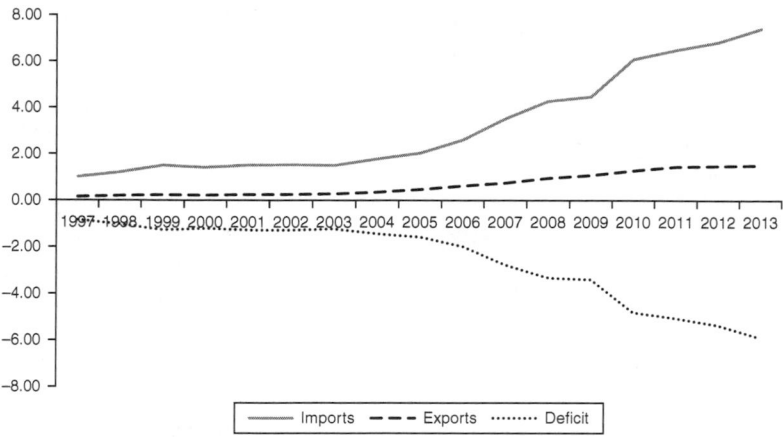

Figure 9.3 Pharmaceutical products: Balance of trade, Brazilian exports and imports (US$ billion FoB)

Source: Drawn by the author from data from MDIC/Secex/Sistema Alice apud, INTERFARMA, 2014.

As well as generating significant savings for the Ministry (estimated at approximately R$4 billion a year) and reducing the country's dependence on importing products (Figure 9.3), the partnerships signed thus far have also benefitted the population, since they guarantee the supply of essential medicines to the SUS network. In 2012, more than R$250 million was invested in public pharmaceutical companies' infrastructure and workforce training – more than five times the average investment for the previous twelve years (R$42 million). Between 2000 and 2011, total government investment was R$ 512 million.

At the end of 2014, the Ministry of Health was involved in 104 product development partnerships, involving 19 public and 57 private laboratories. These agreements provide for the development of 101 products (66 medicines, 7 vaccines and 28 other health products).

Partnerships are focussed on the production of biological medicines, which have an average value significantly higher than traditional medicines and are principally used for the treatment of non-communicable diseases, such as various types of cancer and rheumatic problems. Although biological medicines represent approximately 5% of the medicines purchased by the Ministry of Health (measured by unit sales), they represent 49% of spending. Importing these products has been one of the main reasons for the increase in the health trade deficit, which leapt from approximately US$1 billion in 1997 to more than US$5 billion in 2013.

Reducing dependence on imported biopharmaceuticals by taking advantage of the predicted expiry of a series of product patents over the next few years may extend the population's access to treatments for those diseases for which the technology is demonstrably more effective than traditional medicine. In 2015, more than 25 biopharmaceutical products are available in SUS for the treatment of cancer, rheumatoid arthritis and other chronic diseases. Almost all are in the process of technology transfer to the national public companies.

In the specific case of cancer, the ability to introduce biopharmaceuticals for treatment has proven to be important in reducing inequality in access to this type of treatment. The Aragão et al. (2012) study demonstrated that biopharmaceuticals not incorporated into SUS were usually accessed via legal proceedings and that their implementation was restricted to such demands, prioritizing users of the private health system. In 2010, the federal government spent US$3.4 million on responding to judicial demands related to the supply of biological therapies to treat cancer; since 2012, some of these have been incorporated into SUS. This signifies per capita spending of up to US$183,300 in 2009 and 2010.

The public health system is responsible for the treatment of approximately 80% of cancer cases in Brazil. From 1999 to 2010, federal expenditure on chemotherapy alone rose in real terms from R$780 million to more than R$1 billion. In 2010, total expenditure, including spending on radiotherapy, surgery and radioiodine therapy, passed a landmark R$1.5 billion, or US$852 million (Aragão et al., 2014; MS, 2011). Spending on oncology medication represented more than 10% of total spending on medicines, with the largest burden coming from the acquisition of biological medication. With the exception of immunobiologicals (serum and vaccines) and one group of high-cost medicines aimed at a broad range of rare pathologies, oncology drugs accounted for the largest share of total Ministry of Health spending on medicines. Biopharmaceuticals, which will be produced through PDPs, currently represent R$1.8 billion per year of Ministry of Health public procurement expenditure (MS/DECIIS, 2015).

In the case of cancer, considered here as an example, one needs to remember that treatment based on biological medicines is very costly, given that this is a high-complexity production category and, therefore, one with higher costs. Furthermore, it is more difficult to copy biological medicines once their patents have expired. Unlike chemicals, which may be copied as a whole, proteins are not amenable to identical copying; such copies are therefore biosimilar and require specific regulation. Moreover, companies in this sector have extremely high powers of negotiation, given the market concentration in a very small set of businesses.

Making use of public purchasing power and establishing policies to promote the domestic pharmaceutical industry, including public laboratories, are strategies to protect against the monopolistic practices exercised by the large pharmaceutical companies. These practices are made possible by a regime of intellectual protection highly favourable to economies in developed countries. In a sector in which the substitution of goods is highly limited, the persistence of such practices will certainly deepen social inequalities at both international and national level. From this perspective, policies that take into account the degree of market concentration may ensure the introduction of innovative technologies, while at the same time reducing inequalities in access to medicine.

Concluding reflections

Since the promulgation of Brazil's 1988 Constitution, significant progress has been made in improving the population's access to health services, including to pharmaceutical health care. A series of legal and regulatory frameworks have been established in order to guarantee the free or subsidized provision of medicine to the population. To guarantee the domestic production of essential products, the Ministry of Health has become the country's central pivot in ensuring the local development of production capacity in order to develop technologies to meet SUS needs.

The Ministry of Health has managed to use its purchasing power to guide public and private investment in the interests of the SUS. This has reduced the main risk of technological innovation, which is the absence of a market. Product Development Partnerships have had huge success in transferring technology from the private sector (particularly the sector's large company leaders) to the public sector, which receives the technology and jointly develops the ingredients. Thus, even if production is shared with the private sector, the technology domain has moved to the public sector, as the regulatory framework indicates. However, the final results of the new model of partnerships established from 2012 should also be evaluated in the future, in relation to the ability to internalize the skills for production of APIs. Previous partnerships between private and public companies, as in the case of anti-retroviral drugs, allowed domestic production, but the country continued to depend on imports of the APIs.

What we observe is the construction of public policies to guide a range of health industry actors towards a social need, in this case the demand for medicine. To achieve this, the Ministry of Health has begun to coordinate policies traditionally regarded in Brazil as belonging to the economic sphere. Such orientation shifts the production logic of capitalist reproduction guided by the market, directing public and private investment towards the production of goods aimed at meeting SUS's priority health needs.

Such initiatives have led to successful actions, such as improved access to treatment for HIV/AIDS, cancer, diabetes, hypertension and a series of other diseases prevalent in the country, either through direct SUS provision or mediated through the PFPB in the form of free or low-cost distribution through the country's network of pharmacies. These initiatives in turn have contributed to the development of a domestic generic medicine industry capable of producing technologies to meet public and private health demands at competitive prices, as well as developing production capacity in more innovative areas, such as biopharmaceuticals.

The use of procurement powers and the policies to incentivize the domestic pharmaceutical industry, including public pharmaceutical companies, are forms of protection from the monopolistic practices exercised by the large pharmaceutical corporations. Such practices are made possible through an intellectual protection regime which is extremely favourable to the economies of high-income countries. In a sector in which the substitution of goods is extremely limited, the persistence of such practices clearly deepens social inequalities at both national and international level.

However, huge challenges remain. The country remains a large-scale importer of pharmaceuticals and medicine. The construction of internal production capacity to reduce external dependency is a long-term process, involving heavy investment.

The production of generic medicines is extremely important in meeting domestic health needs, but it does not help to reduce the deficit because it is based on the import of active ingredients and, in certain cases, of formulations which are then combined. There is now a need for a policy that enables Brazilian companies to grow and acquire know-how in the development of generic medicines so they can make the leap towards the production of a more intensive local technology synthesis and broaden their portfolio of similar and innovative medicines for the market.

Notes

1. The research project that was the basis for this chapter received financial support from the National Council for Technological and Scientific Development (CNPq) through a grant to the Instituto Nacional de Ciência e Tecnologia em Saúde (CITECS) – National Institute of Science and Health Technology. The authors would like to thank Cressida Evans for the translation into English from the Portuguese version of this paper.
2. Federal Constitution law: Article 194: Social security encompasses a set of integrated actions by the public power and the civil society geared to assure the rights related to health, social security and social assistance. Article 196. Health is a right assured to all citizens and a state duty warranted through social and economic policies with the objective of reducing the risk of disease and other health impairment, and universal and egalitarian access to health actions for prevention, protection and recovery care (Brasil, 1988).
3. Law 12349/2010 and regulated by Decree 7546/2011.
4. Redrafted in Law no 12349, 2010.

10
Healthy Industries and Unhealthy Populations: Lessons from Indian Problem-Solving

Smita Srinivas

Introduction

The Indian health industry, with substantial pharmaceuticals and biopharmaceuticals capability, has been called 'Supplier to the World'. This industry has had three defining policy environments running from 1950 to 2000, the last of which is arguably still ongoing. These three environments are distinct *market* environments, in which the range of market instruments used has been notable and the public gains to which they have been put have been noteworthy (Srinivas, 2004; 2012).

In earlier work (Srinivas, 2012) I have provided an explanatory framework for addressing the long timeline this history represents in the political economy of health plans in a late industrial push. In the process of analyzing 50 years of capability building, that study demonstrated that India had accomplished a great deal on the supply of medicines, especially generics, vaccines, and diagnostic kits, but was far less impressive in its health outcomes. This chapter builds further on the analysis in that work, but specifically turns its attention to *problem-solving*: the type of state capacity required to reconcile industrial and health goals as an essential part of development plans (Srinivas, 2014a). In examining the experience of the First Market Environment, this chapter argues that no explanation of its history is complete, indeed at all relevant, unless we attend to why a state so capable along one dimension can be so wanting in another (Srinivas, 2004; 2012).[1]

The importance of India's 'First Market Environment'

The First Market Environment (FME) had two distinct market phases: Phase I, from 1950 through the 1960s, and then Phase II running still powerfully until the late 1970s. Phase I was the *public sector* production effort under immense state regulation. This period included the Industries Development and Regulation Act (IDRA) of the 1950s that had been designed to boost indigenous production, diversification and investment, followed by the Industrial Policy Resolution of 1956, the Monopoly and Restrictive Trade Practices Act of 1969 and the Drugs (Display of Prices) Order promulgated in 1962 which was then adapted many times over in both the First and Second Market Environments.

In contrast to Phase I of the FME during which the public sector led in most respects, Phase II of the FME was marked by a focus on Indian *private firms*. Again, the state was busy. Its actions included the withdrawal of permissions for industrial diversification to foreign-owned firms in 1970, the Drug Price Control Order (DPCO) in 1970 and two changes to the Indian Patent Act in 1970 and 1972. Then, in 1978, the New Drug Policy (NDP) of the Government of India followed. The NDP provided explicit goals (although some in conflict) and three powerful categories of its own for drugs and their production licenses: 17 essential drugs preferentially and solely allocated to the public sector, 27 drugs for production only by Indian firms and 64 drugs open to production by anyone (for details, see Srinivas, 2012: chapter 3).

The Second Market Environment (SME) overlaps slightly with Phase II of the FME in the continuing focus on essential medicines. It runs from the 1980s and into the 1990s. However, the SME is distinct in the receding power of the state and the visibility instead of three powerful international effects on Indian firms especially in the 1980s. These included the three 'Ws': the Waxman-Hatch Act of the US (1984), which provided strong incentives for foreign companies that manufactured generics; the WTO's new pressures (1985) on the Trade in Intellectual Property Rights (TRIPs) harmonization and patent reforms; and the WHO and other multilateral agencies' procurement efforts for vaccines and other drugs which disproportionately influenced the technical standards of production (Srinivas, 2004; 2012).

In summary, Phase I of the FME built a political rhetoric of universal access while using strong state controls of the market and privileges of the public sector; Phase II of the FME showed a strong push to domestic, private sector capabilities while using public health drugs such as antibiotics to channel both policy design and private sector behaviour. Indigenous supply capabilities were therefore built over the two Phases, first in the public, then in the private sector, of deep investments, slow technological learning and directed technology transfer. By the end of the FME in the early 1980s, India had emerged as a redoubtable contender amongst developing nations with pharmaceutical capability, and was challenging even some industrialized economies.

The industrial capabilities of the FME were built with clearer plans for public health – such as the supply of essential medicines – than in any subsequent period (Srinivas, 2004; 2012). Unlike the FME, which was inward-looking in order to build indigenous capabilities, the state in the SME especially from the early 1980s used a variety of market and non-market instruments to induce firms to export. Because of the considerable capabilities built in the FME, private indigenous firms stood to make lucrative gains from export markets. Unlike the FME, the SME through the overseas buying instruments of the 1980s was determinedly focussed on upgrading for export markets and on what I have argued elsewhere is the welfare-state priorities of other nations, not necessarily those of India (Srinivas, 2011; 2012).

The SME acted as an important culling zone for firms that were internationally uncompetitive. It also heralded international influences on Indian firms that could not be carefully scripted and regulated by the state. With growing vaccine capability alongside generics, the SME also signalled the growing attraction of large-scale procurement from multilateral agency buyers such as UNICEF and the WHO. The state was undoubtedly less able to control export markets.

Finally, what followed and arguably still exists is a less distinct Third Market Environment (TME) associated with technological shifts in biopharmaceuticals begun in the 1980s and into the 2000s. In important respects these capabilities grew alongside and converged with vaccines in the SME, and with a range of other products and processes in the TME. The state in the TME was far less visible relative to the FME, but more decisive than in the SME. Yet, because of shifting technological considerations, the state's control of domestically owned indigenous private firms far was less than in even the SME.

This Third Market Environment provides an uncertain regulatory environment for new technological frontiers, where the national ownership and national priorities are more ambiguous. Substantial mergers and acquisitions have occurred, new technology capabilities are emerging and new regulatory zones in science and engineering are being explored. Furthermore, manufacturing capabilities have taken something of a backseat to the build-out of private sector opportunities in insurance, logistics, clinics, hospitals and so forth. Technological advances have created the need for a fundamental new balancing between production capabilities and the certainty of access to medicines.

Problem-solving versus state capacity

The three market environments exemplify different tensions arising from growing supply capabilities. How then can industrial and health goals be reconciled as an essential element of development planning? The argument here is that to address this question it is insufficient to focus on the diffuse notion of state capacity. Rather, much more can be induced from a focus on problem-solving, to see how industrial capabilities can inch closer to health outcomes. Should the health industry be an economic engine or a means to healthier populations? If it is a means, then the outcomes should be measured in terms of healthier populations. If it is an end, then some troubling developmental tensions remain.

What, then, is missing in the explanations to date? The two-decade period of the FME requires dissection because it is tempting to see the technological supply-side gains from start to finish in the relatively straightforward terms of a move from less to more capable state and firms. Without the detailed analysis of subsequent environments and of the state's struggle to align industry and health, the FME is itself difficult to bookend and resolve. What becomes hidden is substantial variation in the health climate within which the industry was steeped, and the obscure logics by which certain industrial policies were prioritized over health needs.

For late industrial economies such as India, the means rhetoric is far more visible in the FME, contrasting with the ends rhetoric in the SME and TME. The FME offers the first environment in which the nation-state appears explicitly and self-consciously to foster industrial and health policies moving closer together. It was the first and only environment (Srinivas, 2012) where the range of instruments for policy and planning were so wide across both industry and healthcare; they are far less visible in later phases (see also Chaudhuri, 1986; Sahu, 1998; Srinivas, 2004).

These national politics of the FME include autonomous nation-building faced with immense hurdles of technology transfer and the realpolitik of picking international partner nations. The crucial point is that the FME was an important industrial development 'First', as well as a 'Market' first. It was the epitome of a nationally structured and regulated set of market environments across two phases (public and private sector industrial capabilities) aimed at building health successes.

The lion's share of attention has focussed on the technical details of the FME. Indeed, there is much to extol on the industry side. In comparison with Brazil, for instance, the sheer volume of Indian firms, and the concerted set of national industrial policies to keep out foreign firms, boost inward technology transfer and develop close state-business compacts, points to a redoubtable Indian advance. The broader notion of state capacity helps us less in explaining why the state was much less successful in ensuring better health delivery in later years, precisely when industrial capabilities were growing stronger. It is clear that simple causal explanations from industry to health or vice versa offer an incomplete analysis.

Sahu (1998), for example, clearly demonstrates how tenuous was the link to the technology frontier, and how contested in many respects (although ultimately collaborative) the relationship between firms and the government became in the effort to research, develop and manufacture at home. Indeed, some of the contention between domestic firms and the government was ultimately resolved precisely because the needs of the nation rose to the top, and this was accomplished both rhetorically as well as pragmatically (Chaudhuri, 1986; Sahu, 1998). This pragmatism at least at national policy levels allowed a series of joint initiatives for technology transfer to be put into place between Indian and foreign firms and research institutes. It is clear that some types of problem-solving – such as those focussed on technological learning – were privileged over others.

The FME can be understood as a concerted national policy effort to synchronize the production of essential items to address several subsectors of health care needs and ensuring access for the population. This entailed an effort across multiple geographic territories, institutional navigation in India's complex quasi-federal system of central and state governments, and of different urban and rural development planning and governance contexts (Srinivas, 2012). Evidence of this diversity is seen today, where adjacent subnational states may vary noticeably in strategies and instruments to regulate their health industry and its firms.[2] Indeed, we could argue that state capacity not only varies but that the need to problem-solve becomes more acute, not less, as technological capabilities advance. Waiting for industrial capabilities to evolve fully before systematically addressing health outcomes appears to be a dubious recipe.

Problem-solving capacity can therefore be termed the ability to frame, formulate and attempt to solve complex development challenges (see also Srinivas, 2014a). Problem-solving is arguably like exercising a muscle. The emphasis therefore is on the attempt to solve complex problems, not necessarily on solving them. The more one exercises the muscle (the attempt to solve), the stronger the muscle (ability to problem-solve) becomes. The big difference, however, is that the metaphor of exercising a muscle refers to single individuals, whereas the attempt to problem-solve complex problems requires institutional and organizational muscle. In other words, even if an individual might be able to think ahead to solutions, a truly complex social problem requires institutional and organizational mechanisms to experiment and seed the solution. This is what we might term 'the institutionalization' of the solution.

The tradition of using a grounded problem-solving approach is hardly new in development. Proponents such as Albert Hirschman (1967) used such thinking to probe public performance in development projects and to understand how political and economic reform occurred. Despite such a history of use, however, the more general idea of governance has risen to define and to shape concepts of state capacity, and the more specific problem-solving capacity has been obscured. One might even suggest that such problem-solving muscle should be the core of the state's capacity in development and health, especially for late industrial economies where such substantial technological capabilities are being fostered (Srinivas, 2014a). The FME is an inspirational story when analyzed as state capacity directed towards building technological capabilities. It provides a more cautionary tale when seen through the lens of state efforts in problem-solving for healthier populations.

Problem-solving heuristics as a dynamic element of state capacity

The rhetorical 'states versus markets' development debate is not very helpful in the dilemma of effective policy design. The institutional triad (Figure 10.1) is a heuristic developed in Srinivas (2012) to show a way to understand the evolution of the industry as a whole, and the timeline of the Indian case in comparison with others. It offers a first means of comparative analysis in problem-solving, and a long timeline to understand the difficult process of planning on three particular institutional fronts: (1) production, (2) consumption/demand and (3) delivery. The health industry, after all, has several complex relationships to consider and is not easily divided under traditional ministries and agencies. The Health Ministry, for example, may sometimes control the moral high ground, but the Industries Ministry drives the dynamics of investment and the returns of firms. The triad therefore makes the policy levers and their institutional environment more evident. It reminds us that there is no single good or bad option in absolute terms, but there always exist

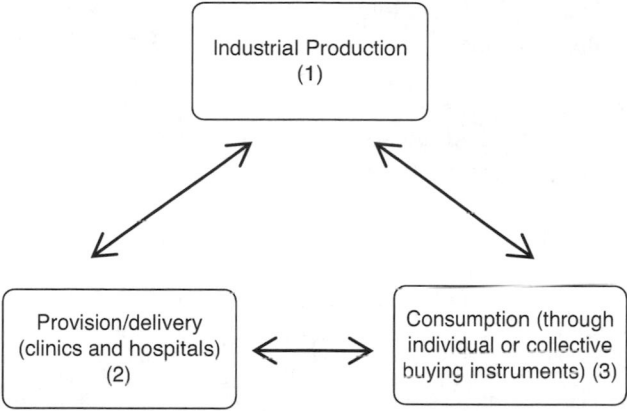

Figure 10.1 Institutional triad of health care
Source: Srinivas (2012: 8; CCBY permission granted)

several, continual problem-solving choices to make in development terms.

The triad's three vertices refer to (1) production, (2) individual or collective consumption or demand and (3) delivery. States not only have to juggle any two; they have to juggle all three. As the Indian nation-state focussed in the FME on (1), the pressure to problem-solve arose in deepening capabilities in (1). For a problem-solving agency, the challenge is that every vertex is connected to every other, and outcomes are rarely causal. With the heuristic, I argued then that very few nations have successfully juggled all three vertices of the triad for any substantial length of time. We can say that developmental success is more likely *as long as state agencies constantly attempt to exercise their problem-solving muscle.*

Inevitably, if somewhere along the way the outcomes of development remain unprioritized, agencies are likely to be solving problems on which they have no agreement, which results in conflict. Yet we know that even in India there have been attempts to address more than one vertex. For example, states such as Karnataka in the south have been experimenting with boosting health insurance programs – often co-operative health insurance models – to build up consumption/demand (2) and improve delivery of hospitalization and certain outpatient services (3). Similarly, private hospital chains such as Apollo have been problem-solving in a more directed way with state health officials and national satellite agencies to boost telemedicine, a technology-driven service (long-distance consultation and diagnostics) which connects (1) and (3). Telemedicine is a way to solve specific types of problems and is not a panacea for all emergency, curative and primary care segments, but it can provide an important solution in many rural areas where access to medicines produced (1), demand (2) and delivery (3), can all face challenges.

Developmental problem-solving is surely context- and place-specific in strategy. Consider a competing, powerful, developmental view: that problem-solving has universal qualities; that what works in Gambia should work in India; or that one problem to be solved is very much like another. Older writing on development long recognized that problems were context-driven, did not require 'big-push' approaches, but had to grapple with the complexity and disequilibria of real-world and situated processes. Albert Hirschman, for instance, recognized that the aphorism of 'One thing at a time' is not always helpful in development, since context-specificity required relational strategies unique to places, so that one-at-a-time sequencing may not move the developmental dial (Hirschman, 1990, and his earlier 1967 work). Later, the idea of 'good enough governance' (Grindle, 2007) signalled relative solutions and relative performance of states, governments and bureaucracies. UNCTAD (2009, IV), for example, connects 'problem-solving energies' to democracy, but while democracy may be helpful to force frequent exercise, it is no guarantee either of setting development priorities or of the state's commitment to continue to exercise its problem-solving muscle.

When one acknowledges that the three vertices in Figure 10.1 are always changing with respect to the other and in response to more systemic factors, a focus on problem-solving can point to *development plans that are patient*. In such plans, long-term and short-term goals are set and process and outcomes can be measured. No state can attend to all three vertices at once, and technological learning, although it has crucial aspects in all dimensions of (1), (2) and (3), is nevertheless not sufficient alone. Therefore, development planning that is patient requires acknowledging that problem-solving is essential, with clear priorities and value-judgements that must be communicated, with measureable outcomes. It requires institutional design that constantly exercises and rewards this problem-solving muscle. For example, vaccine procurement can directly connect production (1) to demand (2) through ambitious buying and clear market signals, but unless the public health system is energized, delivery (3) may be problematic (see comparable arguments for Indian vaccines in Srinivas, 2006; Puliyel and Madhavi, 2008).

Putting patents in their place

Once the emphasis is on problem-solving within the state, the design of realistic industrial policies can also take credible shape. New industrial policies can thus take on this problem-solving character, offering institutional mechanisms through which both productive capabilities and beneficial social indicators can be achieved (Srinivas, 2011; 2012). Technological advance and learning in these industrializing contexts is a specific type of problem-solving capability, but it offers no panacea.

Therefore, policies that are too narrow in terms of technological advance are unlikely to solve end problems. One example is the constant debate on patents. The Indian Patent Act 1970 was a crucial catalyst not just to reform the sector's production and access concerns but of the planning and reform process required to set new health goals. The Indian Patent Act 1970 was a mechanism to protect processes, not products, and was somewhat unexceptional relative to other countries. However, with the rise of Indian public and private sector successes and the use of the Patent Act as a protectionist tool, the Act became more internationally contentious and most visible in the context of the WTO TRIPS negotiations. The 1970 Act represented contested terrain: it was widely praised by those who wished to boost the learning capabilities of Indian firms on the one hand; praised also by those whose goal was more affordable access to medicines; and criticized by others who argued that the fillip it provided to learning was skewed towards 'imitation' and 'reverse engineering' rather than 'real' innovation. Finally, it was criticized for creating protectionist and regressive policies.

However, the First Market Environment shows that such unilinear explanations rely too heavily on patents to explain developmental outcomes; much wider problem-solving gaps existed. The carrots offered to firms were more extensive than just patents, and were ultimately defined by the state's priorities whatever the economic arguments might have been (see also Jacob, 2010: 83). In both the first and second phases of the FME, intellectual property rights (IPR) acted in concert with a range of other industrial instruments for competition, investment, infrastructure and a range of health institutional design issues (many of which remained unsuccessful). Process patents along with the Drug Price Control Order and these other policies forced lowered costs through competition (Abrol and Guha, 1986).

In the Second Market Environment, Indian firms and policy makers faced substantial new pressures to harmonize towards a product patent regime. Conflicting views of reform from bureaucrats and politicians underscored that problem-solving with regard to affordable access had no single narrative or political rhetoric during the trade harmonization negotiations (Jacob, 2010). The elites of the senior Indian Administrative Service (IAS) bureaucracy, for example, possessed considerable discretion and strategic flexibility in shaping policy design and its reform.

Patents offer monopoly protections but are second-best solutions. Acting alone, they rarely solve developmental challenges, although they may resolve trade pressures. Especially in the FME, patents required complementary industrial and social policies including clear foreign direct investment (FDI) guidelines, restrictions on monopolies, price controls, canalization of bulk drugs, rules for pharmacy procurement and use, assumptions about the capacity of clinics and hospitals and so on (Basant, 2010; Rai, 2009; Sahu, 1998; Srinivas, 2011, 2012). Some actively contend that the more one set of capabilities has advanced, the more firms have sought monopoly status and protections of all kinds. Madhavi (2013) states definitely that market guarantees and supports for public-private partnerships have worked to create the public sector's demise in vaccines.

Getting better

The FME's emphasis on universal access pointed policies towards essential medicines, especially public health priorities such as antibiotics. Combined with process patents and price controls, it induced competition and Indian production capabilities in both public and private sectors. The SME saw the introduction of the strongly worded New Drug Policy (NDP) (Government of India, 1978). However, the NDP presumed that item (5) below was necessarily at the right position and compatible with the other goals set out as:

1. To develop self-reliance in drug technology;
2. To provide a leadership role to the public sector;
3. To aim at a quick self-sufficiency in the output of drugs with a view to reduce the quantum of imports;
4. To foster and encourage the growth of the Indian sector;
5. To ensure that the drugs are available in abundance in the country to meet the health needs of our people;
6. To make drugs available at reasonable prices;
7. To keep a careful watch on the quality of production and prevent adulteration and malpractices;

8. To offer special incentives to firms which are engaged in Research and Development; and
9. To provide other parameters to control, regulate and rejuvenate this industry as a whole, with particular reference to containing and channelizing the activity of foreign companies in accord with national objectives and priorities.

The aspirations on the list were noteworthy, but the NDP reflected many unresolved triad questions about value ordering of the vertices and phasing of priorities. They assumed, for example, that cheap and reliable production would solve access to medicines problems. It assumed that domestic production was a necessity, but also that such production combined with other items on the list was sufficient. Only the fifth item in the above list questions this concern most directly.[3] The rest of the points notably address industrial production priorities and incentives.[4]

As Chaudhuri (1986) points out, foreign firms had to be forced into certain roles in the industry. Some of them had been established in India as early as 1923, began the domestic production of formulations only in 1955 and, despite a range of inducements through national pharmaceutical policies, had not begun producing bulk drugs even by 1978. In contrast, several Indian firms had seized the opportunities to do so provided by the state. As I have argued about the FME (Srinivas, 2012: 67), 'India's unique gains in this period were due in part to a multi-pronged policy approach with politically defensible market entry points through "essential" drugs and protectionist restrictions. But politics would have been insufficient without systematic and demonstrable technology outcomes and the development agenda focused on the twin goals of process technology gains and affordable medicines'. By challenging multinational companies in the courts, through national government supports and through a range of bureaucratic interventions, through the use of monopoly restrictions, production allocation licenses, price controls and process patents, Indian problem-solving was already agile on the industrial front. With clearer priorities in health outcomes and deliberate problem-solving rewards, such problem-solving might have reached its highest point yet.

I recently argued that we should consider an evolving spectrum of need and demand (Srinivas, 2014b): Need that is not recognized as need; Need that is recognized as need but not as demand; to Recognized, but unfulfilled demand; and finally, Effective demand (what is traditionally 'demand') and labelled as (2) above. Indeed, part of the toolbox for problem-solving is to identify that which is invisible or for which market signals are inappropriate. Indian examples include the Jaipur Foot prosthetic and the Oral Polio Vaccine cases, both of which required a rich set of actors and organizations that painstakingly problem-solved. In the Jaipur foot prosthetic case, actors progressed from identifying needs to ensuring that those in need had artificial limbs that worked, were caringly customized or could be easily repaired. These were especially rewarding outcomes because while road accidents in India had seen staggering rises, the state responded pitiably. The Jaipur Foot required a strong charitable organization in India to take need to demand in various forms, while all the while improving both the technology of prosthetics appropriate to the country and attempting to meet both domestic and export needs. Ensuring both production and then delivery of Oral Polio Vaccines (introduced in 1978, the same year the NDP came into force) required non-market instruments. This was because although vaccines were free through government programs, they were not easily available or, where available, not taken up. Here, too, an immense effort was state-led but richly enhanced by non-state partnerships.

Two successes further exemplify the potential of well-honed problem-solving led by, but not limited to, the state. One is India's sustained and unsurpassed success in block-level planning and wide administrative and spatial spread for polio immunizations. Private, non-profit organizations, religious groups, labour unions, and many others have thus played vital roles in identifying the needs-demand spectrum for policy makers and health administrators.

The second is emerging urban evidence of success and learning from Surat City. Surat, in dealing with plague and then floods, developed systematic improvements in disease surveillance. In India's polio success and in Surat's ambitious disease surveillance, industrial capabilities for polio vaccines or diagnostic kits and antibiotics were necessary but not sufficient. Challenges after all still remain for Surat in its current response to swine flu and its citywide integration of differentiated and localized community-level surveillance systems. Both polio and Surat have also brought to the fore India's continued administrative challenges in solving last-mile access issues, and the importance of partnerships – local and international – in building experimentation and learning.

Problem-solving in the realm of vertex (2) therefore requires administrators to anticipate how (1) and (3) may be speaking to the effective demand of (3) but not solving the deeper developmental 'hidden' needs (see also Mitra, 1986). At the end of a good problem-solving process, in other words, one should be able to see beyond the obvious. The muscle should begin carrying more problem-solving weight and be more flexible. Problem-solving skills can therefore be collective, both within and outside the state. Both polio and disease surveillance cases exemplify persistent problem-solving exercises through a wider set of governance networks which included the state, firms, NGOs and other community partners. They also exemplify a clear need for connecting market and other instruments to a territorial agenda: national but operating through block-level strategies in the polio case, and citywide and neighbourhood strategies for Surat.

An illustrative case of less successful problem-solving demonstrates the difference between access in principle versus access in practice. Bengaluru (Bangalore) City in Karnataka state is possibly one of India's best sites for medical innovation, and for quality and range of health facilities, yet suffers from an unfortunately common lack of attention to sustained problem-solving.[5] In the 2012 H1N1 outbreak and in the 2015 outbreak of swine flu, Bengaluru faced an unchanged situation: doctors struggled in government research institutes and treatment centres to obtain antibiotics and diagnostic kits. International procurement of diagnostic kits was successful and had ironically steered both state and manufacturer away from production to address the domestic crises (see also Srinivas, 2006).[6] By 2015, little sustained problem-solving had occurred in the state health system in the intervening three years since H1N1, and the city's doctors and patients experienced an alarming sense of *deja vu*.[7]

Yet, problem-solving has to be patient. Oral polio vaccines were introduced in 1978. By 2011, India had become polio-free and by 2014 the three-year cautionary timeline had passed. State problem-solving is never apolitical in this timeline. It may engender bitter debates about the need for privatization or allegations of fraud. For instance, there has been debate about whether national government policies, which in the FME were seen as progenitors of public health, have since deliberately undermined public sector production capabilities in vaccines; furthermore, that such policies exaggerated demand data to justify a growing role for the private sector's profits (Madhavi, 2003; Puliyel and Madhavi, 2008). Worse still is the claim that epidemiological evidence was deliberately sidelined and a 'techno-centrism' adopted in designing vaccine policy (Bajpai and Saraya, 2012), where advance market commitments to new technologies have outstripped 'evidence-based vaccine policies' (Madhavi, 2013). The FME and SME strengthened vaccine production capabilities and created important procurement spaces for priority medicines and vaccines. Multilateral and international vaccine procurement played a much weightier role in the SME in boosting the private sector and creating some tensions between state regulation of exports and domestic uptake.

Therefore, rather than reaching far too wide by seeing state capacity as a normative function across the entire period of productive capabilities, and rather than depending too heavily on the diffuse notion of growing 'good governance', a focus on problem-solving requires policy and planning on the ground to become directed and value-explicit: for example 'Everyone – no matter what their economic or social status – should have real, measurable access to affordable medicines, vaccines, or diagnostic kits. This priority policy will be enforceable by 2020 and will carry explicit penalties for non-performance of government agencies or for those seeking windfall private profits but not delivering better access'.[8] Problem-solving, in other words, is a core state capacity. When done well, problem-solving in the state's line agencies forces dilemmas and discussions about value-propositions that have then to be designed by networks of actors into policy and last-mile planning.

Conclusion: strong production, weak problem-solving in health

The FME was perhaps the most ambitious market environment in the convergence it sought between industry and health goals, and the most overt in these ambitions. These ambitions were seen in decisions by the bureaucracy, through judicial judgements and legal battles against multinational firms, through recognition of personnel and delivery needs. Yet, was this ambition manifested in sustained problem-solving at multiple scales of governance? No.

Indian drug policies, wittingly or not, delinked industrial growth from health needs, even while the state made several market restructuring attempts in order to build capabilities. With the exception of priority national health programs, centralized planning targets were focussed on production capacity and far less on incentives for demand uptake of this capacity and delivery. Despite the rhetoric of grassroots mobilization and rural devolution, there were weak decentralized health plans. The industrial priorities of the pharmaceutical industry were resolved conservatively within the institutional contours of the Ministry of Chemicals and Fertilisers rather than those provided by the Ministry of Health.

While the national government offered carrots and sticks for private domestic firms, these focussed mainly on technological advances and market concentration. These incentives encouraged diversification, dominance in bulk drugs, process patents and price controls that placed caps on health spending and boosted competition. Abrol and Guha (1986), for instance, argue that while the country successfully moved from formulations capability into more challenging bulk drugs, quality consistency suffered. Madhavi (2003) and others have argued that over time and with growing technological capabilities, private suppliers became emboldened in dictating policy design to the state, favouring their own profits over people's health. Technological advance makes domestic resolution of the health industry's priorities more, not less, complex in late industrial economies (Srinivas, 2012).

Yet Indian health and industrial goals were quite decisive and convergent in Phase I of the FME when the public sector was involved. After all, national priorities and institutionalized problem-solving were largely equivalent to the priorities and problem-solving in nationally owned public sector firms. However, the problems and the multitude of actors grew as the FME progressed, and the problem-solving capabilities, although in principle greater, were diffused through the private sector and became more difficult for the state to regulate. At no time during the FME could quality, safety or guaranteed redress be assured. The value priorities related to needs became ironically more obscured by growing technological capabilities and by the attractions of the foreign markets and growing export earnings.

Some nations thus begin problem-solving by creating domestic health delivery as the priority even if they import, while other nations do as India did, developing and deepening their industrial supply. India triumphed in the latter dimension. Yet, there is no 'best' starting point for any problem-solving; its value-basis, systemic linkages and context make it so – points recognized also by Hirschman (1967; 1990). The triad is a perpetually co-evolving system in which states make continual improvements and build institutional ties (Srinivas, 2014a). Problem-solving requires institutions that are agile, staff and rules that are both flexible but oriented towards timely outcomes, and outcome measures that are clear, transparent and can be monitored and enforced. Without these credible commitments to problem-solving towards health outcomes, more generalized state capacities become irrelevant and illegitimate.

Two market environments have now passed, and a third arguably is still under way with biotechnologies changing how we contend with all aspects of health care. The decades since 1950 have demonstrated that Indian production of generic medicines, diagnostic kits, biopharmaceuticals and vaccines has grown stronger and ever more sophisticated. In the absence of regular exercise to connect its vertices, however, the triad remains slack and the state's problem-solving muscles weakened. Rather than resembling a dynamic, co-evolving triad, the result is then an ossified triangle with its base vertices unable to dictate terms to its apex.

Notes

Acknowledgements: My thanks to Maureen Mackintosh and Geoff Banda for the invitation to participate in this book; to them and to Watu Wamae for insightful comments on the draft; and to Radha Ray and the Open University IKD team for making the London stays so pleasurable. This has been an intellectually generous and well-managed research effort. It is my good fortune to have had this opportunity to extend my research, exchange ideas with a great workshop team and receive comments from strong editors.

1. See Sahu's (1998) slightly different periodization but whose emphasis is also on production capabilities.
2. For example, Karnataka state in South India has experimented quite substantially with health care insurance systems (demand) and new pharmaceutical stocking and distribution practices (delivery). Although quite progressive in this regard, it has no deliberate state or urban administrative mechanisms to test the integration regularly.
3. See also Stoker and Jeffery (1988: 565).
4. For the range of specific cases, and contentions and ambiguities, see Sahu (1998) and Srinivas (2006, 2012). Stoker and Jeffrey (1988) discuss the New Drug Policy and foreign firms. The Astra-IDL case emphasized that foreign firms benefitted from the state's unresolved priorities. Most of its arguments about producing a drug already available in India were to emphasize the novelties in production process and the foreign exchange savings to the country. Most questions from bureaucrats to Astra in turn focussed on manufacturing details, employment and local industry effects, and financial priorities such as royalties, branding, export priorities and shares (Ibid: 565).
5. In the Hindu newspaper story, the same leading Head of Department of Neuro-Virology in Bangalore NIMHANS admits to shortages of A(H1N1) testing kits, and although orders had been placed, they had to stop testing because of the unfulfilled orders; http://www.thehindu.com/news/national/karnataka/shortage-of-ah1n1-testing-kits-worries-patients/article3359557.ece, last accessed 27 December 2014.
6. http://www.deccanherald.com/content/459453/state-facing-shortage-swine-flu.html, last accessed 29 March 2015. Srinivas (2006) makes a similar point that international vaccine procurement programs had offered important benefits to Indian firms. However, Indian regulators and health administrators would have to redesign Indian vaccine policies and plans in order to attend to domestic health priorities. Madhavi (2003, 2013) emphasizes the undue influence exerted by private firms on state priorities.
7. See also Kotwani et al. (2007) on uneven availability of common drugs.

8. Although former Prime Minister Indira Gandhi made her famous Alma Ata speech at the WHO on not allowing profiteering from life or death, she did not unfortunately vow to boost problem-solving alongside.

OPEN

Part III
Industrial Policies and Health Needs

The last chapter of Part II framed the development policy challenge of aligning industrial and health goals as 'problem-solving'. This last section of the book draws on case studies and experience to address some of these major policy challenges.

The section starts with a problem health policy makers grapple with across the world: how to control prices of medicines. While most high-income countries closely manage medicines pricing in the context of universalist health systems, most developing countries have low levels of control. Chapter 11 describes an important effort to change this situation in South Africa, a country grappling with the legacy of an inherited and profoundly inegalitarian two-tier health system. The author draws lessons for both policy and process in other African contexts.

A second major industrial policy issue with huge health consequences is the definition and enforcement of quality standards in pharmaccutical manufacturing. Manufacturers and health care providers alike have a shared interest in ensuring the industry grows without compromising public health safety. Standards are both a key technical issue and an arena for international debate on procurement and regulatory strategies. Chapter 12 argues for stronger local African initiative in defining, regulating and harmonizing quality standards.

Procurement of medicines operates as implicit industrial policy, and Part II argued that it is understudied. Chapter 13 investigates innovative approaches, drawing on high-income country initiatives in valuing and pricing innovator medicines for lessons applicable in lower-resource contexts. The chapter picks up from Chapter 11 the issue of price negotiation and its discussion links to Chapter 14, which addresses more broadly the interaction between industry and government through biopharmaceutical business associations.

Chapter 13 also opens up the key issue of business finance for industrial development, a theme addressed further in Chapter 15. Chapter 15 brings together a number of different threads in the book by discussing finance and incentives to support the development of national pharmaceutical industries. The chapter identifies a convergence of thought and initiative recently generated across the African continent for the development of policy incentives for industrial development for health benefit.

11

Policies to Control Prices of Medicines: Does the South African Experience Have Lessons for Other African Countries?

Skhumbuzo Ngozwana

Introduction

Despite the heightened interest in the African pharmaceutical market, there are constraints and challenges that continue to affect access to medicines. One of the key constraints is the high prices of medicines. In the private sector, wholesale and retail mark-ups have been found to range from 2% to 380% and from 10% to 552%, respectively (Cameron et al., 2011). A later study found wholesaler mark-ups between 25% and 50% (IMS Health, 2014a; 2014b), and retail mark-ups between 25% and 500% (Rosen and Rickwood, 2014). Local manufacturers and importers alike have expressed concern over the high mark-ups in the distribution chain, as the exorbitant prices are believed to limit patients' access and sales.

African governments are all grappling with the issue of high medicine prices. Coupled with the increasing momentum for developing local pharmaceutical industries, the issue of medicine prices and how to contain them will come into sharp focus for policy makers. African policy makers are also acutely aware of measures employed by other countries around the world to contain runaway health care costs, and specifically pharmaceutical expenditure. Although price controls are important policy instruments, they are very controversial. The South African experience with pharmaceutical price controls may therefore be a useful case study to inform other African countries' interventions.

This chapter presents the South African experience with the single exit price (SEP) regulations which were enacted to deal with these distortions and to replace the mark-up-based retail pricing systems with fixed professional fees in order ultimately to reduce the price to patient.

Pharmaceutical price control options

Governments have moved to control prices, first, because the innovative pharmaceutical industry has historically been dominated by monopolies, creating the tendency to price products at a premium. Medicines are also different from any other consumer goods in that patient is often price-insensitive, given that the doctor prescribes and a third party pays for the drugs. Furthermore, many consumers and health care professionals equate a higher-priced product with quality, and conversely see a lower-priced product as inferior, resulting in the ready acceptance to prescribe, dispense or ask for high-priced products. The challenge for governments therefore is how to institute proper controls to ensure that medicines are priced fairly and that access is not constrained by high prices.

The literature on pharmaceutical price controls identifies three distinct ways in which expenditure can be controlled: direct controls on the prices of medicines across various levels in the distribution chain; through demand-side measures including financial and reimbursement systems; and finally by influencing demand through the implementation of demand-side measures.

Price controls at the level of the manufacturer

The most difficult step in price controls is arriving at a reasonable or fair price for a medicine. The literature on price controls and the tools employed are mostly from high-income countries. These include the cost-plus method, profit caps, comparative pricing, direct price negotiations and pharmaco-economic evaluations, or a combination of these tools. The cost-plus pricing model is difficult to employ in a country where most suppliers are subsidiaries of international companies or importers of products from other markets. In this scenario, experience shows that it is very difficult to obtain accurate and reliable data to arrive at a determination of real costs and profits.

The second method of price controls, using profit caps, is employed in, for example, the United Kingdom through the Pharmaceutical Price Regulation Scheme (PPRS), whereby the government negotiates a reasonable profit with companies for products sold to the National Health

Service. This method too faces difficulties with arriving at accurate costs and profits when dealing especially with subsidiaries of international companies and importers.

The third method is comparative pricing, comparing prices of products in other markets with local market prices. Complexities include varying dosage forms, strengths and trade names, and the fact that the margins and mark-ups allowed to players in the chain differ across territories. The Netherlands, for example, sets maximum permissible prices using the average wholesale price of similar products in a basket of countries including Belgium, Germany, France and the United Kingdom. It is reported that upon its introduction in 1996, Dutch pharmaceutical prices dropped by an average 20% (Rietveld and Haaijer-Ruskamp, 2002).

The fourth commonly used tool involves direct price negotiations between buyers and pharmaceutical companies. In France, the government directly controls prices through negotiations before a product is launched. Finally, pharmaco-economic evaluations are used by regulators to attempt to arrive at a fair price, taking into consideration the societal costs of the disease and the costs of other treatments. Through economic modelling, the direct and indirect benefits of the drug are calculated and compared with alternative therapies. Pharmaco-economic evaluations are used extensively in the UK, Netherlands, Canada and Australia, among other markets (see also Chapter 13).

Price controls at the wholesale and pharmacy level

Wholesaler margins are controlled through setting either a maximum margin or a maximum price at which wholesalers can sell on to retail pharmacy. Margins in retail pharmacy can be controlled by setting a fixed percentage mark-up to the wholesale price of each medicine, by setting a maximum over all mark-up, or finally by tiered mark-ups where the percentage mark-up reduces as the price of the product increases. The fixed-margin system is widely used in Europe, with margins for prescription drugs normally around 30%, whilst over-the-counter products are freed from price controls. Although margins are fixed, wholesalers may still be able to negotiate discounts and thus increase their profits. The tiered structure is intended to create disincentives for dispensing more expensive products.

Some countries, including China, have a system of price controls that differentiates between imported and locally produced products (Bao, 2000). The Chinese system also differentiates based on drug classes: basic therapeutic and preventive drugs acquired in large volumes, class 1 anti-psychotics, anaesthetic agents, contraceptives and other special classes.

Other measures to influence prices

There are other demand-side measures that can influence prices and expenditure. These include positive and negative lists, reference prices, co-payments, parallel importation, and generic substitution, as well as education of health care professionals and the public. A negative list of products that are not reimbursed forces companies to lower prices in order to gain a listing on the positive list. Similarly, reference prices, which are used to benchmark products in the same therapeutic category that are assigned a certain price cap, and related demand-side measures such as co-payments, are meant to force patients to opt for the cheaper medicines. Generic substitution and closely related educational measures to educate health care professionals and patients about the quality and benefits of generic medicine are other demand-side measures that have been employed to lower medicine expenditure.

The basis of the South African price control regime

Implications of the two-tier South African health care system

When the first democratic government in South Africa came into power in April 1994, it inherited a two-tier health care system (private and public) reflective of the country's divided history. These two tiers have widely differing resources and access medicines via different channels. The private health care tier is a well-resourced private insurance-based world-class platform which serves an estimated 15% of the population (Council for Medical Schemes, 2014). The private pharmaceutical market is valued at $4.1 billion (IMS Health, 2014b) and is supplied with medicines by about 130 manufacturers and importers supplying 5,000 product lines.

The second tier, the public sector health care system, serves the remaining 85% of the population. It is under-resourced, with chronic staff shortages, a quadruple burden of disease and systemic lack of funding. Public sector supplies are obtained through tenders administered by the Central Procurement Unit of the Department of Health. It is supplied with 2,400 product lines by an estimated 90 manufacturers and importers, at an estimated value of $1 billion a year in 2014.[1]

Besides these deep divisions, the democratic government faced spiralling health care costs and an increasingly exclusionary health care system, in which those who served the poor and marginalized were paying more for medicines than those in the affluent areas who were more likely to benefit from price and volume discounts, rebates, bonuses and other incentives. The pricing of medicines had historically been left to market forces, so companies were free to price their products as they wished, to offer bonuses and deals, discounts and rebates, and to discriminate among clients on the basis of volume of purchases and other considerations. The government therefore decided to intervene to correct the distortions.

Despite the large literature on pharmaceutical price controls in highly developed markets with well-developed health insurance schemes and universal coverage (Rietveld and Haaijer-Ruskamp, 2002), there was little from the developing world with similar health care systems to South Africa with a significant portion of patients without health care insurance and with considerable out-of-pocket expenditure on health care and medicines.

The government was also aware of developments internationally, where high medicines prices were receiving global attention from governments and consumers alike. Further, they were acutely aware that price controls have to be enacted in such a way that they still create headroom for market forces to work to exert further downward pressure on pricing. In trying to come up with mechanisms to control prices, the government looked to emulate countries that had successfully introduced controls and managed to reduce, contain and sustain medicine expenditure.

A further challenge faced by South Africa was the huge fragmentation of the distribution channel, unlike the Western world where there are a few distributors and wholesalers controlling the entire distribution chain, and hence enjoying economies of scale. So the choice of policy options to contain drug costs would have to take into consideration the country's unique health care structure.

The South African rationale for price controls

The government believed that medicines were public utility goods, and not mere commodities, and that it could no longer allow a situation where companies priced their products as they pleased. This was reinforced by their view that the prevailing drug prices in South Africa were inflated artificially through the elaborate system of bonuses, discounts, rebates and other perverse incentives systems that led to the dispensing of more expensive drugs, and irrational use of drugs. These perverse incentives, the state alleged, added an additional 50% to the final cost of the drug. The Department of Health claimed that South Africa was among the world's top five most expensive medicine markets.

The Department of Health's position was strongly challenged by the Pharmaceutical Manufacturers Association (PMA) of South Africa, who held the claims were devoid of truth and based on an unfair comparison. The PMA held that the Department of Health was trying to influence the public and create the impression that the pharmaceutical industry was responsible for the high medicine costs, in order to introduce measures to control the industry. To circumvent this, the PMA approached the office of the Public Protector to make a determination whether the statements made by the Department of Health, perceived as laying the groundwork for price controls, were factual.

A key contention was that the Department had compared prices of products sold in the South African retail sector with prices of multi-source products sold by a prominent global NGO, the International Dispensary Association, which supplies developing countries with generics bought internationally in bulk. The PMA's position was that the department was using an untenable comparison to justify the introduction of medicine registration and pricing reform in South Africa, whilst ignoring the fact that patient prices were often double the ex-manufacturer prices, and that various studies had indicated that South African prices were on par with international prices.

Despite the PMA's efforts to block the reforms, the government made clear that they would immediately take measures to correct the disparities and distortions. In this regard, a number of key government policies – legislative and regulatory provisions – were enacted. The next section reviews the constitutional mandate that led to the interventions.

Constitutional enablers of the National Drug Policy

On 8 May 1996, the democratically elected parliament adopted the new Constitution of the Republic of South Africa.[2] This enshrined a Bill of Rights. Section 27 underpinned the legislative and regulatory processes that would follow in reforming the health sector; it read:

> Section 27 (1) (a); everyone has the right to have access to healthcare services, including reproductive health.
>
> Section 27 (2): the state must take all reasonable legislative and other measures within its available resources, to achieve the progressive realisation of each of these rights.

Informed by this provision in the constitution, and acutely aware of the urgency to address the imbalances of the past, to create a new and equitable health care system with universal access to affordable quality health care for all, and ensure the progressive realization of Section 27, the government introduced a number of policy papers which would drive far-reaching regulatory and legislative reforms. The most important was the National Drug Policy (NDP) of 1996. The NDP had far-reaching implications, laying the basis for the Single Exit Price (SEP) regulations discussed below.

National Drug Policy

The NDP (Department of Health, 1996) was aimed broadly at increasing access to safe, affordable quality medicines for all South Africans, and laid the foundation for all the subsequent legislative and regulative revisions and amendments. Specifically, the NDP's objective was '[t]o promote the availability of safe and effective drugs at the lowest possible cost'. The NDP intended to rationalize the pricing structure of drugs and included the following to realize that aim:

- the appointment of a Pricing Committee;
- introducing total transparency in the pricing structure of pharmaceutical manufacturers, wholesalers and dispensers of drugs;
- introducing a non-discriminatory pricing system;
- replacing the wholesale and retail percentage-based mark-up system with a fixed professional fee;
- regulating price increases.

The far-reaching aims of the NDP found expression in the amendment to the Medicines and Related Substances Control Act 101 of 1965. The new Act 90 of 1997 introduced, among others, sections dealing with bonuses and samples (18 A and B), the ethical marketing of pharmaceuticals (18C), generic substitution (22F) and the creation of the Pricing Committee and enactment of the single exit price regulations (22G).

The Medicines and Related Substances Act

Before the introduction of the SEP regulations, the South African pharmaceutical market was dominated by innovator brands, with very little generic penetration. Medicines were promoted directly to doctors and pharmacists, who often received samples, bonuses and many other incentives to drive the prescription or dispensing of particular drugs. These practices led to doctors often prescribing more expensive drugs.

The amended Medicines Act made provisions for the parallel importation of medicines into South Africa by others other than the patent holder (15C), the prohibition of bonusing, rebates and any other incentive scheme (18A), prohibition of sampling of medicines (18B), mandatory generic substitution (22F) and the formation of a Pricing Committee and the clauses governing its mandate[3] (22G), namely that:

(1) The Minister shall appoint such persons as he or she may deem fit to be members of a committee to be known as the pricing committee.
(2) The minister may, on the recommendation of the Pricing Committee make regulations
   (a) on the introduction of a transparent pricing system for all medicines and scheduled substances sold in the republic
   (b) on an appropriate dispensing fee to be charged by a pharmacists or person licensed in terms of Section 22 C (1) (a).
(3) The transparent pricing system contemplated in sub-section (2) (a) shall include a single exit price which shall be the only price at which manufacturers shall sell medicines and scheduled substances to any person other than the state.

The provisions contained in the amendment to the Medicines and Related Substances Control Act 101 of 1965 were immediately challenged in court by the Pharmaceutical Manufacturers Association of South Africa (PMA), who felt that the Department had overreached itself in drafting the act. Although the PMA withdrew its court challenge in 2001 following an international outcry and mounting international and civil society pressure, the regulations pertaining to a Transparent Pricing System for Medicines and Scheduled Substances[4] only came into effect on 2 May 2004.

The Single Exit Price regulations

South Africa's attempt to control prices at wholesale level has elements of a fixed professional fee but with a fixed maximum, based on a tiered scale that considers the price of the product. At retail pharmacy level, the professional fees are also fixed, on a tiered system that endeavours to promote the dispensing of cheaper products. Over-the-counter products are exempted from controls, but pharmacists cannot benefit from discounts as they do in Europe.

The SEP was defined by the regulations as a composite of the manufacturer's exit price, plus the distribution or logistics fee and a 14% value added tax (VAT). The SEP thereby derived would be the one and only price at which wholesalers, pharmacies and other people allowed to dispense in terms of Section 22C (1) (a) could sell the medicine in South Africa, irrespective of the volumes purchased. The SEP would control pricing throughout the pharmaceutical value chain, setting dispensing fees for pharmacists and logistics fees for wholesalers and distributors.

The final price to the end user would include the SEP and the professional (dispensing fee) for the service rendered. Whilst companies would have the freedom to set initial prices, the pricing committee would decide on an annual price increase in accordance with a methodology in the SEP regulations.

Whilst the introduction of the SEP was widely criticized and seen as an anti-private-sector move by the new democratic government, the high prices of medicines had received attention previously from government commissions under the National Party. The three previous commissions – the Snyman Commission (1962), the Steenkamp Commission (1978) and the Browne Commission (1985) – had also made recommendations including curbing excessive medicine promotions, generic substitution, issuing of compulsory licences, calling for the state to participate in the supply of medicines through a tender system and for the state to investigate the introduction of price controls.

Setting the regulations

The Minister of Health appointed a pricing committee with representation from the Departments of Trade and Industry and Finance and the Competition Commission. The committee had pharmacists, lawyers, health economists, pharmaco-economists, academics and consumer representatives, but no industry representation. Their mandate was to establish a new regime of total transparency in the pricing structure of all prescription medicines and over-the-counter products. The committee would also set up regulations for logistics and dispensing fees, international benchmarking of pharmaceuticals and pharmaco-economic evaluation of medicines.

The government stated that, when fully implemented, it expected the SEP regulations to reduce the prices of medicines by 40–70%. In line with the regulations, effective 2 August 2004 and for a year thereafter, the price of medicines would not be higher than 50% of the 'Blue Book' manufacturer net price.[5] The Blue Book was a well-known industry publication that supplied the pharmaceutical industry and health care sector with independent and accurate price lists. The government held that the manufacturer net price listed in the Blue Book was inflated to cater for the complex systems of bonuses, rebates and other incentives at play in the industry, in order to allow the retail chains to acquire drugs at below 50% of the listed Blue Book price.

The SEP regulation 8 allowed for a manufacturer to set their single exit price, which could only be raised once on an annual basis, whilst temporary price reductions were allowed as often as the manufacturer wanted to make them for competitive reasons. The SEP could be increased only once a year based on a predetermined formula[6] that incorporated, among others, the Consumer Price Index (CPI) and Producer Price Index (PPI) for the preceding year; changes in the rates of foreign exchange and purchasing power parity; and the need to ensure the availability, affordability and quality of medicines. The currencies considered are the US Dollar and the Euro, as most South African pharmaceutical companies purchase products and inputs of production from abroad with these two currencies.

The final increase as per formula is calculated as follows:

API Formula = *70% CPI (historical) + 15% (Rand/Dollar variance) + 15% (Rand/Euro variance)*

The exchange rate split of 15% US$ and 15% Euro was based on data provided by the Department of Trade and Industry and data on pharmaceutical imports.

Although this formula has been applied from the beginning, the actual price increases granted by the MoH have displayed a degree of discretion, and the timing has often been delayed, in some cases by up to five months.

Manufacturers can also apply for increases above the formula-based increases, to assist manufacturers and importers to compensate for exchange-rate-related increases in the prices of production inputs or finished products imported from principals overseas. The exceptional circumstances under which the minister would authorize such an increase were adverse financial, operational and other consequences for the manufacturer; adverse effects on the availability of the medicine in South Africa should the increase not be granted; the nature of the disease the medicine was registered for; resultant adverse effects on public health; and lastly, to ensure that the constitutional obligations were not abrogated.

Finally, the Director General of the Department of Health could inform the public if she or he felt that the single exit price of a medicine was unreasonable. Manufacturers and importers were required to inform the Director General six months before the registration of a medicine the intended SEP, the countries where the product was sold and how much it was selling for, the costs of manufacturing, and the marketing and selling costs of the product.

At inception, the regulations stipulated the maximum professional fees that could be added to the single exit price by various players in the distribution chain.

Controversies and challenges

The SEP regulations were immediately challenged in court by various organizations. The pharmacy groups contended that the fees were not sufficient for them to survive, and that the stipulated professional fees threatened the survival of many independent pharmacies. Further, the Pharmaceutical Society of South Africa (PSSA), a large retail pharmacy chain, New Click (Pty) Ltd, and others argued that the Department had overreached itself in promulgating the regulations. The Cape High Court found in favour of the state and dismissed the case, although the dissenting judgment[7] held that it was difficult to understand how the SEP was arrived at; that the logistics fee regulations were contradictory and at odds with other legislation; and that the dispensing fee had been based 'on no more than a thumb suck' and a simplistic 'one size fits all' approach. The PSSA, New Clicks and others appealed the Cape High Court ruling, and the case went to the Supreme Court of Appeal where the Cape High Court decision was overturned.

The Supreme Court of Appeal, in overturning the decision of the Cape High Court, made this finding[8]:

The order of the court below is set aside and replaced with the following order in each application:

(a) The 'Regulations relating to a Transparent Pricing System for Medicines and Scheduled Substances' as published in GN R553 on 30 April 2004 are declared invalid and of no force and effect.

The state in turn appealed, and the case went all the way to the Constitutional Court, which ruled that the Department had indeed acted within the law, but ordered the Department to go back to the drawing board and review the professional fees.

The Department of Health adjusted the proposed dispensing fee to 26% of SEP to a maximum of R26. This proposal was immediately rejected by the Pharmaceutical Society of South Africa, once again on the grounds that it was insufficient and would cause unnecessary hardship to their members and eventual closure of pharmacies. The PSSA proposed a tiered dispensing fee system with average fees of R37, a proposal that found no favour with the Department of Health.

Following these court challenges and negotiations between the various parties, the dispensing fee and the logistic fees have gone through various iterations, and have now been finalized. The June dispensing fee was first published in March 2006, and was immediately rejected by pharmacists. This was then replaced with a new proposal of June 2009. More discussions and consultations followed, and the last iteration was published in June 2014 (Table 11.1). The table shows the complex calculations of the permitted fee for each band of the SEP, at the various revision dates.

The proposed dispensing fees were revised upwards over time as pharmacists complained that their business would be unsustainable (Table 11.1). The lowest tier has stayed below R100 (US$8.50) and the fixed fee was reduced, but the dispensing fee has been revised upwards with the adjustment of the percentage of the total medicine price. In the top tier of products above R799.85 (US$67.80), the fee has also been adjusted upwards through a revision of both the fixed component and the percentage of the medicine price

Logistics fee

Prior to publication of the logistics fee regulation, wholesalers and manufacturers negotiated the logistics fee independently, and there were reports of widely varying logistics fees, with some companies paying in the high double digits. Innovator companies with patent-protected products that wholesalers were desperate to stock would often pay in the low single digits, whilst some did not pay any logistics fees at all. This position put the generic pharmaceutical industry at a distinct disadvantage, as wholesalers would often squeeze generic companies for bigger logistics fees to make up for the loss with innovator companies. The government finally moved to regulate the logistics fee, and in March 2011 published the first draft regulations for Logistics Fees (LF). The second iteration was published in September 2012 following negotiations and discussions with providers of logistical services. The fee involves four tiers, with a LF of 8% of the ex-manufacturer price excluding VAT + R3 ($0.25) for items less that R100 (US$ 8.50), and a LF of R54 (US$4.58) for items exceeding R1,000.00 (US$84)

Table 11.1   Pharmacy dispensing fee: fee in rands (R) plus permitted mark-up (%), by band of SEP in rands (R) and date of publication of schedule

Date of publication of fee schedule

03/2006	06/2009	12/2010	09/2013	06/2014
SEP < R77.00 R7.00 + 28% of SEP	**SEP < R100.00** R6.00 + 36% of SEP	**SEP < R75.00** R6.00 + 46% of SEP	**SEP < R81.00** R6.30 + 46% of SEP	**SEP not > R 85.70** R 6.95 + 46% of SEP
SEP = R75.00 < R 150.00 R 23 + 7% of SEP	**SEP = R100.00 < R 250.00** R 32 + 10% of SEP	**SEP = R75.00 < R 200.00** R 15.75 + 33% of SEP	**SEP = R81.00 < R 216.00** R 16 + 33% of SEP	**SEP R 85.70 < R228.53** R18.55 + 33% of SEP
SEP > R150.00 < R250.00 R 26 + 5% of SEP	**SEP > R150.00 < R1000.00** R 45 + 5% of SEP	**SEP > R200.00 < R700.00** R 51 + 15% of SEP	**SEP > R216.00 < R756.00** R 55 + 15% of SEP	**SEP > 228.53 < R799.85** R59.00 + 15% of SEP
SEP > R 250.00 R 31 + 3% of SEP	**SEP > R 1000.00** R 65 + 3% of SEP	**SEP > R 700.00** R 121 + 5% of SEP	**SEP > R 756.00** R 131 + 5% of SEP	**SEP > R799.85** R 140 + 5% of sep

Source: Government Gazettes, various years, extracted by author.

Despite representations from wholesalers and support from the generics industry for the logistics fee to include a minimum fee and a fixed cap, the department rejected that application on the grounds that having a fixed minimum would be anti-competitive. It published the final logistics fee with only a fixed cap. Manufacturers and importers would be free to negotiate a fee up to the capped level with wholesalers. The regulations also stipulated that where the current logistics fee exceeds the current caps, manufactures and providers of logistical services must negotiate to reduce the fee within 60 days of publication of final logistics fees. The regulations, however, allowed the minister to authorize a manufacturer or importer to increase the logistics fee in exceptional circumstances.

Experience with the Single Exit Price regulations to date

Price increases under the regulations

Table 11.2 below captures the experience with the SEP to date. It shows the quantum as determined by the SEP methodology and the eventual increase granted by the Minister.

It is clear from the table that the minister has not always adhered to the formula, and has exercised discretion in granting increases – a sore point for the industry.

Although the industry has complained about the low increases from inception, experience shows that since the introduction of the SEP, they have not always taken the full increase granted. In fact, temporary price reductions have been taken frequently within the period of an

Table 11.2 SEP increases since the implementation of the SEP (%)

Year	SEP calculation as per methodology (%)	SEP granted by the Minister (%)	Variance
2004/05 &	2.60	5.20	N/A
2006/07	2.60		
2008	8.40	6.50	−1.90
2009	12.12	13.2	+1.08
2010	9.90	7.40	−2.50
2011	−2.10	0.00	N/A
2012	6.90	2.14	−4.76
2013	8.20	5.80	−2.40
2014	8.90	5.80	−3.10

Source: National Department of Health, Pharmaceutical Task Group, author analysis.

SEP increase. This has largely been for competitive reasons, and at times motivated by the need to sell short dated stock before it expires.

A further justifiable complaint is that the Department of Health delays the increases, so companies lose out. For example, in 2010, there was a five-month delay between the increase and the time that companies could take the increase. These delays occurred as a consequence of the 'application' process introduced, and decisions to accept applications only from 1 April. Given the 30-day approval process, the earliest companies can take an increase is 1 May, which leaves companies with just seven months to enjoy the price increase. Besides these delays, there were also frequent rejections due to such matters as formatting issues on the SEP increase application template, Department of Health database discrepancies and missing documentation.

SEP impact on prices

The experience of South Africa with price controls demonstrates that, contrary to popular opinion, the Department of Health conceptualized a regime based on global practice and tried to blend a number of instruments with a good historical record of effectiveness in other countries.

In terms of controls at the manufacturer level, in attempting to arrive at a fair ex-manufacturer price, and considering the complexities of setting a fair price in a predominantly import based industry, the government settled arbitrarily on 50% of the Blue Book price on the basis that prices were inflated by the same figure to make up for the incentives, bonuses, sampling and other perversities in the system. The price negotiation component between companies and government has only been recently employed for state procurement, where besides published reference prices, the Central Procurement Unit can and does directly negotiate prices with manufactures, especially if they are not too far from the reference prices listed. At the same time, elements of comparative pricing were built into the regulations through the International Benchmarking provisions wherein South African prices would be compared to a basket of prices in five countries including Canada, Australia, New Zealand and Spain. Similarly, pharmaco-economic evaluations were also built into the regulations, although these and comparative pricing through benchmarking have yet to be finalized.

When it comes to other measures to control prices, South Africa has not adopted positive and negative lists, whilst experience with demand-side measures such as reference prices, co-payments, and generic substitution and education of health care professionals and the public is mixed. Private health care insurance schemes all have reference pricing systems in place, and accompanying co-payments if patients elect to use more expensive products outside the formulary and reference prices. Government enacted provisions for mandatory generic substitution, and although this and other measures have seen generic usage increase from the mid-20% in 2002 to around 60% by volume (IMS Health, 2014a), there is still scope for more growth. To this extent, the government can do more to educate patients about the safety, quality and efficacy of generic medicines, as well as the benefits for patients and health systems. This is an area that still requires much work.

There is general acceptance that the introduction of the SEP regime has resulted in a downward impact on the prices of medicines. The graph in Figure 11.1 is drawn from data from the Council of Medical Schemes, which publishes an annual report detailing, among other things, total health care expenditure in the private sector, and looks at the contribution of the various players.

The Department of Health reported savings of 19%, made up of 25–50% for generic medicine prices and 12% for originator medicines.[9] IMS Health reported an average drop in medicine prices of 24% between June 2003 and June 2006 (Vokes, 2007) since the introduction of the SEP. Similarly, Emsley and Booysen (2004) reported that the introduction of the SEP had resulted in a reduction of 36.7% in the prices of quetiapine and 13% for haloperidol. Admittedly, that paper was published a few months after the introduction of the SEP, so it is

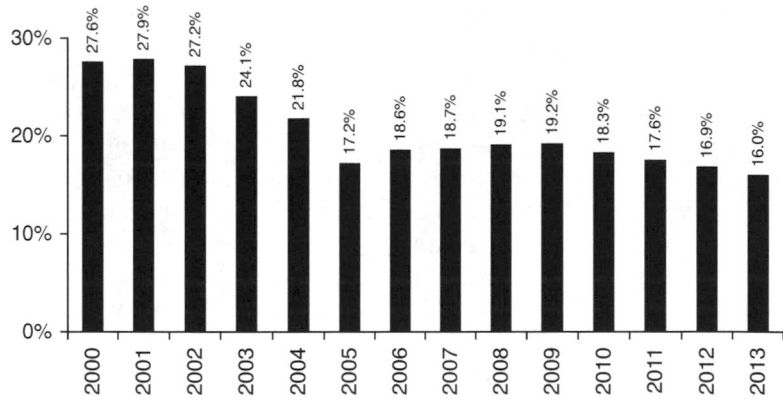

Figure 11.1 Medicine contribution to total private health care costs
Source: Drawn by the author from data from Council for Medical Schemes (2014).

not clear if the reductions have been sustained. Further evidence of the impact of SEP on prices was reported by Steyn et al. (2007), who demonstrated that the SEP regime had reduced the average cost of anti-diabetic medicines by around 29.6%. Finally, the biggest private health insurance company, Discovery Medical Aid, reported: 'Because of the single exit price legislation, these drug price reductions benefit all users in the private healthcare system. Conservative estimates suggest total annual savings of about R 319 million per year are achieved for the scheme in medicine expenditure' (DHMS, 2012).

The media and other parties have also reported extensively on the impact of these price regulations. For example, the *Mail and Guardian*, South Africa's leading weekly newspaper, reported on 26 February 2008: 'The introduction of medicine pricing regulations a few years ago resulted in a 20% drop in prices, and savings of over R 2.3 billion on medicines'.

Other reports and theses, especially looking at the impact of the SEP on the pharmacy profession, and occasionally on the patient, do however offer a different view of the impact. They describe a profession decimated by the regulations, with multiple closures of pharmacies, especially in rural areas. Although critically important and requiring further critical academic enquiry, they are outside the scope of this chapter. There is also anecdotal evidence that the early gains made may be slowly eroding as the contribution of medicines to overall health care costs continues to creep up, albeit slowly. Whether this is purely a factor of the SEP policies starting to fall short, or because of increased medicines usage, or the impact of pseudo-generics which tend to crowd out true generics and inflate prices, or other factors, requires further study.

SEP impact on manufacturers and access to medicines

It is accepted internationally that the entry of generics significantly widens access to medicines, and the size (volume) of the market often expands after patent expiry. The impact of the SEP regime on access to medicines is an area that still requires further investigation.

The reference prices are normally set with the first generic entrants and often undergo revisions with further entry. In certain instances, the revisions have been quite dramatic, leading to wholesale price decreases, further lowering the price of the drug and indirectly promoting access. The case of simvastatin is instructive. Simvastatin is highly genericized, with the first generic product launched in 2002 by Adcock Ingram. Adcock remained the clear market leader despite other generic alternatives. In 2009, Michol, a new simvastatin generic entrant, came in at a very low SEP, and as a consequence the prices of a pack of 30 simvastatin tablets dropped from over R120 to around R25. Arguably, the effect of this would have been to increase access by patients, especially those who pay out of pocket for package deals that include consultation fees and medicines from family practitioners.

The impact of the SEP has also come through in capping prices through private medical schemes' reference pricing systems. All the private medical insurance schemes have their own reference pricing systems to set the maximum price a scheme will pay for a generic drug. The effect has been to force newly launched generics to price below the reference price, and in some instances to compel the innovator to drop their prices or face the risk of their products facing co-payments. Similarly, if, for competitive reasons, a generic manufacturer drops prices drastically and sets a new reference price, other companies are forced to follow suit or face the prospect of co-payments, which will deter patients.

Impact on manufacturers

Manufacturers have complained that the SEP regime has put the sector under pressure, as the SEP increases are insufficient to offset the effect of the weaker Rand, coupled with wage and utilities inflation. This leads to reduced earnings and threatens the commercial viability of some product lines. Given that most companies import both the active pharmaceutical ingredients and other raw materials from overseas, the weakening of the Rand in a price-controlled environment leads to significantly higher cost of goods sold, without the recourse to increase prices to offset that. This is particularly so because although the regulations have a mechanism for extraordinary prices increases, companies complain that the process is onerous, hugely bureaucratic and difficult to access. These pressures have led to some manufacturers discussing discontinuation of some products. Recently, it was reported that Fresenius Kabi had withdrawn one product, Voluven, from the market, although the company stated that the withdrawal was not related to cost pressures (Bateman, 2014).

Delays are also a major problem for manufacturers. When a company applies for an SEP for a new product, or informs the Department of an SEP price adjustment, the Department 'approves' and then notifies price vendors such as Medikredit. The product is then allocated a NAPPI (billing) code, after which it can be sold on the South African market. Companies complain that delays in assessing the SEP applications and informing vendors delays market access for new products, and in the case especially of first-to-market generics, restricts and denies patients access to cheaper products. Although the regulations envisaged that the

SEP would be agreed within 48 hours of notifying the Department of Health, the process has evolved to one of 'approval', and delays of up to a month are not uncommon.

The potential closure of independent community pharmacies in rural and remote areas, mentioned above, may clearly reduce access. The Pharmaceutical Society of South Africa opposed the SEP regulations and the dispensing fees on the basis that they threatened the viability of independent community pharmacy. Since the early court challenges, there have been widespread reports that some community pharmacies did go into bankruptcy. The Pharmaceutical Society of South Africa reports that many small town and rural pharmacies have closed (PSSA, 2014) negatively affecting access. Dodd (2007) demonstrated that independent pharmacies saw net profits fall, that the price controls could push some pharmacies into bankruptcy and that closure of pharmacies in remote and rural areas would render the distribution of medicines economically unviable and thus affect access.

Some contend, furthermore, that the SEP regime has the unintended consequence of keeping prices higher than they would otherwise have been. They argue that late entrants often find it impossible to offer discounts on the prevailing prices, given that medical schemes will still reimburse up to the level of the reference price, so there is no incentive for pharmacists to offer the lower-priced product. This is compounded by the fact that the dispensing fee is calculated as a percentage of the price of the drug, inadvertently incentivizing pharmacists to dispense the highest-priced generic as long as it is within the reference price band.

Finally, it is argued that the SEP regime creates a disincentive for new entrants to offer lower entry prices. Some experts believe that because companies know that they will struggle to get price increases (Medical Chronical, 2012) sufficient to offset inflationary pressures and Rand weakness, among other challenges, they deliberately set high prices from the outset, possibly reducing access. The proponents of this view note that medicine prices in South Africa are artificially inflated, and higher in comparison to the same products in other countries.

Conclusion: are there lessons for other African countries?

South Africa embarked on the SEP path exactly a decade ago, informed by the realization that, as public utility goods, medicine prices could not be left to the vagaries of the market. In that time, there has been much acrimony, public disagreements in the media and other public spaces between the main protagonists. Throughout all of this, the Department of Health, backed by the government and the ruling party, as well as public health and patient advocates, held firm. There have been threats of court cases, and many actual court cases, which have invariably led to iterations of the dispensing and logistics fees. What has emerged, though, is that through proper consultation and a willingness to open up and present the evidence base for positions held on various issues, it is possible to move towards negotiated positions. The first critical lesson for those who would want to embark on the price regulation route, therefore, is the absolute necessity of having clear and unambiguous political support for reform. Without this, there is no hope for success.

The second key lesson from South Africa's journey with price regulations is the necessity of involving all key stakeholders in the process very early on. Governments and policy makers must take the private sector into their confidence and clearly and firmly explain the rationale for their decisions, ensuring that all views and all aspects are taken into consideration beforehand. Arguably, if the South African Department of Health had embarked on an exercise with the pharmacy profession, escorted by reputable independent and honest brokers, to arrive at a reasonable and evidence-based dispensing fee, there would have been no need for court cases, nor for the time spent in the last couple of years on endless consultations and the various iterations of the dispensing fee.

Third, it is imperative to collect the evidence base to guide policy decisions to be taken before embarking on a price reform process. This means making a full and thorough assessment of the entire distribution chain and finding the factors at play with each of the stakeholders. In the South African example, the R26/26% dispensing regime was no danger to the big retail chains, but threatened the survival of the small community pharmacy.

Fourth, it is imperative to make both the interpretation and implementation of any regulatory processes as simple as possible. The complexity that crept into the South African SEP regime and the bureaucratization of the process only served to make the pricing regime more unpopular. A measure of predictability and certainty around the application and approval process, the time periods for taking the increases and so forth would have lessened the tension between industry and the regulators.

Finally, although the SEP regime seems to have had a positive impact on prices, it is clear that supply-side measures on their own have only limited impact. It is thus critical for those governments that intend to regulate prices to devote equal attention to the demand side. This can be done, among other methods, through massive patient education about the benefits of generic medicines, the incentivization of health care professionals to prescribe or dispense the cheapest products – above and beyond the dispensing fee – and the need to adopt generic prescribing across the board.

Notes

1. National Department of Health, South Africa – Tender analysis by author, from data accessed in December 2014 at http://www.doh.gov.za/mpc3.php.
2. The Constitution of the Republic of South African – 'Everyone has the right to have access to – a) health care services, including reproductive health care'. Section 27 (1) (b) of the Constitution further mandates the state to, 'take reasonable legislative and other measures, within its available resources to achieve the progressive realisation of the right'.
3. The Medicines and Related Substances Control Act 101 of 1965 as amended.
4. Department of Health. Regulations Relating to a Transparent Pricing System for Medicines and Scheduled Substances. GG No R 553 30 April 2004.
5. Department of Health. Regulations Relating to a Transparent Pricing System for Medicines and Scheduled Substances. GG No R 553 30 April 2004.
6. National Department of Health – Regulations relating to a transparent pricing system for medicines and scheduled substances made in terms of Section 22G of the Medicines and Related Substances Act, 1965 (Act No 101 of 1965).
7. *New Clicks South Africa (Pty) Ltd v Tshabalala-Msimang and Another NNO; Pharmaceutical Society of South Africa and Others v Tshabalala-Msimang and Another.*
8. The Supreme Court of Appeal of South Africa – In the matter between The Pharmaceutical Society of South Africa AND Others and the Minister of Health and ANOTHER, New Clicks South Africa (Pty) Ltd and Dr Manto Tshabalala-Msimang and ANOTHER, Case No 542/04 & 543/04.
9. A presentation by the Department of Health on Medicine price regulation – the South African experience (2009).

12
Pharmaceutical Standards in Africa: The Road to Improvement and Their Role in Technological Capability Upgrading

Geoffrey Banda, Julius Mugwagwa, Dinar Kale and Margareth Ndomondo-Sigonda

Introduction

This chapter discusses standards, an elusive term and concept. For the African pharmaceutical sector especially, the term is used by the manufacturing sector, regulators, technical experts, procurement agencies, health system actors and policy makers to mean different things. There is a dearth of systematic studies that address what standards are, their classification and the logic behind their set-up and operation, and this has contributed to a huge asymmetry in understanding. The socio-economic, technical and political issues and how they have an impact on local production and industry development, including their effects on access to markets, have also not been systematically explored.

A common understanding of standards, their classifications and development, is important as the continent implements the African Union's Pharmaceutical Manufacturing Plan of Action (see also Chapter 15). Even more important is the need for African technical experts, regulators and policy makers to realize that standards and their development in the pharmaceutical sector is a process under their control. They can drive agenda setting and design realistic and context-sensitive road maps which align local industry development without compromising public health safety. The ability of policy makers to take a critical approach to the meaning and use of standards in the African pharmaceutical sector is an important enabler for designing road maps.

In this chapter we set up some of the issues that need further debate. We deconstruct standards and classify them into two groups; technically based standards and organizational or institutionally based standards. Technically based standards cover product, process, plant and environmental aspects. Organizational or institutionally based standards are those which are important for creating market confidence in firms' output through assuring the credibility and legitimacy of products, quality, production, distribution and recall processes. This credibility and legitimacy arises from physical inspections of production and distribution facilities, and the availability and examination of documentation and data management processes – administrative activities essential for endorsement, certification and accreditation.

We argue that this perspective helps to build an understanding of which types of standards are 'mutable'[1] – that is, judgement-based standards such as inspection, certification and accreditation for which capability building and improvement is a gradual process. By contrast, standards which cannot be compromised are those which deal directly with patient and public health safety concerns, namely quality, safety and efficacy of medicines. Such distinctions aid technical and policy people in designing and implementing appropriate interventions and road maps for technological capability and standards upgrading which do not compromise locally manufactured medicines' quality, safety and efficacy. These distinctions also help in crafting responsive, context-sensitive standards and compliance development processes that do not impose unnecessarily high costs or regulatory barriers on existing local industry. Our discussion of standards is informed by extensive literature searches, fieldwork in India, Kenya, Zimbabwe and South Africa where we interviewed technical experts in 2014, and interaction with regulatory and compliance experts in the UK.

A brief historical perspective

The history of standards in the pharmaceutical industry is traceable to adverse events in patient safety, and one of the notable failures was the 1950–60s thalidomide disaster (Grabowski et al., 1978), in which a morning sickness pill containing thalidomide taken by pregnant mothers resulted in newborns with severe birth defects. The disaster catalysed stringent drug approval and monitoring processes, necessitating the passing of the Kefauver-Harris Drug Amendments Act in 1962 which called for proof of safety and efficacy in the approval process, approvals that now use animal testing and clinical trials that can take up to 12 years. The logic for the development of stringent regulation was that there was a need for an independent government regulatory agency to ensure public health whose goals were not compromised by commercial interests of pharmaceutical companies (Abraham, 2002). All stages of the drug life cycle are regulated from drug discovery to release of the drug on the market (Harper et al., 2007). Table 12.1 summarizes five key stages in the life cycle of a pharmaceutical drug, and the regulatory requirements or standards pertinent for each stage.

For drug discovery, the key guideline is good laboratory practice (GLP), and for phase 1 to 3 clinical trials the guideline is good clinical practice (GCP). When the drug moves to the production phase, good manufacturing practice (GMP) becomes the guiding regulatory requirement, followed by good distribution practice guideline for distribution covering traceability of medicines (systematic identification of products) to aid in organized defective product recall from the market. For post-market surveillance, pharmacovigilance is the regulatory requirement. In addition, there is a wide range of other regulatory requirements at

Table 12.1   Drug life cycle stages and regulatory requirements

Drug life cycle stage	Regulatory requirements/Guidelines
Drug discovery	Good laboratory practice (GLP): these guidelines focus on toxicological safety and protection of the test subject
Clinical trials (phases 1, 2, 3)	Good clinical practice (GCP): these guidelines consider product efficacy and safety evaluation, as well as individual protection and safety during testing
Manufacturing	Good manufacturing practice (GMP): these guidelines are concerned with assuring a manufactured product's quality, safety and efficacy, for both the product and the patient. The process aims to build in quality and ensure quality standards.
Distribution	Good distribution practice: these guidelines deal with storage, transportation and traceability for product recall.
Post-market surveillance	Pharmacovigilance: Sometimes called phase 4, this is monitoring of the product after market authorisation to check for any adverse events or product failure in all respects.

Source: Adapted from Harper et al. (2007) and Muller et al. (1996).

supranational and national levels, inspired by public health concerns and safeguards against drug disasters, to address trade and market entry obligations (Immel, 2001).

The situation is less complex and expensive for generic medicines, which are modelled on branded drugs, since proof of safety and efficacy has already been demonstrated for the branded drug. The generic drug producer needs at the minimum to demonstrate the equivalence of the drug for approval and it does not go through rigorous clinical trials. The bulk of medicines produced in Africa are generics, and consequently the standards that we will discuss in this chapter focus on generics manufacture. We do not cover standards in drug discovery and clinical trials.

While the first set of GMP guidelines for manufacturing, processing, packing or holding finished pharmaceuticals was introduced by the US Food and Drug Administration (FDA) in 1963 (Immel, 2000), the WHO has spearheaded the standards-setting process since the late 1960s, coming up with several amendments and extensions to the guidelines. In this chapter we focus on good manufacturing practice (GMP), defined by the WHO (2004) as the part of quality assurance that ensures that products are consistently produced and controlled to the quality standards appropriate to their intended use and as required by market authorization. Many countries, including India, Kenya and South Africa, have developed their own GMP guidelines based on the WHO guidelines. The WHO is thus a global technical agency responsible for setting standards and normative guidance and for establishing best practice, all of which are implemented through national drug regulatory authorities (DRAs) and other relevant institutions. There is criticism, however, that the WHO sets standards for all its member states regardless of the level of development. There is also some questioning of the way in which the WHO has shifted from a solely advisory body (technical assistance included) towards acting as a regulatory body after it began pre-qualifications of pharmaceutical products for developing countries. WHO pre-qualification has acted as a catalyst for upgrading facilities in developing countries, but its stringent requirements have also been an impediment to market access to global donor-funded medicines purchase, in particularly for HIV/AIDS, TB and anti-malarial drugs.

Standards, their establishment and assurance

A standard can be viewed broadly as a consensus between different agents to do certain key activities according to agreed-upon rules (Nickerson and Muehlen, 2006). This is a definition of standards as a process: a common and agreed understanding of the rules of the game and how it is played, which resonates with the definition of institutions. These standards, therefore, operate on the back of strong institutional and organizational arrangements empowered to certify compliance with set rules through proclamations or a tightly controlled allocation of insignia or certification. Independent validation from a third party is critical for building confidence of other stakeholders who lack inside information or the means to gather credible information to make informed decisions. Standards therefore provide consumers with a basis for making informed consumption decisions and manufacturers with a benchmark of best practice (Nadvi, 1999) and hence a competitive tool.

A technology standard, on the other hand, is defined as 'a set of specifications to which all elements of products, processes, formats or procedures under its jurisdiction must conform' (Tassey, 2000: 58). This form of standards has been credited with the standardization that has significantly reduced manufacturing costs through economies of scale achieved by mass-production of similar or 'standard' components (Katz and Shapiro, 1985; Farrell and Saloner, 1986). It is argued that the presence of standards reduces uncertainty by providing actors with a framework that enables widespread diffusion of a technology (Rosenberg, 1976), as well as a modular approach to the production process where components can be manufactured by different producers.

Organizational or institutionally based standards interact with technology standards through the processes of data or process interrogation against set norms, validation, acceptance and certification. Thus certification and/or accreditation of products or firms affirm that accepted best practice (norms), 'standardized' and imbued with accountability, has been used at various stages in a product's design, development, manufacture, distribution and disposal. Specifically for the pharmaceutical sector, inspection, validation, certification, accreditation and regulation provide a system of traceability and accountability. This is done through detailed verification of quality-dependent procedures through internal and independent audits, quality training of personnel and constant monitoring of quality performance measures (Nadvi, 1999), as well as market performance and rectification in cases of failure.

Government departments, regulatory agencies, pharmaceutical companies' industry associations and other stakeholders play key roles in the design, implementation and refinement of policies and standards governing the sector. The credibility of a standard setting and monitoring process depends on the representativeness of the political process, how well it exploits existing technical knowledge, matches context of application, and how committed participants are to the issue at hand (Fischhoff, 1984). These processes inherently reflect different interests, power structures and the resources of different stakeholders. Consequently and at the heart of this discussion, low-income countries tend to typically be 'standard takers' rather than 'standard makers', with the responsibility for implementation, monitoring and enforcement of the standards resting with the national governments (Stephenson, 1997), which in many African settings are resource-constrained. It is with this background to technical and organizational/institutional standards that we argue that African technical and policy organs need to gain a confident understanding that designing and implementing a road map to improving standards in the pharmaceutical value chain is something that is and should be under their control.

Standards as tools for competition and pressure to improve

The significance of standards has grown over time and they have come to represent an important locus of collective strategy (Astley and Fombrun, 1983) within which the 'rules of the game' are set (Jain, 2012). For many producers and service providers in both the global North and South, compliance with international standards can add a competitive edge and form a necessary condition to access niche markets (Nadvi, 1999). More recent research emphasizes that standards provide opportunities and incentives for low-income countries to modernize local industry and strengthen supply of quality products (Jaffe and Henson, 2004; World Bank, 2005). This growing evidence base suggests that in low-income countries standards can link upgrading local industrial capabilities with supply of medicines and hence better local health service quality and inclusiveness (Nadvi and Waltring, 2002).

It has been argued that good-quality and affordable pharmaceutical products, whether imported or locally produced, depend largely on the outcome of standards-based competition (Narayanan and Chen, 2012). In the international trade literature, research suggests standards can be non-tariff barriers to trade (Stephenson, 1997; Wilson and Abiola, 2003), with regards to labour (Maskus et al., 2004; Maskus and Wilson, 2001) and environmental standards (Anderson, 1996; Anders and Caswell, 2009). These barriers emanate from inadequate provision of finance, local governance and regulatory structures. Kaplinsky et al. (2011) considered how standards such as hazard analysis critical control points (HACCP) and International Standards Organisation (ISO) are used as non-tariff barriers, especially for resource-constrained countries. Supporting this assertion, a growing body of literature shows that without financial and technological support for domestic manufacturers, standards create significant cost and international market entry barriers (EC, 1997; Nadvi, 1999; Stephenson 1997).

International procurement practices and requirements of donors often enforce higher pharmaceutical quality standards than stipulated by national regulatory authorities. Implementation of these higher standards by local firms and achieving certification requires investment in people, equipment and changes in production organization as well as management practices – a costly exercise. Multiple accreditation caused by the need for local, regional and international certification such as WHO pre-qualification has direct negative bottom-line impact. One African firm reported during fieldwork that a WHO pre-qualification inspection can cost as much as US$100,000, a large financial burden especially if accreditation and certification is not supported by success with global health and international medicine supply tenders. As a result, some local industrialists have questioned the logic of solving national-level institutional failure at supranational level. They argue that it is better to strengthen local regulatory authorities or take the harmonization route by solving the institutional challenges at national or regional level. These criticisms inform our critical discussion of standards, what they are and how road maps for improving standards and industry capabilities can be crafted.

The need to deconstruct standards

A respondent from Kenya on being asked what standards were, remarked as follows: 'this is where we have a problem...the word "standard" is misused both at global and national levels'. Such a remark underscores the need to deconstruct standards and classify them. He went on to describe what he considered to be standards, such as the guideline that describes good manufacturing practice (GMP) (which he termed a standard in itself), facility standards and personnel standards, as some of the key issues to be considered. In this section we discuss consecutively the two types of standards identified above: technical standards and institutional or organizational-based standards

Technical and process standards

GMP guidelines are intended to be a set of minimum standards, covering recommendations on quality management, personnel, production facilities and equipment, documentation and records, production and in-process controls, packaging and identification labelling, storage and distribution, laboratory controls, validation, complaints and recalls, and contract manufacturers (WHO, 2004). The diverse range of issues covered by GMP guidelines not only makes them a key and central lens for our discussion of pharmaceutical standards but also highlights why these guidelines are one of the most contested yet key drivers of the pharmaceutical industry. Under GMP we have chosen to focus on four standards that emerged as key in our research. Two of these standards (product and process) were classified as those which should not be compromised because of their direct relationship with patient and public health safety. The GMP process is critical for ensuring product quality, safety and efficacy. As noted in Chapter 3, GMP standards constitute a 'production culture' interwoven with professional judgement as regulators decide on what is deemed adequate especially for processes and facility standards.

Product and process standards

There was consensus among the multinational and local pharmaceutical manufacturers interviewed on the fact that product and process standards cannot be compromised. These they argued, should be the same wherever medicines are produced in the world. These standards are engineered in such a way that quality is built in and checked for at various stages and the evidence meticulously documented. The suppliers of raw materials have their facilities, processes and products vetted, and on receipt, raw materials are sampled and subjected to specific physical, chemical and biological tests. Raw materials are carefully stored ensuring avoidance of cross-contamination. There is a clear and documented chain of custody, traceability and accountability that is established along the whole process. In many African countries the production pharmacist is ultimately responsible and accountable for the release of batches of products after compliance with product and process standards as well as quality control tests. The quality control tests cover chemical, physical and biological characteristics of the product and avoiding contamination in the same three areas. Some of the tests, for example for tablets, include microbial tests, hardness and how well the tablet dissolves.

The drivers of product and quality standards are people, the production equipment and laboratory equipment. Improving standards therefore requires in many instances equipment and skills upgrading. For example, a Zimbabwean firm improved ingredient drying in the wet granulation tablet-making process by investing in a high-capacity fluid bed dryer. They also invested in automatic capsule-filling machines to improve standards and productivity. On the question of whether technical standards change there were diverse opinions in the inter-views. Some respondents argued that technical standards do not change, whereas some regulators reported that technical standards have become more stringent with time. One interesting perspective came from a technical expert who when asked by researchers in Tanzania whether very stringent GMP is necessary, argued that for infusions and injecta-bles (parenterals), it was essential that they have to be sterile because they go straight into the bloodstream. However, he said, for tablets, the minimum safe requirements are different because they go into the stomach. Yet, he argued, current requirements are that they should be 'almost sterile', a standard hard to attain for manufacturers in Tanzania, and more stringent than essential good hygienic standards using good SOPs (standard operating procedures).

It is insights or perspectives such as these that need to be debated by those responsible for designing the road maps for upgrading standards in all their forms for the pharmaceutical sector. Our discussion, however, does not delve into the technicalities of GMP and the specific tests and indicators of quality. Our intention is to spark debate. In separate conver-sations, UK compliance experts acknowledge that there are different interpretations of GMP. What the US FDA means by GMP compliant is not necessarily what Europe's EMA means by GMP compliant and by extension what different African countries mean by GMP compliance. This argument resonates with the standards of the regulators as referred to by a Kenyan technical expert. It therefore becomes difficult according to the Kenyan expert to bring into one country a product produced in another, hence the African regulatory harmonization efforts described later in this chapter.

Facility and personnel standards

Another set of standards that technical experts in Kenya identified are facility and personnel standards. These encompass environmental and structural standards for buildings and health, educational and tech-nical standards for personnel (which are often assumed). One Kenyan respondent remarked that '[facility standards] – that's where the problem of Africa lies'. He reported that facility standards are assumed but not clearly enunciated by regulators, and are especially problematic for old production facilities that have to be refurbished. A Kenyan respondent said, for example, that the WHO talks of 'competent people and suitable premises' in its requirements for pre-qualification – which, however, leaves a lot of room for different interpretations. Facility standards are linked to environmental standards and determine air quality and freedom from contamination through physical separation. Personnel standards include technical know-how, hygiene standards (medical check-ups included) and administrative skills as discussed later. Thus personnel standards cover diverse skills sets depending on functions, which might include but are not limited to analytical and organic chemistry, microbiology, plant engineering, production, pharmacovigilance, quality assurance and research and development. Facility and personnel standards formed the class of standards for which improvement, according to the technical experts we interviewed, should be approached in a gradual and cumulative manner. In Tanzania, regulators reported that they know that the firms are growing and they give them 'timelines' for improvement. These are the classes of standards that we classify as being mutable.

Organizational/institutional aspects of standards

The supply of medicines and other medical products into the health delivery systems is intensively regulated and governed by strict product, process, marketing and institutional standards. The need for regulation comes from information asymmetry between the producers on one side and patients and clinicians on the other side. Patients cannot assess safety or observe quality and efficacy of medicines on their own, and neither can the medical practitioners who decide on their behalf (Harper, 2007). This is where regulatory bodies come in, by seeking evidence of compliance with guidelines, rules and regulations to give credibility and legitimacy to organizations inspected. Accreditation and certification are an institutionally based regime of standards that are built on and meant to validate the technical, process, facility and personnel standards as reflected in the various guidelines such as GLP, GCP, GMP, Good Distribution Practice and pharmacovigilance.

The challenge for Africa rests in skills shortages at the regulator and among compliance managers at firms. As the firm operates, it records data which must be managed and produced as evidence to the regulators (inspectors). This process requires someone with a technical background who also is conversant with data management and documentation. The regulators in addition to the physical inspections also analyse documents and check against the set norms. As discussed earlier, this is where the judgement of the assessor (regulator) comes into play. These standards are of an organizational and institutional nature and are dominated by soft issues of training and retaining human capital.

These institutional/organizational standards tend to be resource-driven and path dependent. Their evolution depends in part on historical legacies of national institutions, industrial capabilities and tertiary training that included practice-based polytechnic training. South Africa and Zimbabwe as a result have relatively well-developed medicines regulatory systems. For South Africa the main piece of legislation shaping pharmaceutical standards is the Medicines and Related Substances Control Act (1965) and its various amendments. The Medicines Control Council (MCC), a public sector body tasked with regulating pharmaceutical products in South Africa has eleven expert committees, which evaluate the safety and efficacy of a drug submitted for approval and they inform the decisions of the MCC. Apart from the Registrar of Medicines, all members of the MCC committees are engaged on a part-time basis, including the evaluators, who are often in full-time employment elsewhere. There is, however, concern on such a heavy reliance on external expertise.

The Medicines Control Council (MCC) comprises four units, inspectorate and law enforcement, operations and administration, clinical and medicines registration. These units perform an administrative and coordinating role, facilitating the work of the expert committees. The MCC works within, and is influenced by, the public sector institutional context, as well as serving as the local competent authority for monitoring implementation of requirements from agencies such as the WHO, FDA and ICH in pharmaceutical manufacturers operating in South Africa. In terms of skills, respondents in South Africa also identified loss of regulatory skills especially at regulatory bodies as a key challenge. They reported that it took a long time to train a competent regulatory person, especially those with industrial experience, and as a result they are perpetually in training mode. The firms also reported that they face the same skills training and retention problems.

Harmonization to upgrade regulatory standards

An interesting issue identified by experts in the Kenyan pharmaceutical industry was the issue of the 'standard' of the regulatory bodies themselves. Different countries have different regulatory capacities and capabilities. Highly resource-limited countries do not have the same capacity and capabilities as resource-rich countries. As a result, manufacturers fear that accreditation by one country does not equate to the same level of stringency as accreditation by another. Interviewees reported that some countries in the East African region had few regulatory pharmacists who looked at dossiers and at the same time had to do factory inspections – an impossible task.

These realities are some of the catalysts for regional medicines harmonization initiatives such as the African Medicines Regulatory

Harmonisation (AMRH) initiative led by the New Partnership for Africa's Development (NEPAD). In recognition of regulatory capacity limitations for some countries and its consequent socio-economic impact, NEPAD Agency undertook, in collaboration with partners[2] to initiate the African Medicines Regulatory Harmonization (AMRH) Programme since 2009. The AMRH initiative is part and parcel of the implementation of the African Union Pharmaceutical Manufacturing Plan for Africa (PMPA) (see Chapter 15) and aims to facilitate access to quality, safe and efficacious medicines to the African people by working through the existing political structures, and the regional economic communities (RECs).

In particular, the initiative aims to catalyse the establishment of effective national, regional and continental medicines regulatory agencies, and has made significant progress since 2009 in Eastern, Western and Southern Africa towards transparent, efficient and effective regulatory systems that provide assurance of faster approval of medical products and technologies that meet internationally acceptable standards of quality, safety and efficacy. Some of the key aspects focussed on are harmonized guidelines for registration of medicines, good manufacturing practice (GMP) inspection guidelines, quality management systems (QMS) and information management system (IMS).

Through NEPAD Agency's coordination, the East African Community (EAC) successfully launched the Medicines Regulatory Harmonization (MRH) programme in March 2012, and is now at implementation stage with substantial progress made in the endorsement of the harmonized guidelines for registration of medicines, good manufacturing practice (GMP) inspection guidelines, quality management systems (QMS) and information management systems (IMS). The NEPAD Agency has undertaken to expand the AMRH programme to other RECs beginning with the Economic Community of West African States (ECOWAS) through its health agency, the West African Health Agency (WAHO) in collaboration with the West African Economic and Monetary Union (UEMOA). The MRH Programme for West Africa was launched on 2 February 2015. Progress has also been made on implementation of the programme in the Southern African Development Community and central African regions.

Cost implications of standards

Regulation raises numerous questions concerning compliance costs in relation to benefits obtained, transaction costs associated with regulatory administration and enforcement, and unanticipated or unwanted responses on the part of the regulated industry. Regulations may have high individual compliance costs, which are compounded by the fact that organizations are simultaneously attempting to comply with other, possibly conflicting regulations. When regulatory standards or mechanisms conflict, they may prevent one another from achieving their intended benefit. Increasing legislative controls in highly complex, and heavily regulated arenas such as health care can lead to 'regulatory inflation' rather than enhanced compliance. Moreover, the risks of compliance failures and regulatory inflation are heightened in the field of healthcare because jurisdiction is often fragmented and operates at multiple layers from global to local levels (Mugwagwa et al., 2015).

The consensus from South African respondents with respect to standards was that innovation, technological capability upgrading and health delivery were cost-sensitive processes, and that while adopting and keeping standards came at a cost, higher costs were being incurred from policy and regulatory uncertainties on the one hand and inefficient quality assurance systems on the other. Trying to curb costs today by compromising on standards would lead to 'fewer drugs to treat current and future generations', but taming the policy and regulatory jungle to ensure cost-effective and sustainable compliance with standards would be good for companies, regulators and patients in the short and long runs. Multiple accreditation has direct bottom-line impact.

The Kenyan standards and upgrading road map

Respondents in Kenya were in general agreement that product and process standards are necessary and that they should be seen as 'minimum regulatory expectations' required to manufacture a product that meets specific needs, that is, fits the purpose for which it is made. Kenya has developed a road map for upgrading standards. They acknowledge that it is a gradual process requiring multi-sectoral coordination and concerted efforts. In an interview, an industry expert involved in designing and developing the road map for the country said:

> So we came up and said you must solve the problem, but it's not a small one … we looked at the whole scenario and came up with seven key areas

which are detailed below as direct quotes:

1. You must have a road map for the local industry to improve because you cannot shut down any one of them because they have been producing.

2. You must have a system where you check the quality of the product on the market and remove the ones which are not performing and remain with those which are performing well.
3. You must have someone overseeing the market and industry and that is the regulator, you must incentivize the capacity and improve its capacity.
4. Whereas the industry is trying to achieve the standards, it's going to cost money, so you should look for a way where they can get the money.
5. You must provide the incentives for the time the industry is improving, they must not improve and lose their market, so you must protect it and come up with incentives that will help them.
6. You must come up with a strategy for capacity building of human [skills], their capacity to undertake this both in the regulatory and in the private sector
7. There are those items which are essential for the industry to place their products on the market, but not one single company can do it alone, so you must put them together and see how they can be shared, and this is what you call the support services or shared platform.

Recognizing that they could not do all seven activities at once, they prioritized the first initiative. They developed the road map, and by mid-2014 the technical aspect had been completed and they were waiting for the narrative part of the document, endorsements and final launch. A concerted effort to involve industry, regulators and the Ministry of Industrialization was made during the process of developing the road map (Technical Expert, Kenya, 2014). The technical expert through his networks brought together the ministers for health and industrialization in a joint meeting to discuss the road map.

Money for upgrading processes and standards

Kenya realized that the process of upgrading production facilities and machinery would impose financing constraints on affected firms. The fourth point in the strategy above deals with the need to facilitate funds availability. To that end they engaged the Kenyan Bankers Association, who informed them of their fears about funding pharmaceuticals production. According to the pharmaceutical industry respondent, the bankers said: 'We are risk-based institutions, we go only where there is less risk, but in pharmaceuticals the risks are so high that we dare not'. This statement points to issues of finance capability on the part of banks (see Chapter 15). Reinforcing the challenge of finance capability, one respondent cited an example of a Development Bank which refused to fund a quality control laboratory because they said they could not demonstrate what would come out of the laboratory. The pharmaceutical technical expert argued that the bank failed to see the overall picture and how the quality control laboratory would result in better production processes and products. The bankers themselves acknowledged that they lack a deep appreciation of the industry dynamics:

> We have never got an expert who we can trust to go there [pharmaceutical industry] and do an evaluation; and I said to them then I should become a banker. (Technical expert, Kenyan pharmaceutical sector, 2014)

Efforts are under way to bring industrialists and bankers together to try and bridge the gap in knowledge about the sector and hence improve risk analysis. Kenya's road map, however, evidences a purposive and integrated approach to improving standards and upgrading facilities. In interviews the technical experts acknowledged that this would be a long process the success of which depends on availability of resources for investment in equipment and people. The programme in Kenya is being supported by UNIDO, supplementing limited national resources allocated to this important initiative. Kenya appears to be taking control of the issue of standards, and although they are still at the initial steps of implementing the programme, there are lessons that other African technical and policy people can learn.

Initiatives focusing on building capacity and capabilities on standards in local manufactures require coherence/harmony between different approaches. Some global institutions working with African countries, such as the WHO, take a product-by-product approach to standards (WHO pre-qualification), whereas UNIDO and GIZ take a systemic technological approach. This helps to explain different approaches to improving standards in African countries. UNIDO and GIZ prefer to build local technical skills by training local industry. In the next section we look at the Indian standards upgrading to extract lessons that Africa can use.

What lessons can Africa learn from the Indian GMP upgrading road map?

Over the last three decades the Indian pharmaceutical industry has emerged as a major supplier of cheap generic drugs across the world.

The Indian government was credited for infusing life into the Indian pharmaceutical industry through industrial and regulatory policy intervention, and the success of the Indian firms made these interventions a recipe for pharmaceutical industrial development in other emerging countries (see also Chapter 10).

Pharmaceutical production in India is governed by the Drugs and Cosmetic Act of 1940 and the much amended Drug and Cosmetics Rules of 1945. The Act and Rules regulate drugs imported, manufactured, distributed and sold. No pharmaceutical products can be imported, manufactured, stocked, distributed or sold unless they meet the quality standards laid down in the Act. An Indian Pharmacopoeia was published in 1955, and over the years problems in controlling spurious or counterfeit medicines have dominated Indian policy agendas. The Indian government initially aimed to enforce GMP standards in all pharmaceutical manufacturing firms via the Drug Policy of 1986. This laid down requirements for GMP adherence in Schedule M of the Rules, which came into force in 1987. Schedule M was strengthened to require WHO-GMP standards, by amendment in 2001, with the aims of ensuring that firms upgraded and of eradicating counterfeit and substandard drugs. Those pharmaceutical firms that did not comply with these regulations have been refused manufacturing licenses from each State Drug Control Administration office. In the case of manufacturing plants approved before December 2001, non-compliance led to their licenses being revoked, forcing closure of these manufacturing facilities.

The financial cost involved in complying with GMP has proved a significant barrier for small companies in India to upgrade manufacturing facilities. Upgrading of manufacturing plants by small scale firms would result in those firms graduating to become medium-scale firms, thereby losing the tax benefits and other concessions available to small scale enterprises. The Indian government responded to this issue by providing some concessions for the Indian firms, increasing investment limits and turnover thresholds for eligibility as a small-scale firm. On the other hand, several large-scale companies upgraded their plants to access high-income country markets, and their significant financial resources made this transition feasible. The deadline for implementation of GMP was postponed from 31 December 2003 to 31 December 2004, and then postponed again until 30 June 2005. Each State Drug Control Administration office also had the authority to extend the deadline of compliance within its area of jurisdiction.

In spite of these concessions, this mandatory application of GMP had a significant impact on the Indian pharmaceutical firms. According to official estimates, in 2001, 327 pharmaceutical manufacturing plants closed, had their licenses suspended, or were forced to shift to some other state. A total of 370 plants were not in a position to comply with GMP and have closed since 2005 (Planning Commission, 2002, par. 7.1.192). In addition to an increase in competitive pressure, GMP compliance has been another force that has induced the exit of small firms from the market. However, the introduction of GMP has also contributed to the enhancement of trust in Indian products in the global market. In addition, complying with GMP standards of the US and Europe has increased exports to Western countries and expanded the opportunity for contract manufacturing.

Since 2000, the strong presence of the Indian firms in the markets of advanced countries, and specifically in the US, has brought severe scrutiny from regulatory agencies around the world. More numerous FDA inspections led to an increase in the number of warning letters and import bans for the Indian firms (see also Chapter 6). The FDA has identified a number of Indian pharmaceutical manufacturers who have had problems with data integrity and GMP at their respective facilities. Gaffney (2015) notes that since GMP data are intended to ensure that products meet pre-established specifications, absence of credible data management creates concern that these products cannot be trusted.

The case of Ranbaxy provides a prime example of the FDA attitude towards implementation of GMP in the Indian firms. The FDA has repeatedly issued warning letters and import bans to two of the company's manufacturing plants because of data integrity issues. The warning letters note that the FDA has concerns about non-compliance with US current Good Manufacturing Practices requirements, although 'FDA has no evidence of harm to any patients who have taken drugs made in these two facilities' (Jeffrey et al., 2001; US Food and Drug Administration, 2008). Elaborating on their concerns at one of the manufacturing plants, the FDA warning letter focuses on concern that 'written records of major equipment cleaning and use are inaccurate' (USFDA, 2008) and notes that their investigative team uncovered 14 instances 'where ... records for equipment used in manufacturing operations ... included initials or signatures of employees who reportedly verified cleaning of equipment but were not shown as present by security log records' (USFDA, 2008).

Jeffrey (2001) argues that this experience highlights the way in which international regulatory authorities play a crucial and detailed role in setting production and data management standards at the Indian manufacturing sites, using the set of regulations and rules developed to protect high-income countries' consumers. The cost of implementing and complying with these regulations is incurred by the Indian manufacturers and government and in most cases passed on to the Indian consumers. Further, these regulatory troubles have caused the Indian firms significant revenue losses and reduced competition in generic markets, contributing to profit margins of multinational pharmaceutical companies. This experience raises issues about the authority of developing country governments in setting standards, and about the appropriateness of international standards to the local context in the developing countries.

Concluding discussion

Pharmaceutical standards and regulations are necessary yet complex institutions which change over time, operate at various vertical and horizontal scales, are subject to different interpretations and applications and have potential to assist the manufacturing of, and access to, safe efficacious medicines. However, they can also act as undesirable market entry barriers. African pharmaceutical industry players accept that standards are important, but they contend that the other regions of the world which are more advanced now 'did not themselves improve their standards overnight'. Rather, it was a gradual and long drawn-out process as countries learned best practice from the first movers. African technical experts argue that Africa should not be pressured to catch up 'overnight'. When African and other developing countries look broadly at pharmaceutical standards, they need to view them as a process, and there is therefore a need to introduce clear road maps for a gradual strengthening of the requirements for standards, driven by local or regional regulatory institutions.

We conclude that in order to improve standards and upgrade technological capabilities, first, standards need to be deconstructed and understood based on risk management principles. Second, institutional or organizational standards that are based on judgement and can be gradually improved should be recognized as mutable in that sense. Third, technically based standards should also be viewed from a risk management perspective. Once this has been done, African technical and policy actors need to take control of the issue of pharmaceutical standards and to design and manage context-sensitive regulatory frameworks and road maps backed by an evidence base that draws from a clear understanding of standards, attendant risk profiles and their role in industry development and access to medicines.

Notes

1. We acknowledge Dr Farah Huzair for proposing the terms 'mutable and immutable' standards at an Innogen Knowledge Exchange workshop on African Local Pharmaceutical and Medicines Supply held in London in 2013
2. The African Union Commission (AUC), Pan African Parliament (PAP), the World Health Organization (WHO), the World Bank (WB), the Bill and Melinda Gates Foundation (BMGF), the UK Department for International Development (DFID), the Clinton Health Access Initiative (CHAI) and the Joint United Nations Programme on HIV/AIDS (UNAIDS)

13

Innovative Procurement for Health and Industrial Development

Joanna Chataway, Geoffrey Banda, Gavin Cochrane and Catriona Manville

Introduction

> Procurement is then an integral part of health policy. However, it is of course also a part of industrial policy. This is because the way in which purchasing decisions are structured and regulated impact profoundly on the way in which production happens. Thus, consideration of the pros and cons associated with procurement regimes needs to be in terms, not only of whether immediate health policy priorities are achieved, but also in light of longer term sustainability of supply of innovative health products. Thus, price, value and innovation are closely interwoven. (Srinivas, 2012: 126)

Part II of this book has demonstrated that building synergies between health systems and industrial development is a complex process of reshaping the politics and political economy of the two systems. A key tool for building and sustaining health-industry relationships, as Smita Srinivas observes above and as some Part I chapters also emphasized, is procurement. Yet procurement remains under-researched and over-simplified as a technical, linear, ordering and delivery process (see Chapter 8), rather than an exercise in deepening and strengthening the domestic economy through market and non-market relationships building.

This chapter aims to shift the literature on health sector procurement into a more developmental mould. It is an innovative procurement chapter in the conceptual sense, addressing the question of how health sector procurement can be developmental both by addressing health sector needs and values and by sustaining industrial suppliers. It also puts forward innovative arguments, exploring in some detail how procurement can constitute a business asset, and using the example of value-based pricing (VBP) in medicines procurement to explore how procurement can better address health sector needs in marketized and fragmented lower-income health systems.

The chapter is divided into two sections. The first section focuses on procurement as an industrial policy in African pharmaceutical markets. It takes a detailed microeconomic look at procurement design from the perspective of local pharmaceutical firms, for whom access to working capital is a major developmental constraint. Using illustrative data from Zimbabwe, the chapter shows that procurement can be either a source of finance or a serious drain on the finances of firms that operate in the context of high bank charges and interest rates, and in highly competitive markets. Careful procurement redesign can have a substantial impact on firms' cash flow and investment prospects.

The second section turns to innovative procurement strategies that stitch industrial production and innovation into the values and needs of health sector users in African countries. It explains and examines the emergent practice of value-based pricing (VBP) as a tool to link medicines prices to health needs. So far applied mainly in high-income countries, VBP nevertheless falls within a category of global and local procurement initiatives that try to foreground need in the design of public procurement. The discussion recognizes that public procurement, because of its scale and the values it embodies, is not simply a process of market purchase. Medicines markets and other related institutions are co-created by public and private sectors in complex and diverse ways. Integral to this pattern of interaction and articulation is the way in which medicines are purchased and the way in which prices are determined. These decisions are political as well as economic, as reflected in the Srinivas quote above.

Public procurement as an industrial policy tool

In the economic development literature, and in the debates on public policies such as defence procurement, there is a long-standing recognition that public procurement can operate as industrial policy. 'Buy local' campaigns and local preferences often formed part of import substitution policies of the type discussed in Part I. The liberalization policies of the 1980s, in both lower-income and higher-income countries, generally removed local procurement preferences and employed international competitive tendering to open up domestic markets to external competition. The development economist Sanjaya Lall, whose conceptual framework of industrial capabilities is used throughout this book, was a persistent proponent of the continuing need for industrial development policy in these 'globalized' and fast-moving market contexts. In the early 2000s he posed the question: 'What can poor countries do to strengthen their industrial competitiveness in the international economic setting?' (Lall 2003). His argument that in developing countries, industrial capabilities (technological, financial, organizational and dynamic) develop slowly, and are cumulative and 'path dependent' as industries and institutions build on existing skills (Chapter 2), implied the need for local policy interventions such as local content rules for firms' procurement. Lall (2003) identified firms' procurement capabilities, as well as those of governments, as elements of cumulative industrial improvement, and recognized the importance of developing larger groups of firms in one sector so that they generate 'spill-over' benefits (Chapter 2).

Much writing on procurement focuses on its role in providing a market for locally supplied goods and services, and hence sustaining business development (Ogot et al., 2009; Uyarra and Flanagan, 2009; see also Chapter 3). The market impact of public procurement is very large. Among OECD (high-income) countries in 2011, 13% of GDP on average was spent by government on procurement of goods and services (OECD nd). In some African countries, outsourcing has rapidly increased the size of public procurement. In Kenya for example, public procurement as a percentage of GDP rose from about 6% in 2002 to 27% in 2008 (Ogot et al., 2009).

Lall's framework indicates, however, that public procurement as a developmental tool should go beyond providing a market, to support local industrial innovation. Public health procurement can act as a financing and incentive mechanism to improve technological capabilities, a key element of pharmaceutical industry development as discussed throughout this book. Increasingly, public procurement is promoted as an industrial and innovation policy tool (Kattel and Lember, 2010; Uyarra and Flanagan, 2009). Public procurement creates and enhances markets for new and existing technologies by shaping the demand environment. It can promote sustainable consumption and production patterns: for example, the US government in 1993 issued an Executive Order for all federal agencies to procure energy-efficient computers, resulting in market transformation for Energy Star computer equipment (Kjöllerström, 2008). Procurement can target purchase of goods and services that are new to the country, or new to the world. This chapter explores innovative ways to strengthen the role of procurement in relation to pharmaceutical industry development and the needs of the health sector in Sub-Saharan African countries.

Trade credit and working capital: the view from the firms

To understand how the financial aspects of procurement design can influence industrial development, it helps to start by analysing how pharmaceutical firms in Africa can use trade credit to reduce borrowing and keep down manufacturing costs. Firms can use their input suppliers as an in-kind financing mechanism, via trade credit, in order to reduce their call on their own funds or expensive bank finance. Firms' private sector procurement mechanisms therefore play a critical role in managing working capital financing requirements and cash flows.

By negotiating for generous trade credit terms, firms can fund varying proportions of raw material procurement, production and logistics processes, and sometimes influence the debtors' collection period. Astute use of these options turns the firms' own procurement process into a generator of in-kind finance. Failure to use them causes the firm to haemorrhage cash if it pays suppliers in advance or opts not to stretch its suppliers by paying their invoices early, before reaching the limit of their credit terms.

We describe here how trade credit can aid small to medium enterprises in accessing in-kind finance through contractual relationships with larger and more established firms and organizations with better access to finance. Suppliers endowed with market power and reputation can access formal credit (usually cheaply) from banks and then extend trade credit (an in-kind loan) to buyers with less access to bank or own finance (Nilsen, 2002; Petersen and Rajan, 1997). Because suppliers choose to whom to advance trade credit, trade credit serves as a screening and monitoring device for suppliers (Berlin, 2003). The fact that there are more suppliers, who are better at evaluating credit risk, than there are financial intermediaries makes trade credit an important source of finance in an economy. When suppliers extend credit to buyers, they reduce transactional costs, making business transactions cheaper and easier (Gianetti et al., 2011).

Trade credit is therefore a cheap source of short-term, external, in-kind finance, advanced not as money but goods on credit. If firms understand how to handle finance (if they have good finance capabilities, see Chapter 15), they can use trade credit to reduce cautionary cash holdings thereby alleviating cash flow problems.

Thus for firms in poorly developed markets, trade credit assumes great importance: there is evidence that industries have an elevated dependence on trade credit in countries with poorly developed financial markets (Fisman and Love, 2003). For Zimbabwe, Fafchamps (1997), using evidence from the 1993 Regional Program for Enterprise Development (RPED) panel survey of 200 Zimbabwean companies, found that trade credit indeed played a significant role in financing enterprises. Trade credit as a percentage of outstanding balances constituted 27% for micro enterprises, 26% for small enterprises, 30% for medium enterprises and 30% for large enterprises.

However the economic deterioration of the 2000s decade in Zimbabwe caused a high level of uncertainty, shortage of foreign currency and increased country risk. Consequently, local firms found it difficult to access trade credit from suppliers for APIs and excipients. The dearth of trade credit and reliance on expensive bank finance throttled financial breathing space for the companies.

In those circumstances, firms can find themselves in a perverse situation, whereby local pharmaceutical firms are funding suppliers instead of vice versa. Local companies had low bargaining power because they purchased small quantities of raw materials, and their suppliers were not worried if they lost them as customers. Local firms procured raw materials from merchants and brokers with critical mass to move 15 to 30 tonnes of products, and the brokers then sold smaller quantities at higher margins to local firms. APIs and excipients were paid for in advance because suppliers feared country political risk and foreign currency risk, a legacy from the times when Zimbabwe had serious foreign currency shortages despite the country's subsequent shift to using a basket of foreign currencies. Zimbabwean firms, because they paid in advance, were therefore financing economically stronger suppliers in India and China.

Where international suppliers sold to local firms, they also reduced their perceived risk by demanding a letter of credit (LC). The LC costs 2.5% of value, plus charges for establishing the LC and transaction charges. Local firms sought to reduce these high financing costs by negotiating for in-country bonded warehouses to hold goods for purchase, reducing delays due to shipping and customs clearance and hence the period when the firm would be out of pocket while awaiting the raw materials. Broadly, the trade financing pattern became another example of a perverse subsidy from weaker African economies to stronger trade partners, which one can find reflected also in other markets.

Public procurement terms as a financial asset for businesses

The discussion above demonstrates just how strongly a pattern of trade financing can influence the cash flow and business development of local firms. It follows that the design of the payment and credit systems used in public sector procurement can strongly affect the businesses from which the government purchases goods and services. The payment mechanisms in public procurement constitute implicit business financing mechanisms – or a drain on the business.

Public drug procurement payments can be made in at least in three ways; advance payment, cash on delivery or credit terms. Each of these payment modes affects the manufacturers' cash flows, cost of finance and eventually the cost of manufacturing pharmaceuticals. The payment terms can be a source of finance for the firm to use in the production process, or they can cause the producer to seek external expensive finance whilst awaiting payment for goods produced and delivered for periods ranging up to six months.

Advance payment provides direct business funding, as payment is made in advance of goods and services delivery. Advance payment reduces the need for manufacturing firms to borrow expensive bank finance when it does not have sufficient cash holdings. With advance payment, the firm uses these funds to purchase raw material, fund the production process and pay labour. While advance payment, in accounting terms, becomes a short-term liability on the balance sheet of the firm, nevertheless the funds obtained for the pharmaceutical products to be supplied constitute an asset (cash holding) that the firm uses for production and logistics.

With the cash-on-delivery payment method, the buyer pays on receipt of goods and services. The manufacturing firm therefore funds raw material acquisition, production and logistics with either own or borrowed (expensive) funds. Compared to the advance payment method, cash on delivery therefore imposes varying degrees of financing costs on the firm. If the firm uses its own funds, the financing costs are lower than bank borrowing, though accountants will argue that using internally generated funds has important opportunity costs for the business.

The third payment method involves credit terms. The manufacturing firm delivers goods to the procurement agency, which pays after a certain pre-agreed period of time from the date they receive the invoice. The period can generally range from 30 to 90 days and in some instances as much as 180 days. This is the most strenuous payment method of the three described for the manufacturing firm's cash flows. The firm must fund raw materials acquisition, production and logistics processes through the period up to payment. The firm must also have skills in chasing on-time payment by the buyer. This chasing process is especially difficult in many instances when the government or state agencies are the buyer, and they need to wait for disbursement of funds from central treasury (see, e.g. Chapter 3). Onerous credit terms of this kind have constrained many African pharmaceutical manufacturing firms to resort to very expensive bank financing prior to receiving payment.

In effect, many local pharmaceutical firms have no option but to provide the government with credit terms: they are effectively helping to finance the local health system. This generates recurrent cash flow problems as they try to fund successive operating cycles. The process of waiting for payment, especially on an order which is large relative to the firm's capacity, can undermine the firm's ability to procure raw materials and pay labour and associated production costs for the next production cycle, as well as constraining effective sales and distribution.

In these constrained situations, there are ways in which a confirmed order or an invoice can be used by a firm to fund production cycles. Two possibilities are a supply chain structured-credit finance approach, and invoice discounting or factoring.

In the first, supply chain structured-credit approach, the firm can use the strength of the procurement agency's own high credit standing. Once the firm has a confirmed order, it can go to a bank to approve a credit facility with conditions. One of the conditions could be the firm assigns the amount payable after fulfilment of the order to the bank. By assigning the firm's (creditworthy) debtors to the bank, it gives the bank control over the funds to be paid. Because funds are disbursed before products have been produced, the firm needs to procure raw material and produce and deliver products before the buyer pays. Consequently, this type of financing carries production, performance and payment risk, hence the need for the firm to have an acceptable production reputation and for the buyer to have good payment reputation. What is key is that the firm can access funds based on a confirmed order from a reputable buyer: an efficient public procurement body that pays reliably can fulfil this role.

The second approach of invoice discounting and factoring requires a much broader and deeper financial institution architecture in the country, including banks and factoring and discounting institutions. This financing method involves a financial institution paying a proportion (up to 85%) of invoice value to a firm in advance, against invoices billed to the firm's buyers. Factoring and invoice discounting are prepayment methods against a sales ledger for a firm – in other words, it offers advance or early payment to the firm that sold its goods. Instead of the firm waiting for payment by the buyer after, say, 180 days, the firm is able to access working capital finance to fund its production cycles. In this instance, instead of getting advance payment from the customer, the firm gets the advance payment (a proportion) from the financial institution.

Essentially invoice discounting and factoring work in the same way, the difference residing in who has credit control over collection of the debt (amount payable to the supplier). With discounting, the firm has control on debt collection, while in factoring, the firm hands over the collection of the debt to the financial institution, writing formally to its customers to pay the bank directly; the bank then carries the responsibility of collecting the debt.

It follows that if the public procurement agency for the health sector has a good track record for paying on time, it opens up an avenue for firms to access funds based on invoices. This financing approach is attractive because production risk is no longer an issue as the products have already been manufactured. The greatest risk is payment risk by the procurement agency, since many agencies procuring medicines using African government funds may find it hard to pay consistently on time, since their own funding may be erratic (see Chapter 8).

Procurement as an asset: a Zimbabwean example

Where there is political will and substantial financing, public – including donor-backed –procurement can become a substantial asset for local manufacturing firms and the health systems they supply. An example is the support generated for manufacturing anti-retroviral (ARV) drugs in Zimbabwe. The Zimbabwean government initially created and assured the market for locally produced ARVs by providing a funding mechanism, in a context where there were strong local manufacturing capabilities. As a result, Zimbabwe became one of the first African countries to manufacture ARVs locally, in 2003. We explore how this came to pass.

During the economic challenges of the late 1980s and 1990s, Zimbabwe faced a huge social and health challenge emanating from the HIV/AIDS pandemic. HIV/AIDS was placing a huge strain on an overburdened and underfunded health system. In response, the government converted an existing drought levy into the AIDS levy to finance the HIV/AIDS programme. The government set up the National Aids Council and the National Aids Trust to collect and administers the AIDS levy, set at 3% of salaries for formally employed people. Fifty per cent of the AIDS levy is reserved for medicines procurement, with the balance allocated to prevention, awareness and administration costs.

The government issued a compulsory license to manufacture ARVs and promised to purchase 75% of the locally manufactured medicines (Osewe et al., 2008). It is important to recognize that the government could only issue a compulsory license because Zimbabwe had built the infrastructure and capabilities to locally manufacture pharmaceutical drugs from the 1950s (Chapter 1). Transferring the technology in order to manufacture ARVs locally was thus possible because of this industrial background.

However, in spite of government's intentions, the hyperinflationary environment of the 2000s constrained public health financing capacity, culminating in the collapse of the public health system (2003 to 2009). The result was a shift to high donor dependence for financing the public health system and medicines procurement. This shift incapacitated public procurement as an industrial policy tool (NECF, 2010), and was the greatest cause of decline in local industry capacity utilization. Reliance on donor funding that fragments public procurement policies continues to pose a demand-side constraint for local pharmaceutical manufacturing.

However, there are exceptions: one donor-funded programme in Zimbabwe provides an unusual example of support from donors for local pharmaceutical production. Ordinarily, in many African health settings, donor-funded health programmes tend to import medicines from India or China independently of public procurement mechanisms. For example, in Zimbabwe the principal purchaser of anti-retroviral drugs for The Global Fund is the United Nations Development Programme (UNDP), which procures the drugs through their pooled procurement base in Copenhagen.[1] This removes public procurement as an industrial policy tool from the available policy arsenal for stimulating and supporting innovation and industrial development in the African context. In such situations, the market becomes unreachable for local manufacturers.

However in this case, purposive support for local manufacturing was provided. The Extended Support Programme funded by the European Union and DFID (the UK Department For International Development) supported local manufacturers CAPS Pharmaceuticals and Varichem in Zimbabwe to manufacture and supply medicines to the local health system during the era of economic collapse (Table 13.1). This example shows that donor-funded programmes can support local industry and operate as an effective industrial policy tool. Table 13.1 shows that CAPS and Varichem were contracted to supply more than US$4 million worth of drugs to the programme. The contract value shows the values

Table 13.1 Donor support for local industry through contracting for local health supplies: Zimbabwe

Contracts for drug supply by some pharmaceutical manufacturing firms and importers

Supplier	Contract Value (Euro)	Value Delivered (Euro)	% Completion of Supply
Varichem Lot 2	1,788,800	1,522,404	85.11
Varichem Lot 4	198,500	198,500	100
CAPS Lot 1	2,289,784	961,139	41.98
PCD Lot 2	433,967	433,967	100
PCD Lot 3	570,235	570,235	100
PCD Lot 4	198,500	198,500	100
GHC	1,585,464	1,585,379	99.99
Mission Pharma Lot 1	986,615	981,044	99.44
Mission Pharma Lot 2	63,000	63,000	100
SJV	253,280	253,280	100
Total	8,368,145	6,767,488	80.87

Source: EU, 2010.

of medicines that were supposed to be delivered, and value delivered shows what the companies had actually delivered by the time the report was compiled (EU, 2010). Table 13.1 also shows that locally based pharmaceutical wholesalers, including PCD, GHC, Mission Pharma and SJV, were allocated quotas that they filled through imports.

A key issue raised by this example is the political scope for governments to incentivize or compel large donors to purchase locally manufactured pharmaceutical products. Such a move can increase governments' space for policy manoeuvre. The South African government, for example, insists on local suppliers in many circumstances: when foreign companies win tenders, they must go into an agency arrangement with a local South African firm, as exemplified by a case where a Zimbabwean firm won a tender to supply ARVs to the South African public health system and had to partner with a South African firm. Other African governments have been less energetic or effective in imposing local partner requirements on overseas suppliers.

Public industrial procurement to serve health needs and values

The previous section has centred on the scope for aligning demand for health commodities with industrial development needs. This section reverses the view, to ask: To what extent can medicines procurement be shaped to ensure that local industrial development increasingly serves the health needs of the populations dependent on the local health system? This is a question raised and addressed for the Brazilian health-industrial complex and its policy development in Chapter 9. Here, we examine schemes that link reimbursement and assessment of a product's value to the impact that products have in real-world contexts. These efforts can be seen as reflecting a desire to link the introduction of new products to competent health care, which allow for maximum access and benefit. The objective is to bring local industrial production and innovation closer to the health needs it should serve

Our focus is on a particular innovative procurement mechanism: value-based pricing of medicines. While this is to date a mechanism largely experimented with in high-income countries, we think it is important because it shifts the attention of procurement policy from a market (often monopoly) price for an already developed drug to an assessment of how a drug will actually work in particular country contexts and for identified needs. Its attractiveness is in indicating ways forward in adapting procurement to a focus on population health benefit and patient needs.

The broader lessons are particularly pertinent for developing country contexts, where fragmented and marketized health systems may generate wide gaps between population needs and market demand. Public and donor procurement mechanism then need to specify as well as address population health needs. An early and widespread example of such an innovative procurement mechanism was the essential medicines lists, developed by the WHO and by health activists, that specify priorities for procurement of essential medicines, by generic names, to support access to drugs that are deemed essential for particular populations (Laing et al., 2003). The parallel to the discussion of VBP here is that the essential medicines lists also aimed to shift the design of public procurement towards better serving needs.

Public procurement and industrial innovation for unmet need

The use of VBP has focussed to date on the role it can play in relation to innovator drugs targeted for currently unmet or poorly met health needs. The dominant framework of thought on incentives for industrial innovation identifies an imbalance between investment risk in innovation and reward for the innovation. This 'market failure' is then put forward as the rationale for public sector investment in basic science: there is insufficient incentive for the private sector to invest in basic and long-term research, so the public sector should underpin drug discovery with support for early-stage research.

However, this conceptual apparatus does little to explain the actual way in which the public and private sectors invest in drug discovery, development and procurement. At all stages, public and private sectors inform each other in influencing the rate and direction of innovation. As argued in the introduction, markets and other institutions are co-created by public and private sectors. The discussion of VBP locates it as one example of this changing pattern of political and economic interaction and articulation, in this case in the way in which drugs are purchased and prices are determined.

One observation from recent patterns of public and private interaction is that market and institutional failures clearly occur not only at the research stage but also at the other end of value chain – at the market access end. This is especially the case in developing country contexts, and a growing international focus on policy, charitable and public sector initiatives has emerged over the past two decades using procurement to address the problems. The institutional vehicles include The Global Alliance for Vaccines and Immunization (GAVI), set up in 2000, which brings together public and private actors to address the challenge of equal access for new and underused vaccines programmes in the world's poorest countries. As of 2013, GAVI stakeholders have committed US$8.2 billion to achieving their mission and have supported the immunization of an estimated 440 million children (GAVI, 2013).

The Global Fund and access initiatives that are disease specific include other examples of efforts to raise the financial endowment needed to generate innovation, product uptake and access to markets for producers, as well as access to medicines for the patients. Their procurement initiatives are designed to support the skills, finance and technological resource endowment required for innovation. In Europe, there has also been renewed policy thinking about how to construct public and private interaction so that appropriate products get to patients (Chataway et al., 2012). Initiatives such as the European Commission's Innovative Medicines Initiatives support basic and applied research (Morgan Jones et al., 2013).

Other high-income country initiatives such as the Innovate UK stem cell programme support policy thinking and address regulatory, business development, funding and access to market issues. At the same time, new approaches to health technology assessment constitute what has been colloquially termed 'the fourth hurdle'. Going beyond efficacy, effectiveness and product approval, they cover value assessments and relate to pricing and procurement. Procurement and the technology assessment that goes along with it should be seen as a form of regulation.

Previous work has suggested that well-targeted systems of regulation and standard setting result in better outcomes than broadbrush approaches in terms of overall outcomes, including innovation (Chataway et al., 2006). For instance, broad regulatory judgment across Europe that banned all products that left chemical residue in water had the unintended consequence of encouraging use of products that were environmentally damaging in a number of other respects than the products that had been banned. The message this regulation sent out to innovators who had worked on creating more environmentally friendly products was negative. It may well be the case similarly that regulation that bans all use of medicines that have undesirable consequences for a very limited number of patients can result in treatments that are less beneficial for the majority. New regulatory science as conceived of by the US Food and Drug Administration (FDA) and the European Medicines Agency (EMA) hopes to target regulation ever more carefully to those who are at risk.

Value-based pricing

This hope that targeted policy and intervention will deliver better results also underpins value-based pricing. The central idea of VBP is that the price of a drug may differ according to the impact that it has on different groups of patients, and maybe also across different health system contexts (Claxton et al., 2008). The desire to become more targeted and specific is common to both traditional rule-based regulation and innovative procurement-based regulation.

Lying behind VBP is a concept of health benefits and costs. Pricing of new innovator drugs is a question not of how much they cost, but of how much the firm can take out of a health system through the price it manages to charge. Where there is a highly competitive market for a medicine, competitive tendering can drive down prices. Where there is a monopoly supplier, the price is a matter for negotiation if procurement agencies have the competence and methodologies. A recent MSF report reported from contacts with nine pharmaceutical companies that value-based and differential pricing strategies were used predominantly in non-competitive markets for vaccines (e.g. for new products) where manufacturers do not have to compete on price (MSF, 2015).

Since resources in all health systems are limited, health economists use tools for technology assessment to feed into assessments of whether a certain therapy should be reimbursed. The concept of the incremental cost effectiveness ratio (ICER) has become one driver of reimbursement for new drugs. Along with measures of Quality Adjusted Life Years (QALYs), ICER calculations are used to measure health benefit and cost to health care provider, and these metrics are used to compare the attractiveness of different therapies. VBP provides a different approach to the logic of reimbursement. The UK is one of the countries that has been debating the introduction of a new way of determining the price for new drugs. The new UK regime has been partly driven by fiscal austerity in the country, in which funds for the purchase of new drugs may well depend on savings in other aspects of health spending. VBP seems to offer a broader approach to pricing decisions, which looks at the impact of drugs on overall health and social care systems.

The UK Department of Health has traditionally used a pharmaceutical price regulation scheme to control expenditure on branded drugs.[2] Recently, however, it has been considering a move to a more outcomes- or value-based approach (Persson et al., 2010). Like the calculations of quality-adjusted life years (QALYs) gained from using the new drug, VBP would also assess the benefits of a drug to individuals. The difference is that VBP signals a move to determining the price to be paid for the drug on the basis of assessment of a drug's impact in terms of health benefits *and* its contributions to the overall health system. The value-based price is in theory the price that ensures that health benefits for patients and the wider society exceed the health benefits displaced elsewhere in the health system and in the society due to the medicines' additional costs (Camps-Walsh et al., 2009; Claxton et al., 2008). The move is also to a more targeted and perhaps more adaptive system, with ongoing assessments of a drug's value potentially influencing its price. Again in theory, the calculation would take into account the importance of incentives for innovation.

The move has a number of implications, and Verhoef and Morris (2015) provide a summary of what value criteria other than QALYs (or similar measure of patient-level health gains) have been advanced in the literature as possible components of VBP. These include:

- Wider patient- or disease-related value criteria such as severity of disease (e.g. whether it is an acute, chronic, rare or terminal disease); unmet need; size of relevant population; age groups particularly suffering an impact of the disease (e.g. children); socially disadvantaged patients; number of other treatment options.
- Health care-related value criteria: being treated at a convenient time and location and after only a short wait; being treated in a way that

patients consider less unpleasant (e.g. taking a medicine once a week as opposed to three times a day); and the degree of risk of the treatment.

* Wider societal value criteria such as ability of patients (and carers) to resume work or to work more productively; cost savings to other publicly funded services (e.g. social care), patients or carers; and how innovative the medicine is.

Some versions of VBP schemes might also involve differential pricing for different patient cohorts. For example, a group of patients with one genetic makeup may benefit more than another group, and therefore the price paid for the drug being taken by the group that benefits more would be higher.

Value attributes will need to be collected, measured, aggregated and converted to evaluate a 'value metric' (Deloitte, 2012).[3] The data that will feed into this assessment will need to go beyond purely clinical trial data. Real-world data – that is, data relevant to the drug in use, not just in trials – would apply both before the market launch (e.g. up-to-date cost of illness data) and post-launch: comparative real-world data, information on side effects and changes in effectiveness over time (Greiner, 2011). The sources of such data could transcend patients, clinicians, hospitals and social networks. The quality of the data and its format, governance and ethical considerations are likely to influence the feasibility and extent to which VBP can reflect real-world values. There may well be a need for the development of new methods which can assess value in different contexts and under different conditions, and which can incorporate trade-offs.

A move towards VBP is certainly not without its complexities and dangers, and it is important to note that only a limited number of countries have attempted to implement VBP schemes. However, it is also the case that those countries do appear to be experiencing benefits as a result of the schemes they have implemented. Sweden is the most widely cited example of a country that has implemented a workable and successful scheme. Evidence from Sweden summarized in Persson (2012) suggests that a VBP scheme may be well placed to encourage the adoption of innovative medicines, especially those that address unmet needs. This is particularly important in the case of orphan drugs designed to treat rare diseases and which due to their high cost-per-QALY often fail to obtain reimbursement. The Swedish Dental and Pharmaceutical Benefits Agency (TLV), from June 2003 to April 2010, received 30 requests for orphan drugs reimbursements and awarded 29 (Cochrane et al., 2015).

Nevertheless, there is limited evidence about how the approach can work in practice, and the evidence available comes from international examples applying only a few elements of the VBP approach. The situation is made additionally complex because VBP metrics are often used on conjunction with other schemes. Sweden combines VBP with other approaches such as coverage with evidence development (CED) schemes (Cochrane et al., 2015), and this in turn makes gathering evidence on the effectiveness of VBP approaches challenging (Persson, 2012).

Additionally, it is difficult to judge what impact funder silos, which mean that costs and benefits from health and social care, for example, are calculated without reference to each other, will have on the way that treatments are rewarded. How will methodologies be developed to assess the full costs and benefits in the health, social care and domestic settings? Can multiple budgets be brought together and analysed coherently? These and other unresolved issues seem to have led to delays in the introduction of VBP-based schemes, although thinking about how VBP might be introduced on a large scale is beginning to influence approaches to determining price.

So why focus on VBP? Earlier we argued that the classic image of publicly supported fundamental science and private support for more applied work is not useful. Innovation emerges from a more diverse and complicated patterns of interactions between private and public sectors that work across the R&D and product development processes to create new medicines and make them accessible to patients. The public sector has to intervene in multiple ways to ensure that incentives offered for drug development are balanced with broad public interest agendas in ensuring access to medicines in response to need.

Value-based pricing is thus not about the drug; it is about the impact of the drug in the context of the health system and unmet health needs. In this respect, VBP could act as an incentive for innovation that is more focussed on delivery of and access to products that are designed to meet the most pressing needs in particular contexts. Perhaps VBP could be thought alongside other mechanisms to try and address local health needs in developing countries. For example, it could be used in conjunction with product development partnerships (PDP) or market guarantees focussed on particular health challenges.

A shift to pricing mechanisms for procurement that use local health needs assessment is challenging for developing countries. Nguyen et al. (2014) emphasize the difficulties more broadly with pharmaco-economic evaluation in developing countries, citing a lack of capacity due to a shortage of qualified researchers and health care data. Fragmented health systems generate poor data on health needs. However, African and other low- and middle-income public procurement bodies face the challenge of procuring innovator medicines as well as generics, and need to develop assessment skills for price negotiations. More generally, a procurement process that seeks to identify population health needs and then encourage local supply development has to build up tools over time to assess the benefits of local innovations.

Conclusion: procurement as development policy and process

Public procurement is an important development tool, and in medicines it needs to be designed to interlock industrial innovation and development with the huge scale of African unmet health need. Given the scale of medicines procurement, and its life-or-death importance, its institutional design and operation therefore require much more policy and research attention. Medicines procurement is at the same time highly technical – requiring capabilities identified in this chapter in financing and health benefit assessment – and also highly political. It involves sets of rules, but it is also a complex set of social and institutional relationships. When it goes wrong, both health and industry suffers.

We have suggested two innovative aspects of procurement that will occupy much more attention of African policy makers. The first is the procurement payment systems and the ways in which they can be designed to act as assets and incentives for local industrial development. The other is the assessment processes that can underpin pricing systems that go beyond competitive tendering to generate negotiated prices for innovative suppliers. Finally, we have argued that value-based pricing is just one example of potential innovative procurement mechanisms that can be designed to have at their heart the objective of both incentivizing industrial suppliers and directing their efforts to address unmet health need. Public procurement may be underfunded by national budgets, but collaboration with donors and private firms can, if purposively designed, promote local production, innovation and access to medicines.

Notes

The authors would like to thank Sonja Marjanovic from RAND Europe for helpful conversations about this chapter.

1. The Global Fund to Fight AIDS, Tuberculosis and Malaria, http://www.theglobalfund.org/en/ (accessed 25 April 2015).

2. The NHS spends about £11 billion annually on drugs of which £8 billion is on branded drugs. This represents about 13% and 10% of available resources, respectively (Claxton et al., 2008).
3. Figure 6 in this report has some case vignettes of VBP agreements.

14
Industry Associations and the Changing Politics of Making Medicines in South Africa

Theo Papaioannou, Andrew Watkins, Julius Mugwagwa and Dinar Kale

Introduction

The making and delivery of new medicines is not only a process of science and technology, of production and marketing, but also a process that is inherently political. As such, the relational and political interactions between industry and government are key to shaping regulatory environments that either promote or constrain an industry's ability to collectively learn, innovate and grow (Malerba, 2002). Often critical to the governing of these relations over time are intermediary actors such as industry associations and various advocacy groups that through processes of conflict, negotiation and collaboration promote knowledge exchange and institutional capacity building. In developing and emerging countries, such intermediaries are likely to play a particularly prominent role in filling institutional knowledge gaps towards shaping regulation and subsequent industry development (Kshetri and Dholakia, 2009). Moreover, these interactions between industry and government can be particularly complex and often contentious when government views an industry as potentially contributing to the public good, as in the case of the pharmaceutical industry and its role in the provision of health care. In such cases, it can be suggested that the strategies employed by industry associations over time will need to address the needs of the government and the civil society it negotiates with in order to effectively advance the interests of the industry it represents.

This chapter builds on these notions by analysing the changing role of biopharmaceutical industry associations and related umbrella organizations in South Africa since the 1960s when the sector's first industry association was formed. More specifically, we examine the ways in which the changing political context and institutional interplay have shaped a South African industry-government relational trajectory that is historically uneven and reactively contentious. In this case, respective pharmaceutical associations have shifted gradually away from pure, narrowly aimed lobbying tactics to greater cooperation with government and civil society on a host of policy-related issues, from health innovation to national goals of development.

Our analysis considers developments during three main periods through which the South African biopharmaceutical industry has evolved: (1) a period of pre-liberalization; (2) a period of expanding pluralism; and (3) a period characterized by increasing partnership. While the activities of industry associations reside primarily in the second and third periods, a discussion of the first period is deemed essential in understanding the unfolding of industry-government relations in subsequent and more recent periods. Findings indicate that two decades of both increasing pluralism and globalization have created tensions amidst regulatory uncertainties between government and the pharmaceutical industry regarding access to medicines on the one hand and strong intellectual property rights (IPRs) on the other. We suggest that such uncertainties can be reduced through improving interaction between biopharmaceutical industry associations, government and civil society organizations (CSOs). This can result in more legitimate and cumulative platforms for partnering on a number of regulatory issues and broader, more holistic developmental aims.

We begin this chapter by positioning industry associations as intermediaries within a broader policy subsystem and clarifying their importance in the developing and emerging country context. We then consider the activities of industry associations within wider government-industry growth and development coalitions, presenting both the challenges and opportunities towards potentially collaborative yet inherently political relations. We follow this with a brief overview of the South African case and the approach and methodology employed in our analysis. Next, we consider the importance of historically embedded relational dynamics between government and the pharmaceutical industry in South Africa that are punctuated by periods of regulatory uncertainty, mostly involving intellectual property regimes that either reinforce or alter existing relational trajectories. We underpin our analysis with evidence from case studies on four industry associations engaged in the South African pharmaceutical industry.[1] These case studies include interviews with senior managers, biopharmaceutical and other industry association presidents and government policy makers in relevant departments. These findings, along with data collected through various secondary sources, lend insights into the current political strategies of biopharmaceutical industry associations and the possibilities of more development-oriented government-industry coalitions going forward.

Industry associations and the policy subsystem

We define industry associations as industry specific member-based organizations that actively lobby and negotiate with government on their members' behalf to shape government policy and regulation. Included in this are business umbrella groups such as chambers of commerce who represent the interests of a number of industries and sectors, and are engaged in broad industry coalition building. These organizations are part of what Sabatier (1991) describes as the 'policy subsystem' comprised of intermediary bodies regularly involved – through a variety of aggregation processes – in the shaping of policy within their specific domain of interest (Jenkins-Smith and Sabatier, 1994). For developing and emerging countries, this subsystem is bound to be particularly important where given institutional capacities for innovation and industry growth will often be lacking (Frankel, 2006), and where their potential development will be the result of politically contested relations between government, industry and civil society. Furthermore, these are likely to involve considerable negotiation between local and global interests (e.g. international bodies and multinational companies [MNCs]). In this context, industry associations will likely play a leading role in bridging institutional knowledge gaps between government and industry, and between the local and the global (Kshetri and Dholakia, 2009).

To advocate their members' interests successfully, industry associations will generally need to engage in and perform the following activities and functions. First, industry associations will employ far-reaching knowledge and information gathering and dissemination activities that target government, the broader industry community and the public. Second, industry associations will develop and maintain working relations with key individuals and ministries in government, often using 'elite' members and officials to lead outreach and lobbying efforts (Kshetri and Dholakia, 2009). Third, industry associations must be capable of building widespread industry coalitions for engaging with government. Otherwise, industry fragmentation can result in an ineffective industry voice; this can lead to government-industry tensions during times of regulatory uncertainty and less-than-optimal policy outcomes. Finally, industry associations will need to function as 'veto players' which influence politics of development and therefore governing structures of innovation capabilities (Tsebelis, 2002). In the context of developing countries, it is increasingly acknowledged that the political creation of successful institutions of innovation happens under significant pressure from industry associations (Doner and Sheneider, 2000).

Despite their potential contribution to development, negative connotations are often ascribed to industry associations and their activities, as they have been viewed as controversial actors of innovation and development. For instance, as early as the 18th century, Adam Smith, in his *The Wealth of Nations*, accused industry associations of playing a negative role in the economy, conspiring against the public or raising the prices of goods. More recently, industry associations have been viewed as special interest groups and/or elitist organizations that pursue narrow rents for a limited number of members at the expense of the wider sector and economy, discouraging competition and thus curtailing collective innovation within an industry (see Olson, 1982; Schmitter and Streeck, 1999). This aligns with ideas concerning corporatism where national economic policy is formed through closely coordinated collaboration between government, industry and labour, either imposed by the government (state corporatism) or formed voluntarily (neo-corporatism) (see Schmitter, 1974; Cawson, 1986). Examples of these might be apartheid-era South Africa and contemporary Sweden, respectively (Thomas, 2004). Schmitter (1974) was concerned with what he coined 'societal corporatism', where a small number of interest organizations are able to monopolize the policy subsystem, competitively eliminating other interest groups and essentially forcing the government to enter into collaborative relations with industry due to political necessity (Maree, 1993). In some cases, some form of societal corporatism may be beneficial, allowing for more rapid development of national capacities during times of necessity or crisis. The obvious downside of societal corporatism is that the state can become beholden to a few key interest groups, for example a small group of domestic conglomerates or a select number of foreign companies. In this way it is thought that industry associations, in certain political contexts, can even threaten democracy (Cawson, 1982).

State-industry relations and coalitions towards development

While industry associations may influence the shaping of government-industry relations, the strategies they employ and the subsequent extent to which government and industry work together may be determined more by long-standing and embedded relational dynamics between the two. Relations between government and industry are often referred to as coalitions, in that some degree of co-dependence and thus cooperation between government and industry is not only inevitable but necessary. In the context of developing countries, relations between government and industry may be characterized as 'growth coalitions', ranging from 'weak growth coalitions' where there is at least a minimal recognition that 'business needs the support of government to make profits; governments need to share in these profits to finance government and politics' (Moore and Schmitz, 2008: 1), to 'strong growth coalitions' where government and industry engage in active cooperation towards the goal of policies that both parties expect to foster investment and increase in productivity (Brautigam et al., 2002). According to Schneider and Maxfield (1997), strong growth coalitions require government and industry to share information and to have a high degree of 'reciprocity, trust, and credibility' towards one another. However, this does not change the fact that growth coalitions presuppose bargaining or compromises between industrial and political elites and CSOs. Khan (1995, 2000) refers to such coalitions as forms of political settlements – the balance-of-power among contending elites, CSOs and social groups. Political settlements are based on a common understanding of how narrow elitist interests can be served through policies of innovation and development.

Since the 1980s, a main focus of political-industrial settlements or government-industry relations for many developing countries, including South Africa, has been the implementation of neo-liberal economic policies. Cornerstones of this policy approach include currency stabilization, denationalization of industry, trade liberalization through the lowering of trade barriers, providing incentives for exporters and reducing favourable treatment of domestic firms, as well as the cutting of deficits for decreasing inflation and lowering interest rates – all aimed at spurring domestic innovation and growth in conjunction with increased foreign direct investment. Results of such neo-liberal-focussed growth coalitions have been mixed, with many developing countries experiencing sharp yet isolated increases in growth and wealth production amidst continued widespread poverty. For developing countries, therefore, it has been argued that government-industry growth coalitions need to evolve to a more development-oriented model that focuses on poverty alleviation over an extended period of time (Brautigam, 1997, 2009; Handley, 2008). Seekings and Nattrass (2011: 339) argue, however, that development coalitions necessitate 'much deeper deliberation and negotiation than a growth coalition: the objective is not only to agree on the mix of public sticks and carrots that serve to promote economic growth, but to agree on a mix that promotes a particular pattern of growth', one that is focussed on the needs and welfare of the poor. For industry and the associations that negotiate with government on industry's behalf, such a move would require a considerable shift away from pure lobbying to greater partnering with government.

The global pharmaceutical industry and the case of South Africa

The global biopharmaceutical industry is comprised of a relatively small number of large research-oriented MNCs based mainly in the developed North and a large number of both small and large companies that manufacture generic medicines both in the developed North but most prominently and increasingly so in the developing South (see Chapter 6). Most generics manufacturers operate as independent companies while others are subsidiaries of large MNCs. The research-based MNCs make generally large profits through the global sale of patented blockbuster drugs which are more expensive than generics and are at times priced out of the reach of poor patients. The research-based MNCs insist that the high prices for the medicines they sell and the profits they garner are necessary for covering the costs of marketing and continued R&D activities. But the inability of many to pay these prices, including the governments of developing countries, and the increasing expiration of many patented medicines have facilitated the tremendous growth of the generics industry which has substantially lowered the price for a number of essential medicines, including anti-malarial, and anti-retroviral drugs, among many others, some experiencing a 50–90% reduction in price, thus considerably increasing access to these medicines. The growth of the generic medicines industry and its impact on research-based MNCs have created considerable fragmentation and conflict within the pharmaceutical industry and between the pharmaceutical industry and the governments of emerging countries such as South Africa.

South Africa's economic growth for the last few years has averaged 2–3% and it slowed down to 2.0% in 2014. However, as the second-largest African economy after Nigeria the country exerts strong economic and political influence on the African continent. The country made the transition from an apartheid state to a constitutional democratic state in 1994. Since then, South Africa has experienced considerable economic growth, but also increased inequality and extreme poverty in certain sections of the population. In the area of biopharmaceuticals, the country has emerged as the industry forerunner in Africa with a significant presence of both domestic manufacturers and MNCs, although the domestic manufacturing industry is relatively small, with up to 65% of the country's pharmaceuticals still being imported (IPASA, 2013). Furthermore, its private market, worth US$2.8 billion in 2012, is relatively small and constitutes less than 1% of the market globally. In 2011, two leading pharmaceutical companies in South Africa were domestically based MNCs, Aspen Pharmacare and Adcock Ingram; domestic companies import up to 90% of active pharmaceutical ingredients from other countries, including India and China. Meanwhile, historically, and presently, the country has had a number of active biopharmaceutical industry associations, making it an important case study for investigating the realities of pharmaceutical production in Africa and the role of industry associations in it.

With respect to industry associations, companies in this sector are members of different associations depending on the segment of the market that they occupy. Most foreign MNCs are members of the newly formed Innovative Pharmaceutical Association South Africa (IPASA), which emerged from a merger between two former associations, Innovative Medicines South Africa (IMSA), for research-based/innovator MNCs; and Pharmaceutical Industry Association of South Africa (PIASA), whose membership included both innovator and generics companies. The new association, IPASA currently represents 24 innovative pharma companies dedicated to producing or importing innovative medicines in South Africa. According to IPASA, only companies that conduct their own R&D qualify for membership. This means that domestic companies with no intellectual property (IP) are excluded from the new association. Only IP holders, for example MNCs with innovator products, can become members of IPASA. In addition to IPASA, there is also the National Association of Pharmaceutical Manufacturers (NAPM), Pharmaceuticals Made in South Africa (PHARMISA), Self-Medication Manufacturers Association of South Africa (SMASA) and National Association of Pharmaceutical Wholesalers (NAPW), among others. They also all belong to the Pharmaceutical Task Group (PTG), a broad coalition involving IPASA, NAPM, PHARMISA and SMASA. The PTG deals with the government on issues of mutual concern such as pricing, regulation and national health insurance. For example, the PTG has retained an advocate to represent the pharmaceutical industry in the Competition Commission enquiry into high health care prices. That being said, many of these associations and member companies are also members of the leading chambers of commerce, CHAMSA and SACCI, and connect with one another through these platforms. This current status of industry has evolved through two main periods: pre-liberalization and the post-apartheid.

Pre-liberalization era

While disagreements over the past two decades on particular regulatory issues have at times stymied relations between the South African pharmaceutical industry and the South African government, tensions between the two are very much rooted in a long history of tense and generally non-negotiable relations between the South African government and the South African business elites, which have carried over into more recent periods from the apartheid era. As Seekings and Nattrass (2011: 343–44) explain,

> Indeed, relations between state and business in South Africa throughout the 20th century were framed by the coexistence of a strong state and powerful corporate capital. The state enjoyed considerable political autonomy from capital, but remained dependent on capital for continued economic growth. The outcome was often tense relationships, as the state sought to push and bully capital into subordinate co-operation, whilst avoiding genuine deliberation, and being careful not to undermine white prosperity.

As such, during the apartheid era, the South African government was intent on maintaining and enriching the white minority through ever increasing control and exploitation of the black majority. This necessitated a command-oriented state, the brutal subjugation of blacks and the complicity of white-owned industry which was dominated by a small number of large state-supported conglomerates all linked in some manner to the South African gold-mining industry. Offering considerable trade protection (much of this induced through international boycott) and ensuring low-wage black labour, the South African government expected industry to operate within certain constraints and to be 'subservient, as long as it was dependent on state patronage' (Seekings and Nattrass, 2011: 344); this resulted in a state-industry relationship that was generally reactive yet ultimately accommodating in terms of industry response, and largely devoid of negotiated compromise.

With an economy centred on mining and energy extraction, and stagnated by the apartheid system and resulting sanctions and boycotts, the

South African government lacked the ability and capacity to either invest in a broad-based science and technology infrastructure (e.g. weak university R&D) or facilitate the growth of technology-based industries (the exception being defence). A strong domestic pharmaceutical industry was never really established in South Africa during this period. The need for medicines, however, meant that large research-based pharmaceutical MNCs continued to sell and distribute medicines in South Africa, with some operating manufacturing facilities in the country. That being said, two pharmaceutical companies, Sterling Winthrop and Merck, divested their interests in South Africa and left the country due to the boycott. A few domestic generics-based pharmaceutical companies such as Adcock Ingram were able to successfully operate under the constraints of apartheid, but their growth and proliferation would not really occur until after apartheid's end. During this period, two main biopharmaceutical industry associations were established. The first was the South African Pharmaceutical Manufacturers Association (PMA), established in 1967, and the second was the National Association of Pharmaceutical Manufactures (NAPM), established in 1977. The membership of the PMA was a mix of domestic and foreign-owned pharmaceutical companies, but the MNCs were more dominant given their market strength; members of NAPM, by contrast, were almost solely domestic manufacturers of generics. Both associations used to work closely with government and/or play advisory roles in policy areas such as health and drug manufacturing. This was consistent with the corporatist state-industry relations of the apartheid era.

Post-apartheid South Africa

South Africa's transition to democracy in 1994 led to weakening of the corporatist hold of the state and strengthening of the civil society (Lehman, 2008). This does not imply that a pluralist approach to state-industry relationships prevailed. Rather, pluralism and corporatism seem to coexist in post-apartheid South Africa. The relationships between industry associations and state appear to be co-operative; governments tend to view the business elites as a key player in pro-market liberal reforms. Indeed, as Seeking and Nattrass (2011: 339) point out, 'Capitalism not only survived the transition from apartheid to democracy, but high profit rates suggest that capitalism continues to flourish in the post-apartheid environment'. This is precisely the reason why South Africa, despite its exceptional economic performance, experiences increased inequality and extreme poverty in certain sections of population, namely the black majority. The co-operative state-industry relations in the post-apartheid era failed to form a strong 'growth coalition' that could also deliver development. Therefore, within the governing party – the African National Congress (ANC) – the new political elite(s) developed distrust against the business elite(s). The ANC adopted pro-market policies with respect to the global economy without necessarily having a pro-business or pro-industry attitude. According to Seeking and Nattrass (2011: 344), 'In the early 1990s, two views of businesses coexisted within the ANC. On the one hand, business was seen to have been one of the pillars of apartheid, exploitative of workers and abusive of consumers. On the other, there was a growing appreciation of the overall weakness of South African capitalism, in particular its inefficiencies stemming from chronic protection against foreign competition and over-concentration'. The first view clearly supported regulation of employment relations and protection of black businesses. The second view supported trade liberalization and industrial policy. As Seeking and Nattrass (2011) observe, both views entailed a commandist approach to business and industry without so much negotiation.

In this post-apartheid mix of corporatism and pluralism, large pharmaceutical companies began to re-establish themselves in South Africa, insisting on strong protection of patented drugs through TRIPS. On the other hand, CSOs such as non-governmental organizations (NGOs) and advocacy groups began to formally participate in the policy-making process (Lehman, 2008). In 1994 there were more than 50,000 NGOs in South Africa, most of them pursuing development objectives (Fioramonti, 2005). In the post-apartheid era, the state inherited a strong regulatory capacity (ibid) and relied on it to protect public health from the spread of diseases such as HIV/AIDS through the poorest sections of population. According to Seekings and Nattrass (2011: 353), 'Its interventions in the private sector were programmatic rather than targeted in that the state legislated frameworks for change...and then endeavoured – with mixed success – to ensure that private sector complied with the statutory requirement'.

One well-known intervention was the government's 1997 Medicines and Related Substances Control Act that would allow South Africa to import and manufacture cheaper generic HIV drugs. This Act prompted 39 big pharmaceutical companies (mainly MNCs) to file through PMA a patent right lawsuit against the South African government – the so-called Big Pharma v Nelson Mandela case. In response, CSOs and activists accused PMA of violations of the human right to health by making essential medicines unaffordable and called the international community to protect developing countries against big pharmaceutical companies (Wolff, 2012). Although in 2001 PMA agreed to drop the lawsuit as a result of the growing opposition, it was too late. The PMA suffered an international public relations disaster with three MNCs, GlaxoSmithKline, Merck and Bristol-Meyers Squibb, breaking ranks with 36 other companies and pushing hard for a settlement that would stave off increasing damage (*The Guardian*, 2001). Eventually, these 36 companies agreed to go along with the lawsuit withdrawal, but PMA dissolved, splitting into two new associations: the Pharmaceutical Industry Association of South Africa (PIASA) and the Innovative Medicines South Africa (IMSA).

PIASA was established as an association of companies involved in the manufacturing and marketing of medicines in South Africa. Its members were research-based MNCs and local manufacturers of pharmaceuticals. PIASA had about 90 members, consisting of both large and small companies. Other organizations, such as the South Africa Medical Device Industry Association (SAMED), were members of PIASA, testifying to the diversity of the association. The objective of PIASA was to shape strategic regulatory issues relating to clinical trials, registration of medicines and IPRs. In addition to this, the association tried to tackle regulatory hurdles that discourage investment in South Africa's biopharmaceutical sector. PIASA was also engaged in activities to influence the quality and cost of medicines, access to treatment, health insurance, drug laws and pharmaco-economic evaluation. Among such activities advocacy, networking and innovation diffusion appear to be the most crucial ones. PIASA interacted with government but also with other associations, including IMSA in the health policy and regulation arenas. For instance, it had substantial involvement in the formulation of the South African Health Charter and Private Health Care Reform programmes. This close interaction of PIASA with government was often seen as uneven, given the conflict of public and private interests. Another important activity of PIASA was diffusion of knowledge through hiring consultants and providing members with expert advice on pertinent issues in the health innovation and regulation terrains. Such issues included standards for manufacturing facilities, drug registration fees and regulatory harmonization. This range of activities in the institutional context of South Africa indicates that PIASA played a crucial role in influencing the country's innovation system.

By contrast, IMSA was established as an industry association for research-based companies, even though some of its members also used to produce generics. This is not surprising; generics are crucial for the public health service in the country. Among IMSA's members there were 12 MNCs who captured about 53% of the MNC market share in South Africa. Generally speaking, this biopharmaceutical association engaged in R&D policy, innovation regulation and lobbying. IMSA did not always perform such activities alone but in collaboration with other associations. Thus, for instance, in the PTG initiative IMSA played an active role in national health insurance issues, working jointly with PIASA and other public actors of South Africa. Another key focus of IMSA was on IPRs, especially access to drugs and marketing. The association worked with and through its members to exert influence on these issues. IMSA's key contacts in government were the Department of Health, the Department of Science and Technology and the Department of Trade and Industry. It also made policy contributions to parliament's portfolio committee on health. However, IMSA also functioned as a government tool for industrial policy implementation. That is to say, it worked closely with government for the implementation of broader national policies by their members, for example requirements under the Black Economic Empowerment (BEE) programme.

The split of PMA into PIASA and IMSA was not the most negative consequence of the 'Big Pharma v Nelson Mandela' case. After all, in April 2013 these associations came together again, forming the Innovative Pharmaceutical Association South Africa (IPASA). It might be argued that the most negative consequence of the 'Big Pharma v Nelson Mandela' case was the damage to trust between government and biopharmaceutical associations. As one interview respondent pointed out,

> [P]re-1994 I think the industry was more in an advisory role, although perhaps not with lobbying focus, access to government ministries was quite possible. What changed it completely for the industry was the court case of 1998 to 2004 which was all about weakening intellectual property and so created a sense that we [the industry] were against the government. So from that time onward, whenever you went into the halls of government, they [the government] would see you as 'you are that industry that took us to court'; so that created such animosity between the Department of Health, the relationship has never really been constructive. (Interview extract: 23)

This statement confirms that, in South Africa, state-business relations (SBR) in the area of biopharmaceuticals remain fragile and therefore lack essential characteristics of effectiveness. According to Cali and Sen (2011: 1543), such characteristics include:

(i) transparency: whether there is a flow of accurate and reliable information, both ways, between business and government, and from representatives of business to their own members; (ii) reciprocity: whether there is capacity and autonomy of state actions to secure improved performance in return for subsidies; (iii) credibility: whether the state command credibility of the private sector, and whether capitalists are able to believe what state actors say; and (iv) whether there is mutual trust between the state and the business sector.

Clearly, South African SBR in the area of biopharmaceuticals are neither transparent and reciprocal nor credible and mutually trusting. Rather, due to the long-term impact of the 'Big Pharma v Nelson Mandela' case, these relations are based on mutual suspicion and distrust.

Analysis and discussion: resetting the state-industry relationships

Since its formation in 2013, IPASA has been engaged in a highly uneven relationship with government over the latter's policy plan to change the patent rules for medicines. That plan incorporates patent flexibilities after the Doha Declaration (WTO, 2001) and recommends elimination of weak patents, promoting the production of generics (DTI, 2013). In response, IPASA embarked on a campaign against the full implementation of the government plan, lobbying the government and other national and international actors for a stronger IPR regime. Its main objection is that by using TRIPS flexibilities and by promoting generics, the South African government's plan on IP policy will reduce innovation and fail to attract investment, particularly FDI, into knowledge-based firms such as those in biopharmaceuticals (IPASA, 2013). The South African government insists that the issue is not about weakening the TRIPS regime and the country's biopharmaceutical innovation system, but about implementing TRIPS with all the necessary flexibilities for the sake of public good (*The Economist*, 2014). The tension between government and IPASA (the majority of research-based pharma MNCs) heightened substantially when it was made known that IPASA was participating (perhaps leading) a campaign in collaboration with a Washington, DC-based public relations firm that aimed to promote the supposed adverse consequences of a weak IPR regime as proposed by the government, to target the South African public, business community and academic institutions. This bypassing of the government by IPASA in its attempts to thwart government policy, and doing so during an election year, fuelled already high levels of distrust between the South African government and the research-based, primarily foreign-owned pharmaceutical companies.

The above episode is an apparent setback to relations that, while recently punctuated with conflict, have been defined more by increasing collaboration both within industry on key regulatory issues, particularly taxation and medicine registration procedures, and with government on broader health care policy. For example, a number of these biopharmaceutical industry associations have been involved more recently in wider policy discussions with government regarding science and technology workforce development, industry-university collaboration and the role of research-based pharmaceutical companies in the development and implementation of a South African National Health Insurance scheme. Resetting relations will require reengaging government on such issues, but huge differences on IPR will need to be addressed, if not wholly overcome. Even though stronger IPR laws are supported by much of South Africa's business community (e.g. SACCI supports a stronger IPR regime), the research-based pharmaceutical industry, due to its status as an important yet 'reluctant' and untrust-worthy medicines provider, will need to go further. It needs to shed the perception that its interests in South Africa do not go beyond clinical trials and the profit-driven motive of protecting of its patented medicines and future therapies for sale not only in South Africa but the entire African continent.

For its part, the South African government needs to decide what type of role it sees the pharmaceutical industry playing in a relatively poor yet modern South Africa. On one hand, the South African government's approach to access to affordable medicines has indeed increased access, but has also resulted in a growing reliance on foreign generics (e.g. from India) rather than the development of a domestic generics industry. On the other hand, it has recently put forward public-private partnership (PPP) initiatives towards developing indigenous high-tech industries such as biotech, yet has not sufficiently articulated, at least in public, the role of IPR or the pharmaceutical industry in this new policy vision. This seeming contradiction is played out between government ministries, particularly long-standing divisions between the Department of Health, which supports weak IPR laws for ensuring access to affordable medicines, and Science and Technology (DST), which favours stronger IPR laws as a means of fostering innovation more generally and realizing the positive externalities that a robust research-based pharmaceutical industry might provide South Africa. However, DoH and the Department of Trade and Industry (DTI) are aligned in the area of access to health. Such intra-government divisions, while justified, do complicate negotiations with industry and likely reinforce industry fragmentation between research-based MNCs and generics manufacturers. Current fragmentation on both sides of the negotiating table are contributing to tense relations between the South African government and the pharmaceutical industry and probably resulting in policy inertia and far less-than-optimal regulation.

Conclusion

In this chapter, we have considered the neglected role of industry associations in Africa as key intermediaries in innovation that, through evolutionary processes of conflict, negotiation and knowledge diffusion, facilitate institutional capacity building while shaping regulation and subsequent industry development. To do so, we have analysed the shifting strategies over time of biopharmaceutical industry associations and related organizations in South Africa. We have considered the importance of historically embedded relational dynamics between government and the pharmaceutical industry in South Africa involving critical junctures of regulatory uncertainty, mostly involving highly contested intellectual property regimes. Tracing developments during three main periods within different national context, our findings support previous research that suggests industry associations are more effective in lobbying and negotiating with government when industry is relatively cohesive and able to speak with one voice. This chapter, however, also suggests that in the case of the pharmaceutical industry, the extent to which industry associations can effectively engage with government is determined, in large part, by the willingness of government over time to neither demand nor capitulate, but to compromise with industry in ways that meet its own requirement for accessible medicines while recognizing the positive externalities of a robust domestic pharmaceutical industry. When such willingness is limited, either long-standing or temporarily, biopharmaceutical industry associations in South Africa are increasingly asserting themselves as 'partners' with government in attempts to correct these long-held tensions with the aim towards negotiating better policy outcomes.

In the case of South Africa, decades of tension between government and industry in general, which carried over from the apartheid era, have exacerbated long-standing pharmaceutical industry fragmentation on key policy issues such as IPR, particularly those between MNCs and domestic generics companies. In turn, this has inhibited constructive policy dialogue and reinforced industry-government distrust, particularly regarding the pervasive assumption that the growth of an innovation-led biopharmaceutical industry in South Africa is incompatible with widespread access to effective and affordable medicines. Subsequent policy divisions between the DOH and DST both mirror the overall divisions and mistrust between industry and government and may contribute to regulatory inefficiencies. This has placed South Africa's biopharmaceutical industry associations, particularly those representing MNCs, often in direct and open conflict with government.

Finally, the historical trajectory and the shift to greater partnering strategies captured here provide insight into the conditions and processes through which 'growth coalitions' in developing countries such as South Africa either remain weak and ineffective in terms of developing a domestic industry or grow strong in that they effectively promote both the growth of domestic industry and the subsequent realization of positive externalities and spill-overs. In doing so, the challenges of moving government-industry relations to a more effective 'development coalition' model that is focussed on growth and poverty alleviation are laid bare. In the case of South Africa, the government and the pharmaceutical industry seem to be locked, based on decades of tension and mistrust, in a rather weak 'growth coalition' that, while promoting the interest of a few key industry players and keeping prices of medicines low, has kept the domestic South African pharmaceutical industry relatively small, dependent on foreign generic suppliers, with few positive externalities or spill-overs gained. For moving towards a stronger growth coalition, the biopharmaceutical industry associations of South African will need to build trust with government and to reconcile industry divisions among themselves.

Notes

Acknowledgements: This chapter draws on a research project, 'Unpacking the Role of Industry Associations in Diffusion and Governance of Health Innovations in Developing Countries', funded by The Leverhulme Trust UK, during 2013–15, reference number RPG-2013–013. The authors would like to thank Maureen Mackintosh and participants of the *Making Medicines in Africa Workshop* (15–16 December 2014) for reading earlier drafts and providing useful comments and suggestions.

1. In total, 19 interviews were conducted, involving 4 industry associations: Innovative Pharmaceutical Industry Association (IPASA), National Association of Pharmaceutical Manufacturers (NAPM), South African Chambers of Commerce (SACCI) and South African Medical Device Industry Association (SAMED).

15

Finance and Incentives to Support the Development of National Pharmaceutical Industries

Alastair West and Geoffrey Banda

Introduction

There is a now a growing international consensus that development of the pharmaceutical industry in Africa can contribute to both economic development and improved public health. This final chapter begins by identifying the striking convergence of thought and initiative that has recently been generated across continental African representative bodies, international agencies and national governments. We outline this emergent consensus and then examine challenges it faces by focusing on the core interconnected policy issues of financing and incentives for industrial development in pharmaceuticals. A sustainable and expanding pharmaceutical industry must reach essential quality standards and also constantly upgrade, moving up the technology ladder while improving cost efficiency. This requires a cocktail of incentives in which finance is key (Chataway et al., 2009). These incentives, in turn, rely on the building up of appropriate financial capabilities within firms and financial institutions as well as within governments. This chapter innovatively traces the interconnections between micro-level financial capabilities and national government policy competences in the design and effective implementation of financial incentives and associated policies to facilitate industrial development in pharmaceuticals in Africa.

The emerging commitment: transforming pharmaceutical manufacturing in Africa

At the African continental level, the African Union Commission (AUC) identified the imperative of pharmaceutical industry development in their *Pharmaceutical Manufacturing Plan for Africa* (PMPA) (AU, 2007), endorsed at the African Union Heads of State and Government Summit in 2007. Progress on realizing the ambition espoused in this document was initially slow to materialize, prompting the Conference of African Ministers of Health (CAMH) to call at their fifth meeting in 2011 for a 'Business Plan' for the accelerated implementation of the PMPA. A partnership was formed later that year between the AUC and the United Nations Industrial Development Organization (UNIDO) to develop the business plan, and in May 2012 the resulting document (AU, 2012a) was approved by a special session of the CAMH in Geneva. In July 2012 the Business Plan was endorsed by AU Heads of State and Government at their summit in Addis Ababa.

Regionally and institutionally, collaborative work on local pharmaceutical development has snowballed. The African Ministers of Industry have also now recognized the pharmaceutical industry as a priority, in the Accelerated Industrial Development of Africa (AIDA) framework endorsed at their 19th meeting in Algiers in 2011. African Regional Economic Communities have also developed plans. The East African Community Regional Pharmaceutical Manufacturing Plan of Action 2012–16 was launched in 2011 (EACRPMPA, 2011). The West African Health Organization (WAHO) has been developing the Economic Community of West African States (ECOWAS) *Regional Pharmaceutical Plan* (ERPP) and its implementation. The ERPP explicitly aligns with the principles and objectives of the Business Plan for the PMPA, and WAHO has rapidly developed a comprehensive approach, despite wrestling with the unprecedented crisis of the Ebola outbreak in the region.

The public health commitment

International organizations concerned with public health are also now indicating growing support for this agenda. The Joint United Nations Programme on HIV/AIDS (UNAIDS) under the leadership of Michel Sidibé has long been an advocate of the importance of strengthening local production, in particular to address the sustainability of HIV/AIDS treatment, as well as access to medicines for tuberculosis and malaria. It is a central component of Pillar Two of the African Union's *Shared Responsibility and Global Solidarity Roadmap for HIV, TB and Malaria Response in Africa*, developed with support from UNAIDS (AU, 2012b).

In 2008 the World Health Assembly adopted the *Global Plan of Action and Strategy on Public Health*, a broad document that identifies the role that local production of essential medicines could play in improving public health. As part of its implementation, the World Health Organization

(WHO) has run an EU Commission-funded project to assess this role. Phase 1 of the study concludes that the development of the local pharmaceutical industry does not inevitably lead to improved public health, and hence that promoting the public health impact should be central to efforts to strengthen the industry. These initiatives have helped to ensure that public health considerations are central to the Business Plans that are being developed. They plot a practical path whereby the industry can contribute to both public health and economic development agendas that were previously considered by some to be mutually exclusive (Kaplan and Laing, 2005).

The strong current consensus amongst the international community, that the development of the pharmaceutical sector in Africa is an imperative, was notably underlined by the Joint WHO Bulletin Editorial by Mr Sidibé, Mr Li (Director General of UNIDO) and Dr Chan (Director General of WHO) (Sidibé et al., 2014). The authors strongly supported the development of the industry in Africa through the implementation of the PMPA Business Plan.

The challenge of implementation

Practical bilateral and multilateral support for the industry is growing. The German government has a long track record of supporting the pharmaceutical industry in Africa. Since 2006 it has funded a UNIDO project on strengthening the local production of essential medicines in developing and least-developed countries, a project initiated by the previous UNIDO Director General Dr Kandeh Yumkella. Bilaterally through its aid agency Deutsche Gesellschaft für Internationale Zusammenarbeit (GIZ), Germany has supported the EAC pharmaceutical plan and many other initiatives such the bioequivalence centre in Addis Ababa (see Chapter 5) and initial feasibility studies for a similar centre in Ghana.

Other international support includes the United States Pharmacopeial Convention (USP) which, with funding from the United States Agency for International Development (USAID), has been running a programme on Promoting the Quality of Medicines (PQM), including capacity building for manufacturers and regulators. In 2013 it opened the Centre for Advanced Pharmaceutical Training (CePAT) in Ghana, to train regulators and the industry in quality assurance and quality control. The St. Lukes Foundation in Tanzania has similarly been training industry professionals on international standards of production through its Industrial Pharmacy Advanced Training Programme, taught by US academics from Purdue and Howard universities, supported by UNIDO.

The need to exploit opportunities under the exemptions and flexibilities offered by the Trade Related Aspects of Intellectual Property Rights (TRIPS) agreement[1] has led the United Nations Development Programme (UNDP), the United Nations Conference on Trade and Development (UNCTAD) and the African Regional Intellectual Property Organization (ARIPO), amongst others, to establish relevant programmes.

The PMPA *Business Plan* identifies the problem of a piecemeal approach that has not delivered rapid development of the industry, and proposes that coordination across different initiatives is required. The international organizations need to invest in supporting emerging national and regional processes to enable development of the industry. Coordinated technical assistance is required to support relatively weak skills availability in the short term and to engage in capacity development across public and private sectors for the long-term sustainability of the industry. National governments too need to invest to support their industries: this point was underscored during a high-level side event at the Ministers of Finance and Economic Planning meeting co-hosted by the African Union Commission and the United Nations Economic Commission for Africa (UNECA) in Abuja in March 2014.

Ghana is an example of a country where a coordinated agenda is progressing. In October 2013 early implementation of the AUC's PMPA *Business Plan* began in Ghana, following an invitation from President Mahama to the Chairperson of the AUC, Dr Nkosazana Dlamini Zuma. A technical assistance work plan was agreed by the national stakeholders and a consortium of partners including UNIDO, WHO, UNAIDS, UNDP, UNFPA, the New Partnership for Africa's Development (NEPAD), the African Network for Drug and Diagnostic Innovation (ANDI) and the Federation of African Pharmaceutical Manufacturer's Associations (FAPMA). The work plan recognizes both the critical need to build capacity within public sector institutions and the private sector and the need within the industry for time and support to invest in upgrading.

The need for complex cross-institution coordination to implement the work plan is illustrated by the collaboration with the Ghanaian Food and Drug Authority (FDA) to develop and implement a good manufacturing practices (GMP) road map; the development of training modules for industry on developing capital investment plans and managing capital project life cycles; the creation of a business linkages platform to enable companies to access the know-how that they require in the short term whilst internal technical capacity is developed; and a market data initiative to provide market transparency to inform policy makers, industry and investors in their decision making. Technical assistance has also been provided to assist government in assessing investment proposals made by pharmaceutical companies under the Export Development and Agriculture Investment Fund (EDAIF) stimulus package, described below.

Upgrading, market consolidation and the challenge of finance

Central to all this work is the recognition that the pharmaceutical sector in Africa needs to upgrade standards in order to be able to provide safe, efficacious, quality-assured essential medicines. Achieving this objective is a highly complex undertaking requiring coordinated action of many parties at national, regional, continental and international levels (Chapter 12). Africa-based companies are able to compete at international standards, contrary to some earlier expressed views (see Chapter 6; Chaudhuri and West, 2014). The most technically advanced companies such as Universal in Kenya (WHO-prequalified for its Lamivudine Zidovudine FDC), Quality Chemicals International Limited in Uganda (with additional site licence for Cipla's pre-qualified products) and four companies in Nigeria that have recently received WHO-GMP certification (including May and Baker and Evans Pharmaceuticals) have attained high international standards.

However, the industry's contribution to economic development and improved public health requires a broader swathe of companies to upgrade to international quality standards, not just for products to treat the major pandemics but for all medicines that have a critical role to play in treating communicable and non-communicable diseases. As earlier chapters have shown, companies across Africa are striving to upgrade their facilities and their manufacturing processes and procedures. However, whilst there have been no published systematic studies on the range of quality standards to which manufacturers on the continent adhere, it is clear that many companies licensed to manufacture pharmaceuticals in Africa currently operate in premises and/or have quality management systems that fall below what should be acceptable.

The concept of the GMP 'road map' establishes rising quality targets over a defined period of time. During transition to meet these milestones, those companies that are operating below them should be restricted to manufacturing products where the risk to health is minimized. Such a stepwise approach creates a transition process for the industry whilst protecting public health. So long as the requirements are enforced by credible sanctions, the framework can discourage unproductive use of subsidies by manufacturers not in practice investing in upgrading. It also provides some market protection for leading companies that have made significant investment, since they can sell a broader range of products during the transition phase.

The PMPA Business Plan focuses initially on generic small-molecule non-sterile production of final formulations in Africa. Even with this subset of essential medicines, the complexity of the system within which manufacturing takes place is significant (see Chapter 2). The industry has multiple stakeholders, operates in widely varying contexts across countries and regions, and includes manufacturers at significantly different levels of industrial development.

Nevertheless, some general requirements for industry development can be identified, and of these the central requirement is finance. Companies need to access capital to invest in retrofitting facilities or building new plants to meet international standards. The magnitude of investment required will depend on many variables including the specific pharmaceutical forms that a manufacturer wishes to produce, the scale of the plant and the starting point of the organization, but most companies will require at least US$10 million (see also Chapter 5 for the financial requirements for a start-up). The efficient use of this investment requires that companies in this knowledge-intensive industry can access the capabilities to design and build GMP-compliant plants and develop or acquire the capabilities to run them. Companies need assistance to access know-how, time to develop plans and implement them, and more time to develop the capabilities first to operate efficiently and then to adapt and innovate.

Upgrading is done by companies, not governments. But policy makers and international development organizations need to understand the challenges faced by manufacturers, and to work with them and with national and regional entities to enable effective upgrading whilst avoiding wasteful use of scarce resources. The AUC has recognized this need for close collaboration, convening a consortium of continental and international partners, including the Federation of African Pharmaceutical Manufacturers Associations (FAPMA), to implement the PMPA Business Plan. The consortium will work with African trade associations, regions and sovereign states on strategies for upgrading the industry.

Regulatory market shaping

In order to invest sustainably, pharmaceutical companies also need access to a large and effectively regulated market in which returns can be made. Further strengthening of regulatory authorities is needed to ensure that legitimate manufacturers do not face competition from spurious, substandard and counterfeit products. Pharmaceutical manufacturers also need to utilize capacity efficiently in order to be competitive, and market scale is an important contributor to achieving cost efficiency. Since many African countries' populations are relatively small, current efforts to defragment African regional markets, and confidence in their likely success, are vital prerequisites to mobilizing investment for many pharmaceutical manufacturers. While for a few firms international donor-funded markets may offer larger-scale market opportunities, the sustainability of an exclusive focus on these markets in the long term is questionable.

Important progress has been made in the direction of regional market consolidation, through the African Medicines Regulatory Harmonization initiative (AMRH), particularly in the EAC and ECOWAS Regional Economic Communities. The documentation for regulatory approval across member states will at least be standardized, removing significant transaction costs from manufacturers, and boding well for increasingly harmonized regulatory requirements in the future (see Chapter 12).

Finally, as earlier chapters have documented, local manufacturers are frequently at an inherent disadvantage in competition with imported medicines, and corrections to the tax and tariff frameworks are required at regional level. The ECOWAS Regional Pharmaceutical Plan (ERPP) advocates for zero tariffs on raw materials, machinery and equipment for pharmaceutical manufacturing within the Regional Economic Community and exemption of inputs from VAT. It also recognizes the need for an appropriate regional framework to support the stepwise approach to upgrading.

Such initiatives can help investors to assess potential returns. However, the quantification of the market opportunities remains elusive, given the paucity of market data for most African countries and regions. This market opacity increases the perceived risk for investors, leading in turn to higher interest payments through an increased risk coupon required for debt providers, or to a higher internal rate of return required by equity investors. The cost of investment capital for African pharmaceutical investors remains a barrier for many companies in countries where interest rates on bank loans may exceed 25%. The next two sections tackle the funding challenge in more detail, first from the point of view of the manufacturers and private financing institutions, and then from the point of view of governments seeking to enable investment for industrial growth.

Building financial capabilities in manufacturers and financial institutions

The African local pharmaceutical industry is playing technological catch-up based on building technological capabilities (Chapter 2). These technological capabilities are sometimes summarized as know-what, know-how, know-why and know-who (Ernst and Lundvall, 1997). They include the skills needed for investment, production and creating market and non-market linkages (Lall, 1992): using technology effectively for expansion; handling key production systems from quality control and operation and maintenance to adaptation and improvement; and dealing effectively with suppliers and customers. While it is accepted that finance plays a strategic role in funding working capital requirements and capital investment, it is however less well documented that many Africa-based firms lack essential capabilities in raising and managing finance effectively (Banda, 2013).

The essential finance capabilities include the ability to understand a project life cycle and phase finance and to structure the most relevant type of financial product. It also encompasses lending technology, pricing and an overall financial approach that does not choke the financial health of the borrowing firm, but rather enhances its productive capacity. Financial capability involves knowing where to get the most appropriately structured financial products, from whom, and when to use them. These firm-level financial capabilities are particularly important for developing-country contexts, where financial systems are not well developed and growth of capital-intensive enterprises depends on capital investment financing (long-term foreign loans), in most cases from offshore sources.

In this section we explore finance capability in the firm and financial institution. This discussion is grounded in empirical work carried out on Zimbabwean pharmaceutical companies and financial institutions, and additional interviews with pharmaceutical sector players in Uganda, Kenya, Tanzania and Ethiopia up to 2013. We analyse how firms use finance expertise and competencies, to identify and manage short-, medium- and long-term funding cycles. We focus on financial institutions at a micro-level and attempt to tease out the technical knowledge and capabilities needed to competently assess, classify, monitor and manage risks. The classes of risk may include credit, management, performance, regulatory, foreign exchange, payment and market risk which in various combinations manifest during a project lifecycle.

The financing context for pharmaceutical firms in Africa

Economic, social and financial history shows sources of finance for setting up enterprises globally have been predominantly internal or own finance, made up of savings, wealth and loans from family and friends (Lazonick and O'Sullivan, 1997a, 1997b), in the industrialization era. Enterprise growth was funded internally by retained earnings, and externally banks were the most prevalent source of finance historically (Lazonick and O'Sullivan, 1997a, 1997b), specifically for the period from 1970 to 1989 (Corbett and Jenkinson, 1996). Other sources of external finance were venture capitalists and capital markets. The key determinants of financing source were the enterprise's management experience, skills and credit reputation.

Growing companies with experienced management, poor to good future prospects, medium to high risk and established credit reputations are likely to use banks as sources of external funds (Corbett and Jenkinson, 1996). African enterprise financing studies similarly find that of all external funding sources, bank finance has been the most prevalent (Fafchamps et al., 1995.)

For established companies, with established credit records, low credit risk and run by experienced management, capital markets are the most likely source of external finance. However, capital markets did not play a major role in raising capital for industrialization, except to a certain extent in the US (Lazonick and O'Sullivan, 1997a, 1997b). Capital markets were used particularly to transfer ownership of corporate entities from family-run or close-knit ownership structures to publicly quoted companies, rather than to raise finance for industrialization.

Capital markets, however, are of little significance in Sub-Saharan African markets because of their small scale and low capitalization, with the possible exceptions of South Africa, Nigeria and Kenya. Venture capital and capital markets are more the exception than the norm in Africa. A more important source of external finance is foreign direct investment (FDI), which can embody technology flows (Portelli and Narula, 2004). FDI allows the developing country to import technology without payment, since the investor brings in knowledge and skills required to operate the technology. Ensuring effective technology transfer is a challenge. However, data on financing manufacturing industry in seven countries in Sub-Saharan Africa indicate that FDI and external/offshore financing were the main sources of capital, reinforcing Ndlela's (2007) and Riddell's (1990) accounts of FDI as being critical for the emergence of the manufacturing industry in countries such as Zimbabwe.

How then do firms select internal or external avenues for financing investment? Internal funds include retained earnings, depreciation or fresh equity injection from existing shareholders. External funds include bank debt, hybrid bonds or issuing of new equity to new shareholders. When internal funds are limited, management seeks external funds. A 'pecking order' theory (Myers, 1984) argues that in the face of limited information, firms will prefer to use own financial resources such as retained earnings or profits; only if self-financing is insufficient will management use external debt instruments: first bank debt, then hybrid bonds, and the last option will be new equity. The order of preference is determined by the objective of retaining management control. Hybrid securities such as convertible bonds dilute management control less, and carry fewer external accountability (discipline and reporting) requirements compared to stock exchange equity. Equity is a last resort because of onerous reporting standards and controls when dealing with broad shareholding structures and professional managers as agents of shareholders (Myers and Majluf, 1984).

Finance capability gaps in pharmaceutical firms

Faced with these financing constraints and choices, a firm with limited internal funds needs to develop capabilities to scan for potential funders and financial products nationally, regionally and internationally. The firm needs to articulate its organizational, dynamic and technological capabilities in a robust well-argued project finance document with supporting data. In building the project finance document and data, the firm needs to use its external networks to assess economic, industry and business environments and attendant risks, as well as stress-testing project data. The finance department as the key operating contact point with external financiers articulates the firm's competencies and capabilities in procurement (trade credit included), research and development, production and engineering, as well as sales and marketing capabilities. Table 15.1 Column 1 summarizes the financial capabilities the firms require.

The firm then needs to negotiate with financial institutions on appropriate finance products by competently structuring the debt or equity relevant to business needs. If this is not managed properly, financial institutions can push their preferred high-yielding products. The firm may then be burdened with finance products characterized by high charges, onerous covenants, triggers and security (collateral) requirements. Firms thus have a great deal to gain from finance capability to identify and structure appropriate borrowing products and negotiate on pricing.

Table 15.1 Finance capabilities at the firm and financial institution levels

Pharmaceutical firms' required competencies	Funder's (financial institutions') required competencies
Identify the businesses' financial needs: Working capital and capital investment requirements	Understand the industry, business, economic, political, and regulatory environment.
Ascertain the best available financing structure; a mix of short, medium and long term finance through debt, equity or hybrid instruments to structure the funding model for the firm	Sector-specific knowledge to competently identify, analyse and manage risks in business, industry, management, markets and regulation. Some funders have a central set of industry and sector specific skills that assists all business units.
Structuring the funding model requires development of knowledge of lending technologies and funding instruments on the market and outside national borders	Alignment of internal capabilities in prospecting, screening, analysis, structuring financial products/ funding schemes, document perfection, disbursement of funds, monitoring and control and eventual repayment of principal and interest.
Crafting a competent project finance proposal that identifies project risks and how they are managed through the management, organisational and technological capabilities of the firm.	Whilst managing projects identify opportunities and the exhibit flexibility to change within and after the life of the funded project.
Competency to apply financial resources to originally identified funding needs, and through financial management capability run successive asset conversion cycles to generate profit and maintain commercial viability.	Through learning-by-doing transfer skills and capabilities developed to other industrial sectors and within departments in the institution.
Competence to repay interest and principal on time, and meet challenges in restructuring debt after negotiation with the funders.	

Source: Compiled by author from fieldwork in Zimbabwe, 2010–13.

Our interview data show, however, that these finance capabilities are lacking in many firms. One respondent in Zimbabwe remarked that the firms 'were afraid to approach international banks because they are not able to produce a robust project proposal and are afraid of being asked questions'. Crafting a project proposal requires knowledge of the firms' capabilities, what the money is needed for, and how revenue will be generated to repay debt. Based on the dynamics of the proposed project business cycles, the firm needs to be able to know which financing tool would be most advantageous to it instead of waiting for the bank to always propose the mode of financing.

Building finance capabilities in banks

Finance capability in financial institutions refers to their ability to source projects to invest in (investment capability); analyse the risks; structure the finance instrument, price the debt instrument and loan duration; followed by monitoring and control and eventually repayment of the debt by the borrower. Various players within the financial institution interact in the process of financing a project. The internal staff identify and analyse risks that include but are not limited to business, industry, management, country, political and foreign currency risks. The risk management process is closely tied to loan structuring, documentation, disbursement and monitoring and control procedures.

These processes depend on in-depth knowledge of the sector being assessed (Table 15.1). In practice, information is opaque and hard to assess. Our research evidence from Zimbabwe and secondary data evidence from East and West Africa suggests lack of in-depth and relevant pharmaceutical sector knowledge by financial institutions. A repeated claim by pharmaceutical executives is that financial institutions do not understand the business of African pharmaceutical drug manufacture. Evidence from Zimbabwe suggests that financiers also need to develop an in-depth knowledge of the economy, industry and health sector for preliminary analysis of projects. They need to greatly improve their networking within the financial sector and the national economy to acquire relevant information for prospecting and analysing projects.

Table 15.2 maps, using Lall's (1992) concept of firm-level technologies, the capabilities needed by these financial institutions. The table maps prospecting, risk analysis, facility structuring and documentation, loan approval, loan disbursement, monitoring and control and ultimately loan repayment. Under prospecting capabilities, relationship managers use investment and networking capabilities to scout different industrial sectors for potential deals. They need intimate knowledge of the economy, industry, various business sectors, credit policy and underwriting standards. Interview respondents pointed to the use of both codified and tacit knowledge at this early stage. They emphasized the importance of experienced 'old-timers' for connections and

Table 15.2 Finance capabilities required by financial institutions, mapped using Lall's (1992) firm-level technological capability framework

Commercial Bank Activity	Processes Carried Out	Equivalent Technological Capability
Deal Prospecting	Based on local knowledge and economic set-up, the market development and sales team prospect for lending candidates that fall within credit policy and underwriting standards. They use networked capabilities for introductions and access to potential borrowers.	The bank uses **linkage capabilities** and **investment capabilities** in accessing borrowers and internal project finance appraisal systems.
Credit Risk Function	Using the following lending technologies: financial statement lending, leasing/asset backed, small business credit scoring or relationship lending in various combinations risk experts analyse for various forms of risks.	The banks use **investment capabilities** to ascertain their appetite for lending to the borrower. **Linkage capabilities** are used to collect information that informs risk analysis and management.
Approval Process	Internal credit processes are followed to independently assess the project documents produced within the institution. The approvers use their knowledge and networks to make informed decisions in the approval process.	**Investment capability** and **linkage capabilities** are used to assess the project for funding.
Accessing Funds by The Borrower	Internal loan administration departments ensure compliance with internal processes, all conditions precedent, and regulatory requirements.	This is mainly **process engineering capability**.
Ensuring Repayment of Borrowed Funds	Based on conditions laid out in the loan agreement, internal experts in sales, credit and credit administration control and monitor the project loan. They use proprietary data and processes as well as external sources of information such as trade and press reports for adverse or positive information. This can also serve as a source of further deal prospecting.	The main capabilities used are **investment, linkage, product and process engineering capabilities**.

Source: Compiled by author from experience and fieldwork between 2011 and 2013.

networks evidencing the need for linkage capabilities. Risk analysis, loan structuring and approval use codified and tacit knowledge for decision making by way of agreed financial ratios and internal metrics. Chief Risk Officers also acknowledged the inherent use of 'gut feel', implying relevance of tacit knowledge.

Capabilities that need to be built thus include loan disbursement, monitoring and control and finally repayment of the loan (Table 15.2). The process involves agreement of terms and conditions between the borrower and financier through a loan agreement document (commonly called the loan facility). On fulfilment of the conditions precedent, the loan administration department processes the security for the loan facility and disburses the funds. Monitoring and control is based on the conditions set out in the loan facility. The capabilities at this stage include those of product and process engineering and also linkage capabilities. Our evidence from empirical work in Zimbabwe and interviews with pharmaceutical executives from East Africa shows a clear perception of financial institutions' deficit of in-depth knowledge of pharmaceutical manufacturing business dynamics and attendant risks and opportunities. These challenges were acknowledged by financial institution executives who agreed that they did not understand the pharmaceutical industry. This information asymmetry and opacity leads to classification of the African pharmaceutical manufacturing sector as high-risk, negatively influencing loan pricing.

The financiers and pharmaceutical executives interviewed proposed to tackle these failings through training and exposure to the pharmaceutical industry. Finance capability cannot be taken for granted and requires purposive and strategic investment to build these competences. An illustration of what can be done is drawn from an innovative mid-career recruitment programme of one international bank in Zimbabwe; Standard Chartered Bank. This programme allowed the bank to build skills and a broader knowledge base by recruiting non-traditional bank trained professionals (Table 15.3). This formed part of an Africa-wide initiative by Standard Chartered Bank Africa.

A senior manager who has since left the bank said this programme was a short-term strategic move to fill an identified skills gap. This seems paradoxical; an innovative and strategic approach which could have contributed a longer term strategy to generate risk analysis skills for project management and build capabilities was relegated to a short term measure. The senior manager argued that once the identified skills gap had been filled, they could revert to the usual graduate trainee programme and train in-house. He argued that the mid-career entrants

Table 15.3   Recruitment of non-traditional banking skills to build finance capability by one Zimbabwean international bank in 1998–2000

Intake	Skills Sets	Roles in the Bank
1	Engineers, Economists	Credit Risk Analysis, Monitoring and Management; Relationship Management; Processing; Global Markets; Retail Banking
2	Engineers (electrical, mechanical and civil), Scientist, Agriculture and Geo-Sensing, Computing Technology and Programming,	Credit Risk Analysis, Monitoring and Management; Relationship Management; Processing; Marketing; Treasury (Global Markets); Retail Banking; Direct Banking; Branch Management; Credit Operations; Interest Recalculation; Structured Trade Finance; Transactional Banking; Syndicated Lending
3	Accountant, Scientist	Credit Risk Analysis, Monitoring and Management; Finance; Treasury Back Office Operations

Source: Compiled by author from fieldwork in Zimbabwe (2010–13) and experience.

came in at middle-management level, were more expensive to the bank and so reverting to the cheaper junior level graduate trainees helped contain costs. However it is clear that these 'non-traditional bankers' had added value to credit risk analysis, management and monitoring, with their specialist skills and in-depth technical knowledge. They served as a knowledge bank that junior and senior management tapped into to understand once-opaque industrial operations. As Table 15.3 shows, many of these recruits' skills were used to build a deeper technical knowledge of industries that the bank funded. The short lived innovative programme (a flash of strategic brilliance) demonstrates the lost opportunity for long term skills and finance capability building.

Government interventions to assist companies to access investment capital

There is therefore a need for micro-level financial skills to be developed within the industry and within the financial community. However, it is also recognized that governments need to intervene to enable companies to access affordable investment capital. What types of interventions can governments employ to help resolve this critical issue? A government can provide soft loans, or it can use direct intervention to reduce the cost of financing (e.g. interest subsidies). As well as such specific initiatives, it can intervene to create a conducive industry context that makes investment in the sector attractive to various providers of capital, thereby reducing perception of risk and theoretically increasing the availability of and reducing the cost of capital. Finally, a government can employ time-limited incentives to support industry investment.

Direct capital provision

Many industry actors and a number of trade associations have called for their governments to set up designated funds for low-cost investment in the pharmaceutical sector. One example is in Ghana, where in 2014 the President announced that Cedis 50 million would be set aside from the Export Development and Agriculture Investment Fund (EDAIF) for soft loans to the pharmaceutical sector (with recent currency depreciation this is now equivalent to less than USD$20 million). The government of Nigeria proposed a Naira 200 billion (roughly USD$100 million) fund to support the sector, but this has yet to materialize.

These limited examples to date suggest that for most countries, direct capital provision may not be viable or of sufficient impact to enable the transformation of the industry. Where countries (such as Ghana) have more than a handful of manufacturers, it is unlikely that governments have resources to create a fund of sufficient magnitude to tackle the capital funding gap for a meaningful number of companies. Furthermore, a government making direct capital provision must be equipped to make informed decisions, to ensure these scarce public resources are not wasted through poor investment. Public funding of investment capital for the pharmaceutical sector therefore demands the development of financial capabilities of the type just outlined within governments as well as private institutions.

However, where limited resources can be brought to bear, there is the potential for leveraging these public funds to assist a number of companies to achieve an affordable cost of capital. For example the proportion of individual investments that a fund supports could be limited to a certain percentage of capital required. A blended cost of capital combining public with commercial investment can be more affordable than pure commercial capital. Such leverage could be enhanced if governments consider taking a junior debt position, thereby perhaps reducing the risk coupon required by private sector investors.

Assuming that an investment fund can be regularly recapitalized, through a sustainable funding mechanism such as a levy on pharmaceutical imports for example, public resources could be allocated in tranches. In this way the capital requirements of an organization at one particular time during a project lifecycle can be addressed without tying up resources required for total overall capital requirements, and therefore a greater number of companies can be supported simultaneously over a number of years.

Direct government expenditure to reduce the cost of financing

Governments can also facilitate access to affordable investment capital through subsidizing interest payments. Interest subsidies were made available to Indian pharmaceutical manufacturers to support their development. Using public resources to support the servicing of debt rather than providing the capital itself can be a more efficient use of public resources. However, limitations on the political acceptability of direct transfer of public funds to the private sector, given other pressing demands on public expenditure, may make such a model untenable for many countries. At the least, mechanisms are essential to control waste of resources and limit government financial liabilities.

Can criteria be established for companies to be eligible for such subsidies? There is widespread anxiety about governments trying to 'pick winners', or rather failing to spot losers, thereby backing unsustainable manufacturers and losing scarce funds to unintended uses. All industrial policy interventions require the development of industrial skills and capabilities within government.

Another concern may be that an interest subsidy approach can reinforce a debt-financing model, shifting the industry away from equity financing. Equity financing should form an element of the capital structure of firm in which the return on investment is necessarily long term. Hence, parallel mechanisms may be needed to encourage companies to seek some equity financing to cover some of the capital requirements for upgrading. These mechanisms could include facilitating repatriation of profits, to stimulate interest from foreign investors, or levelling the playing field between debt and equity financing through limiting the tax shields that debt conveys.

Interest subsidies provide an investment incentive, but have the advantage that they do not have a direct impact on revenues and operating profitability, unlike preferential pricing or other forms of market protection. They may therefore be a constructive means of support in that they do not encourage uncompetitive practices.

Creating an industry context that attracts capital

Creating a conducive context for pharmaceutical manufacturing involves the combination of multiple interventions, not all of which are necessarily within the purview of individual governments. The importance of a regional market has already been highlighted. However, individual governments can tackle dimensions such as the overall business environment (corporate tax rates and special economic zones, for example), as well as sector-specific aspects such as strengthening regulatory oversight and developing human resources. While credible forward-looking statements from governments help, genuine impact does require observable developments and interventions.

The role of time-limited incentives

The PMPA Business Plan, regional plans and national strategies all call for time-limited incentives. Given the specific nature of the pharmaceutical industry, what is the purpose of these incentives, what are the tools available to governments and how do these vary by country context?

First, there is a clear distinction to be made between time-limited incentives and policies to induce structural change whether on the demand or supply side. For instance, resolving the widespread unequal tax and duty regimes applied to imports versus inputs for local production (Chapters 2–6) is a long-term structural approach that needs to be embedded. However, it is also possible to decide to adjust tax regimes for a limited period of time, to convey a temporary competitive advantage to local producers in competition with imports.

Examples of time-limited incentives that could be utilized can be drawn from the policy actions already implemented within Africa, on other continents, and for other industries. A major concern for manufacturers is funding their working capital requirements. For African companies this is a particularly profound problem, since they need to import the vast majority of inputs from abroad. Often, credit terms are used up before raw materials can even begin to be converted into final formulations. Such concerns can be addressed through provision of working capital credits, an approach that was used successfully in India, or through underwriting letters of credit enabling manufacturers to secure improved credit terms from their suppliers.

Other government incentives can focus on reducing the tax burden for which companies are liable, as a means to free up resources to fund investment. Effectively, this provides an additional margin that can make local products more competitive in the transition period, as companies learn to operate facilities more efficiently. Examples of incentives to achieve these intents are tax holidays and special depreciation provisions. The latter were once again used in India where companies were able to include depreciation over time on the profit and loss statements up to 150% of the capital cost for plants and equipment.

Previous chapters have covered the use of procurement preferences and restricted lists and highlighted the potential for such approaches to give a boost to local manufacturers. There are acknowledged downsides associated with market protection, particularly if done at a national rather than a regional level, since it can, for example, reduce competition. Introducing preferential import tariffs on inputs for local production is another mechanism to provide a degree of protection for nascent industries. Again, a regional approach that consolidates markets can help to implement this while sustaining local competition.

This discussion is far from exhaustive in covering the range of industrial policy incentives available. The relative merits of the different tools depend strongly on context, but their fundamental purpose is to support the industry during a transition phase so that companies can build capabilities, develop plans for upgrading facilities and execute them, whilst continuing to compete viably during the transition. This transition period also provides time for policy makers to put in place longer term initiatives to sustain the economic and technical viability of high-quality manufacturing, including defragmenting markets and building the institutional capacities and skills within government and industry actors. Initiatives are under way to address these structural realities, but a much stronger push is still required, with the support of international technical assistance programmes to build government skills and accelerate industrial knowledge accumulation.

The importance of country context

Each country considering development of its pharmaceutical industry faces a unique context which determines what policies and initiatives are required and feasible. With a large domestic market, a government could employ protective measures to support industry growth, using import substitution as Ethiopia has done (Chapter 4). For smaller countries, however, regional exports are likely to be a critical part of the business mix for a sustainable industry. Botswana has an expressed desire to establish a pharmaceutical industry, but with a population of 2 million, its strategic positioning objective is to become a regional centre for pharmaceutical production.

Another key variable is the state of the public finances. All countries face choices as to where they invest public resources, and where such resources are severely constrained, the Ministry of Finance and the National Revenue Authority are likely to resist policy initiatives that will reduce the contribution of current taxes levied on the sector to government income, or that increase expenditure through for example procurement preferences or industry subsidies. For example, at present, Ghana and Kenya face difficult public finance situations, making budget-neutral support mechanism such as domestic market protection an attractive option. While the options open to governments and their relative power vary according to the specific context, complementary regional initiatives such as tariff harmonization, regulatory harmonization and general collaboration between countries can increase the leverage that national government interventions have to stimulate upgrading and development of the sector.

Conclusion

We began by highlighting recent developments at regional, continental and international levels that have generated a new convergence of high-level political will to support the development of the pharmaceutical manufacturing industry in Africa. The chapter has sought to shift the understanding of the key challenge of investment finance within those strategies, from a focus on access to capital to a framework of collaborative financial capability building in firms, financial institutions and governments. The chapter outlines the shared political recognition of the need for time, protection and incentives to build the industrial base through upgrading and transition to higher skills and quality standards. Development of new skills within interconnected institutions, evolution of regional markets and firms making the requisite investments and learning to operate competitively at international standards cannot happen overnight. This final chapter, framed by the intensive international and regional collaborations that are now under way, also frames the detailed studies in this book as a timely contribution to those endeavours.

Note

1. See the World Trade Organisation website at https://www.wto.org/english/ tratop_e/trips_e/trips_e.htm for more information on TRIPS.

Bibliography

Abbott, F.A. (2011) *Trends in Local Production of Medicines and Related Technology Transfer*, Geneva: World Health Organization Department of Public Health Innovation and Intellectual Property [Online]. Available from: http://www. who.int/phi/publications/local_production_trends/en/ [accessed 10 January 2015].

Abraham, J. (2002) 'Making Regulation Responsive to Commercial Interests', BMJ, 325, 1164–69.

Abrol, D. & Guha, A. (1986) 'Production and Price Controls: The Achilles Heel of National Drug Policy', in *Drug Industry and the Indian People*, A.S. Gupta (ed.), proceedings and papers presented at the 'All India Seminar of National Drug Policy', held in New Delhi, on 28 and 29 April 1986, A Delhi Science Forum (DSF) and Federation of Medical Representatives Association of India (FMRAI) publication.

AfDB (1994) *Project Completion Report: First Line of Credit to Zimbabwe Development Bank; Republic of Zimbabwe*, African Development Bank, Tunis.

AfDB (1997) *Zimbabwe: Economic Structural Adjustment Programme: Project Performance Evaluation Report (PPER)*, African Development Bank Group, Tunis.

AfDB (1998) *Zimbabwe First Line of Credit to Zimbabwe Development Bank: Project Performance Evaluation Report (PPER)*, African Development Bank Group, Tunis.

AfDB (2009) *Zimbabwe Short-Term Strategy: Concept Note*, African Development Bank: Regional Department, South Region A, Tunis.

African Union (AU) (2007) *Pharmaceutical Plan for Africa*. Available from: www. unido.org/fileadmin/user_media/Services/PSD/BEP/Pharmaceutical%20manu-facturing%20plan%20for%20Africa-English.pdf [accessed 22 May 2010].

African Union (AU) (2012a) *Pharmaceutical Manufacturing Plan for Africa Business Plan*, Addis Ababa, Ethiopia. Available from: http://sa.au.int/en/sites/default/files/pmpa%20bp%20ebook.pdf [accessed 30 April 2015].

African Union (AU) (2012b) *Roadmap on Shared Responsibility and Global Solidarity for AIDS, TB and Malaria Response in Africa*, Addis Ababa, Ethiopia, available from: http://www.au.int/en/sites/default/files/Shared_Res_Roadmap_Rev_F%5B1%5D.pdf [accessed 30 April 2015].

Anders, S.M. & Caswell, J.A. (2009) 'Standards as barriers versus standards as catalysis: Assessing the impact of HACCP implementation of US seafood imports', *American Journal of Agricultural Economy*, 91 (2), 310–21.

Anderson, K. (1996) 'Environmental standards and international trade', *Proceedings of the World Bank Annual Conference on Development Economics*, 317–18.

Aragão, E., Loureiro, S. & Temporão, J.G. (2014) 'Trajetórias tecnológicas na indústria farmacêutica: desafios para a equidade no Brasil' in Silva Paim, J. & Almeida-Filho, N. (Eds.) *Saúde Coletiva: Teoria e Prática*, Medbook, Rio de Janeiro.

Aspen Holdings (2013) *Aspen Pharmacare Holdings Limited Integrated Report 2013* [Online]. Available from: http://financialresults.co.za/2013/aspen_ir2013/IR2013/1_about_this_report.php [accessed 30 April 2015].

Assefa, H., Bienen, D. & Ciuriak, D. (2013) 'Ethiopia's investment prospects: A sectoral overview', *African Review of Economics and Finance*, 4 (2), 203–46.

Astley, W.G. & Fombrun, C.J. (1983) 'Collective strategy: social ecology of organizational environments', *Academy of Management Review*, 8, 576–87.

Athreye, S. (2004) 'Trade policy, industrialization and growth in India' in Bromley, S., Mackintosh, M., Brown, W. & Wuyts, M. (eds.) *Making the International: Economic Interdependence and Political Order*, Milton Keynes: The Open University In association with Pluto Press.

Bagachwa, M.S.D. & Mbelle, A.M.Y. (1995) 'Tanzania' in Wangwe (ed.) *Exporting Africa: Technology, Trade and Industrialisation in Sub-Saharan Africa*, UNU/INTECH and Routledge, London.

Bajpai, V. & Saraya, A. (2012) 'Understanding the syndrome of techno-centrism through the epidemiology of vaccines as preventive tools', *Indian Journal of Public Health*, 56 (2), 133–39.

Banda, G. (2013) 'Finance as a "forgotten technological capability" for promoting African local pharmaceutical manufacture', *International Journal of Technology Management & Sustainable Development*, 12 (2), 117–35.

Bao, Q. (2000) 'Paying the price of medicines', *The China Business Review* [Online]. Available from: https://chinabusinessreview.com/ [accessed 15 November 2014]

Barker, C. (1983) 'The Mozambique pharmaceutical policy', *The Lancet*, 2 (8353), 780–82.

Basant, R. (2010) *Intellectual Property Protection, Regulation and Innovation in Developing Economies-The Case of Indian Pharmaceutical Industry*, Indian Institute of Management-Ahmedabad, Working Paper Series.

Bate, R. (2008) *Local Pharmaceutical Production in Developing Countries*. Available from: www.libinst.ch/publikationen/LI-LocalPharmaceuticalProduction.pdf [accessed 3 May 2015].

Bateman, C. (2014) 'Exchange rate hurting chronic drug suppliers – but ARV pipeline safe, says govt', *South African Medical Journal*, 104 (7), 461–63.

Bell, M. & Pavitt, K. (1993) 'Technological accumulation and industrial growth: contrasts between developed and developing countries', *Industrial and Corporate Change*, 2 (1), 157–210.

Berger, M., Murugi, J., Buch, E., Ijsselmuiden, C., Kennedy, A., Moran, M., Guzman, J., Devlin, M. & Kubata, B. (2009) *Strengthening Pharmaceutical Innovation in Africa*, Council on Health Research for Development (COHRED), New Partnership for Africa's Development (NEPAD).

Berlin, M. (2003) 'Trade credit: why do production firms act as financial intermediaries?' *Business Review*, 3, 21–28.

BMI (2013) *Ghana Pharmaceuticals and Healthcare Report Q3 2013*, Business Monitor International, London.

BMI Espicom (2013) *World Pharmaceutical Markets Fact Book 2013*, Espicom Business Intelligence Ltd.

BMI Research (2015) 'Kenya pharmaceuticals and healthcare report Q1 2015', 1 January 2015 [Online]. Available from: http://www.marketresearch.com/Business-Monitor-International-v304/Kenya-Pharmaceuticals-Healthcare-Q1-8494874/ [accessed 3 May 2015].

Bolu, R.B., Ketavarapu, N.R., Indukuri, V.S.K., Gorantia, S.R. & Chava, S. (2012) *Efficient Process to Induce Enantioselectivity in Prochiral Carbonyl Compounds*, US Patent Application 2012/0264933, filed 22 June 2012.

Bond, P. (1998) *Uneven Zimbabwe: A Study of Finance, Development and Underdevelopment*, Africa World Press, Trenton.

Botanical Extracts EPZ (2015) *BEEPZ Project Milestones* [Online]. Available from: http://www.be-epz.com/page5.html [accessed 27 April 2015].

Brasil (1988) Constituição da República Federativa do Brasil. Brasília, DF, Senado, 1998. Available from http://www.senado.gov.br/legislacao/const/con1988/CON1988_16.02.1998/CON1988.shtm [accesses 13 February 2015].

Brasil (1996) Lei de Patentes. Lei n° 9.279, de 14 de maio de 1996. Regula direitos e obrigações relativos à propriedade industrial. Available from http://www.planalto.gov.br/ccivil_03/leis/l9279.htm [accessed 3 February 2015].

Brasil (1998) Ministério da Saúde. PORTARIA N° 3.916, DE 30 DE OUTUBRO DE 1998. Available from http://bvsms.saude.gov.br/bvs/saudelegis/gm/1998/prt3916_30_10_1998.html [accessed 16 April 2015].

Brasil (2004a) Política Nacional de Assistência Farmacêutica (PNAF). Ministério da Saúde/Conselho Nacional de Saúde. Resolução n°. 338, de 6 de maio de 2004. Diário Oficial da União 2004.

Brasil (2004b) Decreto n. 5.090, de 20 de maio de 2004. Regulamenta a Lei 10.858, de 20 de maio de 2004, institui o programa "Farmácia Popular do Brasil", e dá outras providências. Diário Oficial da União, Poder Executivo, Brasília, DF, n. 97, seção 1, p. 6, 21 mai. 2004. Available from http://www2.camara.leg.br/legin/fed/decret/2004/decreto-5090-20-maio-2004-532380-norma-pe.html [accessed 11 January 2015].

Brasil (2004c) Lei no 10.973, de 2 de dezembro de 2004. Dispõe sobre incentivos à inovação e à pesquisa científica e tecnológica no ambiente produtivo e dá outras providências. Available from http://www.planalto.gov.br/ccivil_03/_ato2004–2006/2004/lei/l10.973.htm [accessed 3 April 2015].

Brasil (2005) Lei do Bem. Lei 11.196/05 21 de novembro de 2005. Available from http://www.planalto.gov.br/ccivil_03/_ato2004–2006/2005/lei/l11196.htm [accessed 15 March 2015].

Brasil (2010) Lei n° 12.349, de 15 de dezembro de 2010. Available from http://www.planalto.gov.br/ccivil_03/_Ato2007–2010/2010/Lei/L12349.htm [accessed 25 March 2015].

Brasil (2011) Decreto n° 7.546, de 2 de agosto de 2011. Available from http://www.planalto.gov.br/ccivil_03/_ato2011–2014/2011/Decreto/D7546.htm [accessed 25 March 2015].

Brasil (2012) Ministério da Saúde. Portaria N° 837, de18 de abril de 2012. Define as diretrizes e os critérios para o estabelecimento das Parcerias para o Desenvolvimento Produtivo (PDP). Available from http://bvsms.saude.gov.br/bvs/saudelegis/gm/2012/prt0837_18_04_2012.html [accessed 3 April 2015].

Brasil (2013) Brasil Maior. Acompanhamento das medidas setoriais. Conselho Nacional de Desenvolvimento Nacional.

Brasil (2014) Ministério da Saúde. Aqui Tem Farmácia Popular. Available from http://portalsaude.saude.gov.br/index.php [accessed 13 March 2015].

Bräutigam, D. (1997) 'Institutions, economic reform, and democratic consolidation in Mauritius', *Comparative Politics*, 30 (1), 45–62.

Bräutigam, D., Rakner, L. & Taylor, S. (2002) 'Business associations and growth coalitions in Sub-Saharan Africa', *The Journal of Modern African Studies*, 40 (4), 519–47.

Brautigam, B. (2009) *The Dragon's Gift: The Real Story of China in Africa*, Oxford University Press, Oxford.

Brett, E.A. (2005) 'From corporatism to liberalisation in Zimbabwe: Economic policy regimes and political crisis, 1980–97', *International Political Science Review*, 26 (1), 91–106.

Browne (1985) *White Paper on the Report of the Commission of Inquiry into Health Services*, Government Printer, Pretoria.

Buss, P. (2011) 'Brazil: Structuring cooperation for health', *The Lancet*, 377 (9779), 1722–23.

Cabral, L. (2010) 'Brazil's Development Cooperation with the South: A Global Model in Waiting', *Overseas Development Institute (ODI)*. Available from http://www.odi.org.uk/opinion/4952-brazils-development-cooperation-south-global-model-waiting [accessed 27 April 2015].

Cabral, L., Russo, G. & Weinstock, J. (2014) 'Brazil and the shifting consensus on development co-operation: Salutary diversions from the 'aid-effectiveness' trail?' *Development Policy Review*, 32 (2), 179–202.

Calì, M. & Sen, K. (2011) 'Do effective state business relations matter for economic growth? Evidence from India states', *World Development*, 39 (9), 1542–57.

Cameron, A., Ewen, M., Auton, M. & Abegunde, D. (2011) *The world medicines situation 2011 – Medicine prices, availability and affordability*, World Health Organisation, Geneva. Available from http://www.who.int/medicines/areas/policy/world_medicines_situation/WMS_ch6_wPricing_v6.pdf [accessed 30 April 2015].

Camps-Walsh, G., Aivas, I. & Barratt, H. (2009) *Improving UK Patient Outcomes: How Can Value-Based Pricing Improve Access and Adoption of New Treatments?* Available from http://www.2020health.org/dms/2020health/downloads/reports/2020vpcdoc-sep09.pdf [accessed 1 May 2015].

Capanema, L.X. & Palmeira Filho, P.L. (2004) *A cadeia farmacêutica e a política industrial: uma proposta de inserção do BNDES*, BNDES Setorial, Rio de Janeiro, 19, 23–48.

Cawson, A. (1982) *Corporative and Welfare: Social Policy and State Intervention in Britain*, London: Heinemann Educational Books.

Cawson, A. (1986) *Corporatism and Political Theory*, Basil Blackwell, Oxford.

Central Statistics of Ethiopia (CSA) (2014), *Report on Large and Medium Scale Manufacturing and Electricity Industries Survey, various issues*, Industry Minister, GTP Pharma sector performance report. Available from http://www.eeaecon.org/node/8118 [accessed 3 May 2015].

Chang, H. (2004) 'Regulation of foreign investment in historical perspective', *The European Journal of Development Research*, 16 (3), 687–715.

Chataway, J., Tait, J. & Wield, D. (2006) 'The governance of agro- and pharmaceutical biotechnology innovation: public policy and industrial strategy', *Technology Analysis and Strategic Management*, 18 (2), 169–85.

Chataway, J., Chaturvedi, K., Hanlin, R., Mugwagwa, J., Wield, D. & Smith, J. (2009) 'Technological trends and opportunities to combat diseases of the poor in Africa', in Kalua, F., Awotedu, A., Kamwanja, L. & Saka, J. (eds.) *Science, Technology and Innovation for Public Health in Africa*, NEPAD Office of Science and Technology, Pretoria, 53–93.

Chataway, J., Fry, C., Marjanovic, S. & Yaqub, O. (2012) 'Public private collaborations and partnerships in stratified medicine: making sense of new interactions', *New Biotechnology*, 29 (6), 732–40.

Chaudhuri, S. (1986) 'Licensing Policies and Growth of Drug TNCs in India', in A. S.Gupta (ed.), *Drug Industry and the Indian People,*. New Delhi and Patna: Delhi

Science Forum and Federation of Medical Representatives Associations of India, pp. 243–54.

Chaudhuri, S. (2008) 'Indian Generic Companies, Affordability of Drugs and Local Production in Africa with Special Reference to Tanzania', Milton Keynes: The Open University Research Centre on Innovation, Knowledge and Development, IKD Working Paper No. 37.

Chaudhuri, S. (2012) 'Multinationals and monopolies: Pharmaceutical industry in India after TRIPS', *Economic and Political Weekly*, 47 (2), 46–54.

Chaudhuri, S., Mackintosh, M. & Mujinja, P.G.M. (2010) 'Indian generics producers, access to essential medicines and local production in Africa: An argument with reference to Ghana', *European Journal of Development Research*, 22 (4), 451–68.

Chaudhuri, S. & West, A. (2015) 'Can local producers compete with low cost imports? A simulation study of pharmaceutical industry in low-income Africa', *Innovation and Development, Industrial and Corporate Change*, 5 (1), 23–38.

Chava. S., Gorantla, S.R., Indukuri, V.S.K. & Joga, R. (2014) *Process for the preparation of tenofovir*, US patent 8,791,259 issued 29 July 2014.

Chege, J., Ngui, D. & Kimiyu, P. (2014) *Scoping paper on Kenyan manufacturing*, WIDER Working Paper 2014/136, October 2014, United Nations University – World Institute for Development Economics Research.

Chifamba, R. (2003) *Analysis of Mining Investments in Zimbabwe*, PhD, Goteborg University.

Chuma, J. & Okungu, V. (2011) 'Viewing the Kenyan health system through an equity lens: implications for universal coverage', *International Journal for Equity in Health*, 10 (22).

CIMS (2013) *CIMS Updated Prescribers' Handbook*, Mumbai, UBM Medica India Private Ltd.

Claxton, K., Briggs, A., Buxton, M.J., Culyer, A.J., McCabe, C., Walker, S. & Sculpher, M.J. (2008) 'Value based pricing for NHS drugs: an opportunity not to be missed?' *BMJ: British Medical Journal*, *336* (7638), 251–54.

CMAM (2011) *Proposta de Necessidades E Alocação de Recursos Para Medicamentos*, Ministério da Saúde de Moçambique.

Cochrane, G., Wooding, S., Taylor, J., Kamenetzky, A., Sousa, S. & Parks, S. (2015) *Accelerated Access Review: An international review of emerging and effective practice in improving access to medicines and medical technologies*, RAND Europe.

Corbett, J. & Jenkinson, T. (1996) 'The financing of industry, 1970–1989: An international comparison', *Journal of The Japanese and International Economies*, 10, 71–90.

Cordeiro, H. (1985) *A Indústria da Saúde no Brasil*, Edições Graal, Rio de Janeiro.

Cornia, G.A., Jolly, R. & Stewart, F. (1987) *Adjustment with a Human Face*, Clarendon Press, Oxford.

Council for Medical Schemes (2014) *Annual Report 2013/14*. Available from http://www.medicalschemes.com/files/Annual%20Reports/AR2013_2014LR. pdf [accessed: 4 December 2014].

COWI (2012) *Finalização Do Plano de Negócios Da SMM: Situação Dos Mercados Farmacêuticos Em Moçambique E Na Região Da SADC*, COWI Consulting, Maputo.

Datta, D., Vellanki, S.R.R., Salu, A., Balusu, R.B., Ravi, M.R., Nandipati, H.B., Rama, S., Vadali, L.R., Gorantla, S.S.C., Desari, S.R. & Mitapelly, N. (2014) *Process for the preparation of tenofovir disoproxil fumarate*, US Patent 8,759,515 issued 24 June 2014.

Davies, R. & Ratso, J. (2000) *Zimbabwe: Economic adjustment, income distribution and trade liberalization*, Centre for Economic Policy Analysis, New School University, New York.

D'Ávila Viana, A.L. & Elias, P.E.M. (2007) 'Saúde e desinvolvimento', *Ciência & Saúde Coletiva*, 12, 1765–77.

Deloitte (2012) *Value-Based Pricing for Pharmaceuticals: Implications of the Shift from Volume to Value*. Available from http://deloitte.wsj.com/cfo/files/2012/09/ValueBasedPricingPharma.pdf [accessed 1 May 2015].

De Oliveira, L. (2012) *Nota Informativa Sobre a Iniciativa de Instaliação Da Fábrica de Antiretrovirrais E Outrs Medicamentos Em Moçambique*, Farmanguinhos, Fundação Oswaldo Cruz.

De Oliveira, L. (2013) *Inicitativa de Instalação Da Fábrica de Antiretrovirrais E Outros Medicamentos Em Moçambique; Avaliação Do Projecto*, Farmanguinhos, Fundação Oswaldo Cruz.

Department of Health (1996) *National Drug Policy* for *South Africa*. Available from http://apps.who.int/medicinedocs/en/d/Js17744en/ [accessed 30 April 2015].

DHMS (2012) *Discovery Health Medical Scheme Integrated Annual Report 2012*. Available from http://www.discovery.co.za/discovery_coza/web/linked_content/pdfs/health/health_integrated_annual_report.pdf [accessed 30 April 2015].

Dodd, S.A. (2007) *The Effect of the Drug Price Intervention on Retail Pharmacy in South Africa*, mini-dissertation submitted in partial fulfilment of the requirements for the degree Masters in Business Administration. North-West University. Available from http://dspace.nwu.ac.za/bitstream/handle/10394/4297/dodd_sa(1).pdf?sequence=1 [accessed 30 April 2015].

Doner, R.F. & Sheneider, B.R. (2000) 'Business associations and economic development: Why some associations contribute more than others', *Business and Politics*, 2 (3), 261–88.

Dosi, G., Freeman, C., Nelson, R.R., Silverberg G. & Soete, L. (eds.) (1998) *Technical Change and Economic Theory*, Pinter Publishers, London and New York.

DTI (2013) *Draft National Policy on Intellectual Property, 2013*, Available from: http://ip-unit.org/wp-content/uploads/2013/09/DRAFT-IP-POLICY.pdf [accessed 29 April 2015].

EACRPMPA (2011) *East African Community Regional Pharmaceutical Manufacturing Plan of Action 2012–2016*, Arusha, Tanzania; EAC Secretariat. Available from http://feapm.com/fileadmin/user_upload/documents/EAC_Regional_Pharmaceutical_Manufacturing_Plan_of_Action.pdf [accessed 3 May 2015].

East African Community Secretariat (nd) Guidelines for Good Manufacturing Practice for Medicinal products within the EAC, Report: EAC/TF-MED/GMP/PD/N2R0. Available from http://www.tfda.or.tz/index.php?option=com_phocadownload&view=category&download=129:guidelines-on-good-manufacturing-practice-for-medicinal-products-within-the-eac&id=69:good-manufacturing-practice&Itemid=440 [accessed 30 April 2015].

Economist, The (2014) *The New Drug War Continued*. Available from http://www.economist.com/blogs/schumpeter/2014/01/new-drug-war-continued [accessed 29 April 2015].

EIC (Ethiopian Investment Commission) (2014) Available from http://www.investethiopia.gov.et/images/pdf/incentives.pdf [accessed 12 January 2015].

Emeje, M.O., Izuka, A., Isimi, C.Y., Ofoefule, S.I. & Kunle, O.O. (2011) 'Preparation and standardization of a herbal agent for the therapeutic management of asthma', *Pharmaceutical Development and Technology*, 16 (2), 170–78.

Emeje, M.O. & Kunle, O.O. (2005) 'Effect of two surfactants and mode of incorporation on the compaction characteristics of the hot water leaf extract of Ficus Sur', *Journal of Nutraceuticals and Functional Medical Foods*, 4, 147–56.

Emsely, R. & Booysen, F. (2004) 'Cost effectiveness of an atypical conventional antipsychotic in South Africa', *South African Journal of Psychiatry*, 10 (3), 58–66.

Ernst, D. & Lundvall, B. (1997) *Information Technology in The Learning Economy – Challenges for Developing Countries*, DRUID Working Paper No. 97–12, Danish Research Unit for Industrial Dynamics.

European Union (EU) (2010) *Zimbabwe-Vital Health Services Support Programme, Phase I and II. Draft Evaluation Report*, Harare, Zimbabwe.

Fafchamps, M. (1997) 'Trade credit in Zimbabwean manufacturing', *World Development*, 25 (5), 795–815.

Farrell, J. & Saloner, G. (1986) 'Installed base and compatibility: Innovation, product preannouncements and predation', *American Economic Review*, 76, 940–55.

FDA (2014) *Facts about Good Manufacturing Practices (CGMPs)*. Available from http://www.fda.gov/Drugs/DevelopmentApprovalProcess/Manufacturing/ucm169105.htm [accessed 3 November 2014].

FDRE (2004) 'Labor Proclamation No. 377/2003', *Federal Negarit Gazeta*, Federal Democratic Republic of Ethiopia.

FDRE (2007) 'Drug Fund and Pharmaceuticals Supply Establishment – Proclamation No. 553/2007', *Federal Negarit Gazeta*, Federal Democratic Republic of Ethiopia.

FDRE (2009) 'Food, Medicine and Healthcare Administration and Control – Proclamation No 661/2009', *Federal Negarit Gazeta*, Federal Democratic Republic of Ethiopia.

Fioramonti, L. (2005) 'Civil society and democratisation: Assumptions, dilemmas and the South African experience', *Theoria*, 107, 65–88.

Fiotec/Fiocruz (2007) *Estudo de Viabilidade Técnico-Económica Para a Instalação Da Fábrica de Medicamentos Em Moçambique Para Produção de Medicamentos Anti-Retrovirais E Outros*, Relatório de Estudo, Fundação Oswaldo Cruz, Rio de Janeiro.

Fischhoff, B. (1984) 'Setting standards: A systematic approach to managing public health and safety risks', *Management Science*, 30 (7), 823–43.

Fisman, R. and Love, I. (2003) 'Trade credit, financial intermediary development, and industry growth', *The Journal of Finance*, 58 (1), 353–74.

Flynn, M. (2008) 'Public production of anti-retroviral medicines in Brazil, 1990–2007', *Development and Change*, 39 (4), 513–36.

Flynn, M. (2010) 'Corporate Power and State Resistance: Brazil's Use of TRIPS Flexibilities for Its National AIDS Program', in Shadlen, K. C., Guennif, S., Guzman, A. & Lalitha, N. (eds.) *Intellectual Property, Pharmaceuticals, and Public Health: Access to Drugs in Developing*, Cheltenham: Edward Elgar Publishing.

FMHACA (2013a) *Medicine Manufacturing Establishment Directive Number 12/2013*, available from http://www.fmhaca.gov.et/documents/Directive%20%20for%20Medicine%20Manufucturing%20Establishmen%20%202013.pdf [accessed 3 May 2015].

FMHACA (2013b) *The GMP Road Map – Pharmaceutical Manufacturing*, August, Addis Ababa.

FMoH (2011) *Health and Health Related Indicators*, Policy Planning Directorate, Addis Ababa.

FMoH (2012) 'Health Sector Development Programmes III, IV FMOH, Health Sector Development Programme Annual Performance Report 2011/12', available from: http://www.moh.gov.et/documents/26765/28899/Annual+Perfor mance+Report+2011/3ba3483a-9ee0–4a8b-bc39–4ca5acd8a9eb?version=1.2 [accessed 3 May 2015].

Fojule, G. & Ogunyale, P.O. (2001) 'Efficacy of niprisan in the prophylactic management of patients with sickle cell disease', *Current Theory & Research*, 62(1), 26.

Fortunak, J.M.D. (2014) 'Green Chemistry and Global Access to Medicines', *Gordon Research Conference on Green Chemistry*, Hong Kong, July 30.

Fortunak, J.M.D., Byrn, S.R, Dyson, B., Ekeocha, Z., Ellison, T., King, C.L., Kulkarni, A., Lee, M., Conrad, C. & Fortunak, J.R. (2013) 'An efficient, green chemical synthesis of the malaria drug piperaquine', *Topical Journal of Pharmaceutical Research*, 12 (5), 791–798.

Frankel, R. (2006) 'Associations in China and India: An overview', *European Society of Association Executives*. Available from http://www.esae.org/arti cles/2006_07_004.pdf [accessed 23 October 2014].

Frost and Sullivan (2010) *The Pharmaceutical Industry in Key East African Countries*, Report No M57C-52, May.

Frost and Sullivan (2012) *Analysis of the Pharmaceutical Market of Kenya and Tanzania: Unpacking the Five Key Segments Driving Growth*, Report No M72B-5G, April.

Gadelha, C. A. G. (2006) 'Desenvolvimento, complexo industrial da saúde e política industrial' *Revista de Saúde Pública*, 40 (N Especial), 11–23.

Gadelha, C.A.G. & Costa, L.S. (2012) 'A saúde na política nacional de desenvolvi mento: um novo olhar sobre os desafios da saúde', in Fundação Oswaldo Cruz, et al. *A saúde no Brasil em 2030: diretrizes para a prospecção estratégica do sistema de saúde brasileiro*, Rio de Janeiro: Fiocruz.

Gadelha, C.A.G, Costa, L.S. & Maldonado, J.O. (2012) 'O complexo econômico-industrial da saúde e a dimensão social e econômica do desenvolvimento', *Revista de Saúde Pública (Impresso)*, 46, 21–28.

Gadelha, C.A.G., Costa, L.S., Santos de Varge Maldonado, J.M., Barbosa, P.R. & Vargas, M.A. (2013) 'The health care economic-industrial complex: concepts and general characteristics', *Health*, 5 (10), 1607–21.

Gadelha, C.A.G., Maldonado, J.M.S.V. & Costa, L.S. (2014)'Complexo produtivo da saúde: inovação, desenvolvimento e estado', in Silva Paim, J. & Almeida-Filho, N. (eds.), *Saúde Coletiva: Teoria e Prática*, Medbook, Rio de Janeiro.

Gaffney, A. (2015) 'India's data integrity problems', *Regulatory Affairs Professionals Society*, 3 February 2015. Available from http://www.raps.org/Regulatory-Focus/News/2014/08/19/18980/Indias-Data-Integrity-Problems-Updated-17-June-2014/ [accessed 3 May 2015].

Garwood, P. (2007) 'Kenya rejects bid to remove government's compulsory licensing flexibilities', *Intellectual Property Watch* .Available from http://www. ip-watch.org/2007/09/14/kenyan-parliament-rejects-bid-to-remove-govern ments-compulsory-licensing-option/ [accessed 27 April 2015].

GAVI (2013) *The GAVI Alliance 2013 Annual Progress Report*. Available from http://gaviprogressreport.org/2013/ [accessed 17 November 2014].

Gebre-Mariam, T. & Nikolayev, A.S. (1993) 'Evaluation of starch obtained from Ensete ventricosum as a binder and disintegrant for compressed tablets', *Journal of Pharmacy and Pharmacology*, 45, 317–20.

Gebre-Mariam, T. & Schmidt, P.C. (1996a) 'Isolation and physico-chemical properties of Enset starch', *Starch/Stärke*, 48, 208–14.

Gebre-Mariam, T. & Schmidt, P.C. (1996b) 'Characterization of Enset starch and its use as a binder and disintegrant for tablets', *Pharmazie*, 51, 303–11.

Gebre-Mariam, T. & Schmidt, P.C. (1998) 'Some physico-chemical properties of Dioscorea abyssinica starch', *Starch/Stärke*, 50, 241–46.

Gebre-Mariam, T., Winnemöller, M. & Schmidt, P.C. (1996a) 'An evaluation of the disintegration efficiency of a sodium starch glycolate prepared from Enset starch in compressed tablets', *European Journal of Pharmaceuticals and Biopharmaceuticals*, 43, 124–32.

Gebre-Mariam, T., Winnemöller, M. & Schmidt, P.C. (1996b) 'The use of a starch obtained from Dioscorea abyssinica in tablet formulations. Part (II): The sodium starch glycolate from Dioscorea abyssinica as a disintegrant', *Pharmaceutical Industry*, 58, 255–59.

Gianetti, M., Burkart, M. & Ellingsen, T. (2011) 'What you sell is what you lend? Explaining trade credit contracts', *The Review of Financial Studies*, 24 (4), 1261–98.

Goldman, D. & Smith, J. (2005) *Socioeconomic Differences in the Adoption of New Medical Technologies*, National Bureau of Economic Research. NBER Working Paper Series, no. 11218.

Gomes, R., Pimentel, V., Lousada, M. & Pieroni, J.P. (2014) *O novo cenário de concorrência na indústria farmacêutica brasileira*, Complexo Industrial da Saúde BNDES Setorial 39, p. 97–134. Available from http://www.bndes.gov.br/SiteBNDES/export/sites/default/bndes_pt/Galerias/Arquivos/conhecimento/bnset/set3903.pdf [accessed 9 April 2015].

Goodluck, C. (2014) 'Role of family resources in firm performance: Evidence from Tanzania', *Journal of African Business*, 15 (2), 122–35.

Government of India (GOI) (1978) *New Drugs Policy*, Ministry of Chemicals and Fertilisers, New Delhi.

Grabowski, H.G., Vernon, J.M. & Thomas, G.L. (1978) 'Estimating the effects of regulation on innovation: An international comparative analysis of the pharmaceutical industry', *Journal of Law and Economics*, 21 (1), 133–63.

Greiner, W. (2011) 'Germany's drug pricing after AMNOG – What comes next?' Presentation at the 7th America and German Healthcare Forum, Minneapolis. Available from http://cges.umn.edu/docs/Greiner.Workshop.GermanyDrugPricingafterAMNOG.pdf [accessed 1 May 2015].

Griliches, Z. and Mairesse, J. (1995) 'Production functions: the search for identification', NBER Working Paper No. 5067, National Bureau of Economic Research, Cambridge, MA.

Grindle, M. (2007) *Going Local: Decentralization, Democratization, and the Promise of Good Governance*. Princeton University Press, Princeton.

Guardian, The (2001) 'Firms Split Over Deal in Cheap Drugs Lawsuit'. Available from http://www.theguardian.com/world/2001/apr/18/medicalscience.aids [accessed 29 April 2015].

Guimer, J., Lee, E. & Grupper, M. (2004) *Processes and Issues for Improving Access to Medicines: The Evidence Base for Domestic Production and Greater Access to Medicines*, DFID Health Systems Resource Centre, London.

Handley, A. (2008) *Business and the State in Africa: Economic Policy-making in the Neo-liberal Era*, Cambridge University Press, Cambridge.

Harper, I., Brhlikova, P. & Pollock, A. (2007) *Good Manufacturing Practice in the Pharmaceutical Industry – Working Paper 3*, prepared for Workshop on 'Tracing Pharmaceuticals in South Asia', 2–3 July, University of Edinburgh.

Hebrault, D. (2014) *New Continuous Flow Chemistry Webinar – Recent Advances in Organic Chemistry Part 8*. Available from http://us.mt.com/us/en/home/events/webinar/ondemand/continuous-flow-chemistry-II-organic-chemistry.html [accessed 10 November 2014].

Helmsing, A.H.J. (1990) 'Industrialization in Zimbabwe: A non-replicable model?' *Africa Focus*, 6, 267–82.

Herzer, D. & Grimm, M. (2012) 'Does foreign aid increase private investment? Evidence from panel cointegration', *Applied Economics*, 44 (20), 2537–50.

Himbara, D. (1993) 'Myths and realities of Kenyan capitalism', *Journal of Modern African Studies*, 31 (1), 93–107.

Hirschman, A. O. (1967) *Development Projects Observed*. The Brookings Institution, Washington, DC.

Hirschman, A. O. (1990). 'The case against "one thing at a time"', *World Development*, 18 (8), 1119–22.

Immel, B. (2000) 'A brief history of the GMPs', *Regulatory Compliance Newsletter*, Winter.

Immel, B. (2001) 'A Brief History of GMPs for Pharmaceuticals', *Pharmaceutical Technology*. Available from www.gmpnews.ru/wp-content/uploads/2010/05/History-gmp.pdf [accessed 4 May 2015].

IMS (2012) *Africa: A Ripe Opportunity. Understanding the Pharmaceutical Market Opportunity and Developing Sustainable Business Models in Africa*, IMS Health. Available from http://www.imshealth.com/ims/Global/Content/Insights/Featured%20Topics/Emerging%20Markets/IMS_Africa_Opportunity_Whitepaper.pdf [accessed 27 April 2015].

IMS Health (2014a) Total Private Market, South Africa October 2014.

IMS Health (2014b) Total Private Market, South Africa November 2014.

IMS Institute for Healthcare Informatics (2014) *Understanding the pharmaceuticals value chain*. Available from http://www.imshealth.com/vgn-ext-templating/v/index.jsp?vgnextoid=a64de5fda6370410VgnVCM10000076192ca2RCRD&vg nextchannel=a64de5fda6370410VgnVCM10000076192ca2RCRD# [accessed 3 May 2015].

Interfarma (2014) *Associação da indústria farmacêutica de pesquisa – Guia 2014*. Available from http://www.interfarma.org.br/biblioteca.php [accessed 21 March 2015].

IPASA (2013) *Draft National Policy on Intellectual Property, 2013: Submission by Innovative Pharmaceutical Association of South Africa (IPASA)*. Available from http://ipasa.co.za/wp-content/uploads/2014/01/Copy-of-IPASA-submission-on-the-draft-national-policy-on-IP-final-131016.pdf [accessed 04 November 2014].

IPEA (2011) *Cooperação Brasileira Para O Desenvolvimento Internacional 2005–2009*, Administração Pública Federal, Brasília: Casa Civil, IPEA e ABC. Available from http:/www.abc.gov.br/api/publicacaoarquivo/328 [accessed 05 April 2014].

IRIN News Africa (2015) 'KENYA: Small farmers cash in on Artemisinin production'. Available from http://www.irinnews.org/report/82486/kenya-small-farmers-cash-in-on-artemisinin-production [accessed 27 April 2015].

Iyamu, E.W., Turner, E.A. & Asakura, T. (2003) 'Niprisan (Nix-0699) improves the survival rates of transgenic sickle cell mice under acute severe hypoxic conditions', *British Journal of Hematology*, 122 (6), 1001.

Jacob, A.G. (2010) *Steering the State: The Politics of Institutional Change in the Pharmaceutical and Telecommunications Sectors in Post Reform India*, Ph.D. dissertation, Rutgers University, New Brunswick, NJ.

Jaffe, S. & Henson, S. (2004) *Standards and Agro-Food Exports from Developing Countries: Rebalancing the Debate*, Policy Research Working Paper 3348, The World Bank, Washington, DC.

Jain, S. (2012) 'Pragmatic agency in technology standards setting: The case of ethernet', *Research Policy*, 41, 1643–54.

Jayaraman, K. (2012) 'Finding the right chemistry', *Nature Medicine*, 19, 1200–03.

Jeffrey, R (2001) *Tracing pharmaceuticals in South Asia, University of Edinburgh*, Centre for Asian Studies Working Paper.

Jeffrey, R., Pollock, A., Jeffrey, P., Harper, I. & Ecks, S. (2010) *Tracing Pharmaceuticals in South Asia: Regulation, Distribution and Consumption*, ESRC End of Award Report, RES-167–25–0110. ESRC, Swindon.

Jenkins-Smith, H.C. & Sabatier, P.A. (1994) 'Evaluating the advocacy coalition framework', *Journal of Public Policy*, 14 (2), 175–203.

Jian. B. & Si, Y. (2008) *Amino Alcohol Ligand and Its Use in Preparation of Chiral Propargylic Alcohols and Tertiary Amines Via Enantioselective Addition Reaction*, US Patent 7,439,400; issued October 21, 2008.

Kaijage, F. & Tibaijuka, A. (1996) *Poverty and Social Exclusion in Tanzania*. International Institute for Labour Studies, Research Series 109, ILO, Geneva.

Kaplan, W. & Laing, R. (2005) *Local Production of Pharmaceuticals: Industrial Policy and Access to Medicines. An Overview of Key Concepts, Issues and Opportunities for Future Research. Health, Nutrition and Population (HNP) Discussion Paper*, The World Bank's Human Development Network, The International Bank for Reconstruction and Development / The World Bank, Washington, DC.

Kaplan, W. A., Wirtz, V.J. & Stephens, P. (2013) 'The Market Dynamics of Generic Medicines in the Private Sector of 19 Low and Middle Income Countries between 2001 and 2011: a descriptive time series analysis', *Public Library of Science – One*. Available from http://www.plosone.org/article/info%3Adoi%2F10.1371%2Fjournal.pone.0074399 [accessed 26 February 2015].

Kaplinsky, R. & Masuma, F. (2010). *What Are the Implications for Global Value Chains When the Market Shifts from the North to the South?* The World Bank, Washington, DC.

Kariuki, J., Njeru, M., Wamae, W. & Mackintosh, M. (2015) 'Local supply chains for medicines and medical supplies in Kenya: understanding the challenges', ACTS Working Paper. Available at http://iphsp.acts-net.org/publications/working-papers [accessed 08/09/15].

Kattel, R. & Lember, V. (2010) 'Public procurement as an industrial policy tool: An option for developing countries?' *Journal of Public Procurement*, 10 (3), 368–404.

Katz, M.L. & Shapiro, C. (1985) 'Network externalities, competition, and compatibility', *American Economic Review*, 75, 424–40.

KEMRI (2015) *Background of KEMRI.* Available from http://www.kemri.org/index. php/about-kemri/background [accessed 27 April 2015].

KEMSA Task Force (2008) *KEMSA Task Force Report,* KEMSA, Nairobi.

Khan, M. (1995) 'State Failure in Weak States: A Critique of New Institutionalist Explanations', in J. Harris, J. Hunter and C. Lewis (eds.), *The New Institutional Economics and Third World Development,* Sage, London.

Khan, M. (2000) 'Rent Seeking as a Process: Inputs, Rent-Outcomes and Net Effects', in M. Khan and K.S. Jomo (eds.), *Rents, Rent-Seeking and Economic Development,* Cambridge University Press, Cambridge.

Khanna, T. & Palepu, K.G. (1997) 'Why focused strategies may be wrong for emerging markets', *Harvard Business Review,* 75 (4) (July–August), 41–51.

Kim, J.Y., Farmer, P.E. & Porter, M.E. (2013) 'Redefining global health-care delivery', *Lancet,* 382, 1060–69.

Kjöllerström, M. (2008) *Public Procurement as a Tool for Promoting More Sustainable Consumption and Production Patterns,* Sustainable Development Innovation Briefs. Issue 5. United Nations Department of Economic and Social Affairs. Available from http://esa.un.org/marrakechprocess/pdf/InnovationBriefs_no5. pdf [accessed 30 April 2015].

Kotwani, A., Ewen, M., Dey, D., Iyer, S. Lakshmi, P.K., Patel, A., Raman, K., Singhal, G.L., Thawani, V., Tripathi, S. & Laing, R. (2007) 'Prices & availability of common medicines at six sites in India using a standard methodology', *Indian Journal of Medical Research,* 125, 645–54.

Kragelund, P. (2008) 'The return of non-DAC donors to Africa: New prospects for African Development?' *Development Policy Review,* 26 (5), 555–84.

Kshetri, N. & Dholakia, N. (2009) 'Professional and trade associations in a nascent and formative sector of a developing economy: A case study of the NASSCOM effect on the Indian offshoring industry', *Journal of International Management,* 15(2), 225–39.

Laing, R., Waning, B., Gray, A., Ford, N. & Hoen, E.T. (2003) '25 years of the WHO essential medicines lists: progress and challenges', *The Lancet,* 361 (9370), 1723–29.

Lall, A. (1992) 'Technological capabilities and industrialisation', *World Development,* 20 (2), 165–86.

Lall, S. (2003) *Reinventing Industrial Strategy: The Role of Government Policy in Building Industrial Competitiveness,* QEH Working Paper Series-QEHWPS111.

Lall, S. & Narula, R. (2004) 'Foreign direct investment and its role in economic development: Do we need a new agenda?' *The European Journal of Development Research,* 16 (3). *Harvard Business Review,* 75 (4), 41–51.

Lall, S. & Wangwe S. (1998) 'Industrial policy and industrialisation in Sub-Saharan Africa', *Journal of African Economies,* 7 (Supp. 1), 70–107.

Lazonick, W. & O'Sullivan, M. (1997a) 'Finance and industrial development. Part I: the United States and the United Kingdom', *Financial History Review,* 4, 7–29.

Lazonick, W. & O'Sullivan, M. (1997b) 'Finance and industrial development: evolution to market control. Part II: Japan and Germany', *Financial History Review,* 4, 117–38.

Lehman, H.P. (2008) 'The emergence of civil society organizations in South Africa', *Journal of Public Affairs,* 8(1–2), 115–27.

Losse, K., Schneider, E. & Spennemann, C. (2007) *The Viability of Local Production in Tanzania*, Deutsche Gesellschaft für Technische Zusammenarbeit (GTZ), Eschborn, Germany.

Loureiro, S.A.L.S., Simões, B., Aragão, E., Mota, F., Moura, H. & Damasceno, L. (2007) 'Diffusion of medical technology and equity in health in Brazil: An exploratory analysis', *European Journal of Development Research*, 19, 66–80.

Loyola, M.A. (2008) 'Medicamentos e saúde pública em tempos de AIDS: metamorfoses de uma política dependente', *Ciênc. Saúde Coletiva*, 13, 763–78.

MacDonald, R. & Yamey, G. (2001) 'The cost to global health of drug company profits', *Western Journal of Medicine*, 174 (5), 302–03.

Mackintosh, M., Chaudhuri, S. & Mujinja, P.G.M. (2011) 'Can NGOs regulate medicines markets? Social enterprise in wholesaling, and access to essential medicines', *Globalization and Health*, 7 (4).

Madhavi, Y. (2003) 'The manufacture of consent? Hepatitis B vaccination', *Economic and Political Weekly*, 38 (24), 2417–24.

Madhavi, Y. (2013) 'Vaccines and vaccine policy for universal health care', *Social Change*, 43 (2), 263–91.

Malerba, F. (2002) 'Sectoral systems of innovation and production', *Research Policy*, 31(2), 247–64.

Maluka, S.O. (2013) 'Why are pro-poor exemption policies in Tanzania better implemented in some districts than in others?' *International Journal for Equity in Health*, 12 (80).

Manning, R. (2006) 'Will "Emerging Donors" Change the Face of International Co-Operation?' *Development Policy Review*, 24 (4), 371–85.

Maree, J. (1993) 'Trade unions and corporatism in South Africa', *Transformation*, 21 (1993), 24–54.

Maskus, K., Otsuki, T. & Wilson, J. (2004) *The Costs of Complying with Foreign Product Standards for Firms in Developing Countries: An Econometric Study*, Research Program on Political and Economic Change, Working Paper PEC2004–0004.

Maskus, K.E. & Wilson, J.S. (2001) 'A Review of Past Attempts and the New Policy Context', in K. E. Maskus and J. S. Wilson (eds.), *Quantifying the Impact of Technical Barriers to Trade: Can It Be Done?* University of Michigan Press, Ann Arbor.

Maxon, R.M. (1992) 'Multinational Corporations', in Ochieng, W.R. and R.M. Maxon (eds.), *An Economic History of Kenya*, East African Publishers, pp. 383–88.

McIntyre, D., Garshong, B., Mtei, G., Meheus, F., Thiede, M., Akazili, J., Ally, M., Aikins, M., Mulligan, J.H. & Goudge, J. (2008) 'Beyond fragmentation and towards universal coverage: insights from Ghana, South Africa and the United Republic of Tanzania', *Bulletin of the World health Organization*, 86, 871–76.

Mckinsey and Company (2013) *Pharmaceutical Sector in Africa*, presentation at the African Pharmaceutical Summit, Hammamet, Tunisia, September 23.

Medical Chronicle (2012) *Medical Schemes Should Plan Properly to Address Rising Demand for Biologics*. Available from http://www.medicalchronicle.co.za/medical-schemes-should-plan-properly-to-address-rising-demand-for-biologics/ [accessed 30 April 2015].

MEDS (Mission for Drugs and Essential Supplies) (2013) *2012 Annual Report and Financial Statements for the Year Ended 31st December 2012*, Nairobi.

Mhamba, M.R. & Mbirigenda, S. (2010) *The Pharmaceutical Industry and Access to Essential Medicines in Tanzania, EQUINET Discussion Paper* 83. Available from http://equinetafrica.org/bibl/docs/DIS83TZN%20medicines%20mhamba.pdf [accessed 30 April 2015].

Ministry of Industrialization (2010) *Kenya National Industrialization Policy Framework, Draft Five.* Available from http://industrialization.eac.int/index.php?option=com_docman&task=doc_download&gid=115&Itemid=70 [accessed 27 April 2015].

Mitra, S. (1986) 'Actual Drug Needs: Facts and Fallacies', in A. S. Gupta (ed.), *Drug Industry and the Indian People*, Delhi Science Forum and Federation of Medical Representatives Associations of India, New Delhi and Patna, pp. 59–68.

Mkandawire, T. (2001) 'Thinking about development states in Africa', *Cambridge Journal of Economics*, 25, 289–313.

Mlambo, A.S., Pangeti, E.S. & Phimister, I. (2000) *Zimbabwe: A History of Manufacturing 1890–1995*, University of Zimbabwe Press, Harare.

MoFED (2006) *Building on Progress – A plan for Accelerated and Sustained Development to End Poverty (PASDEP) 2005/06–2009/10*, Ministry of Finance and Economic Development Ethiopia. Available from http://www.mofed.gov.et/English/Pages/Home.aspx [accessed 3 May 2015].

MoFED (2012) *Growth and Transformation Plan (2010/11–2014/15) – Annual Progress Report for F.Y. 2010/11*, Ministry of Finance and Economic Development Ethiopia. Available from http://www.mofed.gov.et/English/Pages/Home.aspx [accessed 3 May 2015].

MoHSW (Ministry of Health and Social Welfare) (2006) *Strategies for Promotion of Local Production of Pharmaceuticals in Tanzania 2006–2016*, Dar es Salaam.

MoHSW (Ministry of Health and Social Welfare) (2008) *Mapping of the Medicines Procurement and Supply Management System in Tanzania*, Dar es Salaam. Available from: http://www.who.int/medicines/areas/coordination/tanzania_mapping_supply.pdf [accessed 4 May 2015].

MoHSW (Ministry of Health and Social Welfare) (2009) *Annual Health Statistical Tables and Figures: Tanzania Mainland*, Dar es Salaam.

MoHSW (Ministry of Health and Social Welfare) (2012) *Tanzania National Health Accounts Year 2010*, Dar es Salaam. Available from https://www.hfgproject.org/tanzania-national-health-accounts-year-2010-sub-accounts-hiv-aids-malaria-reproductive-child-health/ [accessed 4 May 2015].

MoHSW (Ministry of Health and Social Welfare) (2013) *Mid Term Review of the Health Sector Strategic Plan III 2009–2015*, Main Report, Ministry of Health and Social Welfare, United Republic of Tanzania, p. 34. Available from http://digit-allibrary.ihi.or.tz/2643/ [accessed 30 April 2015].

MoMS (Ministry of Medical Services) (2010) *Kenya Pharmaceutical Country Profile*, Nairobi, November. Available from http://www.who.int/medicines/areas/coordination/kenya_pharmaceuticalprofile_december2010.pdf [accessed 4 May 2015].

MoMS & MPHS (Ministry of Medical Services and Ministry of Public Health and Sanitation) (2010) *Sessional Paper on National Pharmaceutical Policy*, Government of Kenya, Nairobi. Available from http://apps.who.int/medicinedocs/en/d/Js18697en/ [accessed 4 May 2015].

MoMS & MPHS (Ministry of Medical Services and Ministry of Public Health and Sanitation) (nd) *Kenya National Health Accounts 2009/10* Government of Kenya,

Nairobi. Available from http://www.who.int/pmnch/media/events/2013/ kenya_nha.pdf [accessed 4 May 2015].

Moon, S. (2011) *Pharmaceutical Production and Related Technology Transfer*, World Health Organization Department of Public Health Innovation and Intellectual Property, Geneva.

Moore, M. & Schmitz, H. (2008), *Idealism, Realism and the Investment Climate in Developing Countries*, Institute of Development Studies, Working paper series, no. 307. IDS, Brighton.

Morgan Jones, M., Castle-Clarke, S., Brooker, D., Nason, E., Huzair, F. & Chataway, J. (2014) *The Structural Genomics Consortium: A knowledge platform for drug discovery*, A RAND research report. Available from http://www.rand.org/pubs/ research_reports/RR512.html [accessed 1 May 2015].

MoST (2012) *The Green Paper on Science, Technology and Innovation Policy of Ethiopia Building Competitiveness through Innovation of the Ministry of Science and Technology*, Ministry of Science and Technology Ethiopia. Available from http:// www.most.gov.et/ [accessed 3 May 2015].

MoST (2013) *National Science, Technology and Innovation Policy of Ethiopia*, Ministry of Science and Technology Ethiopia. Available from http://www.most.gov.et/ [accessed 3 May 2015].

MS/DECIIS (2015) *Departamento do Complexo Industrial e Inovação em Saúde*. Available from http://portalsaude.saude.gov.br/index.php/o-ministerio/prin cipal/secretarias/sctie [accessed 22 April 2015].

MS/PFPB (2014) *Farmácia Popular do Brasil*. Available from http://portalsaude. saude.gov.br/index.php/o-ministerio/principal/secretarias/sctie/farmacia-popular [accessed 12 February 2015].

MSD (Medical Stores Department) (2013) *Medium Term Strategic Plan II: 2014–2020*, Dar es Salaam. Available from http://msd.or.tz/index.php/medium-term-strategic-plan-2014–2020/category/6-medium-term-strategic-plan [accessed 30 April 2015].

MSF (2015) *The Right Shot: Bringing Down Barriers to Affordable and Adapted Vaccines*. Available from http://www.msf.org.br/sites/default/files/msf_the_right_shot_ report_2nded_2015.pdf [accessed 1 May 2015].

MSH (Management Sciences for Health) (2010) *International Drug Price Indicator Guide 2009*. Available from http://erc.msh.org/mainpage.cfm?file=1.0.htm&m odule=DMP&language=English [accessed 30 April 2015].

MSH (Management Sciences for Health) (2013) *International Drug Price Indicator Guide 2012*. Available from http://erc.msh.org/dmpguide/pdf/ DrugPriceGuide_2012_en.pdf [accessed 30 April 2015].

MTDP (2010) *Medium Term Development Plan – January 2010–December 2015*, Government of Zimbabwe, Harare.

Mugwagwa J., Kale D. & Banda, G. (2015) *Standards and Their Role in Pharmaceutical Upgrading in Low- and Middle-Income Countries*, Innogen Institute Policy Brief, March.

Mujinja, P.G.M., Mackintosh, M., Justin-Temu, M. & Wuyts, M. (2014) 'Local production of pharmaceuticals in Africa and access to essential medicines: "Urban bias" in access to imported medicines in Tanzania and its policy impli-cations', *Globalization and Health*, 10 (12), 1–12.

Muller, K.M., Gempeler, M.R., Scheiwe, M. & Zeugin, B.T. (1996) 'Quality assur-ance for biopharmaceuticals: An overview of regulations, methods and prob-lems', *Pharmaceutics Acta Helvetiae*, 71, 421–38.

Myers, S.C. (1984) 'The capital structure puzzle', *The Journal of Finance*, 39 (3), 575–92.

Myers, S. & Majluf, N. (1984) 'Corporate financing and investment decision when firms have information investors do not have', *Journal of Financial Economics*, 13, 187–221.

Nadvi, K. (1999) 'Collective efficiency and collective failure: the response of Sialkot surgical instrument cluster to global quality pressures', *World Development*, 27 (9), 1605–26.

Nadvi, K. & Halder, G. (2007) 'Local clusters in global value chains: Exploring dynamic linkages between Germany and Pakistan', *Entrepreneurship & Regional Development*, 17 (5), 339–63.

Nadvi, K.M. & Waltring, F. (2004) 'Making Sense of Global Standards', in H. Schmitz (ed.), *Local Enterprises in the Global Economy: Issues of Governance and Upgrading*, Edward Elgar. Cheltenham.

Narayanan, V. & Chen, T. (2012) 'Research on technology standards: Accomplishment and challenges', *Research Policy*, 41, 1375–1406.

National Bureau of Statistics (NBS) (2009) *Annual Survey of Industrial Production*. Available from http://nbs.go.tz/takwimu/Industry/ASIP_2009_Statistical.pdf [accessed 30 April 2015].

Ndlela, D.B. (2007) 'Africa's Industrialisation: An Alternative Approach', in Senghor, J. & Poku, N.K. (eds.), *Towards Africa's Renewal*, Ashgate, Hampshire and Burlington.

NECF (National Economic Consultative Forum) (2011) *The NECF Health Task Force Report On The Current Status Of The Pharmaceutical Industry Of Zimbabwe And Factors Affecting Its Growth Prospects*, Harare, Zimbabwe.

Nelson, R.R. & Winter S.G. (1982) *An Evolutionary Theory of Economic Change*, Belknap Press, Cambridge, MA.

Nguyen, T.A., Knight, R., Roughead, E.E., Brooks, G. & Mant, A. (2014) 'Policy options for pharmaceutical pricing and purchasing: issues for low-and middle-income countries', *Health Policy and Planning*, 30 (2), 267–80.

Nickerson, J.V. & zur Muehlen M. (2006) 'The ecology of standards processes: Insights from internet standards making', *MIS Quarterly*, 30, 467–88.

Nigussu, E., Belete, A. & Gebre-Mariam, T. (2013) 'Acetylation and characterization of enset starch and evaluation of its direct compression and drug release sustaining properties', *International Journal of Pharmacological Science and Research*, 4, 4397–4409.

Nilsen, J.H. (2002) 'Trade credit and the bank lending channel', *Journal of Money, Credit and Banking*, 34 (1), 226–53.

Ogonda, R.T. (1992) 'Kenya's Industrial Progress in the Post-Independence Era', in Ochieng, W.R. and Maxon, R.M. (eds.), *An Economic History of Kenya*, East African Publishers, 297–312. Nairobi.

Ogot, M., Nyandemo, S., Kenduiwo, J., Mokaya, J., Iraki, W., Muriuki, R. & Mulinge, M. (2009) *The Long Term Policy Framework for Public Procurement in Kenya*, PPOA, University of Nairobi.

Olcay, M. & Laing R. (2005) *Pharmaceutical Tariffs: What is their effect on prices, protection of local industry and revenue generation?* Paper prepared for The Commission on Intellectual Property Rights, Innovation and Public Health. Available from http://www.who.int/intellectualproperty/studies/TariffsOnEssentialMedicines.pdf [accessed 19 February 2015].

Oliveira, E. A., Labra, M.E. & Bermudez, J. (2006) 'A produção pública de medicamentos no Brasil: uma visão geral', *Cad. Saúde Pública*, 22 (11), 2379–89.

Olson, M. (1982) *The Rise and Decline of Nations*, Yale University Press, New Haven.

Organisation of Economic Cooperation and Development (OECD) (nd) *Public Procurement for Sustainable and Inclusive Growth*. Available from http://www. oecd.org/gov/ethics/PublicProcurementRev9.pdf [accessed 25 April 2015].

Osewe, P.L., Nkrumah, Y.K. and Sackey, E. (2008) *Improving Access to HIV/AIDS Medicines in Africa: Trade-Related Aspects of Intellectual Property Rights (TRIPS) Flexibilities Utilization*, World Bank, Washington, DC.

Page, J. (2012) 'Can Africa industrialise?' *Journal of African Economies*, 21 (Suppl. 2), ii86–ii125.

Paim, J.S. (2009) 'Uma análise sobre o processo da Reforma Sanitária Brasileira', *Saúde em Debate*, 33, 27–37.

Palmeira-Filho, P.L., Pieroni, J.P., Antunes, A. & Bomtempo, J.V. (2012) 'O desafio do financiamento à inovação farmacêutica no Brasil: a experiência do BNDES Profarma', *Revista do BNDES*, 37, 69–90.

Pangeti, E.S. (2000) 'The Economy Under Siege: Sanctions and the Manufacturing Sector, 1965–1979', in Mlambo, A.S., Pangeti, E.S. & Phimister, I. (eds.), *Zimbabwe: A History of Manufacturing 1890–1995*, University of Zimbabwe Press, Harare.

Patwardhan, B. & Mashelkar, R.A. (2009) 'Traditional medicine-inspired approaches to drug discovery: Can Ayurveda show the way forward?' *Drug Discovery Today*, 14, 804.

Pavignani, E. & Durão, J. R. (1999) 'Managing external resources in Mozambique: Building new aid relationships on shifting sands?' *Health Policy and Planning*, 14 (3), 243–53.

Perampaladas, K., Masum, H., Kapoor, A., Shah, R., Daar, A.S. & Singer, P.A. (2010) 'The road to commercialization in Africa: Lessons from developing the sickle-cell drug Niprisan', *BMC International Health and Human Rights*, 10 (Suppl. 1), S11.

Persson, U. (2012) *Value Based Pricing in Sweden: Lessons for Design?* Seminar Briefing 12. Office of Health Economics, London. Available from https://www. ohe.org/news/value-based-pricing-sweden-lessons-design [accessed 1 May 2015].

Persson, U., Willis, M. & Odegaard, K. (2010) 'A case study of ex ante, value-based price and reimbursement decision-making: TLV and rimonabant in Sweden', *European Journal of Health Economics*, 11 (2), 195–203.

Petersen, M.A. and Rajan, R.G. (1997) 'Trade credit: Theories and evidence', *The Review of Financial Studies*, 10 (3), 661–91.

Pharmaceutical Society of South Africa (2014) *PSSA Submission: Market Enquiry into the Private Healthcare Sector*. Available from http://www.healthinquiry. net/Public%20Submissions/PSSA%201%20submission%20to%20Market%20 Inquiry.pdf [accessed 30 April 2015].

Phimister, I. (1988) *An Economic and Social History of Zimbabwe, 1890–1948*, Longman, London.

Phimister, I. (2000) 'The Origins and Development of Manufacturing in Southern Rhodesia, 1894 – 1939', in Mlambo, A.S., Pangeti, E.S. & Phimister, I. (eds.),

Zimbabwe: A History of Manufacturing 1890–1995, University of Zimbabwe Press, Harare.

Pinheiro, E., Vasan, A., Kim, J.Y., Lee, E., Guimier, J.M. & Perriens, J. (2006) 'Examining the production costs of antiretroviral drugs', *AIDS*, 20 (13), 1745–52.

Pinho, V.D., Gutmann, B., Miranda, L.S.M., de Souza, R. & Kappe, C.O. (2014) 'Continuous flow synthesis of a-halo ketones: essential building blocks of antiretroviral agents', *J. Org. Chem.*, 79, 1555–1562.

PINTEC/ Instituto Brasileiro de Geografia e Estatística IBGE (2011) *Pesquisa de Inovação Tecnológica*, IBGE, Rio de Janeiro. Available from Pesquisa de Inovação – PINTEC, http://www.pintec.ibge.gov.br/index.php?option=com_content_extjs&view=article&id=17&Itemid=6 [accessed 1 March 2015].

Portal Fiocruz (2014) *Produção e Inovação*. Available from http://portal.fiocruz.br/pt-br/content/produ%C3%A7%C3%A3o-e-inova%C3%A7%C3%A3o [accessed 20 March 2015].

Portelli, B. & Narula, R. (2004) *Foreign direct investment through acquisitions and implications for technological upgrading: Case evidence from Tanzania*, Research Memoranda 008, MERIT, Maastricht Economic Research Institute on Innovation and Technology, Maastricht.

Private Sector Innovation Programme for Health (2014). Overview of Experiences in the Pharmaceutical Supply Chain; Implications of the Poor in Kenya. Available from http://www.psp4h.com/ [accessed 3 May 2015].

Progenerico (2014) *Associação Brasileira das Indústrias de Medicamentos Genéricos*. Available from http://www.progenericos.org.br/index.php/noticias [accessed 15 March 2015].

Puliyel, J. M. & Madhavi, Y. (2008) 'Vaccines: Policy for public good or private profit?' *Indian Journal of Medical Research*, 127 (1), 1–3.

Rai, R.K. (2009) 'Effect of the TRIPS-mandated intellectual property rights on pharmaceutical industry', *The Journal of World Intellectual Property*, 11 (5–6), 404–31.

Rajagopal, D. (2013) 'Cipla completes the Medpro deal, buys 100% stake in the South African company', *The Economic Times*, 28 February. Available from http://articles.economictimes.indiatimes.com/2013–02–28/news/37352125_1_cipla-medpro-cipla-chairman-subhanu-saxena [accessed 27 April 2015].

Rajan, R.G. & Subramanian, A. (2011) 'Aid, Dutch disease, and manufacturing growth', *Journal of Development Economics*, 94 (1), 106–18.

Reich, M. (1990) 'Why the Japanese don't export more pharmaceuticals: Health policy as industrial policy', *California Management Review*, Winter, 124–50.

Richardson, C.J. (2005) 'How the loss of property rights caused Zimbabwe's collapse', *CATO Institute Economic Development Bulletin*, Project on Global Economic Liberty 4.

Riddell, R. (1990) *Manufacturing Africa: Performance and Prospects of Seven Countries in Sub-Saharan Africa*, James Curry, London.

Rietveld, A.H. & Haaijer-Ruskamp, F.M. (2002) 'Policy options for cost containment of pharmaceuticals', *International Journal of Risk and Safety in Medicine*, 15, 29–54.

Ripin, D.H.B., Teager, D.S., Fortunak, J., Basha, S.M., Bivins, N., Boddy, C.N., Byrn. S., Catlin, K.K., Houghton, S.R. & Jagadeesh, S.T. (2010) 'Process improvements for the manufacture of tenofovir disoproxil fumarate at commercial scale', *Organic Process R&D Journal*, 14, 1194–1201.

Roa, A.C. & Baptista e Silva, F.R. (2015) 'Fiocruz as an actor in Brazilian foreign relations in the context of the community of Portuguese-speaking countries: An untold story', *História, Ciências, Saúde-Manguinhos*, 22 (1), 153–69.

Rosen, D. & Rickwood, S. (2014) "Supply Chain Optimisation in Africa's Private Sector – Reducing the Price to Patient", IMS Health. Available from http://www.imshealth.com/deployedfiles/imshealth/Global/Content/Healthcare/Driving%20Healthcare%20Performance/High%20Growth%20Markets/IMSH_Africa_Supply_Chain_WP.pdf [accessed 30 April 2015].

Rosenberg, N. (1976) *Perspectives on Technology*, Cambridge University Press, Cambridge.

Rowe, R.C., Sheskey, P.J., Cook, W.G. & Fenton, M.E. (2012) *Handbook of Pharmaceutical Excipients*, 7th ed., Pharmaceutical Press, London.

Russo, G. & Banda, G. (forthcoming) 'Re-thinking pharmaceutical production in Africa; Insights from the analysis of the local manufacturing dynamics in Mozambique and Zimbabwe', *Studies in Comparative International Development*.

Russo, G., Cabral, L. & Ferrinho, P. (2013) 'Brazil-africa technical cooperation in health: What's its relevance to the post-busan debate on "aid effectiveness"?' *Globalization and Health*, 9, 2.

Russo, G., de Oliveira, L., Shankland, A. & Sitoe, T. (2014) 'On the margins of aid orthodoxy: The Brazil-Mozambique collaboration to produce essential medicines in Africa', *Globalization and Health*, 10 (1), 70.

Russo, G. & McPake, B. (2010) 'Medicine prices in urban Mozambique: A public health and economic study of pharmaceutical markets and price determinants in low-income settings', *Health Policy and Planning*, 25 (1), 70–84.

Sabatier, P.A. (1991) 'Toward better theories of the policy process', *PS: Political Science & Politics*, 24 (2), 147–56.

Sahu, S.K. (1998) *Technology Transfer, Dependence, and Self-Reliant Development in Third World: The Pharmaceutical and Machine Tool Industries in India*, Praeger Publishers, London.

Sala de Situação em saúde (2015) Available from http://189.28.128.178/sage/paineis/aqt/tabelaFP.php?ufcidade=Brasil&ufs=&ibges=&cg=&tc=&re_giao=&rm=&qs=&ufcidade=Brasil&qt=5570%20munic%C3%ADpios&pop=20 2799518&cor=005984&output=html&title= > [accessed 7 March 2015].

Schmitter, P.C. (1974) 'Still the century of corporatism?', *The Review of Politics, 36* (1), 85–131.

Schmitter, P. & Streeck, C. (1999), *The Organization of Business Interests: Studying the Associative Action of Business in Advanced Industrial Societies*. No. 99/1. MPIfG discussion paper.

Schneider, B. R. & Maxfield, S. (1997) 'Business, the State, and Economic Performance in Developing Countries', in S. Maxfield and B.R. Schneider (eds.), *Business and the State in Developing Countries*, Cornell University Press, Ithaca.

Seekings, J. & Nattrass, N. (2011) 'State-business relations and pro-poor growth in South Africa', *Journal of International Development*, 23 (3), 338–57.

Seiter, A. & Gyansa-Lutterodt, M. (2009) *Policy Note: The Pharmaceutical sector in Ghana*. Available from http://apps.who.int/medicinedocs/en/m/abstract/Js16765e/ [accessed 28 April 2015].

Shadlen, K. & Massard da Fonseca, E. (2013) 'Health policy as industrial policy: Brazil in comparative perspective', *Politics & Society*, 41 (4), 561–87.

Sheldon, R.A. (2007) 'The E factor: Fifteen years on', *Green Chemistry*, 9, 1273–83.

Shelys Pharmaceuticals. (2008) *Company Profile*, Shelys Pharmaceuticals, Dar es Salaam.

Sidibé M., Yong L. & Chan, M. (2014) 'Commodities for better health in Africa: Time to invest locally.' *Bulletin of the World Health Organization*, 92, 387–387A.

SMM and Farmanguinhos (2013) *Plano de Negócios Da SMM*, Sociedade Moçambicana de Medicamentos, Matola.

Snyman, H.W. (1962) *Report of the Commission of Inquiry Into High Cost of Medical Services and Medicines*, R.P. no. 59/1962, Government Printer, Pretoria.

Srinivas, S. (2004) *Technological Learning and the Evolution of the Indian Pharmaceutical and Biopharmaceutical Sectors*, Unpublished Dissertation, Massachusetts Institute of Technology, Cambridge, MA.

Srinivas, S. (2006) 'Industrial development and innovation: Some lessons from vaccine procurement', *World Development*, 34 (10), 1742–64.

Srinivas, S. (2011) *Well Beyond Market Failure: Development States in Indian pharmaceuticals and biotech*, paper presented at the American Political Science Association annual meeting (APSA) 2011, Seattle, 1–4 September 2011.

Srinivas, S. (2012) *Market Menagerie. Health and Development in Late Industrial States*, Stanford University Press, Stanford.

Srinivas, S. (2014a) *Development planning criteria in local pharmaceutical production*, Paper prepared for the Open University-UNIDO workshop on "Making Medicines in Africa", 15–16 December, London.

Srinivas, S. (2014b) 'Demand and Innovation: Paths to Inclusive Development', in Ramani, S. (ed.), Innovation in India: Combining Economic Growth with Inclusive Development, Cambridge University Press, Cambridge.

Steenkamp, W.F.J. (1978) *The Steenkamp Commission. Report of the Commission of Inquiry into the Pharmaceutical Industry*, Government Printer, Pretoria.

Stephenson, S. (1997) *Standards and conformity assessment as non-tariff barriers to trade*, World Bank Development Research Group Policy Research Working Paper No 1826, World Bank, Washington DC, September.

STERP (2009) *Short Term Emergency Recovery Programme (STERP): Getting Zimbabwe Moving Again*, Government of Zimbabwe, Harare.

Steyn, R., Burger, J.R., Hendrik, J., Serfontein, P. & Lubbe, M.S. (2007) 'Influence of a new reference based pricing system in South Africa on the prevalence and cost of antidiabetic medicines: A pilot study', *International Journal of Pharmacy Practice*, 15 (4), 307–11.

Stoker, A. & Jeffery, R. (1988) 'Pharmaceuticals and health policy: An Indian example', *Social Science and Medicine*, 27 (5), 563–67.

Sutton, J. (2012) *Competing in Capabilities: The Globalization Process*, Oxford University Press, Oxford.

Sutton, J. & Kellow, N. (2010) 'An Enterprise Map of Ethiopia', International Growth Centre. Available from http://personal.lse.ac.uk/sutton/ [accessed 3 May 2015].

Sutton, J. & Olomi, D. (2012) *An Enterprise Map of Tanzania*, International Growth Centre, London.

Tassey, G. (2000) 'Standardization in technology-based markets', *Research Policy*, 29 (4–5), 587–602.

Tempest, B. (2011) *The Structural Changes in the Global Pharmaceutical Marketplace and Their Possible Implications for Intellectual Property*, UNCTAD-ICTSD Project on IPRs and Sustainable Development, Policy Brief Number 10, July. Available from http://ictsd.org/i/publications/111430/ [accessed 28 April 2015].

TGE (1993a) *National Health Policy of the Transitional Government of Ethiopia*, Addis Ababa.

TGE (1993b) *National Drug Policy of the Transitional Government of Ethiopia*. Available from http://apps.who.int/medicinedocs/en/m/abstract/Js17823en/ [accessed 3 May 2015].

Thomas C.S. (ed.) (2004) *Research Guide to U.S. and International Interest Groups*, Praeger, Westport.

Thomas, G.L. (1994) 'Implicit industrial policy: The triumph of Britain and the failure of France in global pharmaceuticals', *Industrial and Corporate Change*, 3 (2), 541–48.

Tibandebage, P., Mackintosh, M., Israel, C., Mhede, E. & Mujinja, P.G.M. (2014) 'The Tanzanian health sector as buyer and user of medicines and other essential supplies, Working Paper 1', in *Industrial Productivity, Health Sector Performance and Policy Synergies for Inclusive Growth (IPHSP) research project*. Available from http://www.repoa.or.tz/documents/REPOA_WP_14_5.pdf [accessed 4 May 2015].

Tsebelis, G. (2002) *Veto Players: How Political Institutions Work*, Princeton University Press, Princeton.

Turshen, M. (2001) 'Reprivatizing pharmaceutical supplies in Africa', *Journal of Public Health Policy*, 22 (2), 198–225.

UNCTAD (2009) *The Least Developed Countries Report 2009: The State and Development Governance*, United Nations Conference on Trade and Development, Geneva.

UNCTAD (2011) *Local Production of Pharmaceuticals and Related Technology Transfer in Developing Countries: a Series of Case Studies by the UNCTAD Secretariat*, United Nations Conference on Trade and Development, Geneva.

UNIDO (United Nations Industrial Development Organisation) (2007) 'Pharmaceutical Sector Profile: Zimbabwe', *Global UNIDO Project: Strengthening the local production of essential generic drugs in least developed and developing countries*, Vienna, Austria.

UNIDO (United Nations Industrial Development Organisation) (2010a) 'Pharmaceutical Sector Profile: Kenya', *Global UNIDO Project: Strengthening the local production of essential generic drugs in least developed and developing countries*, Vienna, Austria.

UNIDO (United Nations Industrial Development Organisation) (2010b) 'Pharmaceutical Sector Profile: Uganda', *Global UNIDO Project: Strengthening the local production of essential generic drugs in least developed and developing countries*, Vienna, Austria.

UNIDO (United Nations Industrial Development Organisation) (2011a) 'Pharmaceutical Sector Profile: Nigeria', *Global UNIDO Project: Strengthening the Local Production of Essential Generic Drugs in Least Developed and Developing Countries*, Vienna, Austria.

UNIDO (United Nations Industrial Development Organisation) (2011b) 'Pharmaceutical Sector Profile: Zimbabwe', *Global UNIDO Project: Strengthening* the Local Production of Essential Generic Drugs in Least Developed and Developing Countries, Vienna, Austria.

UNIDO (2012) *Kenya Pharmaceutical Sector Development Strategy – Strengthening the Local Production of Essential Medicines in Least Developed and Developing Countries*, UNIDO.

UNIDO (2014) *Kenya GMP Roadmap: A Stepwise Approach for the Pharmaceutical Industry to Attain WHO GMP Standards – Strengthening the Local Production of Essential Medicines in Least Developed and Developing Countries*, UNIDO.

UNIDO (2015) *Industrial Pharmacy Advanced Training (IPAT)*. Available from http://www.unido.org/en/what-we-do/poverty-reduction-through-productive-activities/business-investment-and-technology-services/competitiveness-business-environment-and-upgrading/pharmaceuticals/industrial-pharmacy-advanced-training-ipat.html [accessed 27 April 2015].

UNIDO/GoT (2012) *Tanzania Industrial Competitiveness Report*, United Nations Industrial Development Organization (UNIDO) and Government of Tanzania, Ministry of Industry and Trade (GoT). Available from http://www.unido.org/fileadmin/user_media/Services/PSD/TanzaniaIndustrialCompetitivenessRepor t2012-ebook.pdf [accessed 30 April 2015].

UNITAID (2013) *Malaria Medicines Landscape*, WHO, UNITAID, Geneva. Available from http://www.unitaid.eu/images/marketdynamics/publications/UNITAID-MalariaMedicinesLandscape-2013_DEC.pdf [accessed 18 May 2015].

URT (United Republic of Tanzania) (2009) Speech by the Minister for Finance and Economic Affairs, Hon. Mustafa Haidi Mkulo MP, Introducing to the National Assembly the Estimates of Government Revenue and Expenditure for the Financial Year 2009/10. Available from http://www.mof.go.tz/mofdocs/budget/BUDGET%20SPEECH%20ENGLISH%20FINAL%20VERSION.pdf [accessed 30 April 2015].

USFDA (2008) *Warning letter WL: 320–08–02*, Centre for Drug Evaluation and Research, Development of Health and Human Services, Washington, DC. Available from http://www.fiercebiotech.com/press-releases/fda-issues-warning-letter-ranbaxy-regarding-march-inspections [accessed 3 May 2015].

USNLM (2014) Artemisinin derivatives, *United States National Library of Medicine*. Available from http://livertox.nih.gov/ArtemisininDerivatives.htm [accessed 8 November 2014].

Uyarra, E. & Flanagan, K. (2009) *Understanding the Innovation Impacts of Public Procurement*, Manchester Business School Working Paper, Number 574. Available from www.mbs.ac.uk/research/workingpapers/ [accessed 1 December 2014].

Verhoef ,T.I. & Morris, S. (2015) 'Cost-effectiveness and pricing of antibacterial drugs', *Chemical and Biological Drug Research*, 85 (1), 4–13.

Vokes, S. (2007) 'Trade dynamics affecting the face of retail pharmacy in South Africa', *South African Pharmaceutical Journal*, 74 (7), 6–9.

von Hippel, E. (1982) 'Get new products from customers', *Harvard Business Review*, 60 (2), 117–22.

Wafula, F., Molyneaux, C., Mackintosh, M. & Goodman, C. (2013) 'Protecting the public or setting the bar too high? Understanding the causes and consequences of regulatory actions of frontline regulators and specialized drug shop operators in Kenya', *Social Science & Medicine*, 97, 220–27.

Wamae, W. and Kariuki Kungu, J. (2014) 'Pharmaceutical Manufacturing in Kenya: Key trends and Developments', *ACTS Working Brief No.3*, African Centre for Technological Studies. Available from http://iphsp.acts-net.org/publications/policy-briefs [accessed 14 May 2015].

Wamae, W., Kariuki Kungu, J. & Clark, N. (2014) 'Value Added Tax in the Pharmaceutical Industry: What Does It Really Mean for Kenya's Industrialisation?' *ACTS Working Brief No.1*, African Centre for Technological Studies. Available from http://iphsp.acts-net.org/publications/policy-briefs [accessed 14 May 2015].

Wamai, R.G. (2009) 'Reviewing Ethiopia's health system development: International medical community', *Japanese Medical Association Journal*, 52 (4), 279–86.

Wambebe, C.O., Bamgboye, E.A., Badru, B.O., Khamofu, H., Momoh, J.A., Ekpeyong, M., Audu, B.S., Njoku, S.O., Nasipuri, N.R., Kunle, O.O., Okogun, J.I., Enwerem, N.M., Gamaniel, S.K., Obodozie, O.O., Samuel, B., Fojule, G. & Ogunyale, P.O. (2001a) 'Efficacy of niprisan in the prophylactic management of patients with sickle cell disease', *Current Theory & Research*, 62 (1), 26.

Wambebe, C., Khamofu, H., Momoh, J.A.F., Ekpeyong, M., Audu, B.S., Njoku, O.S., Bamgboye, E.A., Nasipuri, R.N., Kunle, O.O., Okogun, J.I., Enwerem, M.N., Audam, J.G., Gamaniel, K.S., Obodozie, O.O., Samuel, B., Fojule, G. & Ogunyale, O. (2001b) 'Double-blind, placebo-controlled, randomised cross-over clinical trial of NIPRISAN® in patients with Sickle Cell Disorder', *Phytomedicine*, 8 (4), 252.

Wangwe, S. (ed.) (1995) *Exporting Africa: Technology, Trade and Industrialisation in Sub-Saharan Africa*, UNU/INTECH and Routledge, London.

Wangwe, S. (2003) *Exporting Africa: Technology, Industrialism and Trade*, Routledge, London.

Wangwe, S., Tibandebage, P. Mhede, E., Israel, C., Mujinja P.G.M. & Mackintosh, M. (2014a) 'Reversing Pharmaceutical Manufacturing Decline in Tanzania: Policy Options and Constraints', *REPOA Brief* 43, July. Available from http://www.repoa.or.tz/documents/REPOA_BRIEF_43.pdf [accessed 30 April 2015].

Wangwe, S., Tibandebage, P., Mackintosh, M., Israel, C., Mhede, E. & Mujinja P.G.M. (2014b) 'From Passive to Active Industrial Policy: Improving Locally Manufactured Supplies to the Tanzanian Health Sector', *REPOA Brief* 46, September. Available from http://www.repoa.or.tz/documents/REPOA_BRIEF_46.pdf [accessed 1 May 2015].

Waning, B., Maddix, J., Tripodis, Y., Laing, R., Leufkens, H.G.M. & Gokhale, M. (2010) 'Towards equitable access to medicines for the rural poor: analyses of insurance claims reveal rural pharmacy initiative triggers price competition in Kyrgyzstan', *International Journal for Equity in Health*, 8 (43).

Warren-Rodríguez, A. (2010) 'Uncovering trends in the accumulation of technological capabilities and skills in the Mozambican manufacturing sector', *Oxford Development Studies*, 38 (2), 171–98.

WHO (World Health Organization) (1995) *Essential Drugs Monitor* No 019. Available from http://apps.who.int/medicinedocs/en/d/Js16518e/4.7.html#Js16518e.4.7 [accessed 11 April 2015].

WHO (World Health Organization) (2004a) *WHO Guidelines on Safety Monitoring of Herbal Medicines in Pharmacovigilance Systems*, WHO Press, Geneva.

WHO (World Health Organization) (2004b) 'WHO good manufacturing practices: main principles for pharmaceutical products', in *WHO Expert Committee on*

Specifications for Pharmaceutical Preparations, 37th report, Geneva, WHO 2003. Annex 4 (WHO Technical Report Series, No. 908).

WHO (World Health Organization) (2005) *Local Production of Essential Medicines, including Antiretrovirals: Issues, Challenges and Perspectives in the African Region*, Report of the Regional Director, regional Committee for Africa, Maputo, Mozambique.

WHO (World Health Organization) (2007a) *WHO Guidelines for Assessing Quality of Herbal Medicines with Reference to Contaminants and Residues*, WHO Press, Geneva.

WHO (World Health Organization) (2007b) *WHO Guidelines on Good Manufacturing Practices (GMP) for Herbal Medicines*, WHO Press, Geneva.

WHO (World Health Organization) (2012) *Estatísticas da Saúde Mundial*. Available from http://www.who.int/gho/publications/world_health_statistics/2012/en/ [accessed 13 March 2015].

Willcox, M.L., Graz, B., Falquet, J., Diakite, C., Giani, S. & Diallo, D. (2011) 'A "reverse pharmacology" approach for developing an anti-malarial phytomedicine', *Malaria Journal*, 10 (Suppl. 1), S8.

Wilson, J.S. & Abiola, V. (2003) *Standards & Global Trade: A Voice for AFRICA*, The World Bank, Washington, DC.

Wolff, J. (2012) *The Human Right to Health*, W.W. Norton & Company, New York and London.

World Bank (2005) *Food safety and agricultural health standards: Challenges and opportunities for developing country exports*, Report no. 31027, Poverty Reduction & Economic Management Trade Unit, Agriculture and Rural Development Department, The World Bank, Washington, DC.

World News (2013) *Cipla Ups Stake in Ugandan Firm, Acquires 14.5% for $15 Million*. Available from http://article.wn.com/view/2013/11/21/Cipla_ups_stake_in_Ugandan_firm_acquires_145_for_15_million_l/ [accessed 27 April 2015].

World Trade Organisation (2001) *Declaration on the TRIPS Agreement and Public Health*. Available from http://www.wto.org/english/thewto_e/minist_e/min01_e/mindecl_trips_e.htm [accessed: 29 April 2015].

Yadav P. (2014) *Kenya Medical Supplies Authority (KEMSA): A case study of the ongoing transition from an ungainly bureaucracy to a competitive and customer focused medical logistics organization*, The World Bank, Washington, DC.

Index

Note: Italic page numbers indicate a table or figure.

15% price preference, 31, 55, 115

AA Pharmaceuticals, 22, 47
access to health care, 1, 3, 99, 145
access to medicines, 3, 166, 169, 203,
 219–20
accreditation, 225, 228, 230, 233
Action Medeor, 157, 158
active pharmaceutical ingredients
 (APIs), 122, 123–4
 costs, 127–8, 131
 in Ethiopia, 70
 imports, 11, 39, 89
 'leap-frogging' technologies, 130–2,
  138–40
 local production in Africa, 129–30
 manufacturing, 124, 126–9
  African capacity for, 137–8
  building skills for, 142–3
 quality management systems and
  GMP, 132–3
Adcock Ingram, 219, 267, 269
Addis Pharmaceuticals Factory, 68
advance payment, 248
African Growth and Opportunity Act,
 28
African manufacturing, *see* local
 manufacturing
African Medicines Regulatory
 Harmonisation (AMRH), 234–5,
 284
African National Congress (ANC), 270
African Union Commission (AUC), 278–9
AIDS, *see* anti-retrovirals (ARVs)
albendazole, *49*, 108
amodiaquine, 139
 artesunate-amodiaquine, 58, 138–9
amoxicillin, *49*, 52–3, *96*
amoxicillin-clavulonate, 108
anti-diabetics, 219
anti-hypertensives, 89
anti-malarials, 36, 138
 suppliers, 162

in Tanzania, 52, 58
anti-retrovirals (ARVs)
 in Brazil, 170–1
 in Brazil–Mozambique programme,
  85–102
 costs, 127–9
 in Kenya, 31, 36, 42
 in Tanzania, 47, 48
 in Zimbabwe, 15, 250–2
antibiotics, 46, 48, 52–3
APIs, *see* active pharmaceutical
 ingredients (APIs)
artemether, *126*
artemisinin, 36, *126*
 combination therapies, 138–9
artemisinin-lumefantrine, 52
artesunate, *126*
artesunate-amodiaquine, 58, 138–9
ARVs, *see* anti-retrovirals (ARVs)
Aspen, 46, 53, 267
asthma, 175

banks, 286, 289, *290*, 291–2
'basket funds', 153, 155
Bengaluru (Bangalore) City, 195
Beta Healthcare International, 22, 46
beta lactams, 52–3
'Big Pharma v Nelson Mandela' case,
 270, 272
Bioavailability, 127
Bioclones, 138
bioequivalence, 81–2
Biomanguinhos, 171
BIOVAC, 137
Blue Book price list, 211–12, 217
Boehringer Ingelheim, 42
'boom and crash' period, 65, 67
Botanical Extract EPZ, 36
braingain, 142
brand names, 104, 107–8
Brazil, 2, 166–82
 government of, *87*, 88, *91*
 health-industry relationships, 147–8

Brazil – *continued*
  industrial policy for
    pharmaceuticals, 171–2
  local manufacturing, 172–3
  Mozambique ARV programme,
    85–102
  Partnerships for Productive
    Development, 177–80
  pharmaceutical health care, 168–73
  pharmaceutical health care policy,
    169–70
  pharmaceutical products imports
    and exports, *178*
  social rights, 168–9
  technological development in
    medicines, 170–1
Brazil Without Extreme Poverty Plan,
  175
Brazilian Federal Constitution, 168
Brazilian Popular Pharmacy Program
  (PFPB), 173, 174–7
'buy local', 17, 28, 29, 42

Cadila Pharmaceuticals Ethiopia
  (CPEL), 68, 112
cancer, 179–80
capacity utilization, 18, 37, 70
capital investment, *see* investment
  capital
capital markets, 286
CAPS Pharmaceuticals, 14, 251, *252*
captopril, 88
cardiovascular disease, 175
cash-on-delivery, 248
Centre for Advanced Pharmaceutical
  Training, 280
Certificate of Pharmaceutical Product,
  111
Certification, 225, 228, 230, 233
chambers of commerce, 263
China
  Ethiopia
    imports to, 70
    joint ventures in, 73–5
  imports, 11
  investment in Tanzania, 22
  price control system, 205–6
Cipla, 108
ciprofloxacin, *49*, 53

civil society organizations (CSOs),
  262, 265, 270
clavulonate, 108
clinical trials, *226*
coalitions, 264–6
collaborative capabilities, 145, 148
  building, 162–4
  local manufacturing, 161–2
COMESA medicines market, 19
  from Kenya, 28, 30, 43
comparative pricing, 205, 217
competitive tendering, 119
compulsory licensing, 41–2
Conference of African Ministers of
  Health, 279
Cosmos, 36, 42
cost efficiency, in Kenya, 37
cost-plus pricing model, 204
costs
  APIs, 127–8, 131
  ARVs, 127–9
  distribution, 35
  overheads and labour, 126
  shipping, 130
  standards, 235–6
country-level capabilities, 33
coverage with evidence development
  (CED), 258
credit risk function, *290*
credit terms, 160, 248–9

Datlabs, 14
Dawa, 27, 42
deindustrialization, 11, 15
depreciation provisions, 295–6
Development Bank of Ethiopia, 78
diabetes, 175, 219
diclofenac, *49*
differential pricing, 255, 257
dihydroartemisinin-piperaquine, 139
dioscorea starch, 141
direct capital provision, 293–4
direct government expenditure, 294
direct price negotiations, 205
Discovery Medical Aid, 219
disease surveillance, 194–5
dispensing fees, 210–11, 213–14, *215*
distribution costs, 35
district medical officer, 153–4

donor funding
  in Kenya, 18, 31
  public sector procurement, 154–7
  in Tanzania, 52–3
  in Zimbabwe, 16, 251, *252*
dosage forms, *30, 35*
drug life cycle stages, *226*
drug master file, 137
Drugs for Neglected Diseases, 58
dual-brand strategy, 108

E-factor, 126–7, 131, 139
East African Community (EAC), 60, 284
East African Pharmaceuticals, 67–8
Economic Community of West African States (ECOWAS), 235, 279, 284
economic crises, 10
  in Tanzania, 20–1
  in Zimbabwe, 15–16
economies of scale, 129, 228
educational system
  for API manufacture, 142
  in Kenya, 38–9
  skills shortages, 233, 234
  in Tanzania, 57
efavirenz (EFV), 127, 131
emerging donors, 97
empty hard gelatin capsules, 73–4
enset starch, 141
entecavir, 130
equity, 287, 294
essential medicines, 55, 60, 150, 151, 253
Ethiopia, 65–84
  developing and supplying the health sector, 70–2
  industry today, 69–70
  joint ventures, 65, 66, 68–9, 73–6
  phases of industrial development, 66–9
  science and technology policies, 79–82
  socio-economic policies and investment environment, 76–82
  starch excipients, 140–2

Ethiopian Pharmaceutical Manufacturing company (EPHARM), 66–7, 70
Ethiopian Pharmaceuticals and Medical Supplies Manufacturing Association (EPMSMA), 67, 68
European Medicines Agency (EMA), 232, 255
evolutionary economics, 32–3
excipients, 123–4, *125*
  importation, 11, 70
  starch, 140–2
Export Promotion Zones, 28
exports
  Brazilian pharmaceuticals, *178*
  Kenyan pharmaceuticals, 17, 19, 28, 29–30
  Tanzanian pharmaceuticals, *23,* 47–8
  see also Indian exports
external funds, 287

facility standards, 232–3
factoring, 249–50
faith-based sector, 150, *151,* 157
family ownership, 49–50
Farmanguinhos, *87,* 88, 89, 92, 99, 171
FDIs, *see* foreign direct investments (FDIs)
financial capabilities, 237–8
  in banks, 289, *290,* 291–2
  investment, 57, 58, 289
  in manufacturers and financial institutions, 285–9
financial institutions, 287, *288,* 289–92
Fine Chemicals Corporation (FCC), 122, 137
finished pharmaceutical products (FPPs), 123–4
  costs, 128
  local manufacturing, 129–30
  quality management systems and GMP, 132–3
Fiocruz, 87, 92, 99, 171, 174
firm-level capabilities, 33, 57–8
  financial, 285–8
  technological, *290*

First Market Environment (FME),
183–5
patents, 191–2
problem-solving and state capacity,
186–8, 189
vaccines, 195
fixed-margin system, 205
flow chemistry, 131, 139–40
folic acid, *49*
Food, Medicine and Healthcare
Administration Control
Authority (FMHACA), 77, 80–1
foreign direct investments (FDIs), 103,
286
in Ghana, 115–20
Indian companies, 112–14
in Kenya, 26–7
foreign experts, 38, 40
FPPs, *see* finished pharmaceutical
products (FPPs)
funds
accession and repayment, *290*
Global Fund, 52, 251, 254
internal and external, 287
see also donor funding

generic companies, 104–5
growth, 266
Indian in Africa, 109–14
generic medicines, 11
manufactured in Kenya, 18
manufactured in Zimbabwe, 16
market in Brazil, 172–3
MNCs and, 106, 108–9
in South Africa, 218, 219–20
standards, 227
Generic Medicines Law, 170, 171
Germany, 11, 280
Ghana, 114–15, 281–2, 293
Indian imports, 109, *110*
industrial policy, 115–20
retail prices of formulations, *118*
GIZ, 82, 238
glibenclamide, *96*
Global Alliance for Vaccines and
Immunization, 254
Global Fund, 52, 251, 254
global pharmaceutical industry, 104–5
anticipated trends, *107*

and South Africa, 266–73
see also multinational corporations
(MNCs)
globalization, 163
good clinical practice (GCP), *226*
good laboratory practice (GLP), *226*
good manufacturing practice (GMP),
226, 227, 230–2, 235
APIs and FPPs, 132–3
in Ethiopia, 67–8, 75, 81
in Ghana, 116
in India, 238–41
'road map', 81, 238–41, 282
in Tanzania, 51–2, 57
government of Brazil (GoB), *87,* 88, *91*
government of Mozambique (GoM),
87, 88, *91,* 101
government policy
in Brazil, 169–70
and collaborative capabilities, 163–4
in Ethiopia, 76–82
in Ghana, 115
and industry associations, 261–3
investment capiital accession, 292–7
leverage over funding, 154–7
licensing and joint ventures, 41–3
subsystem, 263–4
in Tanzania, 54–6, 59–62
see also industrial policies; public
sector; state-industry relations
granules, 124
Green Center for Chemical
Manufacturing, 131
green chemistry, 131
Growth and Transformation Plan
(GTP), 71, 80, 82
growth coalitions, 265–6
GSK, 34, 53, 108

harmonization initiatives, 234–5
hazard analysis critical control points,
229
health care
access to, 1, 3, 99, 145
in Brazil, 168–73
industry-healthcare integration in
Zimbabwe, 14–15
institutional triad of, 188, *189*
in Kenya and Tanzania, 150, *151*

health care – *continued*
two-tier South African system, 206–7
health sector
in Ethiopia, 70–2
market structure, 149–57
non-profit wholesaling, 157–9
organization, 147–9
private sector procurement and
local products, 159–61
Health Sector Development
Programme, 71
Health Sector Services Fund, 154
health-industry relationships, 147–8,
149
hepatitis B virus, 130
herbal medicines, 134–7
H1N1 outbreak, 195
HIV/AIDS, *see* anti-retrovirals (ARVs)
Holley Industrial Group Ltd, 22
horizontal cooperation, 98
human resources
in Kenya, 38–9
in Mozambique, 99–100
hybrid bonds, 287
hydrochlorothiazide, 88, *96*
hypertension, 89, 175

immunobiologicals, 180
Imperial Health Sciences, 107
import duty, 55, 115, 130
import substitution policies, 7
in Kenya, 17, 26, 27, 29, 42
in Tanzania, 20
in Zimbabwe, 13–14
imports/importers, 160–1
APIs, 11, 39, 89
excipients, 11, 70
liberalization of, 8, 21, 28, 30
machinery, 39–40, 50
in Tanzania, 47–8, 50
incremental cost effectiveness ratio,
256
India, 1, 103
experts and training, 38
generic companies in Africa, 109–14
GMP, 238–41
health-industry relationships, 147
industrial capabilities, 184, 186–7
marketing strategy, 107–9

MNCs role in, 193
need and demand, 193–4
New Drug Policy, 184, 192–3
patents, 191–2
pharmaceutical industry, 105
problem-solving and state capacity,
186–90
retail prices of formulations, *118*
strong production, weak problem-
solving, 196–8
see also First Market Environment
(FME)
Indian exports, 11, 18, *112*, 185
to Africa, 109, *110*
to Ethiopia, 70
to Kenya, 39
model followed, 113
to Tanzania, 51, 108
Indian Patent Act, 1970 191
Industrial and Commercial
Development Corporation
(ICDC), 17, 27, 42
industrial capabilities, 2
in India, 184, 186–7
see also technological capabilities
industrial innovation, incentives for,
253–5
industrial policies
in Brazil, 171–2
in Ethiopia, 78–9
in Ghana, 115–20
and health sector organization, 147–9
public sector procurement, 244–52
industry associations, 261–3, 275
policy subsystem and, 263–4
in South Africa, 261–4, 267–9, 271–2
industry-healthcare integration, in
Zimbabwe, 14–15
Infusion Medicare, 27, 42
injectable infusions, 35
in-kind finance, 246
Innovative Medicines South Africa
(IMSA), 267, 271–2
institutional triad of health care, 188,
189
insulin, 76
intellectual property rights (IPR), 191,
262, 273, 274
see also TRIPS

Interchem Pharmaceuticals, 21, 47
interest subsidies, 294
internal funds, 287
International Dispensary Association,
208
international market liberalization, 8
International Reference Prices, 119
International Standards Organisation,
229
international tendering, 119, 154–5
investment
in Ethiopia, 76–82
for industry development, 283
in Mozambique, 90, *91*, 92
pharmaceutical investment
timeline, 8, *9*, 10–11
in Tanzania, 19–20, 46–7
see also foreign direct investments
(FDIs)
investment capabilities, 57, 58, 289
investment capital, 126
accession to, 292–7
country context, 296–7
direct capital provision, 293–4
direct government expenditure,
294
time-limited incentives, 295–6
invoice discounting, 249–50
IPAT program, 133, 139
ISI, *see* import substitution policies

Jaipur Foot prosthetic, 194
joint ventures
in Ethiopia, 65, 66, 68–9, 73–6
in Kenya, 41–3
Julphar Pharmaceuticals, 69, 75–6

Kefauver-Harris Drug Amendments
Act 1962, 225
Keko Pharmaceuticals, 20, 21, 22, 47
KEMSA, 150, 154, 161, 164
Kenya, 25–44
background to pharmaceutical
industry, 25–6, 43–4
collaborative capabilities
building, 162–4
local manufacturing, 161–2
domestic market size for medicines,
156

dominant East African producer,
17–19
donor influence and government
leverage, 154–7
equipment and inputs, 39–40
health-industry relationships, 149
human resources and the
educational system, 38–9
industrial structure, 34–5
investment timeline, 10
knowledge flows, linkage
capabilities and innovation,
40–1
licensing and joint ventures, 41–3
market and supply chain
segmentation, 149–50
market position pharmaceutical
industry, 29–32
market power and local purchasing,
151
non-profit wholesaling, 157–9
post-colonial industrialization, 26–9
private sector procurement and
local products, 159–61
procurement capabilities in the
public sector, 152–4
productivity, capacity utilization
and cost efficiency, 37
products and standards, 35–6
standards, 236–8
technological capabilities and
innovation sectors, 32–44
Kenya Overseas Company, 17
Kilimanjaro School of Pharmacy, 139
knowledge flows, 40–1

Laboratories & Allied Inc, 27, 35
LaGray Pharmaceuticals, 109, 114,
122, 138
Lall, Sanjaya, 244–5
lamivudine, 88, 89, *96*
lamivudine-zidovudine, 36, *96*
lamivudine-zidovudine-nevirapine, *96*
'leap-frogging' technologies, 122, 130–2
for competitive advantage, 138–40
letter of credit, 247
liberalization of imports, 8
in Kenya, 28, 30
in Tanzania, 21

licensing, 41–3
linkage capabilities, 33, 57
loan disbursement, monitoring and
    control, *290*, 291
local manufacturing, 5
  in Africa
    capabilities, 11–12
    transforming, 278–82
  APIs, 129–30
    capacity for manufacturing, 137–8
    'leap-frogging' technologies for,
      130–2
  in Brazil, 172–3
  collaborative capabilities, 161–2
  domestic market share in Tanzania,
    49
  in Ethiopia, 71–2, 83
  expansion today, 23
  FPPs, 129–30
  in Ghana, 117, *118*
  Indian company investment,
    112–14
  investment timeline, 8–11
  MNCs investment, 8
  in Mozambique, 99–102
  three case studies, 12
local procurement, in Kenya and
    Tanzania, 151, 157–9
logistics fees, 214, 216
lumefantrine, 52

machinery
  importation, 39–40, 50
  medical equipment, 154
Mansoor Daya Chemicals Ltd, 19, 21, 47
manufacturing, *see* local
    manufacturing
marketing, 148
marketing strategy, MNCs in Africa,
    105–9
markets
  capital, 286
  generics, 106, 108–9
  market size trends, *107*
medical equipment, 154
Medical Supplies Department (MSD),
    53, 55, 150, 154–5, 156
Medicines and Related Substances Act
    1997, 209–10, 234, 270

Medicines Control Council, 234
Medicines Regulatory Harmonization
    programme, 235
MEDS (Mission for Essential Drugs
    Supply), 31, 157–9, 163, 164
Merck, 269
metronidazole, *96*
MNCs, *see* multinational corporations
    (MNCs)
Mozambican Ministry of Health
    (MISAU), 88, 89, *94*, 101
Mozambique, 85–102
  Brazil-supported pharmaceutical
    factory, 86–9
  company and the market, 92–7
  government of, *87*, 88, *91*, 101
  Indian imports, 109, *110*
  local production of
    pharmaceuticals, 99–102
  south-south collaboration in
    context, 97–9
  technical investment, 90, *91*, 92
Mozambique Pharmaceuticals Ltd
    (SMM), 88, 95–7, 102
multinational corporations (MNCs),
    103, 104–5
  in India, 193
  investment, 8
  marketing strategy in Africa, 105–9
  moving out of Kenya, 30, 34
  research-based, 266
  in South Africa, 267, 269, 272

National Association of
    Pharmaceutical Manufacturers,
    269
National Development Bank, 171–2
National Drug Policy (NDP), Ethiopia,
    77
National Drug Policy (NDP), South
    Africa, 208–10
national drug regulatory agencies
    (NDRAs), 132, 133, 227
National Essential Medicines List,
    174–5
National Health Insurance Scheme
    (NHIS), Ghana, 119
National Health Policy (NHP),
    Ethiopia, 70, 77

National Institute for Pharmaceutical R&D, 134–6
National Medicine Policy (PNM), 169, 170
National Policy of Pharmaceutical Care, 169–70
national tendering, 119
National Veterinary Institute, Ethiopia, 69
NATPHARM, 16
Nelson Mandela Metropolitan University, 139–40
neoclassical economics, 32
neo-liberal economic policies, 265
nevirapine, 42, 88, 89, *96*
New Click (Pty) Ltd, 213
New Drug Policy (NDP), India, 184, 192–3
New Partnership for Africa's Development, 235
Nigeria
  Indian imports, 109, *110*
  investment timeline, 10
  Niprisan™ development, 134–7
Niprisan™, 134–7
non-government organizations (NGOs), 157
  in South Africa, 270
non-profit wholesaling, 157–9
Novartis, 36, 104

oil crises, 10
open tendering, 154–5
ophthalmic products, 35
oral polio vaccines, 194, 195
Organic Health Law, 169
organizational standards, 225, 228, 233–6
organocatalysis, 131
overheads and labour costs, 126

packaging, 39, 50, 160
Partnerships for Productive Development (PDPs), 174, 177–80
patents, 104–5, 106, 107, 191–2, 273
PEPFAR, 31
personnel standards, 232–3
Pharmaceutical Fund and Supply Agency, 72

Pharmaceutical Industry Association of South Africa (IPASA), 267, 271–2, 273
pharmaceutical industry in Africa, 5–6
  historical political economy, 7–24
  upgrading, market consolidation and financial challenges, 282–4
  see also individual countries
pharmaceutical investment timeline, 8, *9*, 10–11
Pharmaceutical Manufacturers Association of South Africa (PMA), 208, 210
Pharmaceutical Manufacturing Plan for Africa (PMPA), 2, 224, 235, 279, 281, 283, 295
Pharmaceutical Price Regulation Scheme, 204
Pharmaceutical Society of South Africa (PSSA), 213–14, 221
Pharmaceutical Task Group, 267
Pharmaceuticals and Poisons Board (PPB), 34, 41
pharmacists
  dispensing fees, 210–11, 213–14, *215*
  in Kenya, 38
pharmacovigilance, *226*
Pharmacure, 69
Pharmanova, 14
phytomedicines, 134–7
piperaquine, 139
Plus 5 Pharmaceuticals, 15
PMPA, *see Pharmaceutical Manufacturing Plan for Africa* (PMPA)
policy subsystem, 263–4
polio immunizations, 194–5
political economy, overview, 7–24
post-colonial industrialization, in Kenya, 26–9
post-independence era, 10
prednisone, *96*
price controls
  options, 204–6
  SEPs, 204, 210–13
  SEPs controversies and challenges, 213–16
  SEPs experience to date, 216–21

price controls – *continued*
  South African regime, 206–8, 221–3
prices/pricing
  15% price preference, 31, 55, 115
  Blue Book price list, 211–12, 217
  comparative, 205, 217
  differential, 255, 257
  high, 203
  International Reference Prices, 119
  private sector local products, 159–60
  unit, 95, *96*
  value-based, 244, 253, 255–9
  see also retail prices
private sector
  in Ethiopia, 78
  imports in Mozambique, 94–5
  in India, 184
  in Kenya and Tanzania, 150, *151*
  price mark-ups, 203
  procurement and local products,
    159–61
  in South Africa, 206
  in Tanzania, 53
problem-solving, 186–90
  successes and failures, 193–5
  weak, 196–8
process standards, 231–2, 237–8
PROCIS, 177–8
procurement, 148, 243–4, 259
  capabilities in the public sector,
    152–4
  improved, 128
  local, 151, 157–9
  practices in the public sector, 154–7
  private sector and local products,
    159–61
  public sector, 119
    health needs and values, 252–9
    industrial policy tool, 244–52
  in Zimbabwe, 250–2
product development packages, 122,
  142
product standards, 231–2
production capabilities, 57, 58
PROFARMA, 172
professional fees, 210–11, 213–14, *215*
profit caps, 204–5
project finance document, 287
prospecting capabilities, 289, *290*

public health
  challenge of implementation, 280–2
  commitment to, 279–80
public sector
  imports in Mozambique, 93, *94*
  in India, 184, 197
  investment in Tanzania, 19–20
  in Kenya and Tanzania, 150, *151*
  procurement, 119
    health needs and values, 252–9
    industrial policy tool, 244–52
  procurement capabilities, 152–4
  procurement practices, 154–7
  in South Africa, 206
purchasing, *see* procurement
pyrimethamine, 52

Quality Adjusted Life Years, 256
Quality Chemicals International, 282
quality control tests, 231
quality management systems (QMSs),
  132–3, 235

Ranbaxy, 105, 240
raw materials
  costs, 127–9
  standards, 231
  see also active pharmaceutical
    ingredients (APIs); excipients
reference pricing, 217, 219–20
'reform and revival' period, 68
Regional Bioequivalence Centre, 81–2
regional centres of excellence, 133,
  142
regulatory environment
  in Africa, 111, 283–4
  in Brazil, 177
  in Zimbabwe, 234
  see also standards
Regulatory Sciences Institute, 132
repayment, *290*
research and development (R&D), 36,
  167, 172
retail prices
  controls, 205–6
  in India and Ghana, *118*
  mark-ups, 203
reverse pharmacology (RP), 122,
  133–4, 136

Rwanda, 109, *110*
Rx Africa (Ethiopia), 69

St Lukes Foundation, Tanzania, 280
Sandoz, 109
Sanitary Reform, 168
Second Market Environment (SME),
    184–5, 186, 191–2
    vaccines, 195
sectoral systems of innovation, 32–4
SEPs, *see* single exit price regulations
    (SEPs)
Shelys Pharmaceuticals, 20, 21, 22,
    23, 108
    investment and consolidation, 46
    sold to Aspen, 53–4
shipping costs, 130
Short term Economic Recovery
    Programme, 16
sickle-cell disease, 134–6
simvastatin, 219–20
single exit price regulations (SEPs),
    204, 210–13
    controversies and challenges,
        213–16
    impact on manufacturers and access
        to medicines, 219–21
    price increases under, 216–17
    setting, 211–13
Sino-Ethiop Associate (Africa), 68,
    73–5
skills shortages, 233, 234
Smith & Nephew, 66
social rights, 168–9
sodium starch glycolate, 141
South Africa
    API manufacturing, 137–8, 139–40
    economic growth, 266–7
    and the global pharmaceutical
        industry, 266–73
    industry associations, 261–4, 267–9,
        271–2
    investment timeline, 10
    National Drug Policy, 208–10
    post-apartheid, 269–73
    pre-liberalization era, 268–9
    price control regime, 206–8, 221–3
    regulatory system, 234
    SEPs, 204, 210–13

SEPs controversies and challenges,
    213–16
SEPs experience to date, 216–21
state-industry relations and
    coalitions, 264–6
two-tier health care system, 206–7
South African Pharmaceutical
    Manufacturers Association
    (PMA), 269, 270–1, 272
South-South cooperation programme,
    Brazil–Mozambique ARVs,
    85–102
SRA approvals, 132, 142
Standard Chartered Bank, 291, *292*
standard operating procedures (SOPs),
    134, 232
standards, 224–41
    classification, 225
    competitive tools and pressure to
        improve, 229–30
    cost implications, 235–6
    drug life cycle, *226*
    establishment and assurance,
        227–9
    facility and personnel, 232–3
    historical perspective, 225–7
    Kenyan, 236–8
    organizational aspects of, 233–6
    technical and process, 230–2
    upgrading, 237–8
    see also good manufacturing practice
        (GMP); WHO-prequalification
        standards
starch, 140–2
state capacity, 186–90
state-industry relations, 275–6
    post-apartheid, 269–72
    pre-liberalization, 268
    resetting, 273–5
    in South Africa, 264–6
Sterling Winthrop, 269
'stock-outs', 153
strategic partnerships, in Ethiopia,
    73–6
structural adjustment programmes,
    10–11
structured-credit approach, 249
sulphadoxine-pyrimethamine, 52
Sumaria group, 46

Sun Pharmaceuticals, 105
suppliers
  anti-malarials, 162
  as knowledge source, 40
supply chain segmentation, 149–50
Surat City, 194–5
sustainability of health systems, 166–7
Sweden, 257–8
swine flu, 195

Tanzania, 19–22, 45–63
  collaborative capabilities
    building, 162–4
    local manufacturing, 161–2
  competitiveness and upgrading,
    21–2
  domestic market size for medicines,
    156
  donor influence and government
    leverage, 154–7
  economic crisis and liberalization,
    20–1
  health-industry relationships, 149
  Indian imports, 51, 108
  industrial strengths and
    vulnerabilities, 49–54
  investment and consolidation,
    19–20, 46–7
  market and supply chain
    segmentation, 149–50
  market power and local purchasing,
    151
  non-profit wholesaling, 157–8
  pioneering firms and public sector
    investment, 19–20
  private sector procurement and
    local products, 159–61
  procurement capabilities in the
    public sector, 152–4
  production and exports, 23
  recent industrial decline, 47–9
  turnaround strategies, 54–62
Tanzania Food and Drug Authority
  (TFDA), 52, 60, 62
Tanzania Pharmaceutical Industries
  Ltd (TPI), 20, 21, 22, 23, 47
Tanzansino, 22, 47
technical investment, in Mozambique,
  90, 91, 92

technological capabilities, 12
  in Brazil, 167
  at firm-level, 290
  in Kenya, 32–44
  in Tanzania, 21, 56–9
  upgrading, 51–2, 285
technology standards, 225, 228,
  230–2
technology transfer packages, 122,
  142
telemedicine, 190
tendering processes
  competitive, 119
  donors, 52–3
  open, 154–5
tenofovir disoproxil fumarate (TDF),
  127–8, 129, 131
test kits, 154
Teva Jerusalem, 67
thalidomide, 225
Third Market Environment (TME),
  185, 186
time-limited incentives, 295–6
topical preparations, 35
trade credit, 56, 246–7
triad of health care, 188, 189
TRIPS, 41–2, 171, 184, 191, 270, 273,
  281
two-tier South African system,
  206–7

Uganda, 109, 110
UK, drug prices, 256
UN agencies, 2
UN Development Programme
  (UNDP), 251
UNAIDS, 279
UNCTAD, 190
UNIDO, 2, 38, 238, 280
Unified Health System (SUS), Brazil,
  166, 167, 168–70, 177
unit prices, SMMs, 95, 96
Universal Corporation, 19, 28, 36, 43,
  282
universality of care, 166, 170
US African Growth and Opportunity
  Act, 28
US Food and Drug Administration
  (FDA), 227, 240, 255

US PEPFAR, 31
US Pharmacopeia (USP), 132, 138, 280

vaccines, 137, 190, 194, 195
VALE S.A., *87*, 88, 90, *91*
value-based pricing (VBP), 244, 253, 255–9
Varichem Pharmaceuticals, 14, 251, *252*
VAT regulations, 60, 115, 162
venture capital, 286
'vertical programmes', 155, 156

waste management, 126, 138
Waxman-Hatch Act 1984, 184
wet granulation, 124
WHO
    public health assessment, 279–80
    standards guidelines, 227
WHO-prequalification standards, 155, 230, 238
    in Ethiopia, 81
    in Kenya, 36, 43
    in Tanzania, 52, 58
wholesaling, 150–1
    complaints about, 153
    non-profit, 157–9

price controls, 205–6
price mark-ups, 203
private sector, 159–61
working capital, 56, 246–7
working capital credits, 295
WTO Agreement on Government Procurement, 119

Zaf Pharmaceuticals, 73
Zenufa laboratories, 22, 47
zidovudine, 89
    lamivudine-zidovudine, 36, *96*
Zimbabwe
    current pharmaceutical manufacturing, 16–17
    early import substitution, 13–14
    era of economic collapse, 15–16
    finance capabilities, 289, 291, *292*
    industry–healthcare integration, 14–15
    investment timeline, 10
    loss of early industrial advantage, 13–17
    procurement as an asset, 250–2
    regulatory system, 234
    trade credit, 247